BIRDS, BEASTS, AND RELATIVES

By Gerald Durrell

* Available in Viking Compass edition

GERALD DURRELL

Birds, Beasts, and Relatives

NEW YORK THE VIKING PRESS

Viking Compass Edition
Issued in 1971 by The Viking Press, Inc.
625 Madison Avenue, New York, N.Y. 10022

SBN 670-16775-4 (hardbound)
670-00315-8 (paperback)
Library of Congress catalog card number: 77-83247
Fourth printing December 1973
Printed in U.S.A.

TO THEODORE STEPHANIDES,

in gratitude for laughter and for learning

CONTENTS

Conversation

It had been a hard winter, and even when spring was supposed to have taken over, the crocuses—which seemed to have a touching and unshaken faith in the seasons—were having to push their way grimly through a thin crust of snow. The sky was low and grey, liable to discharge another fall of snow at any minute, and a biting wind howled round the house. Taken altogether, weather conditions were not ideal for a family reunion, particularly when it was my family.

It was a pity, I felt, that when they had all forgathered in England for the first time since World War II, they should be treated to something approaching a blizzard. It did not bring out the best in them; it made them more touchy than usual, quicker to take offence, and less likely to lend a sympathetic ear to anyone's point of view but their own.

They were grouped, like a pride of moody lions, round a fire so large and flamboyant that there was immediate danger of its setting fire to the chimney. My sister Margo had just added to it by the simple method of dragging in the carcass of a small tree from the garden and pushing one end into the fireplace, while the remainder of the trunk lay across the hearth-rug. My mother was knitting, but you could tell by the slightly vacant look on her face and the way her lips moved occasionally, as if she were in silent prayer, that she was really occupied with the menu for tomorrow's lunch. My brother

Leslie was buried behind a large manual on ballistics, while my elder brother Lawrence, clad in a roll-top pullover of the type usually worn by fishermen (several sizes too large for him), was standing by the window sneezing wetly and regularly into a large scarlet handkerchief.

"Really, this is a *frightful* country," he said, turning on us belligerently, as though we were all directly responsible for the climatic conditions prevailing. "You set foot on shore at Dover and you're met by a positive barrage of cold germs. . . . D'you realize that this is the first cold I've had in twelve years? Simply because I had the sense to keep away from Pudding Island. Everyone I've met so far has a cold. The entire population of the British Isles seems to do absolutely nothing from one year's end to another except shuffle round in small circles sneezing voluptuously into each other's faces . . . a sort of merry-go-round of reinfection. What chance of survival has one got?"

"Just because *you've* got a cold you carry on as though the world was coming to an end," said Margo. "I can't understand why men always make such a fuss."

Larry gave her a withering look from watering eyes. "The trouble with you all is that you like being martyrs. No one free from masochistic tendencies would stay in this—this virus's paradise. You've all stagnated; you *like* wallowing here in a sea of infection. One excuses people who have never known anything else, but you all had a taste of the sun in Greece; you should know better."

"Yes, dear," said Mother soothingly, "but you've just come at a bad time. It can be very nice, you know. In the spring, for example."

Larry glared at her. "I hate to jolt you out of your Rip Van Winkle-like trance," he said, "but this is supposed to *be* the spring . . . and look at it! You need a team of huskies to go down to post a letter."

"Half an inch of snow," snorted Margo. "You do exaggerate."

"I agree with Larry," Leslie said, appearing from behind his book suddenly. "It's bloody cold out. Makes you feel you don't want to do anything. You can't even get any decent shooting."

"Exactly," said Larry triumphantly, "while in a sensible country like Greece one would be having breakfast outside and then going down to the sea for a morning bathe. Here my teeth chatter so much it's only with difficulty that I can eat any breakfast."

"I do wish you'd stop harping on Greece," said Leslie. "It reminds me of that bloody book of Gerry's. It took me ages to live that down."

"Took *you* ages?" said Larry caustically. "What about me? You've no idea what damage that Dickens-like caricature did to my literary image."

"But the way he wrote about me, you would think I never thought about anything but guns and boats," said Leslie.

"Well, you never do think about anything but guns and boats."

"I was the one that suffered most," said Margo. "He did nothing but talk about my acne."

"I thought it was quite an accurate picture of you all," said Mother, "but he made me out to be a *positive imbecile*."

"I wouldn't mind being lampooned in decent prose," Larry pointed out, blowing his nose vigorously, "but to be lampooned in bad English is unbearable."

"The title alone is insulting," said Margo. "*My Family and Other Animals!* I get sick of people saying, 'And which other animal are you?'"

"I thought the title was rather funny, dear," said Mother. "The only thing I thought was that he hadn't used all the best stories."

"Yes, I agree," said Leslie.

"What best stories?" Larry demanded suspiciously.

"Well, what about the time you sailed Max's yacht round the island? That was damned funny."

"If that story had appeared in print I would have sued him."

"I don't see why, it was very funny," said Margo.

"And what about the time you took up spiritualism—supposing he'd written about that? I suppose you'd enjoy *that?*" inquired Larry caustically.

"No, I would not—he couldn't write that," said Margo in horror.

"Well, there you are," said Larry in triumph. "And what about Leslie's court case?"

"I don't see why you have to bring me into it," said Leslie.

"You were the one who was going on about him not using the best incidents," Larry pointed out.

"Yes, I'd forgotten about those stories," said Mother, chuckling. "I think they were funnier than the ones you used, Gerry."

"I'm glad you think that," I said thoughtfully.

"Why?" asked Larry, glaring at me.

"Because I've decided to write another book on Corfu and use all those stories," I explained innocently.

The uproar was immediate.

"I forbid it," roared Larry, sneezing violently. "I absolutely forbid it."

"You're not to write about my spiritualism," Margo cried out. "Mother, tell him he's not to write about that."

"Nor my court case," snarled Leslie. "I won't have it."

"And if you so much as mention yachts . . ." Larry began.

"Larry dear, do keep your voice down," said Mother.

"Well, forbid him to write a sequel then," shouted Larry.

"Don't be silly, dear, *I* can't stop him," said Mother.

"Do you want it all to happen again?" demanded Larry hoarsely. "The bank writing to ask if you will kindly remove your overdraft, the tradesmen looking at you askance, anonymous parcels full of strait-jackets being left on the doorstep, being cut dead by all the relatives. You are supposed to be head of the family—stop him writing it."

"You do exaggerate, Larry dear," said Mother. "Anyway, I can't stop him if he wants to write it. I don't think it will do any harm and those stories are the best ones, I think. I don't see why he shouldn't write a sequel."

The family rose in a body and told her loudly and vociferously why I should not write a sequel. I waited for the noise to die down.

"And apart from those stories, there are quite a number of others," I said.

"Which ones, dear?" inquired Mother.

The family, red-faced, bristling, glowered at me in an expectant silence.

"Well," I said thoughtfully, "I want to give a description of your love affair with Captain Creech, Mother."

"What?" squeaked Mother. "You'll do no such thing . . . love affair with that disgusting old creature, indeed. I won't have you writing about *that*."

"Well, I think that's the best story of the lot," said Larry unctuously, "the vibrant passion of the romance, the sweet, archaic charm of the leading man . . . the way you led the poor old chap on . . ."

"Oh, do be quiet, Larry," said Mother crossly. "You do make me angry when you talk like that. I don't think it's a good idea for you to write this book, Gerry."

"I second that," said Larry. "If you publish we'll sue you in a body."

Faced with such a firm and united family, bristling in their resolve to prevent me at all costs, there was only one thing I could do. I sat down and wrote this book.

Writing something of this sort presents many pitfalls for the author. His new readers do not want to be constantly irritated by references to a previous book that they have not read, and the ones who have read the previous book do not want to be irritated by constant repetition of events with which they are familiar. I hope that I have managed to steer a fairly steady course between the two.

PART ONE

Perama

Here great trees cool-shaded grow, pear, pomegranate, rich apple, honey-sweet fig and blossoming olive, forever bearing fruit, winter and summer never stripped, but everblowing the western wind brings fruit to birth and ripens others. Pear follows pear, apple after apple grows, fig after fig, and grape yields grape again.

—HOMER

1

THE CHRISTENING

The island lies off the Albanian and Greek coast-lines like a long, rust-eroded scimitar. The hilt of the scimitar is the mountain region of the island, for the most part barren and stony, with towering rock cliffs haunted by blue rock-thrushes and peregrine falcons. In the valleys in this mountain region, however, where water gushes plentifully from the red-and-gold rocks, you get forests of almond and walnut trees, casting shade as cool as a well, thick battalions of spear-like cypress and silver-trunked fig trees with leaves as large as a salver. The blade of the scimitar is made up of rolling greeny-silver eiderdowns of giant olive trees, some reputedly over five hundred years old and each one unique in its hunched, arthritic shape, its trunk pitted with a hundred holes like pumice-stone. Towards the tip of the blade you have Lefkimi, with its twinkling, eye-aching sand dunes and great salt marshes, decorated with acres of bamboos that creak and rustle and whisper to each other surreptitiously. The island is called Corfu.

That August, when we arrived, the island lay breathless and sun-drugged in a smouldering, peacock-blue sea under a sky that had been faded to a pale powder-blue by the fierce rays of the sun. Our reasons for packing up and leaving the gloomy shores of England were somewhat nebulous, but based loosely on the fact that we were tired of the drab suburbanness of life in England and its accompanying bleak and unpleasant climate. So we had fled to Corfu, hoping that the sunshine of Greece would cure us of the mental and physical inertia which so long a sojourn in England had brought about. Very soon after we had landed, we had acquired our first villa and our first friend on the island.

The friend was Spiro, a waddling, barrel-shaped man with huge powerful hands and a brown, leathery, scowling face. He had perfected an odd but adequate command over English and he possessed an ancient Dodge which he used as a taxi. We soon found that Spiro, like most of the Corfu characters, was unique. There seemed to be no one that he did not know and nothing that he could not obtain or get done for you. Even the most bizarre requests from the family would be met by him with the remark, "Don'ts yous worrys about thats. I'll fixes thats." And fix it he would. His first major piece of fixing was the acquisition of our villa, for Mother had been insistent that we must have a bathroom, and this very necessary adjunct of wholesome living was in short supply in Corfu. But, needless to say, Spiro knew of a villa with a bath, and very soon, after much shouting and roaring, gesticulation, sweating, and waddling to and fro carrying armfuls of our goods and chattels, Spiro had us safely installed. From that moment he ceased to be merely a taxi driver that we hired and became our guide, philosopher, and friend.

The villa that Spiro had found was shaped not unlike a brick and was a bright crushed-strawberry pink with green shutters. It crouched in a cathedral-like grove of olives that sloped down the hillside to the sea, and it was surrounded by a pocket-handkerchief-size garden, the flower-beds laid out with a geometrical accuracy so dear to the Victorians, and the whole thing guarded by a tall, thick hedge of fuchsias that rustled mysteriously with birds. Coming, as we had done, from a number of years' torture in the cold grey of England, the sunshine and the brilliant colours and scents it evoked acted on us all like a heady draft of wine.

It affected each member of the family in a different way. Larry wandered about in a sort of daze, periodically quoting long stanzas of poetry to Mother, who either did not listen or else said, "Very nice, dear," absently. She, entranced by the variety of fruit and vegetables available, spent most of her time closeted in the kitchen preparing complicated and delicious menus for every meal. Margo, convinced that the sunshine would do for her acne what all the pills and potions of the medical profession had so far failed to do, sun-bathed with strenuous earnestness in the olive groves and in consequence got herself badly burnt. Leslie discovered, to his delight, that one could purchase lethal weapons without a permit in Greece and so he kept disappearing into town and reappearing carrying a variety of fowling pieces ranging from ancient Turkish muzzle-loaders to revolvers and shot guns. As he insisted on practising with each new acquisition, our nerves became somewhat frayed, and as Larry remarked somewhat bitterly, it was rather like living in a villa surrounded by revolutionary forces.

The garden, for long untended, was an overgrown riot of uninhibited flowers and weeds in which whirled, squeaked, rustled, and jumped a multi-coloured merry-go-round of insect life, and so it was the garden that held my immediate attention.

However luxurious our various gardens had been in England, they had never provided me with such an assortment of living creatures. I found myself prey to the most curious sensation of unreality. It was rather like being born for the first time. In that brilliant, brittle light I could appreciate the true huntsman's-red of a lady-bird's wing case, the magnificent chocolate and amber of an earwig, and the deep shining agate of the ants. Then I could feast my eyes on a bewildering number of creatures unfamiliar to me: the great, furry carpenter-bees, which prowled like electric-blue teddy bears, humming to themselves, from flower to flower; the sulphur-yellow, black-striped swallow-tailed butterflies, with their elegant cut-away coats, that pirouetted up and down the fuchsia hedge doing complicated minuets with each other; and the humming-bird hawk-moths that hung, stationary, suspended by a blur of wings, in front of the flowers, while they probed each bloom with their long, delicate proboscises.

I was exceedingly ignorant as to even the simplest facts about these creatures and I had no books to guide me. All I could do was to watch them as they went about their business in the garden or capture them so that I could study them more carefully at first hand. Very soon my bedroom was filled with a battalion of jam jars and biscuit tins containing the prizes that I had found in our tiny garden. These had to be smuggled surreptitiously into the house, for the family, with the possible exception of Mother, viewed the introduction of this fauna into the villa with considerable alarm.

Each brilliant day brought some new puzzles of behaviour to underline my ignorance. One of the creatures that intrigued and irritated me most was the dung-beetle. I would lie on my stomach with Roger, my dog, squatting like a mountain of black curls, panting, by my side, watching two shiny black dung-beetles, each with a delicately curved rhino horn on its head, rolling between them (with immense dedication) a beautifully shaped ball of cow dung. To begin with I wanted to know how they managed to make the ball so completely and beautifully round. I knew from my own experiments with clay and Plasticine that it was extremely difficult to get a completely round ball, however hard you rubbed and manipulated the material, yet the dung-beetles, with only their spiky legs as instruments, devoid of calipers or any other aid, managed to produce these lovely balls of dung, as round as the moon. Then there was the second problem. Why had they made it and where were they taking it?

I solved this problem, or part of it, by devoting one entire morning to a pair of dung-beetles, refusing to be deviated from my task by the other insects in the garden or by the faint moans and yawns of boredom that came from Roger. Slowly, on all fours, I followed them foot by laborious foot across the garden, which was so small to me and yet such a vast world to the beetles. Eventually they came to a small hummock of soft earth under the fuchsia hedge. Rolling the ball of dung uphill was a mammoth task, and several times the beetle's foot-work was at fault and the ball would break away and roll back to the bottom of the little incline, the beetles hurrying after it and, I liked to imagine, shouting abuse at each other. Eventually, however, they got it to the top of the rise and started down the opposite slope. At the bottom of the slope, I noticed for the first time, was a round hole like a well, which had been sunk into the earth, and it was for this that the beetles were heading. When they were within a couple of inches of the hole, one of the beetles hurried ahead and backed into the hole where he sat, gesticulating wildly with his front legs, while the other beetle, with a considerable effort (I could almost convince myself that I heard him panting), rolled the ball of dung up to the mouth of the burrow. After a considerable length of time spent in pushing and pulling, the ball slowly disappeared into the depths of the earth and the beetles with it. This annoyed me. After all, they were obviously going to do something with the ball of dung, but if they did it under ground, how could I be expected to see what they did? Hoping for some enlightenment on this problem, I put it to the family at lunch time. What, I inquired, did dung-beetles do with dung? There was a moment's startled silence.

"Well, I expect they find it useful, dear," said Mother vaguely.

"I trust you're not hoping to smuggle some into the house?" Larry inquired. "I refuse to live in a villa whose decor consists of balls of dung all over the floor."

"No, no, dear, I'm sure he won't," said Mother peaceably and untruthfully.

"Well, I'm just warning you, that's all," said Larry. "As it is, he appears to have all the more dangerous insects out of the garden closeted in his bedroom."

"They probably want it for warmth," said Leslie, who had been giving the matter of dung-beetles some thought. "Very warm stuff, dung. Ferments."

"Should we, at any time, require central heating," said Larry, "I'll bear that in mind."

"They probably eat it," said Margo.

"Margo, dear," said Mother. "Not while we're having lunch."

As usual, my family's lack of biological knowledge had let me down.

"What you want to read," said Larry, absentmindedly helping himself to another plateful of stew, which he had just described to Mother as being lacking in flavour, "what you want to read is some Fabre."

I inquired what or who Fabre was, more out of politeness than anything else, because, as the suggestion had come from Larry, I was convinced that Fabre would turn out to be some obscure medieval poet.

"Naturalist," said Larry, his mouth full, waving his fork at me. "Wrote about insects and things. I'll try and get you a copy."

Overwhelmed with such unlooked-for magnanimity on the part of my elder brother, I made a point of being very careful within the next two or three days not to do anything to incur his wrath; but the days passed and no book appeared and eventually I forgot about it and devoted my time to the other insects in the garden.

But the word "why" pursued and frustrated me on every hand. Why did the carpenter-bees cut out little circular pieces from the rose leaves and fly away with them? Why did the ants conduct what appeared to be passionate love affairs with the massed battalions of green fly that infested many of the plants in the garden? What were the strange, amber, transparent insect corpses or shells that I found sticking to grass stalks and to olive trees? They were the empty skins, as fragile as ash, of some creature with a bulbous body, bulbous eyes, and a pair of thick, well-barbed forelegs. Why did each of these shells have a split down its back? Had they been attacked and had all their life juices sucked out of them? If so, what had attacked them and what were they? I was a bubbling cauldron of questions which the family were unable to answer.

I was in the kitchen when Spiro arrived one morning some days later, as I was showing Mother my latest acquisition, a long, thin, caramel-coloured centipede which I was insisting, in spite of her disbelief, glowed with a white light at night. Spiro waddled into the kitchen, sweating profusely, looking, as he always did, truculent and worried.

"I've broughts yours mails, Mrs. Durrells," he said to Mother, and then, glancing at me, "Mornings, Masters Gerrys."

Thinking, in my innocence, that Spiro would share my enthusiasm for my latest pet, I pushed the jam jar under his nose and urged him to feast his eyes upon it. He took one swift look at the centipede, now going round and round in the bottom of the jar like a clock-work train, dropped the mail on the floor, and retreated hurriedly behind the kitchen table.

"Gollys, Masters Gerrys," he said, "what's you doing with *thats?*"

I explained it was only a centipede, puzzled at his reaction.

"Thems bastards are poisonous, Mrs. Durrells," said Spiro earnestly, to Mother. "Honest to Gods Masters Gerrys shouldn't *have* things like thats."

"Well, perhaps not," said Mother vaguely. "But he's so interested in all these things. Take it outside, dear, where Spiro can't see it."

"Makes me scarce," I heard Spiro say as I left the kitchen with my precious jar. "Honest to Gods, Mrs. Durrells, makes me scarce what that boy *finds.*"

I managed to get the centipede into my bedroom without meeting any other members of the family and I bedded him down in a small dish, tastefully decorated with moss and bits of bark. I was determined that the family should appreciate the fact that I had found a centipede that glowed in the dark. I had planned that night to put on a special pyrotechnic display after dinner. However, all thoughts of the centipede and his phosphorescence were completely driven from my mind, for in with the mail was a fat, brown parcel which Larry, having glanced at, tossed across to me while we were eating lunch.

"Fabre," he said succinctly.

Forgetting my food, I tore the parcel open, and there inside was a squat, green book entitled *The Sacred Beetle and Others* by Jean Henri Fabre. Opening it, I was transported by delight, for the frontispiece was a picture of two dung-beetles, and they looked so familiar they might well have been close cousins of my own dung-beetles. They were rolling a beautiful ball of dung between them. Enraptured, savouring every moment, I turned the pages slowly. The text was charming. No erudite or confusing tome, this. It was written in such a simple and straightforward way that even I could understand it.

"Leave the book till later, dear. Eat your lunch before it gets cold," said Mother.

Reluctantly I put the book on my lap and then attacked my food with such speed and ferocity that I had acute indigestion for the rest of the afternoon. This in no way detracted from the charm of delving into Fabre for the first time. While the family siestaed, I lay in the garden in the shade of the tangerine trees and devoured the book, page by page, until by tea-time—to my disappointment—I had reached the end. But nothing could describe my elation. I was now armed with knowledge. I knew, I felt, everything there was to know about dung-beetles. Now they were not merely mysterious insects crawling ponderously throughout the olive groves—they were my intimate friends.

About this time another thing that extended and encouraged my interest in natural history—though I cannot say that I appreciated it at the time—was the acquisition of my first tutor, George. George was a friend of Larry's, tall, lanky, brown-bearded and bespectacled, possessed of a quiet and sardonic sense of humour. It is probable that no tutor has ever had to battle with such a reluctant pupil. I could see absolutely no reason for having to learn anything that was not connected with natural history, and so our early lessons were fraught with difficulty. Then George discovered that, by correlating such subjects as history, geography, and mathematics with zoology, he could get some results, and so we made fair progress. However, the best thing as far as I was concerned was that one morning a week was devoted exclusively to natural history, when George and I would peer earnestly at my newly acquired specimens and endeavour to identify them and work out their life histories. A meticulous diary was kept which contained a large number of flamboyant and somewhat shaky pictures, purporting to be of the specimens in question, done by me in a variety of coloured inks and water-colours.

Looking back, I have a sneaking feeling that George enjoyed the mornings devoted to natural history as much as I did. It was, for example, the only morning during the week that I would go to meet him. I would amble through the olive groves half-way to the tiny villa that he occupied, and then Roger and I would conceal ourselves in a clump of myrtle and await his approach. Presently he would appear, clad in nothing but a pair of sandals, faded shorts, and a gigantic, tattered straw hat, carrying under one arm a pile of books and swinging a long, slender walking-stick in the other hand. The reason for going to meet George, I regret to say, was of an entirely mercenary nature. Roger and I would squat in the sweet-scented myrtles and lay bets with each other as to whether or not, on this particular morning, George was going to fight an olive tree.

George was an expert fencer and had a quantity of cups and medals to prove it, so the desire to fight something frequently overcame him. He would be striding along the path, his spectacles glittering, swinging his walking-stick, when suddenly one olive tree would become an evil and malignant thing that had to be taught a lesson. Dropping his books and hat by the side of the path, he would advance cautiously towards the tree in question, his walking-stick, now transformed into a sword, held in his right hand at the ready, his left arm held out elegantly behind him. Slowly, stiff-legged, like a terrier approaching a bull mastiff, he would circle the tree, watching with narrowed eyes for its first unfriendly move. Suddenly he would lunge forward and the point of his stick would disappear in one of the holes in the olive tree's trunk and he would utter a pleased "Ha," and immediately dodge back out of range, before the tree could retaliate. I noticed that if he succeeded in driving his sword into one of the smaller of the olive tree's holes, this did not constitute a death wound, merely a slight scratch, which apparently had the effect of rousing his antagonist to a fury, for in a second he would be fighting grimly for his life, dancing nimble-footed round the olive tree, lunging and parrying, leaping away with a downward slash of his sword, turning aside the vicious lunge that the olive tree had aimed at him, but so rapidly that I had missed the move. Some olive trees he would finish off quickly with a deadly thrust through one of the larger holes, into which his sword disappeared almost up to the hilt, but on several occasions he met with an olive tree that was almost more than a match for him, and for perhaps a quarter of an hour or so, it would be a fight to the death, with George, grim-faced, using every cunning trick he knew to break through the defences of the giant tree and kill it. Once he had successfully killed his antagonist, George would wipe the blood off his sword fastidiously, put on his hat, pick up his books, and continue, humming to himself, down the path. I always let him get a considerable distance away before joining him, for fear he should realize I had watched his imaginary battle and become embarrassed by it.

It was about this time that George introduced me to someone who was going to become immediately the most important person in my life, Dr. Theodore Stephanides. To me, Theodore was one of the most remarkable people I had ever met (and thirty-three years later I am still of the same opinion). With his ash-blond hair and beard and his handsome aquiline features, Theodore looked like a Greek god, and certainly he seemed as omniscient as one. Apart from being medically qualified, he was also a biologist (his particular study being freshwater biology), poet, author, translator, astronomer, and historian, and he found time between these multifarious activities to help run an X-ray laboratory, the only one of its kind, in the town of Corfu. I had first met him over a little problem of trap-door spiders, a creature that I had only recently discovered, and he had imparted to me such fascinating information about them, so diffidently and shyly, that I was captivated, not only by the information, but by Theodore himself, for he treated me exactly as though I were an adult.

After our first meeting, I was convinced that I should probably never see him again, as anyone as omniscient and famous as he was could not possibly have the time to spare for a ten-year-old. But the following day I received a present of a small pocket microscope from him and a note asking me to go to tea with him in his flat in town. Here I plied him with eager questions and breathlessly ran riot through the enormous library in his study and peered for hours through the gleaming barrels of microscopes at the strange and beautiful forms of pond life that Theodore, like a magician, seemed able to conjure out of any drab, dirty stretch of water. After my first visit to Theodore, I asked Mother tentatively whether I might ask him to come to tea with us.

"I suppose so, dear," said Mother. "I hope he speaks English, though."

Mother's battle with the Greek language was a losing one. Only the day previously she had spent an exhausting morning preparing a particularly delicious soup for lunch, and having concluded this to her satisfaction, she put it into a soup tureen and handed it to the maid. The maid looked at her inquiringly, whereupon Mother used one of the few Greek words that she had managed to commit to memory. "*Exo*," she had said firmly, waving her arms. "*Exo*." She then went on with her cooking and turned round just in time to see the maid pouring the last of the soup down the sink. This had, not unnaturally, given her a phobia about her linguistic abilities.

I said indignantly that Theodore could speak excellent English—in fact, if anything, better English than we could. Soothed by this, Mother suggested that I write Theodore a note and invite him out for the following Thursday. I spent an agonizing two hours hanging about in the garden waiting for him to arrive, peering every few minutes through the fuchsia hedge, a prey to the most terrible emotions. Perhaps the note had never reached him. Or perhaps he had put it in his pocket and forgotten about it and was, at this moment, gallivanting eruditely at the southernmost tip of the island. Or perhaps he had heard about the family and just didn't want to come. If that was the case, I vowed, I would not lightly forgive them. But presently I saw him, neatly tweed-suited, his Homburg squarely on his head, striding up through the olive trees, swinging his stick and humming to himself. Hung over his shoulder was his collecting bag, which was as much a part of him as his arms and legs, for he was rarely seen anywhere without it.

To my delight, Theodore was an immediate, uproarious success with the family. He could, with a shy urbanity, discuss mythology, Greek poetry, and Venetian history with Larry, ballistics and the best hunting areas on the island with Leslie, good slimming diets and acne cures with Margaret, and peasant recipes and detective stories with Mother. The family behaved much in the same way that I had behaved when I went to tea with him. He seemed such an endless mine of information that they bombarded him ceaselessly with questions, and Theodore, as effortlessly as a walking encyclopedia, answered them all, adding for good measure a sprinkling of incredibly bad puns and hilarious anecdotes about the island and the islanders.

At one point, to my indignation, Larry said that Theodore ought to desist from encouraging me in my interest in natural history, for, as he pointed out, the villa was a small one and already stuffed to capacity with practically every revolting bug and beetle that I could lay my hands on.

"It isn't that," said Mother, "that worries me. It's the mess that he gets himself into. Really, Theodore, after he's been out for a walk with Roger he has to change into completely clean clothes. I don't know what he does with them."

Theodore gave a tiny grunt of amusement.

"I remember once," he said, popping a piece of cake into his mouth and chewing it methodically, his beard bristling and his eyes kindling happily, "I was coming to tea with some, . . . um . . . you know, *friends* of mine here in Perama. At that time I was in the army and I was rather proud of the fact that I had just been made a captain. So . . . er . . . you know . . . er . . . to show off I wore my uniform, which included beautifully polished boots and spurs. I was rowed across by the ferry to Perama, and as I was walking through the little marshy bit I saw a plant that was new to me. So I stepped over to collect it. Treading on what . . . you know. . . seemed to be firm ground, I suddenly found that I had sunk up to my armpits in very foul smelling mud. Fortunately there was a small tree near by and I . . . er . . . managed to grab hold of it and pull myself *out*. But now I was covered from the waist downwards with stinking black mud. The sea was . . . er, you know . . . quite close, so I . . . er . . . thought it would be better to be wet with clean sea-water than covered with mud, so I waded out into it and walked up and down. Just at that moment, a bus happened to pass on the road above and as soon as they saw me with my cap on and my uniform coat, walking about in the sea, the bus driver immediately stopped so that all his passengers could . . . er . . . get a better view of the spectacle. They all seemed considerably puzzled, but they were even more astonished when I walked out of the sea and they saw that I was wearing boots and spurs as well."

Solemnly, Theodore waited for the laughter to subside.

"I think, you know," he said meditatively and quite seriously, "that I definitely undermined their faith in the sanity of the army."

Theodore was a huge success with the family and ever after that he came out to spend at least one day a week with us, preferably more if we could inveigle him away from his numerous activities.

By this time we had made innumerable friends among the peasant families that lived around us, and so vociferously hospitable were they that even the shortest walk was almost indefinitely prolonged, for at every little house we came to we would have to sit down and drink a glass of wine or eat some fruit with its owners and pass the time of day. Indirectly, this was very good for us, for each of these meetings strengthened our rather shaky command over the Greek language, so that soon we found that we were fairly proficient in conducting quite complicated conversations with our peasant friends.

Then came the accolade, the gesture that proved to us we had been accepted by the community in general. We were asked to a wedding. It was the wedding of Katerina, the sister of our maid, Maria. Katerina was a voluptuous girl, with a wide, glittering smile and brown eyes as large and as soft as pansies. Gay, provocative, and as melodious as a nightingale, she had been breaking hearts in the district for most of her twenty years. Now she had settled on Stephanos, a sturdy, handsome boy whom the mere sight of Katerina rendered tongue-tied, inarticulate, and blushing with love.

When you were invited to a wedding, we soon discovered, the thing was not done in half-measures. The first festivity was the engagement party, when you all went to the bride's house carrying your presents and she thanked you prettily for them and plied you with wine. Having suitably mellowed the guests, the future bride and groom would start walking to what was to be their future home, preceded by the village band (two violins, a flute, and a guitar) playing sprightly airs, and followed by the guests, all carrying their presents. Katerina's presents were a fairly mixed bag. The most important was a gigantic double brass bed and this led the procession, carried by four of Stephanos' friends. Thereafter followed a string of guests carrying sheets, pillow cases, cushions, a wooden chair, frying pans, large bottles of oil, and similar gifts. Having installed the presents in the new cottage, we then drank to the health of the couple and thus warmed their future home for them. We then all retired to our homes, slightly light-headedly, and waited for the next act in the drama, which was the wedding itself.

We had asked, somewhat diffidently, if Theodore might attend the wedding with us and the bride and her parents were enchanted with the idea, since, as they explained with becoming ingenuousness, very few weddings in the district could boast of having a whole English family *and* a genuine doctor as guests.

The great day came, and donning our best clothes and collecting Theodore from town, we made our way down to Katerina's parents' house, which stood among olive trees overlooking the sparkling sea. This was where the ceremony was to take place. When we got there we found it a hive of activity. Relatives had come on their donkeys from villages as far as ten miles away. All round the house, groups of ancient men and decrepit old women sat engulfing wine in vast quantities, gossiping as ceaselessly and as animatedly as magpies. For them this was a great day, not only because of the wedding, but because, living as much as ten miles distant, they were probably having their first opportunity in twenty years to exchange news and scandal. The village band was in full spate—the violins whining, the guitar rumbling, and the flute making periodic squeaks like a neglected puppy—and to this all the younger guests were dancing under the trees, while near by the carcasses of four lambs were sizzling and bubbling on spits over a great chrysanthemum blaze of charcoal.

"Aha!" said Theodore, his eyes alight with interest. "Now that dance they are doing is the Corfu dance. It and the . . . er . . . tune *originated* here in Corfu. There are some authorities, of course, who believe that the dance . . . that is to say, the *steps* . . . originated in Crete, but for myself, I believe it is . . . um . . . an entirely Corfu product."

The girls in their goldfinch-bright costumes revolved prettily in a half-moon while ahead of them pranced a swarthy young male with a crimson handkerchief, bucking, leaping, twisting, and bowing like an exuberant cockerel to his admiring entourage of hens. Katerina and her family came forward to greet us and ushered us to the place of honour, a rickety wooden table that had been spread with a white cloth and at which was already sitting a magnificent old priest who was going to perform the ceremony. He had a girth like that of a whale, snow-white eyebrows, and moustache and beard so thick and luxuriant that almost all that could be seen of his face were two twinkling, olive-black eyes and a great, jutting, wine-red nose. On hearing that Theodore was a doctor, the priest, out of the kindness of his heart, described in graphic detail the innumerable symptoms of his several diseases (which God had seen fit to inflict him with) and at the end of the recital laughed uproariously at Theodore's childish diagnosis that a little less wine and a little more exercise might alleviate his ailments.

Larry eyed Katerina, who, clad in her white bridal gown, had joined the circle of the dancers. In her tight, white satin,

Katerina's stomach was more prominent and noticeable than it would have been otherwise.

"This wedding," said Larry, "is taking place not a moment too soon."

"Do be quiet, dear," whispered Mother. "Some of them might speak English."

"It's a curious fact," said Theodore, oblivious to Mother's stricture, "that at a lot of the weddings you will find the bride in . . . er . . . um . . . a *similar* condition. The peasants here are very Victorian in their outlook. If a young man is . . . er . . . seriously *courting* a girl, neither family dreams for a moment that he will not marry her. In fact, if he did try to . . . um . . . you know . . . run off, both his family and the bride's family would be after him. This leads to a situation where, when the young man is courting, he is . . . er . . . chaffed, that is to say, has his *leg* pulled by all the young men of the district, who say that they doubt his . . . um . . . prowess as a . . . um . . . you know . . . potential father. They get the poor fellow into such a state that he is almost forced to . . . er . . . you know . . . um . . . *prove* himself."

"Very unwise, I would have thought," said Mother.

"No, no," said Theodore, endeavouring to correct Mother's unscientific approach to the problem. "In fact, it is considered quite a *good* thing for the bride to be pregnant. It proves her . . . um . . . fecundity."

Presently the priest heaved his vast bulk onto his gouty feet and made his way into the main room of the house, which had been prepared for the ceremony. When he was ready, Stephanos, perspiring profusely, his suit half a size too small for him and looking slightly dazed at his good fortune, was propelled towards the house by a laughing, joking band of young men, while a group of shrilly chattering young women fulfilled the same function for Katerina.

The main room of the house was extremely tiny, so that by

the time the bulk of the well-larded priest had been inserted into it, plus all the accoutrements of his trade, there was only just about enough room for the happy couple to stand in front of him. The rest of us had to be content with peering through the door or through the windows. The service was incredibly long and, to us, incomprehensible, though I could hear Theodore translating bits of it to Larry. It seemed to me to involve quite an unnecessary amount of intoning, accompanied by innumerable signs of the cross and the splashing of tidal waves of holy water. Then two little garlands of flowers like twin haloes were held over the heads of Katerina and Stephanos, and while the priest droned on, these were exchanged at intervals. As it had been some considerable time since the people who held these garlands had been to a wedding, they occasionally misinterpreted the priest's instructions and there was, so to speak, a clash of garlands over the heads of the bridal pair; but at long last rings were exchanged and placed upon the brown, work-calloused fingers, and Katerina and Stephanos were truly and, we hoped, irretrievably wed.

The silence during the ceremony had been almost complete, broken only by the odd, drowsy chuckle of a hen or the shrill, and instantly repressed, squall of a baby; but now the stern part of the ceremony was over and the party blossomed once again. The band dug down into its repertoire and produced gayer and more sprightly tunes. Laughter and raucous badinage arose on every side. The wine flowed guggling from the bottles and the guests danced round and round and round, flushed and happy, as inexorably as the hands on a clock face.

The party did not end till well after twelve. All the older guests had already made their way homewards on drooping donkeys. The great fires, with the remains of the sheep carcasses over them, had died in a shroud of grey ash with only a sprinkling of garnet embers winking in it. We took a last glass of wine with Katerina and Stephanos and then made our way sleepily through the olive groves, silvered by a moon as large and as white as a magnolia blossom. The scops owls chimed mournfully to each other, and the odd firefly winked emerald-green as we passed. The warm air smelled of the day's sunshine, of dew, and of a hundred aromatic leaf scents. Mellow and drugged with wine, walking between the great hunched olives, their trunks striped with cool moonlight, I think we all felt we had arrived, that we had been accepted by the island. We were now, under the quiet, bland eye of the moon, christened Corfiotes. The night was beautiful, and tomorrow, we knew, another tiger-golden day lay ahead of us. It was as though England had never really existed.

2

THE BAY OF OLIVES

As you left the villa and walked down through the olive groves, you eventually reached the road with its thick coating of white dust, as soft as silk. If you walked along this for half a mile or so, you came to a goat track which led down a steep slope through the olives and then you reached a small half-moon bay, rimmed with white sands and great piles of dried ribbon-weed that had been thrown up by the winter storms and lay along the beach like large, badly made birds' nests. The two arms of the bay were composed of small cliffs, at the base of which were innumerable rock pools, filled with the glint and glitter of sea life.

As soon as George realized that to incarcerate me every morning of the week in the villa impaired my concentration, he instituted the novel educational gambit of "outdoor lessons." The sandy beach and the shaggy piles of weed soon became scorching deserts or impenetrable jungles, and with the aid of a reluctant crab or sand-hopper to play the part of Cortez or Marco Polo, we would explore them diligently. Geography lessons done under these circumstances I found had immense charm. We once decided, with the aid of rocks, to do a map of the world along the edge of the sea, so that we had real sea. It was an immensely absorbing task, for, to begin with, it was not all that easy to find rocks shaped like Africa or India or South America, and sometimes two or three rocks had to be joined together to give the required shape to the continent. Then, of course, when you were obtaining a rock, you turned it over very carefully and found a host of sea life underneath it which would keep us both happily absorbed for a quarter of an hour or so, till George realized with a start that this was not getting on with our map of the world.

This little bay became one of my favourite haunts, and nearly every afternoon while the family were having their siesta, Roger and I would make our way down through the breathless olive groves, vibrating with the cries of the cicadas, and pad our way along the dusty road, Roger sneezing voluptuously as his great paws stirred up the dust, which went up his nose like snuff. Once we reached the bay, whose waters in the afternoon sun were so still and transparent they did not seem to be there at all, we would swim for a while in the shallows and then each of us would go about his own particular hobbies.

For Roger, this consisted of desperate and unsuccessful attempts to catch some of the small fish that flicked and trembled in the shallow water. He would stalk along slowly, muttering to himself, his ears cocked, gazing down into the water. Then, suddenly, he would plunge his head beneath the surface, and you heard his jaws clop together and he would pull his head out, sneeze violently, and shake the water off his fur, while the goby or blenny that he had attempted to catch would flip a couple of yards farther on and squat on a rock pouting at him and trembling its tail seductively.

For me the tiny bay was so full of life that I scarcely knew where to begin my collecting. Under and on top of the rocks were the chalky white tunnels of the tube-worms, like some swirling and complicated pattern of icing on a cake, and in the slightly deeper water there were stuck in the sand what appeared to be lengths of miniature hose pipe. If you stood and watched carefully, a delicate, feathery, flowerlike cluster of tentacles would appear at the ends of the hose pipes— tentacles of iridescent blue and red and brown that would revolve slowly round and round. These were the bristle-worms; a rather ugly name, I felt, for such a beautiful creature. Sometimes there would be little clusters of them and they looked like a flower-bed whose flowers could move. You had to approach them with infinite caution, for should you move your feet too rapidly through the water you would set up currents that telegraphed your approach and the tentacles would bunch together and dive with incredible speed back into the tube.

Here and there on the sandy floor of the bay were half-moons of black, shiny ribbon-weed, looking like dark feather boas, anchored to the sand, and in these you would find pipe-fish, whose heads looked extraordinarily like elongated sea-horses, perched on the end of a long, slender body. The pipe-fishes would float upright among the ribbon-weeds, which they resembled so closely it required a lot of concentrated searching to find them.

Along the shore, under the rocks, you could find tiny crabs or beadlet anemones like little scarlet-and-blue jewelled pin-cushions, or the snakelocks anemones, their slender, coffee-coloured stalks and long, writhing tentacles giving them a hair style that Medusa might well have envied. Every rock was encrusted with pink or white or green coral, fine forests of minute seaweeds, including a delicate growth of *acetabularia mediterranea* with slender threadlike stalks, and perched on the top of each stalk something that looked like a small green parasol turned inside out by some submarine wind. Occasionally a rock would be encrusted with a great black lump of sponge covered with gaping, protuberant mouths like miniature volcanoes. You could pull these sponges off the rocks and split them open with a razor blade, for sometimes, inside, you would find curious forms of life; but the sponge, in retaliation, would coat your hands with a mucus that smelt horribly of stale garlic and took hours to wear off.

Scattered along the shore and in the rock pools, I would find new shells to add to my collection; half the delight of collecting these was not only the beautiful shapes of the shells themselves, but the extraordinary evocative names that had been given to them. A pointed shell like a large winkle, the lip of whose mouth had been elongated into a series of semi-webbed fingers, was, I discovered to my delight, called the pelican's foot. An almost circular, white, conical, limpet-like shell went under the name of Chinaman's hat. Then there were the ark-shells, and the two sides of these strange, boxlike shells, when separated, did look (if one used a modicum of imagination) like the hulks of two little arks. Then there were the tower-shells, twisted and pointed as a narwhal's horn, and the top-shells, gaily striped with a zigzag pattern of scarlet, black, or blue. Under some of the bigger rocks, you would find keyhole limpets, each one of which had, as the name implied, a strange keyhole-like aperture in the top of the shell, through which the creature breathed. And then, best of all, if you were lucky, you would find the flattened ormers, scaly grey with a row of holes along one side; but if you turned it over and extracted its rightful occupant, you would find the whole interior of the shell glowing in opalescent, sunset colours, magical in their beauty. I had at that time no aquariums, so I was forced to construct for myself, in one corner of the bay, a rock pool some eight feet long by four feet wide. Into this I would put my various captures so that I could be almost certain of knowing where they were on the following day.

It was in this bay that I caught my first spider-crab, and I would have walked right past him, thinking him to be a weed-covered rock, if he had not made an incautious movement. His body was about the size and shape of a small flattened pear, and at the pointed end it was decorated with a series of spikes, ending in two hornlike protuberances over his eyes. His legs and his pincers were long, slender, and spindly. But the thing that intrigued me most about him was the fact that he was wearing, on his back and on his legs, a complete suit of tiny seaweeds, which appeared to be growing out of his shell. Enchanted by this weird creature, I carried him triumphantly along the beach to my rock pool and placed him in it. The firm grip with which I had had to hold him (for once having discovered that he was recognized as a crab, he made desperate efforts to escape) had rubbed off quite a lot of his seaweed suit by the time I got him to the pool. I placed him in the shallow, clear water, and lying on my stomach, watched him to see what he would do. Standing high on his toes, like a spider in a hurry, he scuttled a foot or so away from where I had put him and then froze. He sat like this for a long time, so long in fact that I was just deciding that he was going to remain immobile for the rest of the morning, recovering from the shock of capture, when he suddenly extended a long, delicate claw and very daintily, almost shyly, proceeded to pluck a tiny piece of seaweed that was growing on a near-by rock. He put the seaweed to his mouth and I could see him mumbling at it. At first I thought he was eating it, but I soon realized I was mistaken, for, with an angular grace, he placed his claw over his back, felt around in a rather fumbling sort of way, and then proceeded to plant the tiny piece of weed on his carapace. I presumed that he had been making the base of the weed sticky with saliva or some similar substance to make it adhere to his back. As I watched him, he trundled slowly round the pool, collecting a variety of seaweed with the assiduous dedication of a professional botanist in a hitherto unexplored jungle. Within an hour or so his back was covered with such a thick layer of growth that, if he sat still and I took my eyes off him for a moment, I had difficulty in knowing exactly where he was.

Being intrigued by this cunning form of camouflage, I searched the bay carefully until I found another spider-crab. For him I built a special small pool with a sandy floor, completely devoid of weed. I put him in and he settled down quite happily. The following day I returned, carrying with me a nail brush (which subsequently, rather unfortunately, turned out to be Larry's) and taking up the unfortunate spider-crab, I scrubbed him vigorously until not an atom of weed remained upon his back or legs. Then I dropped into his pool a variety of things: a number of tiny top-shells and some broken fragments of coral, some small sea anemones and some minute bits of bottle-glass that had been sand-papered by the sea so that they looked like misty jewels. Then I sat down to watch.

The crab, when returned to his pool, sat quite still for several minutes, obviously recovering from the indignity of the scrubbing I had given him. Then, as if he could not quite believe the terrible fate that had overtaken him, he put his two pincers over his head and proceeded to feel his back with the utmost delicacy, presumably hoping against hope that at least one frond of seaweed remained. But I had done my task well and his back was shining and bare. He walked a few paces tentatively and then squatted down and sulked for half an hour. Then he roused himself out of his gloom and walked over to the edge of the pond, where he endeavoured to wedge himself under a dark ridge of rock. There he sat brooding miserably over his lack of camouflage until it was time for me to go home.

I returned very early the following morning, and to my delight, I saw that the crab had been busy while I had been away. Making the best of a bad job, he had decorated the top of his shell with a number of the ingredients that I had left for him. He looked extremely gaudy and had an air of carnival about him. Striped top-shells had been pasted on, interspersed with bits of coral, and up near his head he was wearing two beadlet anemones, like an extremely saucy bonnet with ribbons. I thought, as I watched him crawling about the sand, that he looked exceedingly conspicuous, but, curiously enough, when he went over and squatted by his favourite overhang of rock, he turned into what appeared to be a little pile of shell and coral debris, with a couple of anemones perched on top of it.

To the left of the little bay, a quarter of a mile or so from the shore, lay an island called Pondikonissi, or Mouse Island. It was shaped not unlike an isosceles triangle and was thick with elderly cypress trees and oleander bushes, which guarded a small snow-white church and tiny living quarters adjoining it. This island was inhabited by an elderly and extremely verminous monk, with long black robes and a stove-pipe hat, whose major function in life appeared to be ringing the bell in the match-box-size church at intervals and rowing slowly over to a neighbouring headland in the evening, where there was a small nunnery, inhabited by three ancient nuns. Here he would partake of ouzo and a cup of coffee and discuss, presumably, the state of sin in the world today, and then, as the sun set and turned the calm waters round his island to a multi-coloured sheet of shot-silk, he would row back again, like a hunched black crow, in his creaking, leaking boat.

Margo, having discovered that constant sun-bathing, if anything, inflamed her acne, now decided on another of Mother Nature's cures—sea-bathing. Every morning she would get up at about half past five, rout me out of bed, and together we would make our way down to the shore and plunge into the clear water, still chilly from the moon's gaze, and then swim slowly and languidly across to Pondikonissi. Here Margo would drape herself on a rock and I would potter happily in the rock pools on the shore. Unfortunately, our visitations to the island seemed to have a detrimental effect upon the monk, for no sooner had Margo landed and arranged herself attractively on a rock than he would come stamping down the long flight of stone steps that led up to the church, shaking his fist at her, and mouthing incomprehensible Greek from the depths of his long, unkempt beard. Margo would always greet him with a bright smile and a cheerful wave of her hand, and this generally made him almost apoplectic with rage. He would stamp to and fro, his black robes swishing, pointing one dirty and trembling finger at the heavens above and another at Margo. After this had happened on numerous occasions, I managed to commit to memory several of the monk's favourite phrases, for his vocabulary was not an extensive one. I then asked my friend Philemon what they meant. Philemon was convulsed with laughter. He laughed so much that he was almost incapable of explaining to me, but I at length understood that the monk had several derogatory terms that he used for Margo, the mildest of these being "white witch."

When I related this to Mother, she was, to my astonishment, considerably shocked.

"Really," she said, "we ought to report him to somebody. They'd never be able to carry on like that in the Church of England."

Eventually, however, the whole thing became a sort of game. When Margo and I swam across, we would take some cigarettes over for the monk and he would come flying down the stone steps, shaking his fist and threatening us with the wrath of God, and then, having done his duty, as it were, he would hitch up his robes, squat on the wall, and with great good humour smoke the cigarettes we had brought him. Occasionally he would even trot back to the church to bring us a handful of figs from his tree or a few almonds, milky and fresh, which we would crack between the smooth stones on the beach.

Between Pondikonissi and my favourite bay there stretched a whole string of reefs. Most of these were flat-topped, some of them only the size of a table and others the size of a small garden. The majority of them lay perhaps two inches below the surface of the water, so that if you hauled yourself out and stood on them, from a distance it looked exactly as though you were walking on the surface of the sea. I had long wanted to investigate these reefs, for they contained a lot of sea life that you did not find in the shallow waters of the bay. But this presented insurmountable difficulties, for I could not get my equipment out there. I had tried to swim out to one reef with two large jam jars slung round my neck on a string and carrying my net in one hand, but half-way there the jam jars suddenly and maliciously filled with water, and their combined weight dragged me under. It was a few seconds before I managed to disentangle myself from them and rise gasping and spluttering to the surface, by which time my jars were lying glinting and rolling in a fathom of water, as irretrievable as though they had been on the moon.

Then, one hot afternoon, I was down in the bay turning over rocks in an effort to find some of the long, multi-coloured ribbon-worms that inhabited that sort of terrain. So absorbed was I in my task that the prow of a rowing-boat had scrunched and whispered its way into the sandy shore beside me before I was aware of it. Standing in the stern, leaning on his single oar—which he used, as did all the fishermen, twisting it in the water like a fish's tail—was a young man, burnt almost black by the sun. He had a mop of dark, curly hair, eyes as bright and as black as mulberries, and his teeth gleamed astonishingly white in his brown face.

"*Yasu*," he said. "Your health."

I returned his greeting and watched him as he jumped nimbly out of the boat, carrying a small rusty anchor which he wedged firmly behind a great double bed of drying seaweed on the beach. He was wearing nothing but a very tattered singlet and a pair of trousers that had once been blue, but were now bleached almost white by the sun. He came over and squatted companionably beside me and produced from his pocket a tin containing tobacco and cigarette papers.

"It is hot today," he said, making a grimace, while his blunt, calloused fingers rolled a cigarette with extraordinary deftness. He stuck it in his mouth and lit it with the aid of a large, tin lighter, inhaled deeply, and then sighed. He cocked an eyebrow at me, his eyes as bright as a robin's.

"You're one of the strangers that live up on the hill?" he inquired.

By this time my Greek had become reasonably fluent, so I admitted that, yes, I was one of the strangers.

"And the others?" he asked. "The others in the villa, who are they?"

I had quickly learned that every Corfiote, particularly the peasants, loved to know all about you and would, in return for this information, vouchsafe to you the most intimate details of their private lives. I explained that the others at the villa were my mother, my two brothers, and my sister. He nodded gravely, as though this information were of the utmost importance.

"And your father?" he continued. "Where is your father?"

I explained that my father was dead.

"Poor thing," he said, quickly commiserating. "And your poor mother with four children to bring up."

He sighed lugubriously at this terrible thought and then brightened.

"Still," he said philosophically, "thus is life. What are you looking for here under these stones?"

I explained as best I could, though I always found it difficult to get the peasants to understand why I was so interested in such a variety of creatures that were either obnoxious or not worth worrying about and all of which were inedible.

"What's your name?" he asked.

I said that it was Gerasimos, which was the closest approach to Gerald that one could come to in Greek. But, I explained, my friends called me Gerry.

"I'm Taki," he said. "Taki Thanatos. I live at Benitses."

I asked him what he was doing up here so comparatively far from his village. He shrugged.

"I have come from Benitses," he said, "and I fish on the way. Then I eat and I sleep and when it's night I light my lights and go back to Benitses, fishing again."

This news excited me, for not long before, we had been returning late from town, and standing on the road by the little path that led up to the villa, we had seen a boat passing below us, being rowed very slowly, with a large carbon lamp fixed to the bows. As the fisherman manœuvred the boat slowly through the dark, shallow waters, the pool of light cast by his lamp had illuminated great patches of sea-bed with the utmost vividness, reefs smouldering citron green, pink, yellow, and brown as the boat moved slowly along. I had thought at the time that this must be a fascinating occupation, but I had known no fishermen. Now I began to view Taki with some enthusiasm.

I asked him eagerly what time he intended to start his fishing and whether he meant to go round the reefs that lay scattered between the bay and Pondikonissi.

"I start about ten," he said. "I work round the island, then I head towards Benitses."

I asked him whether it would be possible for me to join him, because, as I explained, there were lots of strange creatures living on the reef which I could not obtain without the aid of a boat.

"Why not?" he said. "I shall be down below Menelaos'. You come at ten. I'll take you round the reefs and then drop you back at Menelaos' before I go to Benitses."

I assured him fervently that I would be there at ten o'clock. Then, gathering up my net and bottles and whistling for Roger, I beat a hasty retreat before Taki could change his mind. Once I was safely out of earshot, I slowed down and gave a considerable amount of thought to how I was going to persuade the family in general, and Mother in particular, to let me go out to sea at ten o'clock at night.

Mother, I knew, had always been worried about my refusal to have a siesta during the heat of the day. I had explained to her that this was generally the best time for insects and things like that, but she was not convinced that this was a valid argument. However, the result was that at night, just when something interesting was happening (such as Larry locked in a verbal battle with Leslie), Mother would say, "It's time you went to bed, dear. After all, remember, you don't have a siesta."

This I felt might be the answer to the night fishing. It was scarcely three o'clock and I knew that the family would be lying supine behind closed shutters, only to awake and start to buzz at each other, drowsily, like sun-drugged flies, at about half past five.

I made my way back to the villa with the utmost speed. When I was a hundred yards away, I took off my shirt and wrapped it carefully round my jam jars full of specimens so that not a chink or a rattle would betray my presence; then, cautioning Roger upon pain of death not to utter a sound, we made our way cautiously into the villa and slipped like shadows into my bedroom. Roger squatted panting in the middle of the floor and viewed me with considerable surprise as I took off all my clothes and climbed into bed. He was not at all sure that he approved of this untoward behaviour. As far as he was concerned, the whole afternoon stretched ahead of us, littered with exciting adventures, and here was I preparing to go to sleep. He whined experimentally and I shushed him with such fierceness that his ears drooped, and putting his stumpy tail between his legs, he crept under the bed and curled up with a rueful sigh. I took a book and tried to concentrate on it. The half-closed shutters made the room look like a cool, green aquarium, but in fact the air was still and hot and the sweat rolled in rivulets down my ribs. What on earth, I thought, shifting uncomfortably on the already sodden sheet, could the family possibly see in a siesta? What good did it do them? In fact, how they managed to sleep at all was a mystery to me. At this moment I sank swiftly into oblivion.

I woke at half past five and staggered out, half-asleep, to the veranda, where the family were having tea.

"Good heavens," said Mother. "Have you been sleeping?"

I said, as casually as I could, that I thought a siesta a good thing that afternoon.

"Are you feeling well, dear?" she asked anxiously.

I said, yes, I felt fine. I had decided to have a siesta in order to prepare myself for that evening.

"Why, what's happening, dear?" asked Mother.

I said, with all the nonchalance I could muster, that I was going out at ten o'clock with a fisherman who was going to take me night-fishing, for, as I explained, there were certain creatures that came out only at night and this was the best method of obtaining them.

"I hope this does not mean," said Larry ominously, "that we're going to have octopus and conger eels flopping around the floor. Better stop him, Mother. Before you know where you are the whole villa will look and smell like Grimsby."

I replied, somewhat heatedly, that I did not intend to bring the specimens back to the villa, but to put them straight into my special rock pool.

"Ten o'clock's rather *late*, dear," said Mother. "What time will you be back?"

Lying valiantly, I said I thought I would be back at about eleven.

"Well, mind you wrap up warmly," said Mother, who was always convinced that, in spite of the nights' being warm and balmy, I would inevitably end up with double pneumonia if I did not wear a jersey. Promising faithfully to wrap up warmly, I finished my tea and then spent an exciting and satisfying hour or so in marshalling my collecting gear. There was my long-handled net, a long bamboo with three wire hooks on the end for pulling interesting clumps of seaweed nearer to one, eight wide-mouthed jam jars, and several tins and boxes for putting such things as crabs or shells in. Making sure that Mother was not around, I put on my bathing trunks under my shorts and hid a towel in the bottom of my collecting bag, for I felt sure that I might have to dive for some of the specimens. I knew that Mother's fears of double pneumonia would increase a hundredfold if she thought I was going to do this.

Then at a quarter to ten I slung my bag on my back and, taking a torch, made my way down through the olive groves. The moon was a pale, smudged sickle in a star-lit sky, shedding only the feeblest light. In the black recesses among the olive roots, glow-worms gleamed like emeralds, and I could hear the scops owls calling "toink, toink" to each other from the shadows.

When I reached the beach I found Taki squatting in his boat, smoking. He had already lighted the carbon lamp and it hissed angrily to itself and smelt strongly of garlic as it cast a brilliant circle of white light into the shallow water by the bows. Already I could see that a host of life had been attracted to it. Gobies and blennies had come out of their holes and were sitting on the seaweed-covered rocks, pouting and gulping expectantly like an audience in the theatre waiting for the curtain to go up. Shore-crabs scuttled to and fro, pausing now and then to pluck some seaweed delicately and stuff it carefully into their mouths; and everywhere there trundled top-shells, dragged by small, choleric-looking hermit-crabs, who now occupied the shells in place of their rightful owners.

I arranged my collecting gear in the bottom of the boat and sat down with a contented sigh. Taki pushed off and then, using the oar, punted us along through the shallow water and the beds of ribbon-weed that rustled and whispered along the side of the boat. As soon as we were in deeper water, he fixed both his oars and then rowed standing up. We progressed very slowly, Taki keeping a careful eye on the nimbus of light that illuminated the sea bottom for some twelve feet in every direction. The oars squeaked musically and Taki hummed to himself. Along one side of the boat lay an eight-foot pole ending in a five-pronged, savagely barbed trident. In the bow I could see the little bottle of olive oil, such a necessary accoutrement to the fisherman, for should a slight wind blow up and ruffle the waters, a sprinkling of oil would have a magically calming effect on the pleated surface of the sea. Slowly and steadily we crept out towards the black triangular silhouette of Pondikonissi to where the reefs lay. When we neared them Taki rested on his oars for a moment and looked at me.

"We'll go round and round for five minutes," he said, "so that I may catch what there is. Then after that I will take you round to catch the things that you want."

I readily agreed to this, for I was anxious to see how Taki fished with his massive trident. Very slowly we edged our way round the biggest of the reefs, the light illuminating the strange submarine cliffs covered with pink and purple sea-weeds that looked like fluffy oak trees. Peering down into the water, one felt as though one were a kestrel, floating smoothly on outstretched wings over a multi-coloured autumn forest.

Suddenly Taki stopped rowing and dug his oars gently into the water to act as a brake. The boat came to an almost complete standstill as he picked up the trident.

"Look," he said, pointing to the sandy bottom under a great bulwark of submarine cliff. "Scorpios."

At first glance I could see nothing, then suddenly I saw what he meant. Lying on the sand was a fish some two feet long with a great filigree of sharp spines like a dragon's crest along its back, and enormous petrel fins spread out on the sand. It had a tremendously wide head with golden eyes and a sulky, pouting mouth. But it was the colours that astonished me, for it was decked out in a series of reds ranging from scarlet to wine, pricked out and accentuated here and there with white. It looked immensely sure of itself as it lay there, flamboyant, on the sand, and immensely dangerous, too.

"This is good eating," whispered Taki to my surprise, for the fish, if anything, looked highly poisonous.

Slowly and delicately he lowered the trident into the water, easing the barbed fork inch by inch towards the fish. There was no sound except the peevish hissing of the lamp. Slowly, inexorably, the trident got closer and closer. I held my breath. Surely that great fish with its gold-flecked eyes must notice its approaching doom? A sudden flip of the tail, I thought, and a swirl of sand and it would be gone. But no. It just lay there gulping methodically and pompously to itself. When the trident was within a foot of it, Taki paused. I saw him gently shift his grip on the haft. He stood immobile for a second, although it seemed an interminable time to me, and then suddenly, so speedily that I did not actually see the movement, he drove the five prongs swiftly and neatly through the back of the great fish's head. There was a swirl of sand and blood and the fish twisted and writhed on the prongs, curling its body so that the spines along its back jabbed at the trident. But Taki had driven the trident home too skilfully and it could not escape. Quickly, hand over hand, he pulled in the pole, and the fish came over the side and into the boat, flapping and writhing. I came forward to help him get it off the prongs, but he pushed me back roughly.

"Take care," he said, "the scorpios is a bad fish."

I watched while, with the aid of the oar blade, he got the fish off the trident, and although to all intents and purposes it must have been dead, it still wriggled and flapped and tried to drive the spines on its back into the side of the boat.

"Look, look," said Taki. "You see now why we call it scorpios. If he can stab you with those spines, Saint Spiridion, what pain you would have! You would have to go to the hospital quickly."

With the aid of the oar and the trident, and a dexterous bit of juggling, he managed to lift the scorpion fish up and drop it into an empty kerosene tin where it could do no harm. I wanted to know why, if it was poisonous, it was supposed to be good eating.

"Ah," said Taki, "it's only the spines. You cut those off, The flesh is sweet, as sweet as honey. I will give it to you to take home with you."

He bent over his oars once more and we proceeded to squeak our way along the edge of the reef again. Presently he paused once more. Here the sea-bed was sandy with just a few scattered tufts of young green ribbon-weed. Again, he slowed the boat to a standstill and picked up his trident.

"Look," he said. "Octopus."

My stomach gave a clutch of excitement, for the only octopuses I had seen had been the dead ones on sale in the town, and these, I felt sure, bore no resemblance to the living creature. But peer as hard as I could, the sandy bottom appeared to be completely devoid of life.

"There, *there*," said Taki, lowering the trident gently into the water and pointing. "Can't you see it? Did you leave your eyes behind? There, *there*. Look, I am almost touching it."

Still I could not see it. He lowered the trident another foot.

"Now can you see it, foolish one?" he chuckled. "Just at the end of the prongs."

And suddenly I could see it. I had been looking at it all the time, but it was so grey and sandlike that I had mistaken it for part of the sea-bed. It squatted on the sand in a nest of tentacles, and there under its bald, domed head its eyes, uncannily human, peered up at us forlornly.

"It's a big one," said Taki.

He shifted the trident slightly in his grasp, but the movement was incautious. Suddenly the octopus turned from a drab sandy colour to a bright and startling iridescent green. It squirted a jet of water out of its syphon, and projected by this, in a swirl of sand, it shot off the sea-bed. Its tentacles trailed out behind it, and as it sped through the water, it looked like a runaway balloon.

"Ah, *gammoto!*" said Taki.

He threw the trident down and seizing the oars he rowed swiftly in the wake of the octopus. The octopus obviously possessed a touching faith in its camouflage, for it had come to rest on the sea-bed some thirty-five feet away.

Once again, Taki eased the boat up to it and once again he lowered the trident carefully into the water. This time he took no risks and made no incautious movements. When the pronged fork was within a foot of the octopus's domed head, Taki strengthened his grip on the pole and plunged it home. Immediately the silver sand boiled up in a cloud as the octopus's tentacles threshed and writhed and wound themselves round the trident. Ink spurted from its body and hung like a trembling curtain of black lace or coiled like smoke across the sand. Taki was chuckling now with pleasure. He hauled the trident up swiftly, and as the octopus came into the boat, two of its tentacles seized and adhered to the side. Taki gave a sharp tug and the tentacles were pulled free with a ripping, rasping noise that was like the sound of sticking plaster being removed, a thousand times magnified. Swiftly, Taki grabbed the round, slimy body of the octopus and deftly removed it from the prongs and then, to my astonishment, he lifted this writhing Medusa head and put it to his face so that the tentacles wound round his forehead, his cheeks, and his neck, the suckers leaving white impressions against his dark skin. Then, choosing his spot carefully, he suddenly buried his teeth in the very core of the creature with a snap and a sideways jerk, reminiscent of a terrier breaking the back of a rat. He had obviously bitten through some vital nerve-centre, for immediately the tentacles released their grip on his head and fell limply, only their very extremities twitching and curling slightly. Taki threw the octopus into the tin with the scorpion fish and spat over the side of the boat and then, reaching over, cupped a handful of sea-water and swilled his mouth out with it.

"You have brought me luck," he said, grinning and wiping his mouth. "It is not many nights that I get an octopus *and* a scorpios."

But apparently Taki's luck stopped short at the octopus, for although we circled the reef several times, we caught nothing more. We did see the head of a moray eel sticking out of its hole in the reef, an extremely vicious-looking head the size of a small dog's. But when Taki lowered the trident, the moray eel, very smoothly and with much dignity, retreated with fluid grace into the depths of the reef and we did not see him again. For myself, I was quite glad, for I imagined he must have been about six feet long, and to wrestle about in a dimly lit boat with a six-foot moray eel was an experience that even I, ardent naturalist though I was, felt I could do without.

"Ah, well," said Taki philosophically. "Now let's go and do your fishing."

He rowed me out to the largest of the reefs and landed me with my gear on its flat top. Armed with my net, I prowled along the edge of the reef while Taki rowed the boat some six feet behind me, illuminating the smouldering beauty of the rocks. There was so much life that I despaired of being able to capture it all.

There were fragile blennies, decked out in gold and scarlet; tiny fish half the size of a match-stick with great black eyes and pillar-box red bodies; and others, the same size, whose colouring was a combination of deep Prussian- and pale powder-blue. There were blood-red starfish and purple, brittle starfish, their long, slender, spiky arms forever coiling and uncoiling. These had to be lifted in the net with the utmost delicacy, for the slightest shock and they would, with gay abandon, shed all their arms lavishly. There were slipper limpets that, when you turned them over, you found had half the underside covered by a neat flange of shell, so that the whole thing *did* look rather like a baggy, shapeless carpet-slipper designed for a gouty foot. Then there were cowries, some as white as snow and delicately ribbed, others a pale cream, heavily blotched and smudged with purple-black markings. Then there were the coat-of-mail shells, or chitons, some two and a half inches long, that clung to crannies in the rocks, looking like gigantic wood-lice. I saw a baby cuttlefish the size of a match-box and almost fell off the edge of the reef in my efforts to capture him, but to my immense chagrin, he escaped. After only half an hour's collecting I found that my jars, tins, and boxes were crammed to overflowing with life, and I knew that, albeit reluctantly, I would have to stop.

Taki, very goodhumouredly, rowed me over to my favourite bay and stood watching with amusement while I carefully emptied my jars of specimens into my rock pool. Then he rowed me back to the jetty below Menelaos'. Here he strung a cord through the gills of the now dead scorpion fish and handed it to me.

"Tell your mother," he said, "to cook it with hot paprika and oil and potatoes and little marrows. It is very sweet."

I thanked him for this and for the fact that he had been so patient with me.

"Come fishing again," he said. "I shall be up here next week. Probably Wednesday or Thursday. I'll send a message to you when I arrive."

I thanked him and said I would look forward to it. He pushed the boat off and poled his way through the shallow waters heading in the direction of Benitses.

I shouted "Be happy" after him.

"*Pasto calo*," he answered. "Go to the good."

I turned and trudged my way wearily up the hill. I discovered to my horror that it was half past two and I knew Mother would by now have convinced herself that I had been drowned or eaten by a shark or overtaken by some similar fate. However, I hoped that the scorpion fish would placate her.

3

THE MYRTLE FORESTS

About half a mile north of the villa the olive grove thinned out and there was a great flat basin, fifty or sixty acres in extent, on which no olives grew. Here was only a great green forest of myrtle bushes, interspersed with dry, stony grassland, decorated with the strange candelabras of the thistles, glowing a vivid electric blue, and the huge flaky bulb of squills. This was one of my favourite hunting grounds, for it contained a remarkable selection of insect life. Roger and I would squat in the heavily scented shade of the myrtle bushes and watch the array of creatures that passed us; at certain times of the day the branches were as busy as the main street of a town.

The myrtle forests were full of mantises some three inches long, with vivid green wings. They would sway through the myrtle branches on their slender legs, their wickedly barbed front arms held up in an attitude of hypocritical prayer, their little pointed faces with their bulbous straw-coloured eyes turning this way and that, missing nothing, like angular, embittered spinsters at a cocktail party. Should a cabbage white or a fritillary land on the glossy myrtle leaves, the mantises would approach them with the utmost caution, moving almost imperceptibly, pausing now and then to sway gently to and fro on their legs, beseeching the butterfly to believe they were really wind-ruffled leaves.

I once saw a mantis stalk and finally launch himself at a large swallow-tail which was sitting in the sun gently moving its wings and meditating. At the last minute, however, the mantis missed its footing and instead of catching the swallow-tail by the body, as it had intended to do, caught it by one wing. The swallow-tail came out of its trance with a start and flapped its wings so vigorously that it succeeded in lifting the forequarters of the mantis off the leaves. A few more vigorous flappings and, to the mantis' annoyance, the swallow-tail flew lopsidedly away with a large section missing from one wing. The mantis philosophically sat down and ate the piece of wing that it had retained in its claws.

Under the rocks that littered the ground among the thistles there lived a surprising variety of creatures, in spite of the fact that the earth was baked rock-hard by the sun and was almost hot enough to poach an egg. Here lived a beast that always gave me the creeps. It was a flattened centipede some two inches long, with a thick fringe of long spiky legs along each side of its body. It was so flat that it could get into the most minute crevice and it moved with tremendous speed, seeming more to glide over the ground than run, as smoothly as a flat pebble skims across ice. These creatures were called Scutigeridae, and I could think of no other name which would be so apt in conjuring up their particularly obnoxious form of locomotion.

Scattered among the rocks, you would find holes that had been driven into the hard ground, each the size of a half-crown or larger. They were silk-lined and with a web spread to a three-inch circle around the mouth of the burrow. These were the lairs of the tarantulas, great, fat, chocolate-coloured spiders with fawn-and-cinnamon markings. With their legs spread out, they covered an area perhaps the size of a coffee saucer and their bodies were about the size of half a small walnut. They were immensely powerful spiders, quick and cruel in their hunting, and displaying a remarkable sort of inimical intelligence. For the most part, they hunted at night,

but occasionally you would see them during the day, striding swiftly through the thistles on their long legs, in search of
their prey. Generally, as soon as they saw you, they would
scuttle off and soon be lost among the myrtles, but one day
I saw one who was so completely absorbed that he let me
approach quite close.

He was some six or seven feet away from his burrow, and
he was standing half-way up a blue thistle, waving his front
legs and peering about him, reminding me irresistibly of a
hunter who had climbed up a tree in order to see if there is
any game about. He continued to do this for about five minutes while I squatted on my haunches and watched him. Presently he climbed carefully down the thistle and set off in a
very determined manner. It was almost as though he had seen
something from his lofty perch, but searching the ground
around, I could see no sign of life, and in any case I was not
at all sure that a tarantula's eyesight was as good as all that.
But he marched along in a determined fashion until he came
to a large clump of Job's tears, a fine trembling grass whose
seed heads look like little white plaited rolls of bread. Going
closer to this, I suddenly realized what the tarantula appeared
to be after, for under the delicate fountain of white grass
there was a lark's nest. It had four eggs in it and one of them
had just hatched, and the tiny, pink, downy offspring was still
struggling feebly in the remains of the shell.

Before I could do anything sensible to save it, the tarantula had marched up over the edge of the nest. He loomed
there for a moment, monstrous and terrifying, and then
swiftly he drew the quivering baby to him and sank his long,
curved mandibles into its back. The baby gave two minute,
almost inaudible squeaks and opened its mouth wide as it
writhed briefly in the hairy embrace of the spider. The poison
took effect and it went rigid for a brief moment and then
hung limply. The spider waited, immobile, till he was certain
the poison had done its work, and then he turned and
marched off, the baby hanging limply from his jaws. He looked

like some strange, leggy retriever, bringing in his first grouse of the season. Without a pause, he hurried back to his burrow and disappeared inside it, carrying the limp, pathetic little body of the fledgling.

I was amazed by this encounter, for two reasons: firstly, because I did not realize that tarantulas would tackle anything the size of a baby bird, and secondly, because I could not see how he knew the nest was there—and he obviously *did* know, for he walked, unhesitatingly, straight to it. The distance from the thistle he had climbed to the nest was about thirty-five feet, as I found out by pacing it, and I was positive that no spider had the eyesight to be able to spot such a well-camouflaged nest and the fledgling from that distance. This left only smell, and here again, although I knew animals could smell subtle scents which our blunted nostrils could not pick up, I felt that on a breathlessly still day at thirty-five feet it would take a remarkable olfactory sense to be able to pinpoint the baby lark. The only solution I could come to was that the spider had, during his perambulations, discovered the nest and kept checking on it periodically to see whether the young had hatched. But this did not satisfy me as an explanation, for it attributed a thought process to an insect which I was pretty certain it did not possess. Even my oracle, Theodore, could not explain this puzzle satisfactorily. All I knew was that that particular pair of larks did not succeed in rearing a single young one that year.

Other creatures that fascinated me greatly in the myrtle forests were the ant-lion larvae. Adult ant-lions come in a variety of sizes and, for the most part, rather drab colouring. They look like extremely untidy and demented dragon-flies. They have wings that seem to be out of all proportion to their bodies and these they flap with a desperate air, as though it required the maximum amount of energy to prevent them from crashing to the earth. They were a good-natured, bumbling sort of beast, and did no harm to anybody. But the same could not be said of their larvae. What the rapacious dragonfly larvae were to the pond, the ant-lion larvae were to the dry, sandy areas that lay between the myrtle bushes. The only sign that there were ant-lion larvae about was a series of curious, cone-shaped depressions in areas where the soil was fine and soft enough to be dug. The first time I discovered these cones, I was greatly puzzled as to what had made them. I wondered if perhaps some mice had been excavating for roots or something similar; I was unaware that at the base of each cone was the architect, waiting taut and ready in the sand, as dangerous as a hidden man-trap. Then I saw one of these cones in action and realized for the first time that it was not only the larva's home, but also a gigantic trap.

An ant would come trotting along (I always felt they hummed to themselves as they went about their work); it might be one of the little, busy, black variety or one of the large, red, solitary ants that staggered about the countryside with their red abdomens pointing to the sky, for some obscure reason, like anti-aircraft guns. Whichever species it was, if it happened to walk over the edge of one of the little pits, it immediately found that the sloping sides shifted so that it very soon started to slide down towards the base of the cone. It would then turn and try to climb out of the pit, but the earth or sand would shift in little avalanches under its feet. As soon as one of these avalanches had trickled down to the base of the cone, it would be the signal for the larva to come into action. Suddenly the ant would find itself bombarded with a rapid machine-gun fire of sand or earth, projected up from the bottom of the pit with incredible speed by the head of the larva. With the shifting ground underfoot and being bombarded with earth or sand, the ant would miss its foothold and roll ignominiously down to the bottom of the pit. Out of the sand, with utmost speed, would appear the head of the ant-lion larva, a flattened, ant-like head, with a pair of enormous curved jaws, like sickles. These would be plunged into the unfortunate ant's body and the larva would sink back beneath the sand, dragging the kicking and struggling ant with it to its grave. As I felt the ant-lion larvae took an unfair advantage over the dim-witted and rather earnest ants, I had no compunction in digging them up when I found them, taking them home, and making them hatch out eventually in little muslin cages, so that if they were a species new to me, I could add them to my collection.

One day we had one of those freak storms when the sky turned blue-black and the lightning fretted a silver filigree across it. And then had come the rain—great, fat, heavy drops, as warm as blood. When the storm had passed, the sky had been washed to the clear blue of a hedge-sparrow's egg and the damp earth sent out wonderfully rich, almost gastronomic smells as of fruit-cake or plum pudding; and the olive trunks steamed as the rain was dried off them by the sun, each trunk looking as though it were on fire. Roger and I liked these summer storms. It was fun to be able to splash through the puddles and feel one's clothes getting wetter and wetter in the warm rain. In addition to this, Roger derived considerable amusement by barking at the lightning. When the rain ceased we were passing the myrtle forests, and I went in on the off-chance that the storm might have brought out some creatures that would normally be sheltering from the heat of the day. Sure enough, on a myrtle branch there were two fat, honey- and amber-coloured snails gliding smoothly towards each other, their horns waving provocatively. Normally, I knew, in the height of the summer, these snails would aestivate. They would attach themselves to a convenient branch, construct a thin, paperlike front door over the mouth of the shell, and then retreat deep into its convolutions in order to husband the moisture in their bodies from the fierce heat of the sun. This freak storm had obviously awakened them and made them feel gay and romantic. As I watched them they glided up to each other until their horns touched. Then they paused and gazed long and earnestly into each other's eyes. One of them then shifted his position slightly so that he could glide alongside the other one. When he was alongside, something happened that made me doubt the evidence of my own eyes. From his side, and almost simultaneously from the side of the other snail, there shot what appeared to be two minute, fragile white darts, each attached to a slender white cord. The dart from snail one pierced the side of snail two and disappeared, and the dart from snail two performed a similar function on snail one. So, there they were, side by side attached to each other by the two little white cords. And there they sat like two curious sailing ships roped together. This was amazing enough, but stranger things were to follow. The cords gradually appeared to get shorter and shorter and drew the two snails together. Peering at them so closely that my nose was almost touching them, I came to the incredulous conclusion that each snail, by some incredible mechanism in its body, was winching its rope in, thus hauling the other until presently their bodies were pressed tightly together. I knew they must be mating, but their bodies had become so amalgamated that I could not see the precise nature of the act. They stayed rapturously side by side for some fifteen minutes and then, without so much as a nod or a thank you, they glided away in opposite directions, neither one displaying any signs of darts or ropes, or indeed any sign of enthusiasm at having culminated their love affair successfully.

I was so intrigued by this piece of behaviour that I could hardly wait until the following Thursday, when Theodore came to tea, to tell him about it. Theodore listened, rocking gently on his toes and nodding gravely while I graphically described what I had witnessed.

"Aha, yes," he said when I had finished. "You were . . . um . . . you know . . . um . . . extremely lucky to see that. I have watched any number of snails and I have never seen it."

I asked whether I had imagined the little darts and the ropes.

"No, no," said Theodore. "That's quite correct. The darts are formed of a sort of . . . um . . . calcium-like substance and once they have penetrated the snail, they, you know, disappear . . . dissolve. It seems there is some evidence to think that the darts cause a *tingling* sensation which the snails . . . um . . . apparently find pleasant."

I asked whether I was right in assuming that each snail had winched its rope in.

"Yes, yes, that's quite correct," said Theodore. "They apparently have some . . . um . . . sort of mechanism inside which can pull the rope back again."

I said I thought it was one of the most remarkable things I had ever seen.

"Yes, indeed. Extremely curious," said Theodore, and then added a bomb-shell that took my breath away. "Once they are alongside, the . . . um . . . male half of one snail mates with the, um . . . female half of the other snail and . . . um, *vice versa*, as it were."

It took me a moment or so to absorb this astonishing information. Was I correct in assuming, I inquired cautiously, that each snail was both male *and* female?

"Um. Yes," said Theodore, "hermaphrodite."

His eyes twinkled at me and he rasped the side of his beard with his thumb. Larry, who had been wearing the pained expression he normally wore when Theodore and I discussed natural history, was equally astonished by this amazing revelation of the snails' sex life.

"Surely you're joking, Theodore?" he protested. "You mean to say that each snail is both a male and a female?"

"Yes, indeed," said Theodore, adding with masterly understatement, "it's very curious."

"Good God," cried Larry. "I think it's unfair. All those damned slimy things wandering about seducing each other like mad all over the bushes, and having the pleasures of both sensations. Why couldn't such a gift be given to the human race? That's what I want to know."

"Aha, yes. But then you would have to lay eggs," Theodore pointed out.

"True," said Larry, "but what a marvellous way of getting out of cocktail parties—'I'm terribly sorry I can't come,' you would say. 'I've got to sit on my eggs.'"

Theodore gave a little snort of laughter.

"But snails don't sit on their eggs," he explained. "They bury them in damp earth and leave them."

"The ideal way of bringing up a family," said Mother, unexpectedly but with immense conviction. "I wish I'd been able to bury you all in some damp earth and leave you."

"That's an extremely harsh and ungrateful thing to say," said Larry. "You've probably given Gerry a complex for the rest of his life."

But if the conversation had given me a complex, it was one about snails, for I was already planning vast snail-hunting expeditions with Roger, so that I could bring dozens of them back to the villa and keep them in tins, where I could observe them shooting their love darts at each other to my heart's content. But, in spite of the fact that I caught hundreds of snails during the next few weeks, kept them incarcerated in tins and lavished every care and attention on them (even gave them simulated thunder-storms with the aid of a watering can), I could not get them to mate.

The only other time I saw snails indulging in this curious love-play was when I succeeded in obtaining a pair of the giant Roman, or apple, snails that lived on the stony outcrops of the Mountain of the Ten Saints, and the only reason I was able to get up there and capture these snails was because, on my birthday, Mother had purchased for me my heart's desire, a sturdy baby donkey.

Although, ever since we arrived in Corfu, I had been aware that there were vast quantities of donkeys there—indeed the entire agricultural economy of the island depended on them —I had not really concentrated on them until we had gone to Katerina's wedding. Here a great number of the donkeys had brought with them their babies, many of them only a few days old. I was enchanted by their bulbous knees, their great ears, and their wobbling, uncertain walk and I had determined then, come what might, that I would possess a donkey of my own.

As I explained to Mother, while trying to argue her into agreeing to this, if I had a donkey to carry me and my equipment, I could go so much farther afield. Why couldn't I have it for Christmas, I asked? Because, Mother replied, firstly, they were too expensive, and secondly, there were not any babies available at that precise time. But if they were too expensive, I argued, why couldn't I have one as a Christmas *and* birthday present? I would willingly forgo all other presents in lieu of a donkey. Mother said she would see, which I knew from bitter experience generally meant that she would forget about the matter as rapidly and as comprehensively as possible. As it got near to my birthday, I once again reiterated all the arguments in favour of having a donkey. Mother just repeated that we would see.

Then one day, Costas, the brother of our maid, made his appearance in the olive grove just outside our little garden carrying on his shoulders a great bundle of tall bamboos. Whistling happily to himself he proceeded to dig holes in the ground and to set the bamboos upright so that they formed a small square. Peering at him through the fuchsia hedge, I wondered what on earth he was doing, so, whistling Roger, I went round to see.

"I am building," said Costas, "a house for your mother."

I was astonished. What on earth could Mother want a bamboo house for? Had she, perhaps, decided to sleep out of doors? I felt this was unlikely. What, I inquired of Costas, did Mother want with a bamboo house?

He gazed at me wall-eyed.

"Who knows?" he said shrugging. "Perhaps she wants to keep plants in it or store sweet potatoes for the winter."

I thought this was extremely unlikely as well, but having watched Costas for half an hour I grew bored and went off for a walk with Roger.

By the next day the framework of the bamboo hut had been finished and Costas was now busy twining bundles of reeds between the bamboos to form solid walls and the roof. By the next day it was completed and looked exactly like one of Robinson Crusoe's earlier attempts at house-building. When I inquired of Mother what she intended to use the house for, she said that she was not quite sure, but she felt it would come in useful. With that vague information I had to be content.

The day before my birthday, everybody started acting in a slightly more eccentric manner than usual. Larry, for some reason best known to himself, went about the house shouting "Tantivy!" and "Tally-ho" and similar hunting slogans. As he was fairly frequently afflicted in this way, I did not take much notice.

Margo kept dodging about the house carrying mysterious bundles under her arms, and at one point I came face to face with her in the hall and noted, with astonishment, that her arms were full of multi-coloured decorations left over from Christmas. On seeing me she uttered a squeak of dismay and rushed into her bedroom in such a guilty and furtive manner that I was left staring after her with open mouth.

Even Leslie and Spiro were afflicted, it seemed, and they kept going into mysterious huddles in the garden. From the snippets of their conversation that I heard, I could not make head or tail of what they were planning.

"In the backs seats," Spiro said, scowling. "Honest to Gods, Masters Leslies, I have dones it befores."

"Well, if you're sure, Spiro," Leslie replied doubtfully, "but we don't want any broken legs or anything."

Then Leslie saw me undisguisedly eavesdropping and asked me truculently what the hell I thought I was doing, eavesdropping on people's private conversations? Why didn't I go down to the nearest cliff and jump off? Feeling that the family were in no mood to be amicable, I took Roger off into the olive groves and for the rest of the day we ineffectually chased green lizards.

That night I had just turned down the lamp and snuggled down in bed when I heard sounds of raucous singing, accompanied by gales of laughter, coming through the olive groves. As the uproar got closer, I could recognize Leslie's and Larry's voices, combined with Spiro's, each of them appearing to be singing a different song. It seemed as though they had been somewhere and celebrated too well. From the indignant whispering and shuffling going on in the corridor, I could tell that Margo and Mother had reached the same conclusion.

They burst into the villa, laughing hysterically at some witticism that Larry had produced, and were shushed fiercely by Margo and Mother.

"Do be quiet," said Mother. "You'll wake Gerry. What have you been drinking?"

"Wine," said Larry in a dignified voice. He hiccuped.

"Wine," said Leslie. "And then we danced, and Spiro danced, and I danced, and Larry danced. And Spiro danced and then Larry danced and then I danced."

"I think you had better go to bed," said Mother.

"And then Spiro danced again," said Leslie, "and then Larry danced."

"All right, dear, all right," said Mother. "Go to *bed*, for heaven's sake. Really, Spiro, I do feel that you shouldn't have let them drink so much."

"Spiro danced," said Leslie, driving the point home.

"I'll take him to bed," said Larry. "I'm the only sober member of the party."

There was the sound of lurching feet on the tiles as Leslie and Larry, clasped in each other's arms, staggered down the corridor.

"I'm now dancing with *you*," came Leslie's voice as Larry dragged him into his bedroom and put him to bed.

"I'm sorrys, Mrs. Durrells," said Spiro, his deep voice thickened with wine, "but I couldn't stops thems."

"Did you get it?" said Margo.

"Yes, Missy Margos. Don'ts you worrys," said Spiro. "It's down with Costas."

Eventually Spiro left and I heard Mother and Margaret going to bed. It made a fittingly mysterious end to what had been a highly confusing day as far as I was concerned. But I soon forgot about the family's behaviour, as, lying in the dark wondering what my presents were going to be the following day, I drifted off to sleep.

The following morning I woke and lay for a moment wondering what was so special about that day, and then I remembered. It was my birthday. I lay there savouring the feeling of having a whole day to myself when people would give me presents and the family would be forced to accede to any reasonable requests. I was just about to get out of bed and go and see what my presents were, when a curious uproar broke out in the hall.

"Hold its head. Hold its *head*," came Leslie's voice.

"Look out, you're spoiling the decorations," wailed Margo.

"Damn the bloody decorations," said Leslie. "Hold its *head*."

"Now, now, dears," said Mother, "don't quarrel."

"Dear God," said Larry in disgust, "dung all over the floor."

The whole of this mysterious conversation was accompanied by a strange pitter-pattering noise, as though someone were bouncing ping-pong balls on the tile floor of the hall. What on earth, I wondered, was the family up to now? Normally at this time they were still lying, semi-conscious, groping bleary-eyed for their early morning cups of tea. I sat up in bed, preparatory to going into the hall to join in whatever fun was afoot, when my bedroom door burst open and a donkey, clad in festoons of coloured crepe paper, Christmas decorations, and with three enormous feathers attached skilfully between its large ears, came galloping into the bedroom, Leslie hanging grimly on to its tail, shouting, "Woa, you bastard!"

"Language, dear," said Mother, looking flustered in the doorway.

"You're spoiling the decorations," screamed Margo.

"The sooner that animal gets out of here," said Larry, "the better. There's dung all over the hall now."

"You frightened it," said Margo.

"I didn't do anything," said Larry indignantly. "I just gave it a little push."

The donkey skidded to a halt by my bedside and gazed at me out of enormous brown eyes. It seemed rather surprised. It shook itself vigorously so that the feathers between its ears fell off and then very dexterously it hacked Leslie on the shin with its hind leg.

"Jesus!" roared Leslie, hopping around on one leg. "It's broken my bloody leg."

"Leslie, dear, there is no need to swear so much," said Mother. "Remember Gerry."

"The sooner you get it out of that bedroom the better," said Larry. "Otherwise the whole place will smell like a midden."

"You've simply *ruined* its decorations," said Margo, "and it took me hours to put them on."

But I was taking no notice of the family. The donkey had approached the edge of my bed and stared at me inquisitively for a moment and then had given a little throaty chuckle and thrust in my outstretched hands a grey muzzle as soft as everything soft I could think of—silkworm cocoons, newly born puppies, sea pebbles, or the velvety feel of a tree frog. Leslie had now removed his trousers and was examining the bruise on his shin, cursing fluently.

"Do you like it dear?" asked Mother.

Like it! I was speechless.

The donkey was a rich dark brown, almost a plum colour,

with enormous ears like arum lilies, white socks over tiny polished hooves as neat as a tap-dancer's shoes. Running along
her back was the broad black cross that denotes so proudly
that her race carried Christ into Jerusalem (and has since
continued to be one of the most maligned domestic animals
ever), and round each great shining eye she had a neat white
circle which denoted that she came from the village of Gastouri.

"You remember Katerina's donkey that you liked so much?"
said Margo. "Well, this is her baby."

This, of course, made the donkey even more special. The
donkey stood there looking like a refugee from a circus, chewing a piece of tinsel meditatively, while I scrambled out of bed
and flung on my clothes. Where, I inquired breathlessly of
Mother, was I to keep her? Obviously I couldn't keep her in
the villa in view of the fact that Larry had just pointed out
to Mother that she could, if she so wished, grow a good crop
of potatoes in the hall.

"That's what that house Costas built is for," said
Mother.

I was beside myself with delight. What a noble, kindly,
benevolent family I had! How cunningly they had kept
the secret from me! How hard they had worked to deck the
donkey out in its finery! Slowly and gently, as though she were
some fragile piece of china, I led my steed out through the
garden and round into the olive grove, opened the door of
the little bamboo hut, and took her inside. I thought I ought
to just try her for size, because Costas was a notoriously bad
workman. The little house was splendid. Just big enough for
her. I took her out again and tethered her to an olive tree on a
long length of rope, then I stayed for half an hour in a dream-
like trance admiring her from every angle while she grazed
placidly. Eventually I heard Mother calling me in to breakfast and I sighed with satisfaction. I had decided that, without any doubt whatsoever, and without wishing in any way to
be partisan, this donkey was the finest donkey in the whole

of the island of Corfu. For no reason that I could think of, I decided to call her Sally. I gave her a quick kiss on her silken muzzle and then went in to breakfast.

After breakfast, to my astonishment, Larry, with a magnanimous air, said that if I liked he would teach me to ride. I said that I didn't know he could ride.

"Of course," said Larry airily. "When we were in India I was always galloping about on ponies and things. I used to groom them and feed them and so forth. Have to know what you're doing, of course."

So, armed with a blanket and a large piece of webbing, we went out into the olive grove, placed the blanket on Sally's back, and tied it in position. She viewed these preparations with interest but a lack of enthusiasm. With a certain amount of difficulty, for Sally would persist in walking round and round in a tight circle, Larry succeeded in getting me onto her back. He then exchanged her tether for a rope halter and rope reins.

"Now," he said, "you just steer her as though she's a boat. When you want her to go faster, just simply kick her in the ribs with your heels."

If that was all there was to riding, I felt, it was going to be simplicity itself. I jerked on the reins and dug my heels into Sally's ribs. It was unfortunate that my fall was broken by a large and exceptionally luxuriant bramble bush. Sally peered at me as I extricated myself, with a look of astonishment on her face.

"Perhaps," said Larry, "you ought to have a stick so then you can use your legs for gripping on to her and you won't fall off."

He cut me a short stick and once again I mounted Sally. This time I wrapped my legs tightly round her barrel body and gave her a sharp tap with my switch. She bucked several times, indignantly, but I clung on like a limpet, and to my delight, within half an hour, I had her trotting to and fro between the olive trees, responding neatly to tugs on the rein.

Larry had been lying under the olives smoking and watching my progress. Now, as I appeared to have mastered the equestrian art, he rose to his feet and took a penknife out of his pocket.

"Now," he said, as I dismounted, "I'll show you how to look after her. First of all, you must brush her down every morning. We'll get a brush for you in town. Then you must make sure her hooves are clean. You must do that every day."

I inquired, puzzled, how did one clean donkeys' hooves?

"I'll show you," said Larry nonchalantly.

He walked up to Sally, bent down, and picked up her hind leg.

"In here," he said, pointing with the blade of the knife at Sally's hoof, "an awful lot of muck gets trapped. This can lead to all sorts of things. Foot-rot and so forth, and it's very important to keep them clean."

So saying, he dug his penknife blade into Sally's hoof. What Larry had not realized was that donkeys in Corfu were unshod and that a baby donkey's hoof is still, comparatively speaking, soft and very delicate. So, not unnaturally, Sally reacted as though Larry had jabbed her with a red-hot skewer. She wrenched her hoof out of his hands and as he straightened up and turned in astonishment, she did a pretty pirouette and kicked him neatly in the pit of the stomach with both hind legs. Larry sat down heavily, his face went white, and he doubled up, clasping his stomach and making strange rattling noises. The alarm I felt was not for Larry but for Sally, for I was quite sure that he would extract the most terrible retribution when he recovered. Hastily I undid Sally's rope and flicked her on the rump with the stick and watched her canter off into the olives. Then I ran into the house and informed Mother that Larry had had an accident. The entire family, including Spiro, who had just arrived, came running out into the olive grove where Larry was still writhing about uttering great sobbing, wheezing noises.

"Larry, dear," said Mother distraught, "what *have* you been doing?"

"Attacked," gasped Larry between wheezes. "Unprovoked . . . Creature mad . . . Probably rabies . . . Ruptured appendix."

With Leslie on one side of him and Spiro on the other they carted Larry slowly back to the villa, with Mother and Margo fluttering commiseratingly and ineffectually around him. In a crisis of this magnitude, involving my family, one had to keep one's wits about one or all was lost. I ran swiftly round to the kitchen door where, panting but innocent, I informed our maid that I was going to spend the day out and could she give me some food to eat. She put half a loaf of bread, some onions, some olives, and a hunk of cold meat into a paper bag and gave it to me. Fruit I knew I could obtain from any of my peasant friends. Then I raced through the olive groves, carrying this provender, in search of Sally.

I eventually found her half a mile away, grazing on a succulent patch of grass. After several ineffectual attempts, I managed to scramble up onto her back and then, belabouring her behind with a stick, I urged her to a brisk trot as far away from the villa as possible.

I had to return to the villa for tea because Theodore was coming. When I got back I found Larry, swathed in blankets, lying on the sofa giving Theodore a graphic description of the incident.

"And then, absolutely unprovoked, it suddenly turned on me with slavering jaws, like the charge of the Light Brigade." He broke off to glare at me as I entered the room. "Oh, so you decided to come back. And what, may I inquire, have you done with that equine menace?"

I replied that Sally was safely bedded down in her stable and had, fortunately, suffered no ill effects from the incident. Larry glared at me.

"Well, I'm delighted to hear that," he said caustically.

"The fact that I am lying here with my spleen ruptured in three places is of apparently little or no moment."

"I have brought you . . . um . . . a little, you know . . . er . . . gift," said Theodore, and he presented me with a replica of his own collecting box, complete with tubes and a fine muslin net. I could not have asked for anything nicer and I thanked him volubly.

"You had better go and thank Katerina too, dear," said Mother. "She didn't really want to part with Sally, you know."

"I am surprised," said Larry. "I'd have thought she'd have been only too *glad* to get rid of her."

"You'd better not go and see Katerina now," said Margo. "She's getting near her time."

Intrigued by this unusual phrase, I asked what "getting near her time" meant.

"She's going to have a baby, dear," said Mother.

"The wonder of it is," said Larry, "as I thought when we went to the wedding, she didn't have it in the vestry."

"Larry, dear," said Mother. "Not in front of Gerry."

"Well, it's true," said Larry. "I've never seen such a pregnant bride in white."

I said I thought it would be a good idea if I went to thank Katerina *before* she had the baby because after she had it she would probably be very busy. Reluctantly, Mother agreed to this, and so the following morning I mounted Sally and rode off through the olive trees in the direction of Gastouri, Roger trotting behind and indulging in a game which he and Sally had invented between them, which consisted of Roger darting in at intervals and nibbling her heels gently, growling furiously, whereupon Sally would give a skittish little buck and attempt to kick him in the ribs.

Presently we came to the little low white house, with the flattened area outside its front door neatly ringed with old rusty cans filled with flowers. To my astonishment I saw that we were not the only visitors that day. There were several elderly gentlemen sitting round a small table, hunched over glasses of wine, their enormous, swooping, nicotine-stained moustaches flapping up and down as they talked to each other. Clustered in the doorway of the house and peering eagerly through the one small window that illuminated its interior, there was a solid wedge of female relatives, all chattering and gesticulating at once.

From inside the house came a series of piercing shrieks, interspersed with cries for help from the Almighty, the Virgin Mary, and St. Spiridion. I gathered from all this uproar and activity that I had arrived in the middle of a family row. This interfamily warfare was quite a common thing among the peasants and something I always found very enjoyable, for any quarrel, however trivial, was carried on with grim determination until it was sucked dry of the very last juices of drama, with people shouting abuse at one another through the olive trees and the men periodically chasing each other with bamboos.

I tethered Sally and made my way to the front door of the house, wondering, as I did so, what this particular row was about. The last one in this area that I remembered had lasted for a prodigious length of time (three weeks) and had all been started by a small boy who told his cousin that his grandfather cheated at cards. I wriggled and pushed my way determinedly through the knot of people who blocked the doorway and finally got inside, only to find the entire room seemed to be filled with Katerina's relatives, packed shoulder to shoulder like a football crowd. I had, quite early in life, discovered that the only way of dealing with a situation like this was to get down on one's hands and knees and crawl. This I did and by this means successfully achieved the front row in the circle of relatives that surrounded the great double bed.

Now I could see that something much more interesting than a family row was taking place. Katerina was lying on the bed with her cheap print frock rolled right up above her great, swollen breasts. Her hands were tightly clasping the head of the big brass bedstead, her white mound of a stomach quivered and strained with what appeared to be a life of its own, and she kept drawing her legs up and screaming, rolling her head from side to side, the sweat pouring down her face. Near her by the bedside, and obviously in charge of the proceedings, was a tiny, dirty, wizened little witch of a woman holding a bucket in one hand full of well water. Periodically she would dip a bundle of filthy rags into this and mop Katerina's face and her thighs with it. On the table by the bedstead a jug full of wine and a glass stood, and every time the old crone had finished the ablutions, she would put a drop of wine in the glass and force it into Katerina's mouth; then she would fill the glass and drain it herself, for presumably, in her capacity as midwife, she needed to keep up her strength as much as Katerina.

I congratulated myself warmly on the fact that I had not been deviated on my ride up to Katerina's house by several interesting things I had seen. If, for example, I had stopped to climb up to what I was pretty certain was a magpie's nest, I would probably have missed this whole exciting scene. Curiously enough, I was so used to the shrill indignation of the peasants over the most trivial circumstances that I did not really, consciously, associate Katerina's falsetto screams with pain. It was obvious that she was in some pain. Her face was white, crumpled, and old-looking, but I automatically subtracted ninety per cent of the screaming as exaggeration. Now and then, when she uttered a particularly loud scream and implored St. Spiridion for his aid, all the relatives would scream in sympathy and also implore the Saint's intervention. The resulting cacophony in that tiny space had to be heard to be believed.

Suddenly Katerina clasped the bed-head still more tightly, the muscles in her brown arms showing taut. She writhed, drew up her legs and spread them wide apart.

"It is coming. It is coming. Praised be Saint Spiridion," shouted all the relatives in chorus, and I noticed in the middle of the tangled, matted mass of Katerina's pubic hairs a round white object appear, rather like the top of an egg. There was a moment's pause and Katerina strained again and uttered a moaning gasp. Then, to my entranced delight, the baby's head suddenly popped out of her like a rabbit out of a hat, to be quickly followed by its pink, twitching body. Its face and its limbs were as crumpled and as delicate as a rose's petals. But it was its minuteness and the fact that it was so perfectly formed that intrigued me. The midwife shuffled forward shouting prayers and instructions to Katerina and seized the baby from between her blood-stained thighs. At that moment, to my intense annoyance, the ring of relatives all moved forward a pace in their eagerness to see the sex of the child, so that I missed the next piece of the drama, for all I could see were the large and extremely well padded rumps of two of Katerina's larger aunts.

By the time I had burrowed between their legs and voluminous skirts and got to the front of the circle again, the midwife —at shouts of delight from everybody—declared the baby to be a boy and had severed the umbilical cord with a large and very ancient penknife she had extracted from a pocket in her skirt. One of the aunts surged forward and together she and the midwife tied the cord. Then, while the aunt held the squalling, twitching, pink blob of life, the midwife dipped her bundle of rags into the bucket and proceeded to swab the baby down. This done, she then filled a glass with wine and gave a couple of sips to Katerina and then filled her mouth with wine and proceeded to spit it from her toothless gums all over the baby's head, making the sign of the cross over its little body as she did so. Then she clasped the baby to her bosom and turned fiercely on the crowd of relatives.

"Come now, come now," she shrilled. "It is done. He has arrived. Go now, go now."

Laughing and chattering excitedly, the relatives poured out of the little house and immediately started drinking wine and congratulating each other as though they had all personally been responsible for the successful birth of the baby.

In the airless little room, smelling so strongly of sweat and garlic, Katerina lay exhausted on the bed, making feeble attempts to pull her dress down to cover her nakedness. I went to the edge of the bed and looked down at her.

"*Yasu*, Gerry mine," she said and sketched a white travesty of her normal brilliant smile. She looked incredibly old, lying there. I congratulated her politely on the birth of her first son and then thanked her for the donkey. She smiled again.

"Go outside," she said. "They will give you some wine."

I left the little room and hurried after the midwife, for I was anxious to see what the next stage was in her treatment of the baby. Out at the back of the house she had spread a white linen cloth over a small table and placed the child on it. Then she picked up great rolls of previously prepared cloth, like very wide bandage, and with the aid of one of the more nimble and sober aunts, she proceeded to wind this round and round the baby's tiny body, pausing frequently to make sure its arms lay flat by its sides and its legs were together. Slowly and methodically she bound it up as straight as a guardsman. It lay there with only its head sticking out from this cocoon of webbing. Greatly intrigued by this, I asked the midwife why she was binding the baby up.

"Why? Why?" she said, her grizzled grey eyebrows flapping over her eyes, milky with cataracts, that peered at me fiercely. "Because, if you don't bind up the baby, its limbs won't grow straight. Its bones are as soft as an egg. If you don't bind it up, its limbs will grow crooked or when it kicks and waves its arms about, it will break its bones, like little sticks of charcoal."

I knew that babies in England were not bound up in this way, and I wondered whether this was because the British were in some way tougher-boned. Otherwise, it seemed to me, there would have been an awful lot of deformities inhabiting the British Isles. I made a mental note to discuss this medical problem with Theodore at the first opportunity.

After I had drunk several glasses of wine to honour the baby and eaten a large bunch of grapes, I got on Sally's back and rode slowly home. I would not have missed that morning for anything, I decided. But, thinking about it as we jogged through the dappled shade of the olives, the thing that amazed me was that anything so perfect and so beautiful should have matured and come forth from the interior of what, to me, was an old woman. It was like, I reflected, breaking open the old, brown, prickly husk of a chestnut and finding the lovely gleaming trophy inside.

PART TWO

Kontokali

Hospitality is, indeed, now no less than in classical times, a sacred duty in these islands, and it is a duty most conscientiously performed.

—PROFESSOR ANSTEAD

4

THE PYGMY JUNGLE

It was a warm spring day, as blue as a jay's wing, and I waited impatiently for Theodore to arrive, for we were going to take a picnic lunch and walk two or three miles to a small lake that was one of our happiest hunting grounds. These days spent with Theodore, these "excursions" as he called them, were of absorbing interest to me, but they must have been very exhausting for Theodore, for, from the moment of his arrival till his departure, I would ply him with a ceaseless string of questions.

Eventually, Theodore's cab clopped and tinkled its way up the drive and Theodore dismounted, clad, as always, in the most unsuitable attire for collecting: a neat tweed suit, respectable, highly polished boots, and a grey Homburg perched squarely on his head. The only ungracious note in this city gentleman's outfit was his collecting box, full of tubes and bottles, slung over one shoulder, and a small net with a bottle dangling from the end, attached to the end of his walking-stick.

"Ah, um," he said, shaking me gravely by the hand. "How are you? I see that we have got, um . . . a nice day for our excursion."

As at that time of year one got weeks on end of nice days, this was scarcely surprising, but Theodore always insisted on mentioning it as though it was some special privilege that had been granted us by the gods of collecting. Quickly we gathered up the bag of food and the little stone bottles of ginger beer Mother had prepared for us, and slung these on our backs, together with my collecting equipment, which was slightly more extensive than Theodore's, since everything was grist to my mill and I had to be prepared for any eventuality.

Then, whistling for Roger, we went off through the sunlit olive groves, striped with shade, the whole island, spring-fresh and brilliant, lying before us. At this time of the year the olive groves would be full of flowers. Pale anemones with the tips of their petals dyed red as though they had been sipping wine, pyramid orchids that looked as though they had been made of pink icing, and yellow crocuses so fat, glossy, and waxy-looking you felt they would light like a candle if you set a match to their stamens. We would tramp through the rough stone paths among the olives, then for a mile or so follow the road lined with tall and ancient cypresses, each covered in a layer of white dust, like a hundred dark paint brushes loaded with chalk white. Presently we would strike off from the road and make our way over the crest of a small hill and there, lying below us, would be the lake, perhaps four acres in extent, its rim shaggy with reeds and its water green with plants.

On this particular day, as we made our way down the hillside towards the lake, I was walking a little ahead of Theodore and I suddenly came to an abrupt halt and stared with amazement at the path ahead of me. Alongside the edge of the path was the bed of a tiny stream which meandered its way down to join the lake. The stream was such a tiny one that even the early spring sun had succeeded in drying it up, so that there was only the smallest trickle of water. Through the bed of the stream and then up across the path and into the stream again lay what at first sight appeared to be a thick cable which seemed to be mysteriously possessed of a life of its own. When I looked closely I could see that the cable was made up of what looked like hundreds of small, dusty snakes. I shouted eagerly to Theodore and when he came I pointed this phenomenon out to him.

"Aha!" he said, his beard bristling and a keen light of interest in his eyes. "Um, yes. Very interesting. Elvers."

What kind of snake was an elver, I inquired, and why were they all travelling in a procession?

"No, no," said Theodore. "They are not snakes. They are baby eels and they appear to be, um . . . you know, making their way down to the lake."

Fascinated, I crouched over the long column of baby eels, wriggling determinedly through the stone and grass and prickly thistles, their skins dry and dusty. There seemed to be millions of them. Who, in this dry, dusty place, would expect to find eels wriggling about?

"The whole, um . . . history of the eel," said Theodore, putting his collecting box on the ground and seating himself on a convenient rock, "is very curious. You see, at certain times the adult eels leave the ponds or rivers where they have been living and, er . . . make their way down to the sea. All the European eels do this and so do the North American eels. Where they went to was, for a long time, a mystery. The only thing, um . . . you know . . . scientists knew was that they never came *back*, but that eventually these baby eels would return and repopulate the same rivers and streams. It was not until after quite a number of years that people discovered what really happened."

He paused and scratched his beard thoughtfully.

"All the eels made their way down to the sea and then swam through the Mediterranean, across the Atlantic, until they reached the Sargasso Sea, which is, as you know, off the northeastern coast of South America. The . . . um . . . North American eels, of course, didn't have so far to travel, but they made their way to the same place. Here they mated, laid their eggs, and died. The eel larvae, when it hatches out, is a very curious, um . . . you know . . . leaf-shaped creature and transparent, so unlike the adult eel that for a long time it was classified in a separate genera. Well, these larvae make their way slowly backwards to the place where their parents have come from and by the time they reach the Mediterranean or the North American shore, they look like these."

Here Theodore paused and rasped his beard again and delicately inserted the end of his cane into the moving column of elvers so that they writhed indignantly.

"They seem to have a very um . . . you know . . . strong homing instinct," said Theodore. "We must be some two miles from the sea, I suppose, and yet all these little elvers are making their way across this countryside in order to get back to the same lake that their parents left."

He paused and glanced about him keenly and then pointed with his stick.

"It's quite a hazardous journey," he observed, and I saw what he meant, for a kestrel was flying like a little black cross just above the line of baby eels, and as we watched he swooped and flew away with his claws firmly gripping a writhing mass of them.

As we walked on, following the line of eels, since they were going in the same direction, we saw other predators at work. Groups of magpies and jackdaws and a couple of jays flew up at our approach and we caught, out of the corner of our eye, the red glint of a fox disappearing into the myrtle bushes.

When we reached the lake-side, we had a set pattern of behaviour. First we would have a prolonged discussion as to which olive tree would be the best to put some of our equipment and our food under—which one would cast the deepest and the best shade at noon. Having decided on this, we would make a little pile of our possessions under it and then, armed with our nets and collecting boxes, we would approach the lake. Here we would potter happily for the rest of the morning, pacing with the slow concentration of a pair of fishing herons, dipping our nets into the weed-filigreed water. Here Theodore came into his own more than anywhere else. From the depths of the lake, as he stood there with the big scarlet dragon-flies zooming like arrows round him, he would extract magic that Merlin would have envied.

Here in the still, wine-gold waters, lay a pygmy jungle. On the lake bottom prowled the deadly dragon-fly larvae, as cunning a predator as the tiger, inching its way through the debris of a million last year's leaves. Here the black tadpoles, sleek and shiny as licorice drops, disported in the shallows like plump herds of hippo in some African river. Through green forests of weed the multi-coloured swarms of microscopic creatures twitched and fluttered like flocks of exotic birds, while among the roots of the forests the newts, the leeches uncoiled like great snakes in the gloom, stretching out beseechingly, ever hungry. And here the caddis larvae, in their shaggy coats of twigs and debris, crawled dimly like bears fresh from hibernation across the sun-ringed hills and valleys of soft black mud.

"Aha, now, this is rather interesting. You see this, um . . . little maggot-like thing? Now this is the larvae of the China-mark moth. I think, as a matter of fact, you have got one in your collection. What? Well, they're called China-mark moths because of the markings on the wing, which are said to resemble very closely marks that potters put on the base of, er . . . you know, very *good* china. Spode and so forth. Now the China-mark is interesting because it is one of the few moths that have aquatic larvae. The larvae live under water until they are . . . um . . . ready to pupate. The interesting things about this particular species is that they have, er . . . um . . . you know, two forms of female. The male, of course, is fully winged and flies about when it hatches and er . . . so does one of the females. But the other female when it hatches out has, um . . . no wings and continues to live under the water, using its legs to swim with."

Theodore paced a little farther along the bank on the mud that was already dried and jigsawed by the spring sun. A kingfisher exploded like a blue firework from the small willow, and out on the centre of the lake a tern swooped and glided on graceful, sickle-shaped wings. Theodore dipped his net into the weedy water, sweeping it to and fro gently, as though he were stroking a cat. Then the net was lifted and held aloft, while the tiny bottle that dangled from it would be subjected to a minute scrutiny through a magnifying glass.

"Um, yes. Some cyclopes. Two mosquito larvae. Aha, that's interesting. You see this caddis larva has made his case entirely out of baby ram's-horn snail shells. It is . . . you know . . . remarkably pretty. Ah now! Here we have, I think, yes, yes, here we have some rotifers."

In a desperate attempt to keep pace with this flood of knowledge, I asked what rotifers were and peered into the little bottle through the magnifying glass at the twitching, wriggling creatures, as Theodore told me.

"The early naturalists used to call them wheel-animalcules, because of their curious limbs, you know. They wave them about in a very curious fashion, so that they almost look like, um . . . you know, um . . . er . . . like the *wheels* of a watch. When you next come to see me I'll put some of these under the microscope for you. They are really extraordinarily beautiful creatures. These are, of course, all females."

I asked why, of course, they should be females?

"This is one of the interesting things about the rotifer. The females produce virgin eggs. Um . . . that is to say, they produce eggs without having come into contact with a male. Um . . . er . . . somewhat like a chicken, you know. But the difference is that the *rotifer* eggs hatch out into other females which in turn are capable of laying more eggs which . . . um . . . again hatch out into females. But at certain times, the females lay *smaller* eggs, which hatch out into males. Now, as you will see when I put these under the microscope, the female has a—how shall one say?—a quite *complex* body, an alimentary tract, and so on. The male has nothing at all. He is really just, er . . . um . . . a swimming bag of sperm."

I was bereft of speech at the complexities of the private life of the rotifer.

"Another curious thing about them," Theodore continued, happily piling miracle upon miracle, "is that at certain times, er . . . you know, if it is a hot summer or something like that and the pond is liable to dry up, they go down to the bottom and form a sort of hard shell round themselves. It's a sort of *suspended animation*, for the pond can dry up for, er . . . um . . . let us say seven or eight years, and they will just lie there in the dust. But as soon as the first rain falls and fills the pond, they come to life again."

Again we moved forward, sweeping our nets through the balloon-like masses of frogs' spawn and the trailing necklace-like strings of the toad spawn.

"Here is, er . . . if you just take the glass a minute and look . . . an exceptionally fine hydra."

Through the glass there sprang to life a tiny fragment of weed to which was attached a long slender coffee-coloured column, at the top of which was a writhing mass of elegant tentacles. As I watched, a rotund and earnest cyclops, carrying two large and apparently heavy sacks containing pink eggs, swam in a series of breathless jerks too close to the writhing arms of the hydra. In a moment it was engulfed. It gave a couple of violent twitches before it was stung to death. I knew, if you watched long enough, you could watch the cyclops being slowly and steadily engulfed and passing, in the shape of a bulge, down the column of the hydra.

Presently the height and the heat of the sun would tell us that it was lunch-time, and we would make our way back to our olive trees and sit there eating our food and drinking our ginger beer to the accompaniment of the sleepy zithering of the first-hatched cicadas of the year and the gentle, questioning coos of the collared doves.

"In Greek," Theodore said, munching his sandwich methodically, "the name for collared dove is *dekaoctur*—'eighteener,' you know. The story goes that when Christ was . . .

um . . . carrying the cross to Calvary, a Roman soldier, see-ing that He was exhausted, took pity on Him. By the side of the road there was an old woman selling . . . um . . . you know . . . *milk*, and so the Roman soldier went to her and asked her how much a cupful would cost. She replied that it would cost eighteen coins. But the soldier had only seventeen. He . . . er . . . you know . . . pleaded with the woman to let him have a cupful of milk for Christ for seventeen coins, but the woman avariciously held out for eighteen. So, when Christ was crucified, the old woman was turned into a turtle dove and condemned to go about for the rest of her days repeating *dekaocto, dekaocto*—'eighteen, eighteen.' If ever she agrees to say *deka-epta,* seventeen, she will regain her human form. If, out of obstinacy, she says *deka-ennaea*, nineteen, the world will come to an end."

In the cool olive shade the tiny ants, black and shiny as caviare, would be foraging for our left-overs among last year's discarded olive leaves that the past summer's sun had dried and coloured a nut-brown and banana-yellow. They lay there as curled and as crisp as brandy-snaps. On the hillside behind us a herd of goats passed, the leader's bell clonking mournfully. We could hear the tearing sound of their jaws as they ate, indiscriminately, any foliage that came within their reach. The leader paced up to us and gazed for a minute with baleful, yellow eyes, snorting clouds of thyme-laden breath at us.

"They should not, er . . . you know, be left unattended," said Theodore, prodding the goat gently with his stick. "Goats do more damage to the countryside than practically anything else."

The leader uttered a short sardonic "bah" and then moved away, with his destructive troop following him.

We would lie for an hour or so, drowsing, and digesting our food, staring up through the tangled olive branches at a sky that was patterned with tiny white clouds like a child's finger-prints on a blue, frosty, winter window.

"Well," Theodore would say at last, getting to his feet, "I think perhaps we ought to . . . you know . . . just see what the *other* side of the lake has to offer."

So once more we would commence our slow pacing of the rim of the shore. Steadily our test tubes, bottles, and jars would fill with a shimmer of microscopic life, and my boxes and tins and bags would be stuffed with frogs, baby terrapins, and a host of beetles.

"I suppose," Theodore would say at last, reluctantly, glancing up at the sinking sun, "I suppose . . . you know . . . we ought to be getting along home."

And so we would laboriously hoist our now extremely heavy collecting boxes onto our shoulders and trudge homeward on weary feet, Roger, his tongue hanging out like a pink flag, trotting soberly ahead of us. Reaching the villa, our catches would be moved to more capacious quarters. Then Theodore and I would relax and discuss the day's work, drinking gallons of hot, stimulating tea and gorging ourselves on golden scones, bubbling with butter, fresh from Mother's oven.

It was when I paid a visit to this lake without Theodore that I caught, quite by chance, a creature that I had long wanted to meet. As I drew my net up out of the waters and examined the tangled weed mass it contained, I found crouching there, of all unlikely things, a spider. I was delighted, for I had read about this curious beast, which must be one of the most unusual species of spider in the world, for it lives a very strange aquatic existence. It was about half an inch long and marked in a rather vague sort of way with silver and brown. I put it triumphantly into one of my collecting tins and carried it home tenderly.

Here I set up an aquarium with a sandy floor and decorated it with some small dead branches and fronds of water-weed. Putting the spider on one of the twigs that stuck up above the water-level, I watched to see what it would do. It immediately ran down the twig and plunged into the water, where it turned a bright and beautiful silver, owing to the numerous minute air bubbles trapped in the hairs on its body. It spent five minutes or so running about below the surface of the water, investigating all the twigs and water-weed before it finally settled on a spot in which to construct its home.

Now the water-spider was the original inventor of the diving-bell, and sitting absorbed in front of the aquarium, I watched how it was done. First the spider attached several lengthy strands of silk from the weeds to the twigs. These were to act as guy ropes. Then, taking up a position roughly in the centre of these guy ropes, it proceeded to spin an irregular oval-shaped flat web of a more or less conventional type, but of a finer mesh, so that it looked more like a cobweb. This occupied the greater part of two hours. Having got the structure of its home built to its satisfaction, it now had to give it an air supply. This it did by making numerous trips to the surface of the water and into the air. When it returned to the water its body would be silvery with air bubbles. It would then run down and take up its position underneath the web and, by stroking itself with its legs, rid itself of the air bubbles, which rose and were immediately trapped underneath the web. After it had done this five or six times, all the tiny bubbles under the web had amalgamated into one big bubble. As the spider added more and more air to this bubble and the bubble grew bigger and bigger, its strength started to push the web up until eventually the spider had achieved success. Firmly anchored by the guy ropes between the weed and the twigs was suspended a bell-shaped structure full of air. This was now the spider's home in which it could live quite comfortably without even having to pay frequent visits to the surface, for the air in the bell would, I knew, be replenished by the oxygen given up by the weeds, and the carbon monoxide given out by the spider would soak through the silky walls of its house.

Sitting and watching this miraculous piece of craftsmanship, I wondered how on earth the very first water-spider (who wanted to *become* a water-spider) had managed to work out this ingenious method of living below the surface. But the habit of living in its own home-made submarine is not the only peculiar thing about this spider. Unlike the greater majority of species, the male is about twice the size of the female, and once they have mated, the male is not devoured by his wife, as happens so frequently in the married life of the spider. I could tell from her size that my spider was a female and I thought that her abdomen looked rather swollen. It seemed to me she might be expecting a happy event, so I took great pains to make sure that she got plenty of good food. She liked fat green daphnia, which she was extraordinarily adept at catching as they swam past; but probably her favourite food of all was the tiny, newly hatched newt efts which, although they were a bulky prey for her, she never hesitated to tackle. Having captured whatever titbit happened to be passing, she would then carry it up into her bell and eat it there in comfort.

Then came the great day when I saw that she was adding an extension to the bell. She did not hurry over this and it took her two days to complete. Then one morning, on peering into her tank, I saw to my delight that the nursery contained a round ball of eggs. In due course these hatched out into miniature replicas of the mother. I soon had more water spiders than I knew what to do with and I found, to my annoyance, that the mother, with complete lack of parental feeling, was happily feeding off her own progeny. So I was forced to move the babies into another aquarium, but as they grew they took to feeding upon each other and so in the end I just kept the two most intelligent-looking ones and took all the rest down to the lake and let them go.

It was at this time, when I was deeply involved with the water-spiders, that Sven Olson at last turned up. Larry, to Mother's consternation, had developed the habit of inviting hordes of painters, poets, and authors to stay without any reference to her. Sven Olson was a sculptor, and we had had some warning of his impending arrival, for he had been bombarding us for several weeks with contradictory telegrams about his movements, which had driven Mother to distraction because she kept having to make and unmake his bed. Mother and I were having a quiet cup of tea on the veranda when a cab made its appearance, wound its way up the drive, and came to a stop in front of the house. In the back was seated an enormous man who bore a remarkable facial resemblance to the reconstructions of Neanderthal man. He was clad in a white singlet, a pair of voluminous brightly checked plus fours, and sandals. On his massive head was a broad-brimmed straw hat. The two holes situated one each side of the crown argued that this hat had been designed for the use of a horse. He got ponderously out of the cab, carrying a very large and battered Gladstone bag and an accordion. Mother and I went down to greet him. As he saw us approaching, he swept off his hat and bowed, revealing that his enormous cranium was completely devoid of hair except for a strange, grey, tattered duck's tail on the nape of his neck.

"Mrs. Durrell?" he inquired, fixing Mother with large and childlike blue eyes. "I am enchanted to meet you. My name is Sven."

His English was impeccable, with scarcely any trace of an accent, but his voice was quite extraordinary, for it wavered between a deep rich baritone and a quavering falsetto, as though, in spite of his age, his voice was only just breaking. He extended a very large, white, spade-shaped hand to Mother and bowed once again.

"Well, I am glad you have managed to get here at last," said Mother, brightly and untruthfully. "Do come in and have some tea."

I carried his accordion and his Gladstone bag and we all went and sat on the balcony and drank tea and stared at each other. There was a long, long silence while Sven munched on a piece of toast and occasionally smiled lovingly at Mother, while she smiled back and desperately searched her mind for suitable intellectual topics of conversation. Sven swallowed a piece of toast and coughed violently. His eyes filled with tears.

"I love toast," he gasped. "I simply love it. But it always does this to me."

We plied him with more tea and presently his paroxysms of coughing died away. He sat forward, his huge hands folded in his lap, showing white as marble against the hideous pattern of his plus fours, and fixed Mother with an inquiring eye.

"Are you," he inquired wistfully, "are you, by any chance, musically inclined?"

"Well," said Mother, startled, and obviously suffering from the hideous suspicion that if she said "Yes" Sven might ask her to sing, "I like music, of course, but I . . . can't play anything."

"I suppose," said Sven diffidently, "you wouldn't like me to play something for you?"

"Oh, er, yes, by all means," said Mother. "That would be delightful."

Sven beamed lovingly at her, picked up his accordion and unstrapped it. He extended it like a caterpillar and it produced noise like the tail-end of a donkey's bray.

"She," said Sven, lovingly patting the accordion, "has got some sea air in her."

He settled his accordion more comfortably against his broad chest, arranged his sausage-like fingers carefully on the keys, closed his eyes, and began to play. It was a very complicated and extraordinary tune. Sven was wearing such an expression of rapture upon his ugly face that I was dying to laugh and was having to bite the insides of my cheeks to prevent it. Mother sat there with a face of frozen politeness like a world-famous conductor being forced to listen to somebody giving a recital on a penny whistle. Eventually the tune came to a harsh, discordant end. Sven heaved a sigh of pure delight, opened his eyes, and smiled at Mother.

"Bach is so beautiful," he said.

"Oh, yes," said Mother with well-simulated enthusiasm.

"I'm glad you like it," said Sven. "I'll play you some more."

So for the next hour Mother and I sat there, trapped, while Sven played piece after piece. Every time Mother made some move to seek an escape, Sven would hold up one of his huge hands, as though arresting a line of imaginary traffic, and say, "Just one more," archly, and Mother, with a tremulous smile, would sit back in her chair.

It was with considerable relief that we greeted the rest of the family when they arrived back from town. Larry and Sven danced round each other, roaring like a couple of bulls and exchanging passionate embraces, and then Larry dragged Sven off to his room and they were closeted there for hours, the sound of gales of laughter occasionally drifting down to us.

"What's he like?" asked Margo.

"Well, I don't really know, dear," said Mother. "He's been playing to us ever since he arrived."

"Playing?" said Leslie. "Playing what?"

"His barrel organ, or whatever you call it," said Mother.

"My God," said Leslie. "I can't stand those things. I hope he isn't going to play it all over the house."

"No, no, dear. I'm sure he won't," said Mother hastily, but her tone lacked conviction.

Just at that moment Larry appeared on the veranda again.

"Where's Sven's accordion?" he asked. "He wants to play me something."

"Oh, God," said Leslie. "There you are. I told you."

"I hope he isn't going to play that accordion *all* the time, dear," said Mother. "We've already had an hour of it and it's given me a splitting headache."

"Of course he won't play it all the time," said Larry irritably, picking up the accordion. "He just wants to play me one tune. What was he playing to you, anyway?"

"The most weird music," said Mother. "By some man— you know the one—something to do with trees."

The rest of the day was, to say the least, harrying. Sven's repertoire was apparently inexhaustible and when, during dinner, he insisted on giving us an impression of meal-time in a Scottish fortress by marching round and round the table playing one of the more untuneful Scottish reels, I could see the defences of the family crumbling. Even Larry was beginning to look a little pensive. Roger, who was uninhibited and straightforward in his dealings with human beings, summed up his opinion of Sven's performance by throwing back his head and howling dismally, a thing he only did normally when he heard the national anthem.

But by the time Sven had been with us three days, we had become more or less inured to his accordion, and Sven himself charmed us all. He exuded a sort of innocent goodness, so that whatever he did one could not be annoyed with him, any more than you can be annoyed with a baby for wetting its nappy. He quickly endeared himself to Mother, for, she discovered, he was an ardent cook himself and carried round an enormous leather-bound notebook in which he jotted down recipes. He and Mother spent hours in the kitchen, teaching each other how to cook their favourite dishes, and the results were meals of such bulk and splendour that all of us began to feel liverish and out of sorts.

It was about a week after his arrival that Sven wandered one morning into the room I proudly called my study. In that massive villa we had such a superfluity of rooms that I had succeeded in getting Mother to give me a special room of my own in which I could keep all my creatures.

My menagerie at this time was pretty extensive. There was Ulysses, the scop's owl, who spent all day sitting on the pelmet above the window, imitating a decaying olive stump, and occasionally, with a look of great disdain, regurgitating a pellet onto the newspaper spread below him. The dog contingent had been increased to three by a couple of young mongrels who had been given to me for my birthday by a peasant family and who, because of their completely undisciplined behaviour, had been christened Widdle and Puke. There were rows and rows of jam jars, some containing specimens in methylated spirits, others containing microscopic life. And then there were six aquariums that housed a variety of newts, frogs, snakes, and toads. Piles of glass-topped boxes contained my collections of butterflies, beetles, and dragon-flies. Sven, to my astonishment, displayed a deep and almost reverent interest in my collection. Delighted to have somebody displaying enthusiasm for my cherished menagerie, I took him on a carefully conducted tour and showed him everything, even, after swearing him to secrecy, my family of tiny, chocolate-coloured scorpions that I had smuggled into the house unbeknownst to the family. One of the things that impressed Sven most was the underwater bell of the spider, and he stood quite silently in front of it, his great blue eyes fixed on it intensely, watching the spider as she caught her food and carried it up into the little dome. Sven displayed such enthusiasm that I suggested to him, rather tentatively, that he might like to spend a little time in the olive groves with me, so that I could show him some of these creatures in their natural haunts.

"But how kind of you," he said, his great, ugly face lighting up delightedly. "Are you sure I won't be interfering?"

No, I assured him he would not be interfering.

"Then I would be delighted," said Sven. "Absolutely delighted."

So, for the rest of his stay, we would disappear from the villa after breakfast and spend a couple of hours in the olive groves.

On Sven's last day—he was leaving on the evening boat—we held a little farewell lunch party for him and invited Theodore. Delighted at having a new audience, Sven immediately gave Theodore a half-hour recital of Bach on his accordion.

"Um," said Theodore, when Sven had finished, "do you, you know, er . . . know any other tunes?"

"Just name it, Doctor," said Sven, spreading out his hands expansively. "I will play it for you."

Theodore rocked thoughtfully for a moment on his toes.

"You don't by any chance, I suppose, er . . . happen to know a song called 'There Is a Tavern in the Town'?" he inquired shyly.

"Of course!" said Sven and immediately crashed into the opening bars of the song.

Theodore sang vigorously, his beard bristling, his eyes bright, and when he had come to the end, Sven, without pause, switched into "Clementine." Emboldened by Theodore's Philistine attitude towards Bach, Mother asked Sven whether he could play "If I Were a Blackbird" and "The Spinning Wheel Song," which he promptly executed in a masterly fashion.

Then the cab arrived to take him down to the docks, and he embraced each one of us fondly, his eyes full of tears. He climbed into the back of the cab with his Gladstone bag beside him and his precious accordion on his lap, and he waved to us extravagantly as the cab disappeared down the drive.

"Such a *manly* man," said Mother with satisfaction, as we went inside. "Quite one of the old school."

"You should have told him that," said Larry, stretching himself out on the sofa and picking up his book. "There's nothing homo's like better than to be told they are virile and manly."

"Whatever do you mean?" asked Mother, putting on her spectacles and glaring at Larry suspiciously.

Larry lowered his book and looked at her, puzzled.

"Homosexuals like to be told they are virile and manly," he said at length, patiently, and with the air of one explaining a simple problem to a backward child.

Mother continued to glare at him, trying to assess whether or not it was one of Larry's elaborate leg-pulls.

"You are not trying to tell me," she said at last, "that that man is a—is a—is one of *those*?"

"Dear God, Mother, of course he is," said Larry, irritably. "He's a rampaging old queer—the only reason he's gone rushing back to Athens is because he's living with a ravishing seventeen-year-old Cypriot boy and he doesn't trust him."

"Do you mean to say," asked Margo, her eyes wide, "that they get *jealous* of each other?"

"Of course they do," said Larry, and dismissing the subject, he returned to his book.

"How extraordinary," said Margo. "Did you hear that, Mother? They actually get jealous—"

"Margo!" said Mother quellingly. "We won't go into that. What *I* want to know, Larry, is why you invited him here if you knew he was, er, that way inclined?"

"Why not?" Larry inquired.

"Well, you might at least have thought of *Gerry*," said Mother, bristling.

"Gerry?" asked Larry in surprise. "Gerry? What's he got to do with it?"

"What's he got to *do* with it? Really, Larry, you do make me cross. That man could have been a bad influence on the boy if he had had much to do with him."

Larry sat back on the sofa and looked at Mother. He gave a small exasperated sigh and put his book down.

"For the last three mornings," he said, "Gerry's been giving Sven natural history lessons in the olive groves. It doesn't appear to have done either of them irretrievable harm."

"What?" squeaked Mother. "What?"

I felt it was time to intervene. After all, I liked Sven. I explained how, early in his stay, he had wandered into my room and had become immediately absorbed and fascinated by my collection of creatures. Feeling that one convert was worth half a dozen saints, I had offered to take him into the olive groves and show him all my favourite haunts. So every morning we would set off into the olives and Sven would spend hours lying on his stomach peering at the busy lines of ants carrying their grass seeds or watching the bulbous-bodied female mantis laying her frothy egg case on a stone, or peering down the burrows of trap-door spiders, murmuring, "Wonderful! Wonderful!" to himself, in such an ecstatic tone of voice that it warmed my heart.

"Well, dear," said Mother, "I think, in future, if you want to take one of Larry's friends for walks you should tell me first."

5

CUTTLEFISH AND CRABS

Each morning when I awoke the bedroom would be tiger-striped by the sun peering through the shutters. As usual, I would find that the dogs had managed to crawl onto the bed without my realizing it and would now be occupying more than their fair share, sleeping deeply and peacefully. Ulysses would be sitting by the window staring at the bars of golden sunlight, his eyes slit into malevolent disapproval. Outside, one could hear the hoarse, jeering crow of a cockerel and the soft murmuring of the hens (a sound soothing as bubbling porridge) as they fed under the orange and lemon trees, the distant clonk of goat bells, sharp chittering of sparrows in the eaves, and the sudden outburst of wheezing, imploring cries that denoted one of the parent swallows had brought a mouthful of food to their brood in the nest beneath my window. I would throw back the sheet and turf the dogs out onto the floor, where they would shake and stretch and yawn, their pink tongues curled like exotic leaves, and then I would go over to the window and throw back the shutters. Leaning out over the sill, the morning sun warm on my naked body, I would scratch thoughtfully at the little pink seals the dogs' fleas had left on my skin, while I got my eyes adjusted to the light. Then I would peer down over the silver olive tops to the beach and the blue sea which lay half a mile away. It was on this beach that, periodically, the fishermen would pull in their nets, and when they did so this was always a special occasion for me, since the net dragged to shore from the depths of the blue bay would contain a host of fascinating sea life which was otherwise beyond my reach.

If I saw the little fishing boats bobbing on the water I would get dressed hurriedly, and taking my collecting gear I would run through the olive trees down to the road and along it until I reached the beach. I knew most of the fishermen by name, but there was one who was my special friend, a tall, powerful young man with a mop of auburn hair. Inevitably, he was called Spiro after Spiridion, so in order to distinguish him from all the other Spiros I knew, I called him Kokino, or red. Kokino took a great delight in obtaining specimens for me, and although he was not a bit interested in the creatures himself, he got considerable pleasure from my obvious happiness.

One day I went down to the beach and the net was halfway in. The fishermen, brown as walnuts, were hauling on the dripping lines, their toes spreading wide in the sand as they pulled the massive bag of the net nearer and nearer to the shore.

"Your health, *kyrié* Gerry," Kokino cried to me, waving a large freckled hand in greeting, his mop of hair glinting in the sun like a bonfire. "Today we should get some fine animals for you, for we put the net down in a new place."

I squatted on the sand and waited patiently while the fishermen, chattering and joking, hauled away steadily. Presently the top of the net was visible in the shallow waters, and as it broke surface you could see the glitter and wink of the trapped fish inside it. Hauled out onto the sand, it seemed as though the net were alive, pulsating with the fish inside it, and there was the steady, staccato purring noise of their tails, flapping futilely against each other. The baskets were fetched and the fish were picked out of the net and cast into them. Red fish, white fish, fish with wine-coloured stripes, scorpion fish like flamboyant tapestries. Sometimes there would be an

octopus or a cuttlefish leering up from inside the net with a
look of alarm in its human-looking eyes. Once all the edible
contents of the net had been safely stowed away in the baskets, it was my turn.

In the bottom of the net would be a great heap of stones
and seaweed and it was among these that I found my trophies: once a round flat stone from which grew a perfect
coraline tree, pure white. It looked like a young beech tree in
winter, its branches bare of leaves and covered with a layer
of snow. Sometimes there would be cushion starfish, almost
as thick as a sponge-cake and almost as large, the edges not
forming pointed arms as with normal starfish, but rounded
scallops. These starfish would be of a pale fawn colour, with
a bright pattern of scarlet blotches. Once I got two incredible
crabs, whose pincers and legs when pulled in tight fitted with
immaculate precision the sides of their oval shells. These
crabs were white with a rusty-red pattern on the back that
looked not unlike an Oriental face. It was hardly what I
would call protective colouration, and I imagine they must
have had few enemies to be able to move about the sea-bed
wearing such a conspicuous livery.

On this particular morning I was picking over a great pile
of weed, and Kokino, having stowed away the last of the fish
in the baskets, came over to help me. There was the usual
assortment of tiny squids, the size of a match-box, pipe-fish,
spider-crabs, and a variety of tiny fish which, in spite of their
small size, had been unable to escape through the mesh of
the net. Suddenly Kokino gave a little grunt, half surprise and
half amusement, and picked something out of a tangled
skein of seaweed and held it out to me on the calloused palm
of his hand. I could hardly believe my eyes, for it was a sea-
horse. Browny-green, carefully jointed, looking like some
weird chess-man, it lay on Kokino's hand, its strange protruded mouth gasping and its tail coiling and uncoiling frantically. Hurriedly I snatched it from him and plunged it into
a jar full of sea-water, uttering a mental prayer to St. Spir-

idion that I was in time to save it. To my delight it righted itself, then hung suspended in the jar, the tiny fins on each side of its horse's head fluttering themselves into a blur. Pausing only to make sure that it really was all right, I scrabbled through the rest of the weed with the fervour of a gold prospector panning a river-bed where he had found a nugget. My diligence was rewarded, for in a few minutes I had six sea-horses of various sizes hanging suspended in the jar. Enraptured by my good luck, I bid Kokino and the other fishermen a hasty farewell and raced back to the villa.

Here I unceremoniously foreclosed on fourteen slow-worms and usurped their aquarium to house my new catches. I knew that the oxygen in the jar in which the sea-horses were imprisoned would not last for long and if I wanted to keep them alive I would have to move quickly. Carrying the aquarium, I raced down to the sea again, washed it out carefully, filled the bottom with sand and dashed back to the villa with it; then I had to run down to the sea again three times with buckets to fill it up with the required amount of water. By the time I had poured the last bucket into it, I was so hot and sweaty I began to wonder whether the sea-horses were worth it. But as soon as I tipped them into the aquarium I knew that they were. I had placed a small, twiggy, dead olive branch in the aquarium, which I had anchored to the sand, and as the sea-horses plopped out of the jar they righted themselves and then, like ponies freshly released in a field, they sped round and round the aquarium, their fins moving so fast that you could not see them and each one gave the appearance of being driven by some small internal motor. Having, as it were, galloped round their new territory, they all made for the olive branch, entwined their tails round it lovingly, and stood there gravely at attention.

The sea-horses were an instant success. They were about the only animal that I had introduced to the villa that earned the family's unanimous approval. Even Larry used to pay furtive visits to my study in order to watch them zooming and bobbing to and fro in their tank. They took up a considerable amount of my time, for I found that the sea-water soon grew rancid, and in order to keep it clear and fresh I had to go down to the sea with buckets four or five times a day. This was an exhausting process, but I was glad that I kept it up, for otherwise I would not have witnessed a very extraordinary sight.

One of the sea-horses, obviously an old specimen since he was nearly black, had a very well-developed paunch. This I merely attributed to age; then I noticed one morning there was a line along the paunch, almost as though it had been slit with a razor blade. I was watching this and wondering whether the sea-horses had been fighting and if so what they used as a weapon (for they seemed so defenceless), when to my complete and utter astonishment the slit opened a little wider and out swam a minute and fragile replica of the sea-horse. I could hardly believe my eyes, but as soon as the first baby was clear of the pouch and hanging in the clear water, another one joined it and then another and another until there were twenty microscopic sea-horses floating round their giant parent like a little cloud of smoke. Terrified lest the other adult sea-horses eat the babies, I hurriedly set up another aquarium and placed what I fondly imagined to be the mother and her offspring in it. Keeping two aquariums going with fresh water was an even more Herculean task and I began to feel like a pit-pony; but I was determined to continue until Thursday, when Theodore came to tea, so that I could show him my acquisitions.

"Aha," he said, peering into the tanks with professional zeal, "these are really most interesting. Sea-horses are, of course, according to the books, supposed to be found here, but I myself have er . . . you know . . . never seen them previously."

I showed Theodore the mother with her swarm of tiny babies.

"No, no," said Theodore. "That's not the mother, that's the father."

At first I thought that Theodore was pulling my leg, but he went on to explain that when the female laid the eggs and they had been fertilized by the male, they were taken into this special brood-pouch by the male and there they matured and hatched, so what I had thought was a proud mother was in reality a proud father.

Soon the strain of keeping my stable of sea-horses with a supply of microscopic sea-food and fresh water became too great, and so with the utmost reluctance I had to take them down to the sea and release them.

It was Kokino who, as well as contributing specimens from his nets to my collection, showed me one of the most novel fishing methods I had ever come across.

I met him one day down by the shore putting a kerosene tin full of sea-water into his rickety little boat. Reposing in the bottom of the tin was a large and very soulful-looking cuttlefish. Kokino had tied a string round it where the head met the great egg-shaped body. I asked him where he was going and he said he was going to fish for cuttlefish. I was puzzled because his boat did not contain any lines or nets or even a trident. How then did he propose to catch cuttlefish?

"With love," said Kokino mysteriously.

I felt it was my duty, as a naturalist, to investigate every method of capturing animals, so I asked Kokino whether it was possible for me to accompany him in order to see this mysterious process. We rowed the boat out into the blue bay until it hung over a couple of fathoms of crystal clear water. Here Kokino took the end of the long string that was attached to the cuttlefish and tied it carefully round his big toe. Then he picked up the cuttlefish and dropped it over the side of the boat. It floated in the water for a brief moment, looking up at us with what seemed to be an incredulous expression, and then, squirting out jets of water, it shot off in a series of jerks, trailing the string behind it, and soon disappeared in the blue depths. The string trailed gradually over the side of the boat, then tautened against Kokino's toe. He lit a cigarette and rumpled his flaming hair.

"Now," he said, grinning at me, "we will see what love can do."

He bent to his oars and rowed the boat slowly and gently along the surface of the bay, with frequent pauses during which he stared with intense concentration at the string fastened to his toe. Suddenly he gave a little grunt, let the oars fold to the side of the boat like the wings of a moth, and grasping the line, he started to pull it in. I leaned over the side of the boat, staring down into the clear water, my eyes straining towards the end of the taut black line. Presently, in the depths, a dim blur appeared as Kokino hauled more quickly on the line and the cuttlefish came into sight. As it got closer, I saw, to my astonishment, it was not one cuttlefish but two, locked together in a passionate embrace. Swiftly Kokino hauled them alongside and with a quick flip of the line landed them in the bottom of the boat. So engrossed was the male cuttlefish with his lady-love that not even the sudden transition from his watery home to the open air seemed to worry him in the slightest. He was clasping the female so tightly that it took Kokino some time to prise him loose and then drop him into the tin of sea-water.

The novelty of this form of fishing greatly appealed to me, although I had the sneaking feeling that perhaps it was a little unsporting. It was rather like catching dogs by walking around with a bitch in season on the end of a long leash. Within an hour we had caught five male cuttlefish in a comparatively small area of the bay and it amazed me that there should be such a dense population of them in such a small area, for they were a creature that you very rarely saw unless you went fishing at night. The female cuttlefish, throughout this time, played her part with a sort of stoical indifference, but even so I felt that she should be rewarded, so I prevailed upon Kokino to let her go, which he did with obvious reluctance.

I asked him how he knew that the female was ready to attract the males, and he shrugged.

"It is the time," he said.

Could you then at this time, I inquired, put any female on the end of a string and obtain results?

"Yes," said Kokino. "But of course, some females, like some women, are more attractive than others and so you get better results with those."

My mind boggled at the thought of having to work out the comparative merits between two female cuttlefish. I felt it was a great pity that this method could not be employed with other creatures. The idea, for example, of dropping a female sea-horse over the side on a length of cotton and then pulling her up in a tangled entourage of passionate males was very appealing. Kokino was, as far as I knew, the only exponent of this peculiar brand of fishing, for I never saw any other fisherman employ it, and indeed, the ones I mentioned it to had never even heard of it and were inclined to treat my story with raucous disbelief.

This tattered coast-line near the villa was particularly rich in sea life, and as the water was comparatively shallow it made it easier for me to capture things. I had succeeded in inveigling Leslie into making me a boat, which greatly facilitated my investigations. This craft, almost circular, flat-bottomed, and with a heavy list to starboard, had been christened the "Bootle-bumtrinket" and, next to my donkey, was my most cherished possession. Filling the bottom with jars, tins, and nets and taking a large parcel of food with me, I would set sail in the "Bootle-bumtrinket" accompanied by my crew of Widdle, Puke, and Roger and, occasionally, Ulysses, my owl, should he feel so inclined. We would spend the hot, breathless days exploring remote little bays and rocky and weed-encrusted archipelagoes. We had many curious adventures on these expeditions. Once we found a whole acre of sea-bed covered with a great swarm of sea-hares, their royal-purple, egg-shaped bodies with a neat pleated frill along the edge and two strange protuberances on the head looking, in fact, extraordinarily like the long ears of a hare. There were hundreds of them gliding over the rocks and across the sand, all heading towards the south of the island. They did not touch each other or display any interest in each other, so I assumed it was not a mating gathering, but some form of migration.

On another occasion, a group of languid, portly, and good-natured dolphins discovered us riding at anchor in a small bay, and presumably attracted by the friendly colour scheme of orange and white in which the "Bootle-bumtrinket" was painted, they disported themselves around us, leaping and splashing, coming up alongside the boat with their grinning faces, and breathing deep, passionate sighs at us from their blow-holes. A young one, more daring than the adults, even dived under the boat and we felt his back scrape along its flat bottom. My attention was equally divided between enjoying this delightful sight and trying to quell mutiny on the part of my crew, who had all reacted to the arrival of the dolphins in their individual ways. Widdle, never a staunch warrior, had lived up to his name copiously and crouched shivering in the bows, whining to himself. Puke had decided that the only way to save his life was to abandon ship and swim for the shore; he had to be restrained forcibly, as did Roger, who was convinced that if he was only allowed to jump into the sea with the dolphins, he would be able to kill them all, single-handedly, in a matter of moments.

It was during one of these expeditions that I came across a magnificent trophy that was, indirectly, responsible for leading Leslie into court, although I did not know it at the time. The family had all gone into town, with the exception of Leslie, who was recovering from a very severe attack of dysentery. It was his first day's convalescence and he lay on the sofa in the drawing-room as weak as a kitten, sipping iced tea and reading a large manual on ballistics. He had informed me, in no uncertain terms, that he did not want me hanging around making a nuisance of myself and so, as I did not want to go into the town, I had taken the dogs out in "Bootle-bum-trinket."

As I rowed along, I noticed on the smooth waters of the bay what I took to be a large patch of yellow seaweed. Seaweed was always worth investigating, as it invariably contained a host of small life and sometimes, if you were lucky, quite large creatures; so I rowed towards it. But as I got closer, I saw that it was not seaweed, but what appeared to be a yellowish-coloured rock. But what sort of rock could it be that floated in some twenty feet of water? As I looked closer, I saw, to my incredulous delight, that it was a fairly large turtle. Shipping the oars and urging the dogs to silence, I poised myself in the bows and waited, tense with excitement as the "Bootle-bumtrinket" drifted closer and closer. The turtle, outspread, appeared to be floating on the surface of the sea, sound asleep. My problem was to capture him before he woke up. The nets and various other equipment I had in the boat had not been designed for the capture of a turtle measuring some three feet in length, so the only way I felt I could achieve success was by diving in on him, grabbing him, and somehow getting him into the boat before he woke up. In my excitement it never occurred to me that the strength possessed by a turtle of this size was considerable and that it was unlikely he was going to give up without a struggle. When the boat was some six feet away I held my breath and dived. I decided to dive under him so as to cut off his retreat, as it were, and as I plunged into the lukewarm water I uttered a brief prayer that the splash I made would not awaken him and that, even if it did, he would still be too dozy to execute a rapid retreat. I had dived deep and now I turned on my back and there, suspended above me like an enormous golden guinea, was the turtle. I shot up under him and grabbed him firmly by his front flippers, which curved like horny sickles from out of his shell. To my surprise even this action did not wake him, and when I rose, gasping, to the surface, still retaining my grasp on his flippers, and shook the water from my eyes, I discovered the reason. The turtle had been dead for a fair length of time, as my nose and the host of tiny fish nibbling at his scaly limbs told me.

Disappointing though this was, a dead turtle was better than no turtle at all, and so I laboriously towed his body alongside the "Bootle-bumtrinket" and made it fast by one flipper to the side of the boat. The dogs were greatly intrigued, under the impression that this was some exotic and edible delicacy I had procured for their special benefit. The "Bootle-bumtrinket," owing to her shape, had never been the easiest of craft to steer, and now, with the dead weight of the turtle lashed to one side of her, she showed a tendency to revolve in circles. However, after an hour's strenuous rowing, we arrived safely at the jetty, and having tied up the boat, I then hauled the turtle's carcass onto the shore where I could examine it. It was a hawks-bill turtle, the kind whose shell is used for the manufacture of spectacle frames and whose stuffed carcass you occasionally see in opticians' windows. His head was massive, with a great wrinkled jowl of yellow skin and a swooping beak of a nose that did give him an extraordinarily hawk-like look. The shell was battered in places, presumably by ocean storms or by the snap of a passing shark, and here and there it was decorated with little snow-white clusters of baby barnacles. His underside of pale daffodil-yellow was soft and pliable like thick, damp cardboard.

I had recently conducted a long and fascinating dissection of a dead terrapin that I had found and I felt this would be an ideal opportunity to compare the turtle's internal anatomy with that of his fresh-water brother, so I went up the hill, borrowed the gardener's wheelbarrow, and in it transported my prize up to the house and laid him out in state on the front veranda.

I knew there would be repercussions if I endeavoured to

perform my dissection of the turtle inside the house, but I felt that nobody in his right mind would object to the dissection of the turtle on the front veranda. With my notebook at the ready and my row of saws, scalpels, and razor blades neatly laid out as though in an operating theatre, I set to work.

I found that the soft yellow plastern came away quite easily, compared with the underside of the terrapin, which had taken me three quarters of an hour to saw through. When the plastern was free, I lifted it off like a cover off a dish and there, underneath, were all the delicious mysteries of the turtle's internal organs displayed, multi-coloured and odoriferous to a degree. So consumed with curiosity was I that I did not even notice the smell. The dogs, however, who normally considered fresh cow dung to be the ideal scent to add piquancy to their love life, disappeared in a disapproving body, sneezing violently. I discovered, to my delight, that the turtle was a female and had a large quantity of half-formed eggs in her. They were about the size of ping-pong balls, soft, round, and as orange as a nasturtium. There were fourteen of them, and I removed them carefully and laid them in a gleaming, glutinous row on the flagstones. The turtle appeared to have a prodigious quantity of gut, and I decided that I should enter the exact length of this astonishing apparatus in my already blood-stained notebook. With the aid of a scalpel I detached the gut from the rear exit of the turtle and then proceeded to pull it out. It seemed never-ending, but before long I had it all laid out carefully across the veranda in a series of loops and twists, like a rather drunken railway line. One section of it was composed of the stomach, a rather hideous greyish bag like a water-filled balloon. This obviously was full of the turtle's last meal and I felt, in the interests of science, that I ought to check on what it had been eating just prior to its demise. I stuck a scalpel in the great wobbling mound and slashed experimentally. Immediately the whole stomach bag deflated with a ghastly sighing noise and a stench arose from its interior which made all the other smells pale into insignificance. Even I, fascinated as I was by my investigations, reeled back and had to retreat coughing to wait for the smell to subside.

I knew I could get the veranda cleaned up before the family got back from town, but in my excitement with my new acquisition, I had completely overlooked the fact that Leslie was convalescing in the drawing-room. The scent of the turtle's interior, so pungent that it seemed almost solid, floated in through the French windows and enveloped the couch on which he lay. My first intimation of this catastrophe was a blood-curdling roar from inside the drawing-room. Before I could do anything sensible, Leslie, swathed in blankets, appeared in the French windows.

"What's that bloody awful stink?" he inquired throatily. Then, as his glance fell upon the dismembered turtle and its prettily arranged internal organs spread across the flagstones, his eyes bulged and his face took on a heliotrope tinge. "What the hell's *that?*"

I explained, somewhat diffidently, that it was a turtle that I was dissecting. It was a female, I went on hurriedly, hoping to distract Leslie by detail. Here he could see the fascinating eggs that I had extracted from her interior.

"Damn her eggs," shouted Leslie, making it sound like some strange medieval oath. "Get the bloody thing away from here. It's stinking the place out."

I said that I had almost reached the end of my dissection and that I had then planned to bury all the soft parts and merely keep the skeleton and shell to add to my collection.

"You're doing nothing of the sort," shouted Leslie. "You're to take the whole bloody thing and bury it. Then you can come back and scrub the veranda."

Lucretia, our cook, attracted by the uproar, appeared in the French window next to Leslie. She opened her mouth to inquire into the nature of this family quarrel when she was struck amidships by the smell of the turtle. Lucretia always had fifteen or sixteen ailments worrying her at any given moment, which she cherished with the same loving care that other people devote to window-boxes or Pekingese. At this particular time it was her stomach that was causing her the most trouble. In consequence she gasped two or three times, feebly, like a fish, uttered a strangled "Saint Spiridion!" and fell into Leslie's arms in a well-simulated faint.

Just at that moment, to my horror, the car containing the rest of the family swept up the drive and came to a halt below the veranda.

"Hello, dear," said Mother, getting out of the car and coming up to the steps. "Did you have a nice morning?"

Before I could say anything, the turtle, as it were, got in before me. Mother uttered a couple of strange hiccuping cries, pulled out her handkerchief and clapped it to her nose.

"What," she demanded indistinctly, "is that terrible smell?"

"It's that bloody boy," roared Leslie from the French windows, making ineffectual attempts to prop the moaning Lucretia against the door jamb.

Larry and Margo had now followed Mother up the steps and caught sight of the butchered turtle.

"What . . . ?" began Larry and then he too was seized with a convulsive fit of coughing.

"It's that damned boy," he said, gasping.

"Yes, dear," said Mother through her handkerchief. "Leslie's just told me."

"It's disgusting," wailed Margo, fanning herself with her handkerchief. "It looks like a railway accident."

"What *is* it, dear?" Mother asked me.

I explained that it was an exceedingly interesting hawks-bill turtle, female, containing eggs.

"Surely you don't have to chop it up on the veranda?" said Mother.

"The boy's mad," said Larry with conviction. "The whole place smells like a bloody whaling ship."

"I really think you'll have to take it somewhere else, dear," said Mother. "We can't have this smell on the front veranda."

"Tell him to bury the damned thing," said Leslie, clasping his blankets more firmly about him.

"Why don't you get him adopted by a family of Eskimos?" inquired Larry. "They like eating blubber and maggots and things."

"Larry, don't be disgusting," said Margaret. "They can't eat anything like this. The very thought of it makes me feel sick."

"I think we ought to go inside," said Mother faintly. "Perhaps it won't smell as much in there."

"If anything, it smells worse in here," shouted Leslie from the French windows.

"Gerry dear, you must clean this up," said Mother as she picked her way delicately over the turtle's entrails, "and disinfect the flagstones."

The family went inside and I set about the task of clearing up the turtle from the front veranda. Their voices arguing ferociously drifted out to me.

"Bloody menace," said Leslie. "Lying here peacefully reading, and I was suddenly seized by the throat."

"Disgusting," said Margo. "I don't wonder Lucretia fainted."

"High time he had another tutor," said Larry. "You leave the house for five minutes and come back and find him disembowelling Moby Dick on the front porch."

"I'm sure he didn't mean any harm," said Mother, "but it was rather silly of him to do it on the veranda."

"Silly!" said Larry caustically. "We'll be blundering round the house with gas-masks for the next six months."

I piled the remains of the turtle into the wheelbarrow and

took it up to the top of the hill behind the villa. Here I dug a hole and buried all the soft parts and then placed the shell and the bone structure near a nest of friendly ants, who had, on previous occasions, helped me considerably by picking skeletons clean. But the most they had ever tackled had been a very large green lizard, so I was interested to see whether they would tackle the turtle. They ran towards it, their antennae waving eagerly, and then stopped, thought about it for a bit, held a little consultation and then retreated in a body; apparently even the ants were against me, so I returned dispiritedly to the villa.

Here I found that a thin, whining little man, obviously made belligerent by wine, was arguing with Lucretia on the still-odoriferous veranda. I inquired what the man wanted.

"He says," said Lucretia, with fine scorn, "that Roger has been killing his chickens."

"Turkeys," corrected the man. "Turkeys."

"Well, turkeys then," said Lucretia, conceding the point.

My heart sank. One calamity was being succeeded by another. Roger, we knew, had the most reprehensible habit of killing chickens. He derived a lot of innocent amusement in the spring and summer by chasing swallows. They would drive him into an apoplectic fury by zooming past his nose and then flying along the ground just ahead of him while he chased them, bristling with rage, uttering roars of fury. The peasants' chickens used to hide in the myrtle bushes and then, just as Roger was passing, they would leap out with a great flutter of wings and insane hysterical cackling right into his path. Roger, I was sure, was convinced that these chickens were a sort of ungainly swallow that he could get to grips with and so, in spite of yells of protest on our part, he would leap on them and kill them with one swift bite, all his hatred of the teasing summer swallows showing in his action. No punishment had any effect on him. He was normally an extremely obedient dog, except about this one thing, and so, in desperation, all we could do was to recompense the owners, but only on condition that the corpse of the chicken was produced as evidence.

Reluctantly I went in to tell the family that Roger had been at it again.

"Christ!" said Leslie, getting laboriously to his feet. "You and you sodding animals."

"Now, now, dear," said Mother placatingly. "Gerry can't help it if Roger kills chickens."

"Turkeys," said Leslie. "I bet he'll want a hell of a lot for those."

"Have you cleaned up the veranda, dear?" inquired Mother.

Larry removed a large handkerchief, drenched in eau-de-Cologne, which he had spread over his face. "Does it smell as though he's cleaned up the veranda?" he inquired.

I said hastily that I was just about to do it and followed Leslie to see the outcome of his conversation with the turkey owner.

"Well," said Leslie belligerently, striding out onto the veranda, "what do you want?"

The man cringed, humble, servile, and altogether repulsive. "Be happy, *kyrié*, be happy," he said, greeting Leslie.

"Be happy," Leslie replied in a gruff tone of voice that implied he hoped the man would be anything but. "What do you wish to see me about?"

"My turkeys, *kyrié*," explained the man. "I apologize for troubling you, but your dog, you see, he's been killing my turkeys."

"Well," said Leslie, "how many has he killed?"

"Five, *kyrié*," said the man, shaking his head sorrowfully. "Five of my best turkeys. I am a poor man, *kyrié*, otherwise I wouldn't have dreamed . . ."

"Five!" said Leslie startled, and turned an inquiring eye on me.

I said I thought it was quite possible. If five hysterical

turkeys had leaped out of a myrtle bush, I could well believe that Roger would kill them all. For such a benign and friendly dog, he was a very ruthless killer when he got started.

"Roger is a good dog," said Lucretia belligerently.

She had joined us on the veranda and she obviously viewed the turkey owner with the same dislike as I did. Apart from this, in her eyes Roger could do no wrong.

"Well," said Leslie, making the best of a bad job, "if he's killed five turkeys, he's killed five turkeys. Such is life. Where are the bodies?"

There was a moment of silence.

"The bodies, *kyrié?*" queried the turkey owner tentatively.

"The bodies, the bodies," said Leslie impatiently. "You know, the bodies of the turkeys. You know we can't pay until you produce the bodies."

"But that's not possible," said the turkey owner nervously.

"What do you mean, not possible?" inquired Leslie.

"Well, it's not possible to bring the bodies, *kyrié,*" said the turkey owner with a flash of inspiration, "because your dog has eaten them."

The explosion that this statement provoked was considerable. We all knew that Roger was, if anything, slightly over-fed, and that he was of a most fastidious nature. Though he would kill a chicken, nothing would induce him to feed upon the carcass.

"Lies! Lies!" shrilled Lucretia, her eyes swimming with tears of emotion. "He's a good dog."

"He's never eaten anything in his life that he's killed," shouted Leslie. "Never."

"But five of my turkeys!" said the little man. "Five of them he's eaten!"

"When did he kill them?" roared Leslie.

"This morning, *kyrié,* this morning," said the man, crossing himself. "I saw it myself, and he ate them all."

I interrupted to say that Roger had been out that morning

in the "Bootle-bumtrinket" with me and, intelligent dog though he was, I did not see how he could be consuming the prodigious quantity of five turkeys on this man's farm and be out in the boat with me at the same time.

Leslie had had a trying morning. All he had wanted was to lie peacefully on the sofa with his manual of ballistics, but first he had been almost asphyxiated by my investigations into the internal anatomy of the turtle and now he was being faced by a drunken little man, trying to swindle us for the price of five turkeys. His temper, never under the best of control, bubbled over.

"You're a two-faced liar and a cheat," he snarled. The little man backed away and his face went white.

"*You* are the liar and the cheat," he said with drunken belligerence. "*You* are the liar and the cheat. You let your dog kill everybody's chickens and turkeys and then when they come to you for payment, you refuse. *You* are the liar and the cheat."

Even at that stage, I think that sanity could have prevailed, but the little man made a fatal mistake. He spat copiously and wetly at Leslie's feet. Lucretia uttered a shrill wail of horror and grabbed hold of Leslie's arm. Knowing his temper, I grabbed hold of the other one, too. The little man, appalled into a moment of sobriety, backed away. Leslie quivered like a volcano and Lucretia and I hung on like grim death.

"*Excreta* of a pig," roared Leslie. "Illegitimate son of a diseased whore . . ."

The fine Greek oaths rolled out, rich, vulgar, and biological, and the little man turned from white to pink and from pink to red. He had obviously been unaware of the fact that Leslie had such a command over the fruitier of the Greek insults.

"You'll be sorry," he quavered. "You'll be sorry."

He spat once more with a pathetic sort of defiance and then turned and scuttled down the drive.

It took the combined efforts of the family and Lucretia three quarters of an hour to calm Leslie down, with the aid of several large brandies.

"Don't you worry about him, *kyrié* Leslie," was Lucretia's final summing up. "He's well known in the village as a bad character. Don't you worry about him."

But we were forced to worry about him, for the next thing we knew, he had sued Leslie for not paying his debts and for defamation of character.

Spiro, when told the news, was furious.

"Gollys, Mrs. Durrells," he said, his face red with wrath. "Why don'ts yous lets Masters Leslies shoot the son of a bitch?"

"I don't think that would really solve anything, Spiro," said Mother. "What we want to know now is whether this man has any chance of winning his case."

"Winnings!" said Spiro with fine scorn. "That bastard won't wins anythings. You just leaves it to me. I'll fixes it."

"Now, don't go and do anything rash, Spiro," said Mother. "It'll only make matters worse."

"I won'ts do anything rash, Mrs. Durrells. But I'll fixes that bastard."

For several days he went about with an air of conspiratorial gloom, his bushy eyebrows tangled in a frown of immense concentration, only answering our questions monosyllabically. Then, one day, a fortnight or so before the case was due to be heard, we were all in town on a shopping spree. Eventually, weighed down by our purchases, we made our way to the broad, tree-lined Esplanade and sat there having a drink and exchanging greetings with our numerous acquaintances who passed. Presently Spiro, who had been glaring furtively about him with the air of a man who had many enemies, suddenly stiffened. He hitched his great belly up and leaned across the table.

"Master Leslies, you sees that mans over there, that one with the white hair?"

He pointed a sausage-like finger at a small, neat little man who was placidly sipping a cup of coffee under the trees.

"Well, what about him?" inquired Leslie.

"He's the judges," said Spiro.

"What judge?" said Leslie, bewildered.

"The judges who is going to tries your case," said Spiro. "I wants you go to over there and talks to him."

"Do you think that's wise?" said Larry. "He might think I'm trying to muck about with the course of justice and give me ten years in prison or something."

"Gollys, nos," said Spiro, aghast at such a thought. "He wouldn't puts Master Leslies in prison. He knows better than to do thats while I ams here."

"But even so, Spiro, don't you think *he'll* think it a little funny if Leslie suddenly starts talking to him?" asked Mother.

"Gollys nos," said Spiro. He glanced about him to make sure that we weren't overheard, leaned forward, and whispered, "He collects stamps."

The family looked bewildered.

"You mean he's a philatelist?" said Larry at length.

"No, no, Master Larrys," said Spiro. "He's not one of them. He's a married man and he's gots two childrens."

The whole conversation seemed to be getting even more involved than the normal ones that we had with Spiro.

"What," said Leslie patiently, "has his collecting stamps got to do with it?"

"I will takes you over there," said Spiro, laying bare for the first time the Machiavellian intricacies of his plot, "and yous tells hims that you will get him some stamps from England."

"But that's bribery," said Margaret, shocked.

"It isn't bribery, Misses Margos," said Spiro. "He collects stamps. He *wants* stamps."

"I should think if you tried to bribe him with stamps he'd give you about five hundred years' penal servitude," said Larry to Leslie judiciously.

I asked eagerly whether, if Leslie was condemned, he would be sent to Vido, the convict settlement on a small island that lay in the sparkling sea half a mile or so from the town.

"No, no, dear," said Mother, getting increasingly flustered. "Leslie won't be sent to Vido."

I felt this was rather a pity. I already had one convict friend, serving a sentence for the murder of his wife, who lived on Vido. He was a "trusty" and so had been allowed to build his own boat and row home for the week-ends. He had given me a monstrous black-backed gull which tyrannized all my pets and the family. I felt that, exciting though it was to have a real murderer as a friend, it would have been better to have Leslie incarcerated on Vido so that he too could come home for the week-ends. To have a convict brother would, I felt, be rather exotic.

"I don't see that if I just go and *talk* to him it can do any harm," said Leslie.

"I wouldn't," said Margo. "Remember, there's many a slip without a stitch."

"I do think you ought to be careful, dear," said Mother.

"I can see it all," said Larry with relish. "Leslie with a ball and chain; Spiro too, probably, as an accessory. Margo knitting them warm socks for the winter, Mother sending them food parcels and anti-lice ointment."

"Oh, do stop it, Larry," said Mother crossly. "This is no laughing matter."

"All you've gots to dos is to talks to him, Master Leslies," said Spiro earnestly. "Honest to Gods you've got to, otherwise I can't fixes it."

Spiro had, prior to this, never let us down. His advice had always been sound, and even if it hadn't been legal, we had never so far come to grief.

"All right," said Leslie. "Let's give it a bash."

"Do be careful, dear," said Mother as Leslie and Spiro rose and walked over to where the judge was sitting.

The judge greeted them charmingly and for half an hour Leslie and Spiro sat at his table sipping coffee while Leslie talked to him in voluble, but inaccurate, Greek. Presently the judge rose and left them with much handshaking and bowing. They returned to our table where we waited agog for the news.

"Charming old boy," said Leslie. "Couldn't have been nicer. I promised to get him some stamps. Who do we know in England who collects them?"

"Well, your father used to," said Mother. "He was a very keen philatelist when he was alive."

"Gollys, don't says that Mrs. Durrells," said Spiro, in genuine anguish.

A short pause ensued while the family explained to him the meaning of the word philatelist.

"I still don't see how this is going to help the case," said Larry, "even if you inundate him with penny blacks."

"Never yous minds, Masters Larrys," said Spiro darkly. "I said I'd fixes it and I will. You just leaves it to me."

For the next few days Leslie, convinced that Spiro could obstruct the course of justice, wrote to everybody he could think of in England and demanded stamps. The result was that our mail increased threefold and that practically every free space in the villa was taken up by piles of stamps which, whenever a wind blew, would drift like autumn leaves across the room, to the vociferous, snarling delight of the dogs. As a result of this, many of the stamps began to look slightly the worse for wear.

"You're not going to give him *those*, are you?" said Larry, disdainfully surveying a pile of mangled, semi-masticated stamps that Leslie had rescued from the jaws of Roger half an hour previously.

"Well, stamps are supposed to be old, aren't they?" said Leslie belligerently.

"Old, perhaps," said Larry, "but surely not covered with enough spittle to give him hydrophobia."

"Well, if you can think of a better bloody plan, why don't you suggest it?" inquired Leslie.

"My dear fellow, I don't mind," said Larry. "When the judge is running around biting all his colleagues and you are languishing in a Greek prison, don't blame me."

"All I ask is that you mind your own bloody business," cried Leslie.

"Now, now, dear, Larry's only trying to be helpful," said Mother.

"Helpful," snarled Leslie, making a grab at a group of stamps that were being blown off the table. "He's just interfering as usual."

"Well, dear," said Mother, adjusting her spectacles, "I do think he may be right, you know. After all, some of those stamps do look a little, well, you know, second-hand."

"He wants stamps and he's bloody well going to get stamps," said Leslie.

And stamps the poor judge got, in a bewildering variety of sizes, shapes, colours, and stages of disintegration.

Then another thing happened that increased Leslie's confidence in winning the case a hundredfold. We discovered that the turkey man, whom Larry constantly referred to as Crippenopoulos, had been unwise enough to subpoena Lucretia as a witness for the prosecution. Lucretia, furious, wanted to refuse, until it was explained to her that she could not.

"Imagine that man calling me as a witness to help him," she said. "Well, don't you worry, *kyrié* Leslie, I'll tell the court how he forced you to swear at him and call him . . ."

The family rose in a body and vociferously informed Lucretia that she was not to do anything of the sort. It took us half an hour to impress upon her what she should and should not say. At the end of it, since Lucretia, like most Corfiotes, was not very strong on logic, we felt somewhat jaded.

"Well, with her as witness for the prosecution," said Larry, "I should think you'll probably get the death sentence."

"Larry dear, don't say things like that," said Mother. "It's not funny even in a joke."

"I'm not joking," said Larry.

"Rubbish," said Leslie uneasily. "I'm sure she'll be all right."

"I think it would be much safer to disguise Margo as Lucretia," said Larry judicially. "With her sweeping command over the Greek language she would probably do you considerably less harm."

"Yes," said Margo excitedly, struck for the first time by Larry's perspicacity, "why can't I be a witness?"

"Don't be damned silly," said Leslie. "You weren't there. How can you be a witness?"

"I was almost there," said Margo. "I was in the kitchen."

"That's all you need," said Larry to Leslie. "Margo and Lucretia in the witness-box and you won't even need a judge. You'll probably be lynched by the mob."

When the day of the case dawned, Mother rallied the family.

"It's ridiculous for us all to go," said Larry. "If Leslie wants to get himself into prison, that's his affair. I don't see why we should be dragged into it. Besides, I wanted to do some writing this morning."

"It's our duty to go," said Mother firmly. "We must put on a bold front. After all, I don't want people to think that I'm rearing a family of gaol-birds."

So we all put on our best clothes and sat waiting patiently until Spiro came to collect us.

"Now, don'ts yous worrys, Master Leslies," he scowled, with the air of a warder in the condemned cell. "Everything's going to be O.K.'s."

But in spite of this prophecy, Larry insisted on reciting "The Ballad of Reading Gaol" as we drove into town, much to Leslie's annoyance.

The court-room was a bustle of uncoordinated activity. People sipped little cups of coffee, other people shuffled through piles of papers in an aimless but dedicated way, and there was lots of chatter and laughter. Crippenopoulos was there in his best suit, but avoided our eye. Lucretia, for some reason best known to herself, was clad entirely in black. It was, as Larry pointed out, a premature move. Surely she should have reserved her mourning for after the trial.

"Now, Master Leslies," said Spiro, "you stands there, and I stands there and translates for you."

"What for?" inquired Leslie, bewildered.

"Because you don'ts speaks Greeks," said Spiro.

"Really, Spiro," protested Larry, "I admit his Greek is not Homeric, but it is surely perfectly adequate?"

"Masters Larrys," said Spiro, scowling earnestly, "Master Leslies mustn'ts speaks Greeks."

Before we could inquire more deeply into this, there was a general scuffling and the judge came in. He took his seat and his eyes roved round the court and then, catching sight of Leslie, he beamed and bowed.

"Hanging judges always smile like that," said Larry.

"Larry dear, do stop it," said Mother. "You're making me nervous."

There was a long pause while what was presumably the Clerk of the Court read out the indictment. Then Crippenopoulos was called to give his evidence. He put on a lovely performance, at once servile and indignant, placating but belligerent. The judge was obviously impressed and I began to get quite excited. Perhaps I would have a convict for a brother after all. Then it was Leslie's turn.

"You are accused," said the judge, "of having used defamatory and insulting language to this man and endeavouring to deprive him of rightful payment for the loss of five turkeys, killed by your dog."

Leslie stared blank-faced at the judge.

"What's he say?" he inquired of Spiro.

Spiro hitched his stomach up.

"He says, Masters Leslies," and his voice was so pitched

that it rumbled through the court-room like thunder, "he says that you insults this mans and that you tries to swindle him out of moneys for his turkeys."

"That's ridiculous," said Leslie firmly.

He was about to go on when Spiro held up a hand like a ham and stopped him. He turned to the judge.

"The *kyrios* denies the charge," he said. "It would be impossible for him to be guilty anyway, because he doesn't speak Greek."

"Christ!" groaned Larry sepulchrally. "I hope Spiro knows what he's doing."

"What's he saying? What's he doing?" said Mother nervously.

"As far as I can see, putting a noose round Leslie's neck," said Larry.

The judge, who had had so many coffees with Leslie, who had received so many stamps from him, and who had had so many conversations in Greek with him, stared at Leslie impassively. Even if the judge had not known Leslie personally, it would have been impossible for him not to know that Leslie had some command over the Greek language. Nothing anyone did in Corfu was sacrosanct, and if you were a foreigner, of course, the interest in and the knowledge of your private affairs was that much greater. We waited with bated breath for the judge's reactions. Spiro had his massive head slightly lowered like a bull about to charge.

"I see," said the judge dryly.

He shuffled some papers aimlessly for a moment and then glanced up.

"I understand," he said, "that the prosecution has a witness. I suppose we had better hear her."

It was Lucretia's big moment. She rose to her feet, folded her arms, and stared majestically at the judge, her normally pale face pink with excitement, her soulful eyes glowing.

"You are Lucretia Condos and you are employed by these people as a cook?" inquired the judge.

"Yes," said Lucretia, "and a kinder, more generous family you could not wish to meet. Why, only the other day they gave me a frock for myself and for my daughter and it was only a month or two ago that I asked the *kyrios* . . ."

"Yes," interrupted the judge, "I see. Well, this has not got much relevance to the case. I understand that you were there when this man called to see about his turkeys. Now tell me in your own words what happened."

Larry groaned.

"If she tells him in her own words, they'll get Leslie for sure," he said.

"Well," said Lucretia, glancing round the court to make sure she had everybody's attention. "The *kyrios* had been very ill, very ill indeed. At times we despaired for his life. I kept suggesting cupping to his mother, but she wouldn't hear of it . . ."

"Would you mind getting to the point?" said the judge.

"Well," said Lucretia, reluctantly abandoning the subject of illness, which was always a favourite topic with her, "it was the *kyrios'* first day up and he was very weak. Then this man," she said, pointing a scornful finger at Crippenopoulos, "arrived dead drunk and said that their dog had killed five of his turkeys. Now the dog wouldn't do that, *kyrié* judge. A sweeter, kinder, nobler dog was never seen in Corfu."

"The dog is not on trial," said the judge.

"Well," said Lucretia, "when the *kyrios* said, quite rightly, that he would have to see the corpses before he paid the man, the man said he couldn't show them because the dog had eaten them. This is ridiculous, as you can well imagine, *kyrié* judge, as no dog could eat five turkeys."

"You are supposed to be a witness for the prosecution, aren't you?" said the judge. "I ask only because your story doesn't tally with the complainant's."

"Him," said Lucretia, "you don't want to trust him. He's a drunkard and a liar and it is well known in the village that he has got two wives."

"So you are telling me," said the judge, endeavouring to sort out this confusion, "that the *kyrios* didn't swear at him in Greek and refuse payment for the turkeys."

"Of course he didn't," said Lucretia. "A kinder, finer, more upstanding *kyrios* . . ."

"Yes, yes, all right," said the judge.

He sat pondering for some time while we all waited in suspense, then he glanced up and looked at Crippenopoulos.

"I can see no evidence," he said, "that the Englishman behaved in the way you have suggested. Firstly he does not speak Greek."

"He does speak Greek," shouted Crippenopoulos wrathfully. "He called me a . . ."

"Will you be quiet," said the judge coldly. "Firstly, as I was saying, he does not speak Greek. Secondly, your own witness denies all knowledge of the incident. It seems to me clear, however, that you endeavoured to extract payment for turkeys which had not, in fact, been killed and eaten by the defendant's dog. However, you are not on trial here for that, so I will merely find the defendant not guilty, and you will have to pay the costs."

Immediately pandemonium reigned. Crippenopoulos was on his feet, purple with rage, shouting at the top of his voice and calling on St. Spiridion's aid. Spiro, bellowing like a bull, embraced Leslie, kissed him on both cheeks, and was followed by the weeping Lucretia who did likewise. It was some time before we managed to extricate ourselves from the court, and jubilantly we went down to the Esplanade and sat at a table under the trees to celebrate.

Presently the judge came past and we rose in a body to thank him and invite him to sit and have a drink with us. He refused the drink shyly and then fixed Leslie with a penetrating eye.

"I wouldn't like you to think," he said, "that justice in Corfu is always dispensed like that, but I had a long conversation with Spiro about the case and after some deliberation I decided that your crime was not as bad as the man's. I hoped it might teach him not to swindle foreigners in future."

"Well, I really am most grateful to you," said Leslie.

The judge gave a little bow. He glanced at his watch.

"Well, I must be going," he said. "By the way, thank you so much for those stamps you sent me yesterday. Among them were two quite rare ones which were new to my collection."

Raising his hat he trotted off across the Esplanade.

Interlude
for Spirits

What seest thou else in the dark backward and abysm of time?

—The Tempest

INTERLUDE FOR SPIRITS

Not very long after Leslie's court case, Margo was beset by another affliction to keep company with her acne. She suddenly started to put on weight and before long, to her horror, she was almost circular. Androuchelli, our doctor, was called in to view this mystery. He uttered a long series of distressed "Po, po, po's" as he viewed Margo's obesity. He tried her on several pills and potions and a number of diets, to no effect.

"He says," Margo confided to us tearfully at lunch one day, "that he thinks it's glandular."

"Glandular?" said Mother, alarmed. "What does he mean, glandular?"

"I don't know," wailed Margo.

"Must we always discuss your ailments at mealtimes?" inquired Larry.

"Larry dear, Androuchelli says it's glandular," said Mother.

"Rubbish," said Larry airily. "It's puppy fat."

"Puppy fat!" squeaked Margo. "Do you know how much I weigh?"

"What you want is more exercise," said Leslie. "Why don't you take up sailing?"

"Don't think the boat's big enough," said Larry.

"Beast," said Margo, bursting into tears. "You wouldn't say things like that if you knew how I felt."

"Larry dear," said Mother placatingly, "that wasn't a very kind thing to say."

"Well, I can't help it if she's wandering around looking like a water-melon covered with spots," said Larry irritably. "One would think it was *my* fault the way you all go on."

"Something will have to be done," said Mother. "I shall see Androuchelli tomorrow."

But Androuchelli repeated that he thought her condition might be glandular and that in his opinion Margo ought to go to London for treatment. So, after a flurry of telegrams and letters, Margo was despatched to London and into the tender care of two of the only worth-while relatives with whom we were still on speaking terms, my mother's cousin Prudence and her mother, Great-Aunt Fan.

Apart from a brief letter saying she had arrived safely and that she, Cousin Prue, and Aunt Fan had taken up residence at a hotel near Notting Hill Gate and that she had been put in touch with a good doctor, we heard nothing further from Margo for a considerable length of time.

"I do wish she would write," Mother said.

"Don't fuss, Mother," said Larry. "What's she got to write about, anyway, except to give you her new dimensions?"

"Well, I like to know what's going on," said Mother. "After all, she's in *London*."

"What's London got to do with it?" asked Larry.

"In a big city like that anything can happen," said Mother darkly. "You hear all sorts of things about girls in big cities."

"Really, Mother, you do worry unnecessarily," said Larry in exasperation. "What do you think's happened to her, for Heaven's sake? Do you think she's being lured into some den of vice? They'd never get her through the door."

"It's no joking matter, Larry," said Mother severely.

"But you get yourself into a panic about nothing," said Larry. "I ask you, what self-respecting white slaver is going to look at Margo twice? I shouldn't think there's one strong enough to carry her off, anyway."

"Well, I'm worried," said Mother, "and I'm going to send a cable."

So she sent a cable to Cousin Prudence, who replied at length saying that Margaret was associating with people she didn't approve of, that she thought it would be a good thing if Mother came to talk some sense into her. Immediately pandemonium reigned. Mother, distraught, despatched Spiro to buy tickets and started packing frantically, until she suddenly remembered me. Feeling it would do more harm than good to leave me in the tender care of my two elder brothers, she decided that I should accompany her. So Spiro was despatched to get more tickets and yet more packing was done. I regarded the whole situation as heaven-sent, for I had just acquired a new tutor, Mr. Richard Kralefsky, who was endeavouring—with grim determination in the face of my opposition—to instruct me in irregular French verbs, and this trip to England, I thought, would give me a much-needed respite from this torture.

The journey by train was uneventful, except that Mother was in constant fear of being arrested by the Fascist carabinieri. This fear increased a thousandfold when, at Milan, I drew a caricature of Mussolini on the steamy window of the carriage. Mother scrubbed at it for quite ten minutes with her handkerchief, with all the dedication of a washerwoman in a contest, before she was satisfied that it was obliterated.

Coming from the calm, slow, sunlit days of Corfu, our arrival in London, late in the evening, was a shattering experience. So many people were at the station that we did not *know*, all hurrying to and fro, grey-faced and worried. The almost incomprehensible language that the porters spoke, and London aglitter with lights and churning with people. The taxi nosing its way through Piccadilly like a beetle through a firework display. The cold air that made your breath float like a web of smoke in front of your mouth as you talked, so that you felt like a character in a cartoon strip.

Eventually the taxi drew up outside the fake, soot-encrusted Corinthian columns of Balaklava Mansions. We got our luggage into the hotel with the aid of an elderly, bow-legged, Irish porter, but there was no one to greet us, so apparently the telegram signalling our arrival had gone astray. The young lady, we were informed by the porter, had gone to her meeting, and Miss Hughes and the old lady had gone to feed the dogs.

"What did he say, dear?" asked Mother when he had left the room, for his accent was so thick that it sounded almost as though he were talking a foreign language. I said that Margo had gone to a meeting and that Cousin Prue and Aunt Fan were feeding the dogs.

"What *can* he mean?" said Mother, bewildered. "What meeting has Margo gone to? What dogs is he talking about?"

I said I did not know but, from what I had seen of London, what it needed was a few more dogs around.

"Well," said Mother, inexpertly putting a shilling in the meter and lighting the gas fire, "I suppose we'll just have to make ourselves comfortable and wait until they come back."

We had waited an hour when suddenly the door burst open and Cousin Prue rushed in, arms outstretched, crying "Louise, Louise, Louise," like some strange marsh bird. She embraced us both, her sloe dark eyes glowing with love and excitement. Her beautiful face, delicately scented, was soft as a pansy as I kissed her dutifully.

"I began to think that you were never coming," she said. "Mummy is on her way up. She finds the stairs trying, poor dear. Well, now, *don't* you both look well. You must tell me everything. Do you like this hotel, Louise? It's so cheap and convenient, but full of the most peculiar people."

A gentle wheezing sound made itself heard through the open door.

"Ah, there's Mummy," cried Prue. "Mummy! Mummy! Louise's here."

Through the door appeared my Great-Aunt Fan. At first

glance she looked, I thought rather uncharitably, like a walking tent. She was enveloped in a rusty-red tweed suit of incredible style and dimensions. It made her look like a russet-red pyramid of tweed. On her head she wore a somewhat battered velveteen hat of the style that pixies are reputedly wont to use. Her spectacles, through which her eyes stared owlishly, glittered.

"Louise!" she cried throwing her arms wide and casting her eyes up as though Mother were some divine apparition. "Louise and Gerald! You have come!"

Mother and I were kissed and embraced heartily. This was not the feathery, petal-soft embrace of Cousin Prue. This was a hearty, rib-cracking embrace and a firm kiss that left your lips feeling bruised.

"I am so sorry we weren't here to greet you, Louise dear," said Prue, "but we weren't sure when you were arriving and we had the dogs to feed."

"What dogs?" asked Mother.

"Why, my Bedlington puppies, of course," said Prue. "Didn't you know? Mummy and I have become dog-breeders." She gave a coy, tinkling laugh.

"But you had something else last time," said Mother. "Goats or something, wasn't it?"

"Oh, we've still got those," said Aunt Fan. "And my bees and the chickens. But Prudence here thought it would be a good thing to start dog-breeding. She's got such a head for business."

"I really think it's a paying concern, Louise dear," said Prue earnestly. "I bought Tinkerbell and then Lucybell . . ."

"And then Tinybell," interrupted Aunt Fan.

"And Tinybell," said Prue.

"And Lucybell," said Aunt Fan.

"Oh, Mummy, do be quiet. I've already said Lucybell."

"And there's Tinkerbell too," said Aunt Fan.

"Mummy is a little hard of hearing," said Prue unnecessarily, "and they have all had puppies. I brought them up to London to sell and at the same time we have been keeping an eye on Margo."

"Yes, where is Margo?" asked Mother.

Prue tiptoed over to the door and closed it softly.

"She's at a *meeting*, dear," she said.

"I know, but what sort of meeting?" asked Mother.

Prue glanced round nervously.

"A *spiritualist* meeting," she hissed.

"And then there's Lucybell," said Aunt Fan.

"Oh, Mummy, do be quiet."

"Spiritualist meeting?" said Mother. "What on earth's she gone to a spiritualist meeting for?"

"To cure her fatness and her acne," said Prue. "But mark my words, no good will come of it. It's an evil power."

I could see Mother beginning to get alarmed.

"But I don't understand," she said. "I sent Margo home to see that doctor, what's his name?"

"I *know* you did, dear," said Prue. "Then, after she came to this hotel, she fell into the grasp of that evil woman."

"What evil woman?" said Mother, now considerably alarmed.

"The goats are well too," said Aunt Fan, "but their milk yield is down a little this year."

"Oh, Mummy, do shut up," hissed Prue. "I mean that evil woman, Mrs. Haddock."

"Haddock, haddock," said Mother, bewildered. Her train of thought was always liable to be interrupted if anything culinary was mentioned.

"She's a medium, my dear," said Prue, "and she's got her hooks on Margo. She's told Margo that she's got a guide."

"A guide?" said Mother feebly. "What sort of guide?"

I could see, in her distraught condition, that she was now beginning to think Margo had taken up mountaineering or some similar occupation.

"A spirit guide," said Prue. "It's called Mawake. He's supposed to be a Red Indian."

"I have ten hives now," said Aunt Fan proudly. "We get twice as much honey."

"Mother, be quiet," said Prue.

"I don't understand," said Mother plaintively. "Why isn't she still going to the doctor for her injections?"

"Because Mawake told her not to," said Prue triumphantly. "Three séances ago, he said—according to Margaret, and of course the whole thing comes through Mrs. Haddock so you can't trust it for a moment—according to Margaret, Mawake said she was to have no more punctures."

"Punctures?" said Mother.

"Well, I suppose it's Red Indian for injections," said Prue.

"It is nice to see you again, Louise," said Aunt Fan. "I think we ought to have a cup of tea."

"That's a very good idea," said Mother faintly.

"I'm not going down there to order tea, Mummy," said Prue, glancing at the door as if, behind it, were all the fiends of Hell. "Not when they're having a meeting."

"Why, what happens?" asked Mother.

"And some toast would be nice," said Aunt Fan.

"Oh, Mummy, do be quiet," said Prue. "You have no idea what happens at these meetings, Louise. Mrs. Haddock goes into a trance, then becomes covered with ectoplasm."

"Ectoplasm?" said Mother. "What's ectoplasm?"

"I've got a pot of my own honey in my room," said Aunt Fan. "I'm sure you will enjoy it, Louise. So much purer than these synthetic things you buy now."

"It's a sort of stuff that mediums produce," said Prue. "It looks like . . . Well, it looks like, sort of like—I've never actually *seen* it, but I'm told that it looks like *brains*. Then they make trumpets fly about and things. I tell you, my dear, I never go into the lower regions of the hotel when they are holding a meeting."

Fascinated though I was by the conversation, I felt the chance of seeing a woman called Mrs. Haddock covered with brains, with a couple of trumpets floating about, was too good to miss, so I volunteered to go down and order tea.

However, to my disappointment, I saw nothing in the lower regions of the hotel to resemble remotely Cousin Prudence's description, but I did manage to get a tray of tea brought up by the Irish porter. We were sipping this, and I was endeavouring to explain to Aunt Fan what ectoplasm was, when Margaret arrived, carrying a large cabbage under one arm, accompanied by a dumpy little woman with protruding blue eyes and wispy hair.

"Mother!" said Margo dramatically. "You've come!"

"Yes, dear," said Mother grimly. "And not a moment too soon, apparently."

"This is Mrs. Haddock," said Margo. "She's *absolutely marvellous.*"

It became immediately apparent that Mrs. Haddock suffered from a strange affliction. For some obscure reason she seemed to be incapable of breathing while talking. The result was that she would gabble, all her words latched together like a daisy chain and would then, when her breath ran out, pause and suck it in, making a noise that sounded like "Whaaaha."

Now she said to Mother, "IamdelightedtomeetyouMrs.Durrell.   Ofcourse,myspiritguideinformedmeofyourcoming.   Idohopeyouhadacomfortablejourney   . . .   Whaaaha."

Mother, who had been intending to give Mrs. Haddock a very frigid and dignified greeting, was somewhat put off by this strange delivery.

"Oh, yes. Did we?" she said nervously, straining her ears to understand what Mrs. Haddock was saying.

"Mrs. Haddock is a spiritualist, Mother," said Margo proudly, as though she were introducing Leonardo da Vinci or the inventor of the first aeroplane.

"Really, dear?" said Mother, smiling frostily. "How very interesting."

"Itgivesonegreatcomforttoknowthatthosewhohavegonebe-forearestillintouchwithone. . . . Whaaaha," said Mrs. Haddock earnestly. "Somanypeopleareunaware . . . Whaa . . . aha . . . ofthespiritworldthatliessoclose."

"You should have seen the puppies tonight, Margo," observed Aunt Fan. "The little tinkers had torn up all their bedding."

"Mummy, do be quiet," said Prue, eyeing Mrs. Haddock as though she expected her to grow horns and a tail at any moment.

"Yourdaughterisveryluckyinasmuchasshehas . . . Whaa . . . aha . . . managedtoobtainoneofthebetterguides," said Mrs. Haddock, rather as though Margaret had riffled through the *Debrett* before settling on her spirit counsellor.

"He's called Mawake," said Margo. "He's *absolutely marvellous!*"

"He doesn't appear to have done you much good so far," said Mother tartly.

"But he has," said Margo indignantly. "I've lost three ounces."

"Ittakestimeandpatienceandimplicitbeliefinthefuturelife . . . Whaaaha . . . mydearMrs.Durrell," said Mrs. Haddock, smiling at Mother with sickly sweetness.

"Yes, I'm sure," said Mother, "but I really would prefer it if Margo were under a medical practitioner one could see."

"I don't think they meant it," said Aunt Fan. "I think they're teething. Their gums get sore, you know."

"Mummy, we are not *talking* about the puppies," said Prue. "We are talking about Margo's guide."

"That will be nice for her," said Aunt Fan, beaming fondly at Margo.

"Thespiritworldissomuchwiserthananyearthlybeing. . . . Whaaaha," said Mrs. Haddock. "Youcouldn'thaveyour-daughterinbetterhands.Mawakewasagreatmedicinemaninhis-owntribe. OneofthemostknowledgeableinthewholeofNorth-America. . . . Whaaah."

"And he's given me such good advice, Mother," said Margo. "Hasn't he, Mrs. Haddock?"

"Nomorepunctures. Thewhitegirlmusthavenomorepunctures. . . . Whaaaha," intoned Mrs. Haddock.

"There you are," hissed Prue triumphantly, "I told you."

"Have some honey," said Aunt Fan companionably. "It's not like that synthetic stuff you buy in the shops nowadays."

"Mummy, be quiet."

"I still feel, Mrs. Haddock, that I would prefer my daughter to have sensible medical attention rather than this Mawake."

"Oh, Mother, you're so narrow-minded and Victorian," said Margo in exasperation.

"MydearMrs.Durrellyoumustlearntotrustthegreatinfluencesofthespiritworldthatareafterallonlytryingtohelpandguideus. . . . Whaaaha," said Mrs. Haddock. "Ifeelthatifyoucametooneofourmeetingsyouwouldbeconvincedofthegreatpowersofgoodthatourspiritguideshave. . . . Whaaaha."

"I prefer to be guided by my own spirit, thank you very much," said Mother, with dignity.

"Honey isn't what it used to be," said Aunt Fan, who had been giving the matter some thought.

"You are just prejudiced, Mother," said Margo. "You're condemning a thing without even *trying*."

"IfeelsurethatifyoucouldpersuadeyourMothertoattendoneofourmeetings . . . Whaaaha,"said Mrs. Haddock, "shewouldfindawholenewworldopeningupbeforeher."

"Yes, Mother," said Margo, "you must come to a meeting. I'm *sure* you'd be convinced. The things you see and hear! After all, there are no bricks without fire."

I could see that Mother was suffering an inward struggle. For many years she had been deeply interested in superstitions, folk magic, witchcraft, and similar subjects, and now the temptation to accept Mrs. Haddock's offer was very great. I waited breathlessly, hoping that she would accept. There was nothing I wanted more at that moment than to see Mrs. Haddock covered with brains and with trumpets flying round her head.

"Well," said Mother, undecided, "we'll see. We'll talk about it tomorrow."

"I'msurethatoncewebreakthroughthebarrierforyouwe'llbe-abletogiveyoualotofhelpandguidance. . . . Whaaaha," said Mrs. Haddock.

"Oh, yes," said Margo. "Mawake's simply *wonderful!*"

One would have thought she was talking about her favourite film star.

"Wearehaviganothermeetingtomorroweveninghereinthe-hotel. . . . Whaaaha," said Mrs. Haddock, "andIdohopethat-bothyouandMargowillattend. . . . Whaaaha."

She gave us a pallid smile as though reluctantly forgiving us our sins, patted Margo on the cheek, and left.

"Really, Margo," said Mother as the door closed behind Mrs. Haddock, "you do make me cross."

"Oh, Mother, you are so *old-fashioned*," said Margo. "That doctor wasn't doing me any good with his injections, anyway, and Mawake is working miracles."

"Miracles," snorted Mother scornfully. "You still look exactly the same size to me."

"Clover," said Aunt Fan, through a mouthful of toast, "is supposed to be the best, although I prefer heather myself."

"I tell you, dear," said Prue, "this woman's got a grip on you. She's malignant. Be warned before it's too late."

"All I ask is that you just simply come to a meeting and *see*," said Margo.

"Never," said Prue, shuddering. "My nerves wouldn't stand it."

"It's interesting, too, that they have to have bumble-bees to fertilize the clover," observed Aunt Fan.

"Well," said Mother, "I'm much too tired to discuss it now. We will discuss it in the morning."

"Can you help me with my cabbage?" asked Margo.

"Do what?" inquired Mother.

"Help me with my cabbage," said Margo.

"I have often wondered whether one could not cultivate bumble-bees," said Aunt Fan, thoughtfully.

"What do you do with your cabbage?" inquired Mother.

"She puts it on her face," hissed Prue. "Ridiculous!"

"It isn't ridiculous," said Margo, angrily. "It's done my acne a world of good."

"What? Do you mean you boil it or something?" asked Mother.

"No," said Margo, "I put the leaves on my face and you tie them on for me. Mawake advised it and it works wonders."

"It's ridiculous, Louise dear. You should stop her," said Prue, bristling like a plump kitten. "It's nothing more than witchcraft."

"Well, I'm too tired to argue about it," said Mother. "I don't suppose it can do you any harm."

So Margo sat in a chair and held to her face large crinkly cabbage leaves which Mother solemnly fixed to her head with lengths of red twine. I thought she looked like some curious vegetable mummy.

"It's paganism. That's what it is," said Prue.

"Nonsense, Prue, you do fuss," said Margo, her voice muffled by cabbage leaves.

"I sometimes wonder," said Mother, tying the last knot, "whether my family's *all there*."

"Is Margo going to a fancy-dress ball?" inquired Aunt Fan, who had watched the procedure with interest.

"No, Mummy," roared Prue, "it's for her spots."

Margo got up and groped her way to the door. "Well, I'm going to bed," she said.

"If you meet anybody on the landing, you'll give them a terrible shock," said Prue.

"Have a good time," said Aunt Fan. "Don't stay out till all hours. I know what you young things are like."

After Margo had gone, Prue turned to Mother.

"You see, Louise dear? I didn't exaggerate," she said. "That woman is an evil influence. Margo's behaving like a mad thing."

"Well," said Mother, whose maxim in life was always defend your young regardless of how much in the wrong they are, "I think she's being a little *unwise*."

"Unwise!" said Prue. "Cabbage leaves all over her face! Never doing anything that that Mawake doesn't tell her to! It's not healthy!"

"I shouldn't be a bit surprised if she didn't win first prize," said Aunt Fan, chuckling. "I shouldn't think there'd be other people there disguised as a cabbage."

The argument waxed back and forth for a considerable time, interlaced with Aunt Fan's reminiscences of fancy-dress balls she had been to in India. At length Prue and Aunt Fan left us and Mother and I prepared for bed.

"I sometimes think," said Mother, as she pulled the clothes up and switched off the light, "I sometimes think that I'm the only *sane* member of the family."

The following morning we decided to go shopping, since there were a great number of things unobtainable in Corfu that Mother wanted to purchase and take back with us. Prue said this would be an excellent plan, since she could drop her Bedlington puppies off with their new owner en route.

So at nine o'clock we assembled on the pavement outside Balaklava Mansions, and we must have presented a somewhat curious sight to passers-by. Aunt Fan, presumably to celebrate our arrival, had put on a pixie hat with a large feather in it. She stood on the pavement entwined like a maypole by the leashes of the eight Bedlington puppies that romped and fought and urinated round her.

"I think we'd better take a taxi," said Mother, viewing the gambolling puppies with alarm.

"Oh, no, Louise," said Prue. "Think of the expense! We can go by tube."

"With all the puppies?" asked Mother doubtfully.

"Yes, dear," said Prue. "Mummy's quite used to handling them."

Aunt Fan, now bound almost immobile by the puppies' leashes, had to be disentangled before we could walk down the road to the tube station.

"Yeast and maple syrup," said Margo. "You mustn't let me forget yeast and maple syrup, Mother; Mawake says they're excellent for acne."

"If you mention that man once again I shall get seriously angry," said Mother.

Our progress to the tube station was slow, since the puppies circumnavigated any obstacle in their path in different ways, and we had to pause continually to unwind Aunt Fan from the lamp-posts, pillar-boxes, and occasional passers-by.

"Little tinkers!" she would exclaim breathlessly, after each encounter. "They don't mean any harm."

When we finally arrived at the ticket office, Prue had a prolonged and acrimonious argument over the price charged for the Bedlingtons.

"But they're only eight weeks old," she kept protesting. "You don't charge for *children* under three."

Eventually, however, the tickets were purchased and we made our way to the escalators to face a continuous warm blast of air from the bowels of the earth, which the puppies appeared to find invigorating. Yapping and snarling in a tangle of leads, they forged ahead, dragging Aunt Fan, like a massive galleon, behind them. It was only when they saw the escalators that they began to have misgivings about what, hitherto, had appeared to be an exciting adventure. They did not, it appeared, like to stand on things that move and they were unanimous in their decision. Before long we were all wedged in a tight knot at the top of the escalator, struggling with the screaming, hysterical puppies.

A queue formed behind us.

"It shouldn't be allowed," said a frosty-looking man in a bowler hat. "Dogs shouldn't be allowed on the tube."

"I have paid for them," panted Prue. "They have as much right to travel by tube as you have."

"Bloody 'ell," observed another man. "I'm in an 'urry. Can't you let me get by?"

"Little tinkers!" observed Aunt Fan, laughing. "They're so high-spirited at this age."

"Perhaps if we all picked up a puppy each?" suggested Mother, getting increasingly alarmed by the muttering of the mob.

At that moment Aunt Fan stepped backwards onto the first step of the escalator and slipped and fell in a waterfall of tweeds, dragging the shrieking puppies after her.

"Thank God for that," said the man in the bowler hat. "Perhaps now we can get on."

Prue stood at the top of the escalator and peered down. Aunt Fan had now reached the half-way mark and was finding it impossible to rise, owing to the weight of puppies.

"Mummy, Mummy, are you all right?" screamed Prue.

"I'm sure she is, dear," said Mother soothingly.

"Little tinkers!" said Aunt Fan faintly as she was carried down the escalator.

"Now that your dogs have gone, Madam," said the man in the bowler hat, "would it be possible for us, too, to use the amenities of this station?"

Prue turned, bristling to do battle, but Margo and Mother grabbed her and they slid downwards on the staircase towards the heaving heap of tweed and Bedlingtons that was Great-Aunt Fan.

We picked her up and dusted her down and disentangled the puppies. Then we made our way along to the platform. The puppies now would have made a suitable subject for an R.S.P.C.A. poster. Never, at the best of times, a prepossessing breed, Bedlingtons can, in moments of crisis, look more ill-used than any other dog I know. They stood uttering quavering, high-pitched yelps like miniature sea-gulls, shivering violently, periodically squatting down bow-legged to decorate the platform with the results of their fear.

"Poor little things," said a fat woman commiseratingly, as she passed. "It's a shame the way some people treat animals."

"Oh! Did you hear her?" said Prue belligerently. "I've a good mind to follow her and give her a piece of my mind."

Mercifully, at that moment the train arrived with a roar and a blast of hot air, and distracted everybody's attention. The effect on the puppies was immediate. One minute they had been standing there shivering and wailing like a group of half-starved grey lambs and the next minute they had taken off down the platform like a team of virile huskies, dragging Aunt Fan in their wake.

"Mummy, Mummy, come back," screamed Prue as we started off in pursuit.

She had forgotten Aunt Fan's method of leading the dogs, which she had explained to me at great length. Never pull on the lead, because it might hurt their necks. Carrying out this novel method of dog-training, Aunt Fan galloped down the platform with the Bedlingtons streaming before her. We finally caught her and restrained the puppies just as the doors closed with a self-satisfied hiss and the train rumbled out of the station. So we had to wait in a pool of Bedlingtons for the next train to arrive. Once we finally got them in the train the puppies' spirits suddenly revived. They fought each other with enjoyment, snarling and screeching. They wound their leads round people's legs, and one of them, in a fit of exuberance, leaped up and tore a copy of *The Times* from the grasp of a man who looked as though he were the manager of the Bank of England.

We all had headaches by the time we arrived at our destination, with the exception of Aunt Fan, who was enchanted by the virility of the puppies. Acting on Mother's advice, we waited until there was a pause in the flow of human traffic before we attempted the escalator. To our surprise, we got the puppies to the top with little or no trouble. They were obviously becoming seasoned travellers.

"Thank goodness that's over," said Mother as we reached the top.

"I'm afraid the puppies were a little bit trying," said Prue, flustered. "But then you see, they are used to the country. In town they think that everything's wrong."

"Eh?" said Aunt Fan.

"Wrong," shouted Prue. "The puppies. They think that everything's wrong."

"What a pity," said Aunt Fan, and before we could stop her she had led the puppies onto the other escalator and they disappeared once again into the bowels of the earth.

Once we had got rid of the puppies, in spite of feeling somewhat jaded by our experiences, we had quite a satisfactory morning's shopping. Mother got all the things she needed, Margo got her yeast and maple syrup, and I, while they were purchasing these quite unnecessary items, managed to procure a beautiful red cardinal, a black-spotted salamander as fat and as shiny as an eiderdown, and a stuffed crocodile.

Each satisfied in our own way with our purchases, we returned to Balaklava Mansions.

At Margaret's insistence, Mother had decided that she would attend the séance that evening.

"Don't do it, Louise dear," Cousin Prue said. "It's dabbling with the unknown."

Mother justified her action with a remarkable piece of logic.

"I feel I ought to meet this Mawake person," she said to Prue. "After all, he's giving Margaret treatment."

"Well, dear," said Prue, seeing that Mother was adamant, "I think it's madness, but I shall have to come with you. I can't let you attend one of those things on your own."

I begged to be allowed to go too, for, as I pointed out to Mother, I had some little time previously borrowed a book from Theodore on the art of exposing fake mediums, so I felt that my knowledge thus acquired might come in exceedingly useful.

"I don't think we ought to take Mummy," said Prue. "I think it might have a bad effect on her."

So at six o'clock that evening, with Prue palpitating in our midst like a newly caught bird, we made our way down to Mrs. Haddock's basement room. Here we found quite a collection of people. There was Mrs. Glut, the manageress of the hotel; a tall, saturnine Russian with an accent so thick that he sounded as though he were speaking through a mouthful of cheese; a young and very earnest blond girl; and a vapid young man who, rumour had it, was studying to be an actor, but whom we had never seen do anything more strenuous than doze peacefully in the palm-fringed lounge. To my annoyance, Mother would not let me search the room before we started for hidden cords or fake ectoplasm. However, I did manage to tell Mrs. Haddock about the book I had been reading, as I thought that if she was genuine it would be of interest to her. The look she bestowed upon me was anything but benevolent.

We sat in a circle holdings hands and got off to a rather inauspicious start, since, as the lights were switched out, Prue uttered a piercing scream and leaped out of the chair she had been sitting in. It was discovered that the handbag she had leaned against the leg of the chair had slipped and touched her leg with a leathery clutch. When we had calmed Prue and assured her that she had not been assaulted by an evil spirit, we all returned to our chairs and held hands again. The illumination was from a night-light that guttered and blinked in a saucer and sent shadows rippling down the room and made our faces look as though they were newly arisen from a very old grave.

"NowIdon'twantanytalkingandImustaskyoualltokeepyour-handsfirmlyclaspedsothatwedon'tloseanyoftheessence. . . . Whaaaha," said Mrs. Haddock. "Iknowthereareunbelievers-amongstus.NeverthelessIaskyoutomakeyourmindsquietand-receptive."

"What does she mean?" whispered Prue to Mother. "I'm not an unbeliever. My trouble is I believe *too much*."

Having given us our instructions, Mrs. Haddock then took up her position in an arm-chair, and with deceptive ease, went into a trance. I watched her narrowly. I was determined not to miss the ectoplasm. At first she just sat there with her eyes closed, and there was no sound except for the rustle and quiver of the agitated Prue. Then Mrs. Haddock started to breathe deeply; presently she began to snore richly and vibrantly. It sounded like a sack of potatoes being emptied across a loft floor. I was not impressed. Snoring, after all, was one of the easiest things to fake. Prue's hand clutching mine was moist with perspiration and I could feel her shivers of apprehension running down her arm.

"Ahaaaaa," said Mrs. Haddock suddenly, and Prue leaped in her chair and uttered a small, despairing squeak as though she had been stabbed.

"Ahaaaaaaaa," said Mrs. Haddock, extracting the full dramatic possibilities from this simple utterance.

"I don't like it," whispered Prue shakily. "Louise, dear, I don't like it."

"Be quiet or you'll spoil it all," whispered Margaret. "Relax, and make your mind receptive."

"I see strangers among us," said Mrs. Haddock suddenly, with such a strong Indian accent that it made me want to giggle. "Strangers who have come to join our circle. To them I say 'welcome.' "

The only extraordinary thing about this, as far as I was concerned, was that Mrs. Haddock was no longer stringing her words together and no longer uttering that strange inhalation of breath. She mumbled and muttered for a moment or so, incomprehensibly, and then said clearly, "This is Mawake."

"Ooo!" said Margaret, delighted. "He's come! There you are, Mother! That's Mawake!"

"I think I'm going to faint," said Prue.

I stared at Mrs. Haddock in the dim, shaky light and I could not see any signs of ectoplasm or trumpets.

"Mawake says," announced Mrs. Haddock, "that the white girl must have no more punctures."

"There!" said Margaret triumphantly.

"White girl must obey Mawake. Must not be influenced by disbelievers."

I heard Mother snort belligerently in the gloom.

"Mawake says that if white girl trusts him, before the coming of two moons she will be cured. Mawake says . . ."

But what Mawake was about to say was never vouchsafed to us, for, at that moment, a cat that had been drifting round the room, cloudlike and unobserved, jumped onto Prue's lap. Her scream was deafening. She leaped to her feet shouting, "Louise, Louise, Louise!" and blundered like a bedazzled moth round the circle of people, screaming every time she touched anything.

Somebody had the good sense to switch on the lights before Prue, in her chicken-like panic, could do any damage.

"I say, it's a bit much, what?" said the vapid young man.

"You may have done her great harm," said the girl, glaring at Prue and fanning Mrs. Haddock with her handkerchief.

"I was touched by something. It touched me. Got into my lap," said Prue tearfully. "Ectoplasm."

"You spoiled everything," said Margaret angrily. "Just as Mawake was coming through."

"I think we have heard quite enough from Mawake," said Mother. "I think it's high time you stopped fooling around with this nonsense."

Mrs. Haddock, who had remained snoring with dignity throughout this scene, suddenly woke up.

"Nonsense," she said fixing her protuberant blue eyes on Mother. "Youdaretocallitnonsense? . . . Whaaaha."

It was one of the very few occasions when I had seen Mother really annoyed. She drew herself up to her full height of 4 feet 3½ inches and bristled.

"Charlatan," she said uncharitably to Mrs. Haddock. "I said it was nonsense and it *is* nonsense. I am not having *my* family mixed up in any jiggery-pokery like this. Come Margo, come Gerry, come Prue. We will leave."

So astonished were we by this display of determination on the part of our normally placid mother, that we followed her meekly out of the room, leaving the raging Mrs. Haddock and her several disciples.

As soon as we reached the sanctuary of our room, Margo burst into floods of tears.

"You've spoiled it. You've spoiled it," she said, wringing her hands. "Mrs. Haddock will never talk to us again."

"And a good job, too," said Mother grimly, pouring out a brandy for the twitching and still-distraught Prue.

"Did you have a nice time?" asked Aunt Fan, waking suddenly and beaming at us owlishly.

"No," said Mother shortly, "we didn't."

"I can't get the thought of that ectoplasm out of my mind," said Prue, gulping brandy. "It was like a sort of . . . like . . . well, you know, squishy."

"Just as Mawake was coming through," howled Margo. "Just as he was going to tell us something *important*."

"I think you are wise to come back early," said Aunt Fan, "because even at this time of year it gets chilly in the evening."

"I felt sure it was coming for my throat," said Prue. "I felt it going for my throat. It was like a sort of . . . a kind of . . . well a squishy sort of *hand* thing."

"And Mawake's the only one that's done me any good."

"My father used to say that at this time of the year the weather can be very treacherous," said Aunt Fan.

"Margaret, stop behaving so stupidly," said Mother crossly.

"And Louise dear, I could feel this horrible sort of squishy fingers groping up towards my throat," said Prue, ignoring Margo, busy with the embroidery of her experience.

"My father always used to carry an umbrella, winter and summer," said Aunt Fan. "People used to laugh at him, but many's the time, even on quite hot days, when he found he needed it."

"You always *spoil* everything," said Margo. "You always interfere."

"The trouble is I don't interfere enough," said Mother. "I'm telling you, you're to stop all this nonsense, stop crying, and we are going back to Corfu immediately."

"If I hadn't leaped up when I did," said Prue, "it would have fastened itself in my jugular."

"There's nothing more useful than a pair of galoshes, my father used to say," said Aunt Fan.

"I'm not going back to Corfu. I won't. I won't."

"You will do as you're told."

"It wound itself round my throat in such an evil way."

"He never approved of gum-boots, because he said they sent the blood to the head."

I had ceased listening. My whole being was flooded with excitement. We were going back to Corfu. We were leaving the gritty, soulless absurdity of London. We were going back to the enchanted olive groves and blue sea, to the warmth and laughter of our friends, to the long, golden, gentle days.

6

THE OLIVE MERRY-GO-ROUND

By May the olive-picking had been in progress for some time. The fruit had plumped and ripened throughout the hot summer days and now it fell and lay shining in the grass like a harvest of black pearls. The peasant women appeared in droves carrying tins and baskets on their heads. They would then crouch in circles round the base of the olive tree, chattering as shrilly as sparrows as they picked up the fruit and placed it in the containers. Some of the olive trees had been producing crops like this for five hundred years, and for five hundred years the peasants had been gathering the olives in precisely the same way.

It was a great time for gossip and for laughter. I used to move from tree to tree, joining the different groups, squatting on my haunches, helping them pick up the glossy olives, hearing gossip about all the relatives and friends of the olive-pickers and occasionally joining them as they ate under the trees, wolfing down the sour black bread and the little flat cakes wrapped in vine leaves that were made out of last season's dried figs. Songs would be sung, and it was curious that the peasants' voices, so sour and raucous in speech, could be plaintively sweet when raised in harmony together. At that time of year, with the yellow, waxy crocuses just starting to bubble up among the olive roots, and the banks purple with campanulas, the peasants gathered under the trees looked like a moving flower-bed and the songs would echo down the naves between the ancient olives, the sound as melancholy and as sweet as goat bells.

When the containers were piled high with the fruit, they would be hoisted up, and we would carry them down to the olive press in a long, chattering line. The olive press, a gaunt, gloomy building, was down in a valley through which ran a tiny, glittering stream. The press was presided over by Papa Demetrios, a tough old man, as twisted and bent as the olive trees themselves, with a completely bald head and an enormous moustache, snow-white except where it was stained yellow by nicotine, and reputed to be the biggest moustache in the whole of Corfu. Papa Demetrios was a gruff, bad-tempered old man, but for some reason he took a fancy to me and we got along splendidly. He even allowed me into the holy of holies itself, the olive press.

Here was a great circular trough like an ornamental fish-pond and mounted in it a gigantic grindstone with a central strut of wood jutting from it. This strut was harnessed to Papa Demetrios' ancient horse, which, with a sack over its head so that it did not get giddy, would circle the trough, thus rolling the great grindstone round and round so that it could crush the olives as they were poured into it in a glinting cascade. As the olives were crushed, a sharp, sour smell rose in the air. The only sounds were the solid ploddings of the horse's hooves and the rumbling of the great grindstone and the steady drip, drip of the oil trickling out of the vents of the trough, golden as distilled sunlight.

In one corner of the press was a huge black crumbling mound that was the residue from the grinding: the crushed seeds, pulp, and skin of the olives forming black crusty cakes, like coarse peat. It had a rich, sweet-sour smell that almost convinced you it was good to eat. It was in fact fed to the cattle and horses with their winter food and it was also used as a remarkably efficient, if somewhat overpungent, fuel.

Papa Demetrios, because of his bad temper, was left severely alone by the peasants, who would deliver their olives and depart from the press with all speed. For you were never certain whether anybody like Papa Demetrios might not have the evil eye. In consequence, the old man was lonely and so he welcomed my intrusion into his domain. From me he would get all the local gossip: who had given birth and whether it was a boy or a girl; who was courting whom; and sometimes a more juicy item such as that Pepe Condos had been arrested for smuggling tobacco. In return for my acting as a sort of newspaper for him, Papa Demetrios would catch specimens for me. Sometimes it would be a pale-pink gulping gecko, or a praying mantis, or the caterpillar of an oleander hawk-moth, striped like a Persian carpet, pink and silver and green. It was Papa Demetrios who got me one of the most charming pets that I had at that time, a spade-footed toad, which I christened Augustus Tickletummy.

I had been down in the olive groves helping the peasants and I started to feel hungry. I knew that Papa Demetrios always kept a good supply of food at the olive press, so I went down to visit him. It was a sparkling day with a rumbustious, laughing wind that thrummed through the olive grove like a harp. There was a nip in the air, so I ran all the way with the dogs leaping and barking about me, and I arrived flushed and panting to find Papa Demetrios crouched over a fire that he had constructed out of slabs of olive "cake."

"Ah!" he said, glaring at me fiercely. "So you've come, have you? Where have you been? I haven't seen you for two days. I suppose now spring is here you've got no time for an old man like me."

I explained that I had been busy with a variety of things, such as making a new cage for my magpies, since they had just raided Larry's room and stood in peril of their lives if they were not incarcerated.

"Hum," said Papa Demetrios. "Ah, well. Do you want some corn?"

I said, as nonchalantly as I could, that there was nothing I would like better than corn.

He got up and strutted bow-legged to the olive press and reappeared carrying a large frying pan, a sheet of tin, a bottle of oil, and five golden-brown cobs of dried maize, like bars of bullion. He put the frying pan on the fire and scattered a small quantity of oil into it, then waited until the heat of the fire made the oil purr and twinkle and smoke gently in the bottom of the pan. Then he seized a cob of maize and twisted it rapidly between his arthritic hands so that the golden beads of corn pattered into the pan with a sound like rain on a roof. He put the flat sheet of tin over the top, gave a little grunt, and sat back, lighting a cigarette.

"Have you heard about Andreas Papoyakis?" he asked, running his fingers through his luxurious moustache.

No, I said I had not heard.

"Ah," he said with relish. "He's in hospital, that foolish one."

I said I was sorry to hear it because I liked Andreas. He was a gay, kind-hearted, exuberant boy who inevitably managed to do the wrong things. They said of him in the village that he would ride a donkey backwards if he could. What, I inquired, was his affliction?

"Dynamite," said Papa Demetrios, waiting to see my reaction.

I gave a slow whistle of horror and nodded my head slowly. Papa Demetrios, now assured of my undivided attention, settled himself more comfortably.

"This was how it happened," he said. "He's a foolish boy, Andreas is, you know. His head is as empty as a winter swallows' nest. But he's a good boy, though. He's never done anybody any harm. Well, he went dynamite fishing. You know that little bay down near Benitses? Ah, well, he took his boat there because he had been told that the country policeman had gone farther down the coast for the day. Of course, foolish boy, he never thought to check and make sure that the policeman *was* farther down the coast."

I clicked my tongue sorrowfully. The penalty for dynamite fishing was five years in prison and a heavy fine.

"Now," said Papa Demetrios, "he got into his boat and was rowing slowly along when he saw ahead of him, in the shallow water, a big shoal of barbouni. He stopped rowing and lit the fuse on his stick of dynamite."

Papa Demetrios paused dramatically, peered at the corn to see how it was doing, and lit another cigarette.

"That would have been all right," he went on, "but just as he was about to throw the dynamite, the fish swam away, and what do you think that idiot of a boy did? Still holding the dynamite he rowed after them. Bang!"

I said I thought that there could not be very much left of Andreas.

"Oh, yes," said Papa Demetrios scornfully. "He can't even dynamite properly. It was such a tiny stick all it did was blow off his right hand. But even so, he owes his life to the policeman, who *hadn't* gone farther down the coast. Andreas managed to row to the shore and there he fainted from loss of blood and he would undoubtedly have died if the policeman, having heard the bang, had not come down to the shore to see who was dynamiting. Luckily the bus was just passing and the policeman stopped it and they got Andreas into it and into the hospital."

I said I thought it was a great pity that it should happen to anybody as nice as Andreas, but he was lucky to be alive. I presumed that when he was better he would be arrested and sent to Vido for five years.

"No, no," said Papa Demetrios. "The policeman said he thought Andreas had been punished quite enough, so he told the hospital that Andreas had caught his hand in some machinery."

The corn had now started to explode, banging on to the

top of the tin like the explosions of miniature cannons. Papa Demetrios lifted the pan off the fire and took the lid off. There was each grain of corn exploded into a little yellow-and-white cumulus cloud, scrunchy and delicious. Papa Demetrios took a twist of paper from his pocket and un-wrapped it. It was full of coarse grains of grey sea-salt, and into this we dipped the little clouds of corn and scrunched them up with relish.

"I've got something for you," said the old man at last, wiping his moustache carefully with a large red-and-white handkerchief. "Another one of those terrible animals that you are so eager to get."

Stuffing my mouth with the remains of the popcorn and wiping my fingers on the grass, I asked him eagerly what it was.

"I'll fetch it," he said, getting to his feet. "It's a very curious thing. I've never seen one like it before."

I waited impatiently while he went into the olive press and reappeared carrying a battered tin, the neck of which he had stuffed with leaves.

"There you are," he said. "Be careful, because it smells."

I pulled out the plug of leaves and peered into the tin and discovered that Papa Demetrios was quite right; it smelt as strongly of garlic as a peasant bus on market day. In the bottom was crouched a medium-size, rather smooth-skinned, greenish-brown toad with enormous amber eyes and a mouth set in a perpetual, but rather insane, grin. As I put my hand into the tin to pick him up, he ducked his head between his fore-legs, retracted his protuberant eyes into his skull in the odd way that toads have, and uttered a sharp bleating cry rather like that of a miniature sheep. I lifted him out of the tin and he struggled violently, exuding a terrible odour of garlic. I noticed that on each hind foot he had a horny black excrescence, blade-shaped, like a ploughshare. I was delighted with him, for I had spent a considerable amount of time and energy trying to track down spade-footed toads without success.

Thanking Papa Demetrios profusely, I carried him home triumphantly and installed him in an aquarium in my bedroom.

I had placed earth and sand to a depth of two or three inches at the bottom of the aquarium and Augustus, having been christened and released, immediately set to work to build himself a home. With a curious movement of his hind legs, working backwards, using the blades of his feet as spades, he very rapidly dug himself a hole and disappeared from view with the exception of his protuberant eyes and grinning face.

Augustus, I soon discovered, was a remarkably intelligent beast and had many endearing traits of character which made themselves apparent as he got tamer. When I went into the room, he would scuttle out of his hole and make desperate endeavours to reach me through the glass walls of the aquarium. If I took him out and placed him on the floor, he would hop round the room after me and then, if I sat down, would climb laboriously up my leg until he reached my lap, where he would recline in a variety of undignified attitudes, basking in the heat of my body, blinking his eyes slowly, grinning up at me, and gulping. It was then that I discovered he liked to lie on his back and have his stomach gently massaged by my forefinger, and so from this unusual behaviour he derived the surname of Tickletummy. He would also, I learned, sing for his food. If I held a large, writhing earthworm over the top of the equarium, Augustus would go into paroxysms of delight, his eyes seeming to protrude more and more with excitement, and he would utter a series of little pig-like grunts and the strange bleating cry he had given when I first picked him up. When the worm was finally dropped in front of him, he would nod his head vigorously, as if in thanks, grab one end of it and proceed to stuff it into his mouth with his thumbs. Whenever we had any guests, they were treated to an Augustus Tickletummy recital and they all agreed, gravely, that he had the best voice and repertoire of any toad they had met.

It was round about this time that Larry introduced Donald

and Max into our life. Max was an immensely tall Austrian with curly blond hair, a blond moustache perched like an elegant butterfly on his lip, and intensely blue and kindly eyes. Donald, on the other hand, was short and pale-faced; one of those Englishmen who give you a first impression of being not only inarticulate, but completely devoid of personality.

Larry had run into this ill-assorted couple in the town and had lavishly invited them up to have drinks. The fact that they arrived, mellowed by a variety of alcoholic stimuli, at two o'clock in the morning did not strike any of us as being particularly curious, since, by that time, we were inured, or almost inured, to Larry's acquaintances.

Mother had gone to bed early with a severe cold, and the rest of the family had also retired to their rooms. I was the only member of the household awake. The reason for this was that I was waiting for Ulysses to return to the bedroom from his nightly wanderings and devour his supper of meat and minced liver. As I lay there reading, I heard a dim, blurred sound echoing through the olive groves. I thought at first it was a party of peasants returning late from a wedding, and took no notice. Then the cacophony grew closer and closer and from the clop and jingle accompanying it I realized it was some late night revellers passing on the road below in a cab. The song they were singing did not sound particularly Greek and I wondered who they could be. I got out of bed and leaned out the window, staring down through the olive trees. At that moment the cab turned off the road and started up the long drive towards the house. I could see it quite clearly because whoever was sitting in the back had apparently lighted a small bonfire. I watched this, puzzled and intrigued, as it flickered and shook through the trees on its way up to us.

At that moment Ulysses appeared out of the night sky, like a silently drifting dandelion clock, and endeavoured to perch on my naked shoulder. I shook him off and went and fetched his plate of food, which he proceeded to peck and gobble at, uttering tiny throaty noises to himself and blinking his brilliant eyes at me.

By this time the cab had made slow but steady progress and had entered the forecourt of the house. I leaned out the window enraptured by the sight.

It was not, as I had thought, a bonfire in the back of the cab. There were two individuals sitting there, each clasping an enormous silver candelabra in which had been stuck some of the great white candles that one normally bought to put in the church of St. Spiridion. They were singing loudly and untunefully, but with great panache, a song from *The Maid of the Mountains*, endeavouring, wherever possible, to harmonize.

The cab rolled to a halt at the steps that led up to the veranda.

"At seventeen . . ." sighed a very British baritone.

"At seventeen!" intoned the other singer in a rather heavy middle-European accent.

"He falls in love quite madly," said the baritone, waving his candelabra about wildly, "with eyes of tender blue."

"Tender blue," intoned the middle-European accent, giving a lechery to these simple words that had to be heard to be believed.

"At twenty-five," continued the baritone, "he thinks he's got it badly."

"Badly," said the middle-European accent dolefully.

"With eyes of different hue," said the baritone, making such a wild gesture with his candelabra that the candles sped out of their sockets like rockets and fell sizzling onto the grass.

My bedroom door opened and Margo, clad in yards of lace and what appeared to be butter muslin, came in.

"What on earth's that *noise?*" she asked in a hoarse, accusing whisper. "You *know* Mother's not well."

I explained that the noise was nothing whatsoever to do with me, but apparently we had company. Margo leaned out the window and peered down at the cab where the singers had just reached the next verse of their song.

"I say," she called, in muted tones, "do you mind not making quite so much noise. My mother's sick."

Immediate silence enveloped the cab and then a tall, gangling figure rose unsteadily to its feet. He held his candelabra aloft and gazed earnestly up at Margo.

"Must not dear lady," he intoned sepulchrally, "must not disturb Muzzer."

"No, by Jove," agreed the English voice from the interior of the cab.

"Who do you think they are?" Margo whispered to me in agitation.

I said that to me the thing was perfectly clear; they must be friends of Larry's.

"Are you friends of my brother's?" Margo fluted out the window.

"A noble being," said the tall figure, waving the candelabra at her. "He invited us for drinks."

"Er . . . Just a minute, I'll come down," said Margo.

"To look you closer would be to fulfil the ambition of a lifetime," said the tall man, bowing somewhat uncertainly.

"See you closer," corrected a quiet voice from the back of the cab.

"I'll go downstairs," said Margo to me, "and get them inside and keep them quiet. You go and wake Larry."

I pulled on a pair of shorts, picked up Ulysses unceremoniously (who, with half-closed eyes, was digesting his food), and went to the window and threw him out.

"Extraordinary!" said the tall man, watching Ulysses fly away over the moon-silvered olive tops. "Dis like the house of Dracula, no, Donald?"

"By Jove, yes," said Donald.

I pattered down the corridor and burst into Larry's room. It took me some time to shake him awake, for, under the firm impression that Mother had been breathing her cold germs over him, he had taken the precaution of consuming half a bottle of whisky before he went to bed. Eventually he sat up blearily and looked at me.

"What the bloody hell do *you* want?" he inquired.

I explained about the two characters in the cab and that they had said they had been invited to drinks.

"Oh, Christ!" said Larry. "Just tell them I've gone to Dubrovnik."

I explained that I could not very well do this as by now Margo would have lured them into the house and that Mother, in her fragile condition, must not be disturbed. Groaning, Larry got out of bed and put on his dressing-gown and slippers and together we went down the creaking stairs to the drawing-room. Here we found Max, lanky, flamboyant, good-natured, sprawled in a chair waving his candelabra at Margo, all the candles of which had gone out. Donald sat hunched and gloomy in another chair, looking like an undertaker's assistant.

"Your eyes, they are tender blue," said Max, waving a long finger at Margo. "Ve vas singing about blue eyes, vere ve not, Donald?"

"We *were* singing about blue eyes," said Donald.

"Dat's what I said," said Max benevolently.

"You said 'was,'" said Donald.

Max thought about this for a brief moment.

"Anyvay," he said, "de eyes vas blue."

"Were blue," said Donald.

"Oh, there you are," said Margo, breathlessly, as Larry and I came in. "I think these are friends of yours, Larry."

"Larry!" bellowed Max, lurching up with the ungainly grace of a giraffe. "Ve have come like you told us."

"How very nice," said Larry, forcing his sleep-crumpled features into something approaching an ingratiating smile. "Do you mind keeping your voice down, because my mother's sick?"

"Muzzers," said Max, with immense conviction, "are de most important thing in de vorld."

He turned to Donald, laid a long finger across his moustache, and said "Shush" with such violence that Roger, who had sunk into a peaceful sleep, immediately leaped to his feet and started barking wildly. Widdle and Puke joined in vociferously.

"Damned bad form that," observed Donald between the barks. "Guest should not make his host's dogs bark."

Max went down on his knees and engulfed the still barking Roger in his long arms, a manoeuvre that I viewed with some alarm, since Roger, I felt, was quite capable of misinterpreting it.

"Hush, Bow Wow," said Max, beaming into Roger's bristling and belligerent face.

To my astonishment, Roger immediately stopped barking and started to lick Max's face extravagantly.

"Would you . . . er . . . like a drink?" said Larry. "I can't ask you to stop long, of course, because unfortunately my mother's ill."

"Very civil of you," said Donald. "Very civil indeed. I must apologize for him. Foreigner, you know."

"Well, I think I'll just go back to bed," said Margo, edging tentatively towards the door.

"No, you won't," Larry barked. "Somebody's got to pour out the drinks."

"Do not," said Max, reclining on the floor with Roger in his arms and gazing at her piteously, "do not remove doze eyes from my orbit."

"Well, I'll go and get the drinks, then," said Margo breathlessly.

"And I vill help you," said Max, casting Roger from him and leaping to his feet.

Roger had been under the misguided impression that Max had intended to spend the rest of the night cuddling him in front of the dying fire, and so was not unnaturally put out when he was thrown aside like this. He started barking again.

The door of the drawing-room burst open and Leslie, stark

naked except for a shot-gun under his arm, made his appearance.

"What the bloody hell's going on?" he asked.

"Leslie, *do* go and put some clothes on," said Margo. "These are friends of Larry's."

"Oh, God," said Leslie dismally, "not *more.*"

He turned and made his way back upstairs.

"Drinks!" said Max, rapturously seizing Margo in his arms and waltzing her round to the accompaniment of almost hysterical barks on the part of Roger.

"I do wish you would try to be more quiet," said Larry. "*Max*, for Christ's sake."

"Damned bad form," said Donald.

"Remember my mother," said Larry, since this reference had obviously struck a chord in Max's soul.

Immediately he ceased waltzing with the breathless Margo and came to a halt.

"Vere is your Muzzer?" he inquired. "De lady is sick . . . take me to her dat I may secure her."

"Succour," said Donald.

"I'm here," said Mother in a slightly nasal tone of voice from the doorway. "What *is* going on?"

She was clad in her nightie and wearing, for reasons of her cold, a voluminous shawl over her shoulders. She carried under one arm the drooping, panting, apathetic figure of Dodo, her Dandie Dinmont terrier.

"Why, you're just in time, Mother," said Larry. "I want you to meet Donald and Max."

With the first sign of animation that he had shown, Donald rose to his feet, marched swiftly across the room to Mother, seized her hand, and gave a slight bow over it.

"Enchanted," he said. "Terribly sorry about the disturbance. My friend, you know. Continental."

"How nice to see you," said Mother, summoning up all her resources.

At her entrance, Max had thrown his arms wide and was

now gazing upon her with all the devoutness of a Crusader catching his first sight of Jerusalem.

"Muzzer!" he intoned dramatically. "You are de Muzzer!"

"How do you do," said Mother uncertainly.

"You are," Max asked, getting his facts straight, "de sick Muzzer?"

"Oh, it's just a bit of a cold," said Mother deprecatingly.

"Ve have voked you," said Max, clasping his breast, his eyes brimming with tears.

"Awoken or woken," said Donald *sotto voce*.

"Come," said Max and put his long arms round Mother and ushered her to a chair near the fire, pressing her into it with the utmost delicacy. He took off his coat and spread it gently about her knees. Then he squatted by her side, took her hand and peered earnestly into her face.

"Vhat," he inquired, "does Muzzer vant?"

"An uninterrupted night's sleep," said Leslie, who had just returned, more conventionally garbed in a pair of pyjama trousers and sandals.

"Max," said Donald sternly, "stop monopolizing the conversation. Remember what we have come for."

"Of course," said Max delightedly. "Ve have vunderful news, Larry. Donald has decided to become an author."

"Had to," murmured Donald modestly. "Seeing all you chaps living in the lap of luxury. Royalties pouring in. Felt I must try my hand at it."

"That's jolly good," said Larry, with a certain lack of enthusiasm.

"I've just completed the first chapter," said Donald, "and so we came out hot-foot, as it were, so that I could read it to you."

"Oh, God," said Larry, horrified. "No, Donald, really. My critical faculties are completely dehydrated at half past two in the morning. Can't you leave it here and I'll read it tomorrow?"

"It's short," said Donald, taking no notice of Larry and producing a small sheet of paper from his pocket, "but I think you will find the style interesting."

Larry gave an exasperated sigh, and we all sat back and listened expectantly while Donald cleared his throat.

"Suddenly," he began in a deep vibrant voice, "suddenly, suddenly, suddenly, there he was and then suddenly, there she was, suddenly, suddenly, suddenly. And suddenly he looked at her, suddenly, suddenly, suddenly, and she suddenly looked at him, suddenly. She suddenly opened her arms, suddenly, suddenly, and he opened his arms, suddenly. Then suddenly they came together and, suddenly, suddenly, suddenly, he could feel the warmth of her body and suddenly, suddenly she could feel the warmth of his mouth on hers as they suddenly, suddenly, suddenly, suddenly fell on the couch together."

There was a long pause while we waited for Donald to go on. He gulped once or twice as though overcome with emotion at his own writing, folded the piece of paper carefully and put it back in his pocket.

"What do you think?" he inquired of Larry.

"Well, it's a bit short," said Larry cautiously.

"Ah, but what do you think of the style?" said Donald.

"Well, it's, um, interesting," said Larry. "I think you'll find it's been done before, though."

"Couldn't have been," explained Donald. "You see, I only thought of it tonight."

"I don't think he ought to have any more to drink," said Leslie loudly.

"Hush, dear," said Mother. "What do you intend to call it, Donald?"

"I thought," said Donald owlishly, "I thought I would call it *The Suddenly Book*."

"A very trenchant title," said Larry. "I feel, however, that your main characters could be padded out a little bit, in depth, as it were, before you get them all tangled up on the sofa."

"Yes," said Donald. "You could well be right."

"Well, that *is* interesting," said Mother, sneezing violently. "And now I think we really all ought to have a cup of tea."

"I vill make de tea for you, Muzzer," said Max, leaping to his feet and starting all the dogs barking again.

"I will help you," said Donald.

"Margo, dear, you had better go with them and just make sure they find everything," said Mother.

When the three of them had left the room, Mother looked at Larry.

"And these are the people," she said coldly, "you say are not eccentric."

"Well, Donald's not eccentric," said Larry. "He's just a bit high."

"And suddenly, suddenly, suddenly, suddenly he was drunk," intoned Leslie, putting some more logs on the fire and kicking it into some semblance of a blaze.

"They are both of them very good chaps," said Larry. "Donald's already laid half of Corfu by its ears."

"What do you mean?" said Mother.

"Well, you know how the Corfiotes love to worm every hidden secret out of you," said Larry. "They're all convinced that since he appears to have private means and is so incredibly British that he must have a terribly posh background. So he has been amusing himself by telling them all different stories. He has so far, I have been assured, been the elder son of a duke, the cousin of the Bishop of London, and the illegitimate son of Lord Chesterfield. He has been educated at Eton, Harrow, Oxford, Cambridge, and, to my delight, this morning Mrs. Papanopoulos assured me that he had assured her that his formal education had been undertaken at Girton."

Just at that moment Margaret came back into the drawing-room, looking slightly distraught.

"I think you had better come and do something with them, Larry," she said. "Max has just lighted the kitchen fire with a five-pound note and Donald has disappeared and keeps shouting 'Cooee' at us and we can't see where he's gone."

All of us trooped down to the gigantic stone-flagged kitchen where a kettle was starting to sing on one of the charcoal fires and Max was contemplating, woefully, the charred remains of a five-pound note which he held in one hand.

"Really, Max," said Mother, "what a silly thing to do."

Max beamed at her.

"No expense spared for Muzzer," he said, and then, pressing the remains of the fiver into her hand, "Keep it, Muzzer, as a souvenir."

"Cooee," came a doleful, echoing cry.

"That's Donald," said Max proudly.

"Where is he?" said Mother.

"I don't know," said Max. "Ven he vants to hide, he vants to hide."

Leslie strode to the back door and flung it open.

"Donald," he called, "are you there?"

"Cooee," came a quavering cry from Donald with subtle, echoing overtones.

"Christ!" said Leslie. "The silly bastard's fallen down the well."

In the garden at the back of the kitchen there was a large well some fifty feet deep with a thick, round, iron pipe running right down the shaft. From the echoing qualities of Donald's voice, we were quite sure that Leslie's guess was right. Carrying a lamp, we made our way hurriedly up to the edge of the well and peered, in a circle, down into its dark depths. Half-way down the pipe was Donald, his arms and legs entwined firmly round it. He gazed up at us.

"Cooee," he said coyly.

"Donald, don't be a bloody fool," said Larry exasperatedly. "Come up out of there. If you fall into that water you'll drown. Not that I worry about that, but you'll pollute our entire water supply."

"Shan't," said Donald.

"Donald," said Max, "ve vant you. Come. It is cold down dere. Come and have some tea with Muzzer and ve will talk more about your book."

"Do you insist?" asked Donald.

"Yes, yes, we insist," said Larry impatiently.

Slowly and laboriously Donald climbed up the pipe, while we watched him breathlessly. When he was within easy reach, Max and the entire family leaned over the well, grabbed various portions of his anatomy, and hauled him to safety. Then we escorted our guests back into the house and plied them with vast quantities of hot tea until they seemed as sober as they were likely to be without having slept.

"I think you had better go home now," said Larry firmly, "and we'll meet you in town tomorrow."

We escorted them out onto the veranda. The cab stood, with the horse drooping forlornly between the shafts. The cab driver was nowhere to be seen.

"Did they have a cab driver?" Larry asked of me.

I said that, quite honestly, I had been so captivated by the sight of their candelabras that I had not noticed.

"I vill drive," said Max, "and Donald shall sing to me."

Donald arranged himself carefully in the back of the cab with the candelabras and Max took to the driving seat. He cracked the whip in a most professional manner and the horse aroused itself from its comatose condition, gave a sigh, and then shambled off down the drive.

"Good night," shouted Max, waving his whip.

We waited until they had disappeared from sight behind the olive trees and then trooped back inside the house and with sighs of heartfelt relief, closed the front door.

"Really, Larry, you shouldn't invite people at this hour of night," said Mother.

"I *didn't* invite them at this hour of the night," said Larry, annoyed. "They just *came*. I invited them for drinks."

Just at that moment there was a thunderous knocking on the front door.

"Well, I'm off," said Mother and scuttled upstairs with considerable alacrity.

Larry opened the front door and there stood the distraught figure of the cab driver.

"Where's my carrochino?" he shouted.

"Where were you?" retorted Larry. "The kyrios have taken it."

"They have stolen my carrochino?" shouted the man.

"Of course they haven't stolen it, foolish one," said Larry, now tried beyond endurance. "Because you weren't waiting here they took it to get back into town. If you run quickly you can catch them up."

Imploring St. Spiridion to help him, the man ran off through the olive trees and down towards the road.

Determined not to miss the last act in this drama, I ran to a vantage point where I got a clear view of the entrance to our drive and a stretch of moonlit roadway which led into town. The cab had just left the drive and arrived on the road at a brisk walk, Donald and Max singing happily together. At that moment the cab driver appeared through the olives, and screaming imprecations, he started to run after them.

Max, startled, looked over his shoulder.

"Volves, Donald," he shouted. "Hold tight!" He proceeded to belabour the behind of the unfortunate horse who, startled, broke into a gallop. But it was the sort of gallop that only a Corfu cab horse could achieve. It was just sufficiently fast to keep the cab owner running at full stretch some ten paces behind the cab. He was shouting and imploring and almost weeping with rage. Max, determined to save Donald, at all costs, was belabouring the horse unmercifully while Donald leant over the back of the cab and shouted "Bang!" at intervals, and thus they disappeared out of my sight along the Corfu road.

The following morning, at breakfast, all of us felt slightly jaded, and Mother was lecturing Larry severely for allowing people to turn up at two o'clock in the morning for drinks.

Just at that moment, Spiro's car drove up to the front of the house and he waddled onto the veranda where we were sitting, clasping in his arms an enormous, flat brown-paper parcel.

"This is for yous, Mrs. Durrells," he said.

"For me?" said Mother, adjusting her spectacles. "What on earth can it be?"

She unwrapped the brown paper cautiously and there inside, as bright as a rainbow, was the biggest box of chocolates I had ever seen in my life. Pinned to it was a little white card on which had been written in a rather shaky hand, "With apologies for last night. Donald and Max."

7

OWLS AND ARISTOCRACY

Now winter was upon us. Everything was redolent with the
smoke of olive-wood fires. The shutters creaked and slapped
the sides of the house as the wind caught them, and the birds
and leaves were tumbled across a dark lowering sky. The
brown mountains of the mainland wore tattered caps of snow
and the rain filled the eroded, rocky valleys, turning them into
foaming torrents that fled eagerly to the sea carrying mud and
debris with them. Once they reached the sea they spread like
yellow veins through the blue water, and the surface was
dotted with squill bulbs, logs and twisted branches, dead
beetles and butterflies, clumps of brown grass and splintered
canes. Storms would be brewed in among the whitened spikes
of the Albanian mountains and then tumble across to us,
great black piles of cumulus, spitting a stinging rain, with
sheet lightning blooming and dying like yellow ferns across
the sky.

It was at the beginning of the winter that I received a letter.

Dear Gerald Durrell,

I understand from our mutual friend, Dr. Stephanides, that
you are a keen naturalist and possess a number of pets. I was
wondering, therefore, if you would care to have a white owl
which my workmen found in an old shed they were demolish-
ing? He has, unfortunately, a broken wing, but is otherwise in
good health and feeding well.

If you would like him, I suggest you come to lunch on Friday and take him with you when you return home. Perhaps you would be kind enough to let me know. A quarter to one or one o'clock would be suitable.

Yours sincerely,
Countess Mavrodaki

This letter excited me for two reasons. Firstly, because I had always wanted a barn owl, for that was what it obviously was, and secondly, because the whole of Corfu society had been trying unavailingly for years to get to know the Countess. She was the recluse par excellence. Immensely wealthy, she lived in a gigantic, rambling, Venetian villa deep in the country and never entertained or saw anybody except the workmen on her vast estate. Her acquaintance with Theodore was due only to the fact that he was her medical adviser. The Countess was reputed to possess a large and valuable library and for this reason Larry had been most anxious to try to get himself invited to her villa, but without success.

"Dear God," he said bitterly when I showed him my invitation. "Here I've been trying for months to get that old harpy to let me see her books and she invites you to lunch—there's no justice in the world."

I said that after I had lunched with the Countess, maybe I could ask her if he could see her books.

"After she's had lunch with *you* I shouldn't think she would be willing to show me a copy of *The Times*, let alone her library," said Larry witheringly.

However, in spite of my brother's low opinion of my social graces, I was determined to put in a good word for him if I saw a suitable opportunity. It was, I felt, an important, even solemn occasion, and so I dressed with care. My shirt and shorts were carefully laundered and I had prevailed upon Mother to buy me a new pair of sandals and a new straw hat. I rode on Sally—who had a new blanket as a saddle to honour the occasion—for the Countess's estate was some distance away.

The day was dark and the ground mushy under foot. It looked as though we would have a storm, but I hoped this would not be until after I had arrived, for the rain would spoil the crisp whiteness of my shirt. As we jogged along through the olives, the occasional woodcock zooming up from the myrtles in front of us, I became increasingly nervous. I discovered that I was ill-prepared for this occasion. To begin with, I had forgotten to bring my four-legged chicken in spirits. I had felt sure that the Countess would want to see this and in any case I felt it would provide a subject of conversation that would help us in the initial awkward stages of our meeting. Secondly, I had forgotten to consult anybody on the correct way to address a countess. "Your Majesty" would surely be too formal, I thought, especially as she was giving me an owl? Perhaps "Highness" would be better—or maybe just a simple "Mam"?

Puzzling over the intricacies of protocol, I had left Sally to her own devices and so she had promptly fallen into a donkey-doze. Of all the beasts of burden, only the donkey seems capable of falling asleep while still moving. The result was that she ambled close to the ditch at the side of the road, suddenly stumbled and lurched and I, deep in thought, fell off her back into six inches of mud and water. Sally stared down at me with an expression of accusing astonishment that she always wore when she knew she was in the wrong. I was so furious, I could have strangled her. My new sandals oozed, my shorts and shirt—so crisp, so clean, so *well-behaved-looking* a moment before—were now bespattered with mud and bits of decaying water-weed. I could have wept with rage and frustration. We were too far from home to retrace our footsteps so that I could change; there was nothing for it but to go on, damp and miserable, convinced now that it did not matter how I addressed the Countess. She would, I felt sure, take one look at my gypsy-like condition and order me home. Not only would I lose my owl, but any chance I had of getting Larry in to see her library. I was a fool, I thought bitterly. I should have walked instead of trusting myself to this hopeless creature, who was now trotting along at a brisk pace, her ears pricked like furry arum lilies.

Presently we came to the Countess's villa, lying deep in the olive groves, approached by a drive lined with tall green-and-pink-trunked eucalyptus trees. The entrance to the drive was guarded by two columns on which were perched a pair of white-winged lions who stared scornfully at Sally and me as we trotted down the drive. The house was immense, built in a hollow square. It had at one time been a lovely, rich, Venetian red, but this had now faded to a rose-pink, the plaster bulged and cracked in places by the damp, and I noticed that a number of brown tiles were missing from the roof. The eaves had slung under them more swallows' nests—now empty, like small, forgotten, brown ovens—than I had ever seen congregated in one spot before.

I tied Sally up under a convenient tree and made my way to the archway that led into the central patio. Here a rusty chain hung down and when I pulled it I heard a bell jangle faintly somewhere in the depths of the house. I waited patiently for some time and was just about to ring the bell again when the massive wooden doors were opened. There stood a man who looked to me exactly like a bandit. He was tall and powerful, with a great jutting hawk-nose, sweeping flamboyant white moustaches, and a mane of curling white hair. He was wearing a scarlet tarbush, a loose white blouse beautifully embroidered with scarlet-and-gold thread, baggy pleated black pants, and on his feet upturned *charukias* decorated with enormous red-and-white pom-poms. His brown face cracked into a grin and I saw that all his teeth were gold. It was like looking into a mint.

"*Kyrié* Durrell?" he inquired. "Welcome."

I followed him through the patio, full of magnolia trees

and forlorn winter flower-beds, and into the house. He led me down a long corridor tiled in scarlet and blue, threw open a door, and ushered me into a great, gloomy room lined from ceiling to floor with bookshelves. At one end was a large fire-place in which a blaze flapped and hissed and crackled. Over the fire-place was an enormous gold-framed mirror, nearly black with age. Sitting by the fire on a long couch, almost obliterated by coloured shawls and cushions, was the Countess.

She was not a bit what I had expected. I had visualized her as being tall, gaunt, and rather forbidding, but as she rose to her feet and danced across the room to me I saw she was tiny, very fat, and as pink and dimpled as a rosebud. Her honey-coloured hair was piled high on her head in a pompadour style and her eyes, under permanently arched and surprised eyebrows, were as green and shiny as unripe olives. She took my hand in both her warm little pudgy ones and clasped it to her ample breast.

"How kind, how *kind* of you to come," she exclaimed in a musical, little girl's voice, exuding an overpowering odour of Parma violets and brandy in equal quantities. "How very, *very* kind. May I call you Gerry? Of course I may. My friends call me Matilda . . . it isn't my *real* name, of course. That's Stephani Zinia . . . so uncouth—like a patent medicine. I *much* prefer Matilda, don't you?"

I said, cautiously, that I thought Matilda a very nice name.

"Yes, a comforting *old-fashioned* name. Names are *so* important, don't you think? Now he there," she said, gesturing at the man who had shown me in, "*he* calls himself Demetrios. I call him Mustapha."

She glanced at the man and then leaned forward, nearly asphyxiating me with brandy and Parma violets, and hissed suddenly, in Greek, "He's a misbegotten Turk."

The man's face grew red and his moustache bristled, making him look more like a bandit than ever. "I am not a Turk," he snarled. "You lie."

"You are a Turk and your name's Mustapha," she retorted.

"It isn't . . . I'm not . . . It isn't . . . I'm not," said the man, almost incoherent with rage. "You are lying."

"I'm not."

"You are."

"I'm not."

"You are."

"I'm *not*."

"You're a damned elderly liar."

"Elderly," she squeaked, her face growing red. "You dare to call me elderly . . . you . . . you *Turk* you."

"You are elderly and you're fat," said Demetrios-Mustapha coldly.

"That's too much," she screamed. "Elderly . . . fat . . . that's too much. You're sacked. Take a month's notice. No, leave this instant, you son of a misbegotten Turk."

Demetrios-Mustapha drew himself up regally.

"Very well," he said. "Do you wish me to serve the drinks and lunch before I go?"

"Of course," she said.

In silence he crossed the room and extracted a bottle of champagne from an ice bucket behind the sofa. He opened it and poured equal quantities of brandy and champagne into three large glasses. He handed us one each and lifted the third himself.

"I give you a toast," he said to me solemnly. "We will drink to the health of a fat, elderly liar."

I was in a quandary. If I drank the toast it would seem that I was concurring in his opinion of the Countess, and that would scarcely seem polite; and yet, if I did *not* drink the toast, he looked quite capable of doing me an injury. As I hesitated, the Countess, to my astonishment, burst into delighted giggles, her smooth fat cheeks dimpling charmingly.

"You mustn't tease our guest, Mustapha. But I must admit the toast was a good touch," she said, gulping at her drink.

Demetrios-Mustapha grinned at me, his teeth glittering and winking in the fire-light.

"Drink, *kyrié*," he said. "Take no notice of us. She lives for food, drink, and fighting, and it is my job to provide all three."

"Nonsense," said the Countess, seizing my hand and leading me to the sofa, so that I felt as though I were hitched to a small, fat, pink cloud. "Nonsense, I live for a lot of things, a lot of things. Now, don't stand there drinking my drink, you drunkard. Go and see to the food."

Demetrios-Mustapha drained his glass and left the room, while the Countess seated herself on the sofa, clasping my hand in hers, and beamed at me.

"This *is* cosy," she said delightedly. "Just you and I. Tell me, do you always wear mud all over your clothes?"

I hastily and embarrassedly explained about Sally.

"So you came by *donkey*," she said, making it sound a very exotic form of transport. "How *wise* of you. I distrust motorcars myself, noisy, uncontrollable things. Unreliable.

"I remember we had one when my husband was alive, a big yellow one. But my dear, it was a brute. It would obey my husband, but it would not do a thing I told it to do. One day it deliberately backed into a large stall containing fruit and vegetables—in spite of all I was trying to do to stop it—and then went over the edge of the harbour into the sea. When I came out of hospital, I said to my husband, 'Henri,' I said—that was his name—such a nice, *bourgeois* name, don't you think? Where was I? Oh, yes. Well, 'Henri,' I said, 'that car's malevolent,' I said. 'It's possessed of an evil spirit. You must sell it.' And so he did."

Brandy and champagne on an empty stomach combined with the fire to make me feel extremely mellow. My head whirled pleasantly and I nodded and smiled as the Countess chattered on eagerly.

"My husband was a very cultured man, very cultured indeed. He collected books, you know. Books, paintings, stamps, beer-bottle tops, anything cultural appealed to him. Just before he died, he started collecting busts of Napoleon. You would be surprised how many busts they had made of that horrible little Corsican. My husband had five hundred and eighty-two. 'Henri,' I said to him. 'Henri, this must stop. Either you give up collecting busts of Napoleon or I will leave you and go to St. Helena.' I said it as a joke, though, only as a joke, and you know what he said? He said he had been thinking about going to St. Helena for a holiday —with all his busts. My God, what dedication! It was not to be borne! I believe in a little bit of culture in its place, but not to become *obsessed* with it."

Demetrios-Mustapha came into the room, refilled our glasses and said, "Lunch in five minutes," and departed again.

"He was what you might call a *compulsive* collector, my dear. The times that I trembled when I saw that fanatical gleam in his eye. At a state fair once he saw a combine harvester, simply immense it was, and I could *see* the gleam in his eyes, but I put my foot down. 'Henri,' I said to him. 'Henri, we are not going to have combine harvesters all over the place. If you must collect, why not something sensible? Jewels or furs or something?' It may seem harsh, my dear, but what could I do? If I had relaxed for an *instant* he would have had the whole house full of farm machinery."

Demetrios-Mustapha came into the room again. "Lunch is ready," he said.

Still chattering, the Countess led me by the hand out of the room, down the tiled corridor, then down some creaking wooden stairs into a huge kitchen in the cellars. The kitchen at our villa was enormous enough, but this kitchen simply dwarfed it. It was stone-flagged and at one end a positive battery of charcoal fires glowed and winked under the bubbling pots. The walls were covered with a great variety of copper pots, kettles, platters, coffee pots, huge serving dishes, and soup tureens. They all glowed with a pinky-red gleam in the fire-light, glinting and winking like tiger beetles. In the centre of the floor was a twelve-foot-long dining-table of beautiful polished walnut. This was carefully set for two with snowy-white serviettes and gleaming cutlery. In the centre of the table two giant silver candelabras each held a white forest of lighted candles. The whole effect of a kitchen and a state dining-room combined was very odd. It was very hot and so redolent with delicious smells they almost suffocated the Countess's scent.

"I hope you don't mind eating in the kitchen," said the Countess, making it sound as though it were really the most degrading thing to eat food in such humble surroundings.

I said I thought eating in the kitchen was a most sensible idea, especially in winter, as it was warmer.

"Quite right," said the Countess, seating herself as Demetrios-Mustapha held her chair for her. "And, you see, if we eat upstairs I get complaints from this elderly Turk about how far he has to walk."

"It isn't the distance I complain of, it's the weight of the food," said Demetrios-Mustapha, pouring a pale green-gold wine into our glasses. "If you didn't eat so much, it wouldn't be so bad."

"Oh, stop complaining and get on with serving," said the Countess plaintively, tucking her serviette carefully under her dimpled chin.

I, filled with champagne and brandy, was now more than a little drunk and ravenously hungry. I viewed with alarm the number of eating utensils that were flanking my plate, for I was not quite sure which to use first. I remembered Mother's maxim that you started on the outside and worked in, but there were so many utensils that I was uneasy. I decided to wait and see what the Countess used and then follow suit. It was an unwise decision for I soon discovered that she used any and every knife, fork, or spoon with a fine lack of discrimination and so, before long, I became so muddled I was doing the same.

The first course that Demetrios-Mustapha set before us was a fine, clear soup, sequined with tiny golden bubbles of fat, with fingernail-sized croutons floating like crisp little rafts on an amber sea. It was delicious, and the Countess had two helpings, scrunching up the croutons, the noise like someone walking over crisp leaves. Demetrios-Mustapha filled our glasses with more of the pale, musky wine and placed before us a platter of minute baby fish, each one fried a golden brown. Slices of yellow-green lemons in a large dish and a brimming sauce-boat of some exotic sauce unknown to me accompanied it. The Countess piled her plate high with fish, added a lava flow of sauce, and then squeezed lemon juice lavishly over the fish, the table, and herself. She beamed at me, her face now a bright rose-pink, her forehead slightly beaded with sweat. Her prodigious appetite did not appear to impair her conversational powers one jot, for she talked incessantly.

"Don't you love these little fish? Heavenly! Of course, it's such a pity that they should die so *young*, but there we are. So nice to be able to eat *all* of them without worrying about the bones. *Such* a relief! Henri, my husband, you know, started to collect skeletons once. My dear, the house looked and smelt like a mortuary. 'Henri,' I said to him. 'Henri, this must stop. This is an unhealthy death-wish you have developed. You must go and see a psychiatrist.' "

Demetrios-Mustapha removed our empty plates, poured for us a red wine, dark as the heart of a dragon, and then placed before us a dish in which lay snipe, the heads twisted round so that their long beaks could skewer themselves and their empty eye-sockets look at us accusingly. They were plump and brown with cooking, each having its own little square of toast. They were surrounded by thin wafers of fried potatoes like drifts of autumn leaves, pale greeny-white candles of asparagus and small peas.

"I simply cannot understand people who are vegetarians," said the Countess, banging vigorously at a snipe's skull with her fork so that she might crack it and get to the brain. "Henri once tried to be a vegetarian. Would you believe it? But I couldn't endure it. 'Henri,' I said to him, 'this must stop. We have enough food in the larder to feed an army, and I can't eat it single-handed.' Imagine, my dear, I had just ordered two dozen hares. 'Henri,' I said, 'you will have to give up this foolish fad.' "

It struck me that Henri, although obviously a bit of a trial as a husband, had nevertheless led a very frustrated existence.

Demetrios-Mustapha cleared away the debris of the snipe and poured out more wine. I was beginning to feel bloated with food and I hoped that there was not too much more to come. But there was still an army of knives and forks and spoons, unused, beside my plate, so it was with alarm I saw Demetrios-Mustapha approaching through the gloomy kitchen bearing a huge dish.

"Ah!" said the Countess, holding up her plump hands in excitement. "The main dish! What is it, Mustapha, what is it?"

"The wild boar that Makroyannis sent," said Demetrios-Mustapha.

"Oh, the boar! The *boar!*" squeaked the Countess, clasping her fat cheeks in her hands. "Oh, lovely! I had forgotten all about it. You do like wild boar, I hope?"

I said that it was one of my favourite meats, which was true, but could I have a very small helping, please?

"But of course you shall," she said, leaning over the great, brown, gravy-glistening haunch and starting to cut thick pink slabs of it. She placed three of these on a plate—obviously under the impression that this was, by anyone's standards, a small portion—and then proceeded to surround them with the accoutrements. There were piles of the lovely little golden wild mushrooms, chanterelles, with their delicate, almost winy flavour; tiny marrows stuffed with sour cream and capers; potatoes baked in their skins, neatly split and annointed with butter; carrots red as a frosty winter sun and

great tree trunks of white leeks, poached in cream. I surveyed this dish of food and surreptitiously undid the top
three buttons of my shorts.

"We used to get wild boar *such* a lot when Henri was
alive. He used to go to Albania and shoot them, you know.
But now we seldom have it. What a *treat!* Will you have some
more mushrooms? No? *So* good for one. After this, I think we
will have a pause. A pause is essential, I always think, for
a good digestion," said the Countess, adding naïvely, "and it
enables you to eat so much *more*."

The wild bore was fragrant and succulent, having been
marinaded well with herb-scented wine and stuffed with garlic cloves, but even so I only just managed to finish it. The
Countess had two helpings, both identical in size, and then
leaned back, her face congested to a pale puce colour, and
mopped the sweat from her brow with an inadequate lace
handkerchief.

"A pause, eh?" she said thickly, smiling at me. "A pause
to marshal our resources."

I felt that I had not any resources to marshal, but I did not
like to say so. I nodded and smiled and undid all the rest of
the buttons on my shorts.

During the pause, the Countess smoked a long thin che-
root and ate salted peanuts, chatting on interminably about
her husband. The pause did me good. I felt a little less solid
and somnolent with food. When the Countess eventually decided that we had rested our internal organs sufficiently, she
called for the next course, and Demetrios-Mustapha produced two mercifully small omelets, crispy brown on the outside and liquid and succulent on the inside, stuffed with tiny
pink shrimps.

"What have you got for a sweet?" inquired the Countess,
her mouth full of omelet.

"I didn't make one," said Demetrios-Mustapha.

The Countess's eyes grew round and fixed.

"You didn't make a sweet?" she said, in tones of horror, as though he were confessing to some heinous crime.

"I didn't have time," said Demetrios-Mustapha. "You can't expect me to do all this cooking and all the housework."

"But no *sweet*," said the Countess despairingly. "You can't have a lunch without a sweet."

"Well, I bought you some meringues," said Mustapha. "You'll have to make do with those."

"Oh, lovely!" said the Countess glowing and happy again. "Just what's needed."

It was the last thing I needed. The meringues were large and white and brittle as coral and stuffed to overflowing with cream. I wished fervently that I had brought Roger with me, as he could have sat under the table and accepted half my food, since the Countess was far too occupied with her own plate and her reminiscences really to concentrate on me.

"Now," she said at last, swallowing the last mouthful of meringue and brushing the white crumbs from her chin. "Now, do you feel replete? Or would you care for a little something more? Some fruit perhaps? Not that there's very much at this time of the year."

I said no thank you very much, I had had quite sufficient.

The Countess sighed and looked at me soulfully. I think nothing would have pleased her more than to ply me with another two or three courses.

"You don't eat enough," she said. "A growing boy like you should eat more. You're far too thin for your age. Does your Mother feed you properly?"

I could imagine Mother's wrath if she had heard this innuendo. I said yes, Mother was an excellent cook and we all fed like lords.

"I'm glad to hear it," said the Countess. "But you still look a little peaky to me."

I could not say so, but the reason I was beginning to look

peaky was that the assault of food upon my stomach was beginning to make itself felt. I said, as politely as I could, that I thought I ought to be getting back.

"But of course, dear," said the Countess. "Dear me, a quarter past four already. How time flies!"

She sighed at the thought, then brightened perceptibly.

"However, it's nearly time for tea. Are you sure you wouldn't like to stay and have something?"

I said no, that Mother would be worried about me.

"Now, let me see," said the Countess. "What did you come for? Oh, yes, the owl. Mustapha, bring the boy his owl and bring me some coffee and some of those nice Turkish delights up in the lounge."

Mustapha appeared with a cardboard box done up with string and handed it to me.

"I wouldn't open it until you get home," he said. "That's a wild one, that."

I was overcome with the terrifying thought that if I did not hurry my departure, the Countess would ask me to partake of Turkish delight with her. So I thanked them both sincerely for my owl, and made my way to the front door.

"Well," said the Countess, "it has been enchanting having you, *absolutely enchanting.* You must come again. You must come in the spring or the summer when we have more choice of fruit and vegetables. Mustapha's got a way of cooking octopus which makes it simply melt in your mouth."

I said I would love to come again, making a mental vow that if I did, I would starve for three days in advance.

"Here," said the Countess, pressing an orange into my pocket, "take this. You might feel peckish on the way home."

As I mounted Sally and trotted off down the drive, she called, "Drive carefully."

Grim-faced, I sat there with the owl clasped to my bosom till we were outside the gates of the Countess's estate. Then the jogging I was subjected to on Sally's back was too much. I dismounted, went behind an olive tree, and was deliciously and flamboyantly sick.

When I got home I carried the owl up to my bedroom, untied the box and lifted him, struggling and beak-clicking, out onto the floor. The dogs, who had gathered round in a circle to view the new addition, backed away hurriedly. They knew what Ulysses could do when he was in a bad temper, and this owl was three times his size. He was, I thought, one of the most beautiful birds I had ever seen. The feathers on his back and wings were honeycomb golden, smudged with pale ash-grey; his breast was a spotless cream-white; and the mask of white feathers round his dark, strangely Oriental-looking eyes was as crisp and as starched-looking as any Elizabethan's ruff.

His wing was not as bad as I had feared. It was a clean break, and after half an hour's struggle, during which he managed to draw blood on several occasions, I had it splinted up to my satisfaction. The owl, which I had decided to call Lampadusa, simply because the name appealed to me, seemed to be belligerently scared of the dogs, totally unwilling to make friends with Ulysses, and viewed Augustus Tickletummy with undisguised loathing. I felt he might be happier, till he settled down, in a dark, secluded place, so I carried him up to the attic. One of the attic rooms was very tiny and lit by one small window which was so covered with cobwebs and dust that it allowed little light to penetrate the room. It was quiet and as dim as a cave, and I thought that here Lampadusa would enjoy his convalescence. I put him on the floor with a large saucer of chopped meat and locked the door carefully so that he would not be disturbed. That evening, when I went to visit him, taking him a dead mouse by way of a present, he seemed very much improved. He had eaten most of his meat and now hissed and beak-clicked at me with outspread wings and blazing eyes as he pitter-pattered about the floor. Encouraged by his obvious progress, I left him with his mouse and went to bed.

Some hours later I was awakened by the sound of voices emanating from Mother's room. Wondering, sleepily, what on earth the family could be doing at that hour, I got out of bed and stuck my head out of the bedroom door to listen.

"I tell you," Larry was saying, "it's a damned great poltergeist."

"It can't be a poltergeist, dear," said Mother. "Poltergeists throw things."

"Well, whatever it is, it's up there clanking its chains," said Larry, "and I want it exorcised. You and Margo are supposed to be the experts on the after-life. You go up and do it."

"I'm not going up there," said Margo tremulously. "It might be anything. It might be a malignant spirit."

"It's bloody malignant all right," said Larry. "It's been keeping me awake for the last hour."

"Are you sure it isn't the wind or something, dear?" asked Mother.

"I know the difference between wind and a damned ghost playing around with balls and chains," said Larry.

"Perhaps it's burglars," said Margo, more to give herself confidence than anything else. "Perhaps it's burglars and we ought to wake Leslie."

Half-asleep and still bee-drowsy from the liquor I had consumed that day, I could not think what the family were talking about. It seemed as intriguing as any of the other crises that they seemed capable of evoking at the most unexpected hours of the day or night, so I went to Mother's door and peered into the room. Larry was marching up and down, his dressing-gown swishing imperially.

"Something's got to be done," he said. "I can't sleep with rattling chains over my head, and if I can't sleep I can't write."

"I don't see what you expect *us* to do about it, dear," said Mother. "I'm sure it must be the wind."

"Yes, you can't expect us to go up there," said Margo. "You're a man, *you* go."

"Look," said Larry, "you are the one who came back from London covered with ectoplasm and talking about the infinite. It's probably some hellish thing you've conjured up from one of your séances that's followed you here. That makes it *your* pet. You go and deal with it."

The word "pet" penetrated. Surely it could not be Lampadusa? Like all owls, barn owls have wings as soft and as silent as dandelion clocks. Surely he could not be responsible for making a noise like a ball and chain?

I went into the room and inquired what they were all talking about.

"It's only a ghost, dear," said Mother. "Larry's found a ghost."

"It's in the attic," said Margo, excitedly. "Larry thinks it followed me from England. I wonder if it's Mawake?"

"We're not going to start *that* all over again," said Mother firmly.

"I don't care *who* it is," said Larry, "which one of your disembodied friends. I want it removed."

I said I thought there was just the faintest possibility that it might be Lampadusa.

"What's that?" inquired Mother.

I explained that it was the owl the Countess had given me.

"I might have known it," said Larry. "I might have known it. Why it didn't occur to me instantly, I don't know."

"Now, now, dear," said Mother. "It's only an owl."

"Only an owl!" said Larry. "It sounds like a battalion of tanks crashing about up there. Tell him to get it out of the loft."

I said I could not understand why Lampadusa was making a noise since owls were the quietest of things. . . . I said they drifted through the night on silent wings like flakes of ash. . . .

"This one hasn't got silent wings," said Larry. "It sounds like a one-owl jazz band. Go and get it *out*."

Hurriedly I took a lamp and made my way up to the attic When I opened the door I saw at once what the trouble was. Lampadusa had devoured his mouse and then discovered that there was a long shred of meat still lying in his saucer. This, during the course of the long, hot day, had solidified and become welded to the surface of the saucer. Lampadusa, feeling that this shred of meat would do well as a light snack to keep body and soul together until dawn, had endeavoured to pick it off the plate. The curve of his sharp amber beak had gone through the meat, but the meat had refused to part company with the saucer, so that there he was, effectively trapped, flapping ineffectually round the floor, banging and clattering the saucer against the wooden boards in an effort to disentangle it from his beak. So I extricated him from this predicament and carried him down to my bedroom where I shut him in his cardboard box for safe-keeping.

PART THREE

Criseda

This place is wonderfully lovely. I wish you could see it; if you came I could put you up beautifully, and feed you on Ginger-beer and claret and prawns and figs.

—EDWARD LEAR

8

HEDGEHOGS AND SEA-DOGS

When spring came, we moved to a new villa, an elegant, snow-white one shaded by a huge magnolia tree, that lay in the olive groves not far from where our very first villa had been. It was on a hillside overlooking a great flat area marked out like a gigantic chess-board by irrigation ditches, which I knew as the fields. They were in fact the old Venetian salt-pans used long ago for collecting the brine that floated into the channels from the big salt-water lake on whose shores they lay. The lake had long since silted up and the channels, now flooded by fresh water from the hills, provided a grid-work of lush fields. This was an area overflowing with wildlife, and so it was one of my happiest hunting grounds.

Spring in Corfu never seemed to be half-hearted. Almost overnight, it seemed, the winter winds had blown the skies clean of clouds, so that they shone a clear delphinium blue, and overnight the winter rains had flooded the valleys with wildflowers; the pink of pyramid orchids, yellow of crocus, tall pale spikes of the asphodels, the blue eyes of the grape hyacinths peering at you from the grass, and the wine-dipped anemones that bowed in the slightest breeze. The olive groves were alive and rustling with the newly arrived birds: the hoopoes, salmon-pink and black with surprised crests, probed their long, curved beaks at the soft earth between the clumps of emerald grass; goldfinches, chiming and wheezing, danced merrily from twig to twig, their plumage glowing gold and scarlet and black. In the irrigation ditches in the fields, the waters became green with weed, interlaced with the strings of toad spawn, like black-pearl necklaces; emerald-green frogs croaked at each other, and the water tortoises, their shells as black as ebony, crawled up the banks to dig their holes and lay their eggs. Steel-blue dragon-flies, slender as threads, hatched and drifted like smoke through the undergrowth, moving in a curious stiff flight. Now was the time when the banks at night were lit by the throbbing, green-white light of a thousand glow-worms and in the day-time by the glint of wild strawberries hanging like scarlet lanterns in the shade. It was an exciting time, a time for explorations and new discoveries, a time when an overturned log might reveal almost anything from a field-vole's nest to a wriggling glitter of baby slow-worms, looking as though they were cast in burnished bronze.

I was down in the fields one day, endeavouring to catch some of the brown water-snakes that inhabited the irrigation ditches, when an old woman, whom I knew slightly, called me from some six fields away. She had been digging up the ground with her short-handled, broad-bladed hoe, standing up to her ankles in the rich loam, wearing the thick, ungainly sheep's-wool stockings the peasants put on for this operation.

"I've found you something," she called. "Come quickly."

It was impossible for me to get there quickly, for each field was surrounded by an irrigation ditch on all four sides and finding the bridges across these was like finding your way through a maze.

"Quickly! Quickly!" screamed the old woman. "They are running away. Quickly!"

I ran and leaped and scuttled, almost falling into the ditches, racing across the rickety plank bridges, until, panting, I reached her side.

"There," she said, pointing. "There. Mind they don't bite you."

I saw that she had dug up a bundle of leaves from under the earth in which something white was moving. Gingerly I parted the leaves with the handle of my butterfly net and saw to my delight four fat, newly born, baby hedgehogs, pink as cyclamen, with soft, snow-white spines. They were still blind and they wriggled and nosed at each other like a litter of tiny pigs. I picked them up and put them carefully inside my shirt, thanked the old woman, and made my way homewards. I was excited about my new pets, principally because they were so young. I already had two adult hedgehogs, called Itch and Scratch because of the vast quantities of fleas they harboured, but they were not really tame. These babies I thought would grow up differently. I would be, as far as they were concerned, their mother. I visualized myself walking proudly through the olive groves, preceded by the dogs, Ulysses, and my two magpies, and trotting at my heels, four tame hedgehogs, all of which I would have taught to do tricks.

The family were arranged on the veranda under the grapevine, each occupied with his or her own affairs. Mother was knitting, counting the stitches audibly at intervals to herself and saying "damn" periodically when she went wrong. Leslie was squatting on the flag-stones, carefully weighing gunpowder and little piles of silver shot as he filled shiny red cartridge cases. Larry was reading a massive tome and occasionally glancing irritably at Margaret, who was clattering away at her machine, making some diaphanous garment, and singing, off key, the only line she knew of her favourite song of the moment.

"She wore her little jacket of blue," she warbled. "She wore her little jacket of blue, She wore her little jacket of blue, She wore her little jacket of blue."

"The only remarkable thing about your singing is your tenacity," said Larry. "Anybody else, faced with the fact that they could not carry a tune and couldn't remember the simplest lyric, would have given up, defeated, a long time ago."

He threw his cigarette butt down on the flag-stones and this produced a roar of rage from Leslie.

"Watch the gunpowder," he shouted.

"Leslie dear," said Mother, "I do wish you wouldn't shout like that, you've made me lose count."

I produced my hedgehogs proudly and showed them to Mother.

"Aren't they sweet," she said, peering at them benignly through her spectacles.

"Oh, God! He hasn't got something new has he?" asked Larry. He peered at my pink progeny in their white fur coats with distaste.

"What are they?" he inquired.

I explained that they were baby hedgehogs.

"They can't be," he said. "Hedgehogs are all brown."

My family's ignorance of the world they lived in was always a source of worry to me, and I never lost an opportunity of imparting information. I explained that female hedgehogs could not, without suffering the most refined torture, give birth to babies covered with hard spines, and so they were born with these little rubbery white spikes which could be bent between the fingers as easily as a feather. Later, as they grew, the spines would darken and harden.

"How are you going to feed them, dear? They've got such tiny mouths," said Mother, "and they must still be drinking milk, surely?"

I said that I had seen, in a shop in the town, a complete do-it-yourself baby outfit for children, which consisted of several worthless items such as a celluloid doll, nappies, a potty, and so forth, but one article had caught my attention; a miniature feeding bottle with a supply of tiny red teats. This, I said, would be ideal for feeding the baby hedgehogs with, but the potty, doll, and other accoutrements could be given to some deserving peasant child. There was only one slight snag, and that was that I had had some rather heavy expenses to meet recently (such as the wire for the magpie cage) and so I had overspent on my pocket-money.

"Well, dear," said Mother doubtfully, "if it isn't too expensive I suppose I could buy it for you."

I said it was not expensive at all, when you considered that it was more like an investment, for not only would you be getting an invaluable feeding bottle which would come in useful for other animals, but you would be rearing four tame hedgehogs and getting a grateful peasant child into the bargain. What finer way, I asked, of spending money? So the outfit was purchased. A young peasant girl, whom I rather fancied, received with the most satisfactory joy the doll, potty, and other rubbish, and I went about the stern task of rearing my babies.

They lived in a large cardboard box, full of cotton wool, under my bed, and at night, in order to keep them warm, I placed their box on top of a hot-water bottle. I had wanted to have them sleeping in the bed with me, but Mother pointed out that this was not only unhygienic, but that I risked rolling on them in the night and killing them. I found they thrived best on watered cow's milk and I fed them assiduously three times a day and once in the middle of the night. The night feed proved to be a little difficult, for in order to make sure that I woke up I had borrowed a large tin alarm clock from Spiro. This used to go off like a rattle of musketry, and unfortunately woke not only me but the entire family as well. Eventually, so vociferous were the family in their complaints, Mother suggested I give them an extra feed late at night when I went to bed, in lieu of the feed at two o'clock in the morning that woke everybody up. This I did and the hedgehogs thrived and grew. Their eyes opened and their spines turned from snow-white to grey and became firmer. They had now, as I anticipated, convinced themselves that I was their mother, and would come scrambling onto the edge of the box when I opened it, jostling and pushing for first suck at the bottle, uttering tiny wheezy squeaks and grunts. I was immensely proud of them and looked forward happily to the day when they would trot at my heels through the olive groves.

Then Mother and I were invited to spend a week-end with some friends in the extreme south of the island, and I found myself in a quandary. I longed to go, for the sandy, shallow coasts of the south were a fine place for finding heart-urchins which, in fact, looked not unlike baby hedgehogs. Heart-shaped, they were covered with soft spines which formed a tufted tail at one end and a spiky Red-Indian-like head-dress along the back. I had found only one of these, and that had been crushed by the sea and was scarcely recognizable, but I knew from Theodore that they were found in abundance two or three inches under the sand in the south of the island. However, I had my brood of hedgehogs to consider, for I could not very well take them with me, and as Mother was coming too, there was nobody I really trusted to look after them.

"I'll look after them," offered Margo. "Dear little things."

I was doubtful. Did she realize, I asked, the intricacies of looking after the hedgehogs? The fact that, for example, the cotton wool in their box had to be changed three times a day? That they must have only diluted cow's milk? That the milk had to be warmed to blood heat and no more? And most important of all, that they were allowed only half a bottle of milk each at every feed? For I had very soon found out that, if you let them, they would drink themselves comatose at every meal, with the most dire results that entailed the changing of the cotton wool even more frequently.

"Don't be silly," said Margo. "Of course I can look after them. I know about babies and things. You just write down on a piece of paper what I am supposed to do, and they'll be quite all right."

I was torn. I desperately wanted to search for heart-urchins in the golden sands covered by the warm, shallow sea, and yet

I doubted Margo's proclivities as a nursemaid. However, Margo grew so indignant at my doubting her that eventually, reluctantly, I gave in. I had prevailed upon Larry, who happened to be in a good mood, to type out a detailed list of do's and don't's for hedgehog-rearers and I gave Margo a practical course in bottle warming and cotton wool changing.

"They seem awfully hungry," she said as she lifted each writhing, squeaking baby out of the box and pushed the end of the teat into its groping, eager mouth.

I said that they were always like that. One should take no notice of it. They were just naturally greedy.

"Poor little things," said Margo.

I should have been warned.

I spent an exhilarating week-end. I got myself badly sunburnt, for the fragile spring sun was deceptive, but I came back, triumphant, with eight heart-urchins, four shells new to my collection, and a baby sparrow that had fallen out of its nest. At the villa, after I had suffered the barks and licks and nibbles of greeting that the dogs always bestowed upon you if you had been away for more than two hours, I asked Margo eagerly how my baby hedgehogs were.

"They're doing all right now," she said. "But really, Gerry, I do think you ill-treat your pets. You were starving those poor little things to death. They were so hungry. You've no idea."

With a sinking feeling in the pit of my stomach, I listened to my sister.

"Ravenous, poor little dears. Do you know, they've been taking two bottles each at every feed?"

Horrified, I rushed up to my bedroom and pulled the cardboard box out from under my bed. In it lay my four hedgehogs, bloated beyond belief. Their stomachs were so large that they could only paw feebly with their legs without making any progress. They had degenerated into pink sacks full of milk, frosted with spines. They all died that night and Margo wept copiously over their balloon-like corpses. But her grief did not give me any pleasure, for never would my hedgehogs trot obediently at my heels through the olive groves. As a punishment to my overindulgent sister, I dug four little graves and erected four little crosses in the garden as a permanent reminder, and for four days I did not speak to her.

My grief over the death of my hedgehogs was, however, short-lived, for at that time Donald and Max reappeared on the island, triumphantly, with a thirty-foot yacht, and Larry introduced into our midst Captain Creech.

Mother and I had spent a very pleasant afternoon in the olive groves, she collecting wildflowers and herbs and I collecting newly emerged butterflies. Tired but happy, we made our way back to the villa for tea. When we came in sight of the villa, she came to a sudden halt.

"Who's that man sitting on the veranda?" she asked.

I had been busy throwing sticks for the dogs, so I was not really concentrating. Now I saw, stretched out on the veranda, a strange figure in crumpled white ducks.

"Who is he? Can you see?" asked Mother, agitated.

At that time she was suffering under the delusion that the manager of our bank in England was liable, at any moment, to pay a flying visit to Corfu for the express purpose of discussing our overdraft, so this unknown figure on the veranda fermented her fears.

I examined the stranger carefully. He was old, almost completely bald, and what little hair he had adhering to the back of his skull was long and as white and wispy as late summer thistle-down. He had an equally unkempt white beard and moustache. I assured Mother that, as far as I could see, he bore no resemblance to the bank manager.

"Oh, dear," said Mother, annoyed. "He would arrive now. I've got absolutely nothing for tea. I wonder who he is?"

As we got nearer, the stranger, who had been dozing peacefully, suddenly woke up and spotted us.

"Ahoy!" he shouted, so loudly and suddenly that Mother

tripped and almost fell down. "Ahoy! You must be Mother Durrell, and the boy, of course. Larry told me all about you. Welcome aboard."

"Oh, dear," whispered Mother to me, "it's another one of Larry's."

As we got closer, I could see that our guest had a most extraordinary face, pink and as carunculated as a walnut. The cartilage of his nose had obviously received, at one time or another, so many severe blows that it twisted down his face like a snake. His jaw too had suffered the same fate and was now twisted to one side, as though hitched up to his right ear-lobe by an invisible thread.

"Delighted to meet you," he said, as though he owned the villa, his rheumy eyes beaming. "My, you're a better-looking wench than your son described."

Mother stiffened and dropped an anemone from the bunch of flowers she carried.

"I," she said with frigid dignity, "am Mrs. Durrell, and this is my son Gerald."

"My name's Creech," said the old man. "Captain Patrick Creech." He paused and spat accurately and copiously over the veranda rail into Mother's favourite bed of zinnias. "Welcome aboard," he said again, exuding bonhomie. "Glad to know you."

Mother cleared her throat nervously. "Is my son Lawrence here?" she inquired, adopting her fruity, aristocratic voice, which she did only in moments of extreme stress.

"No, no," said Captain Creech. "I left him in town. He told me to come out here for tea. He said he would be aboard shortly."

"Well," said Mother, making the best of a bad job, "do sit down. If you will excuse me a moment I'll just go and make some scones."

"Scones, eh?" said Captain Creech, eyeing Mother with such lasciviousness that she dropped two more wildflowers.

"I like scones, and I like a woman that's handy in the galley."

"Gerry," said Mother frostily, "you entertain Captain Creech while I get the tea."

She made a hurried and slightly undignified exit and I was left to cope with Captain Creech.

He had reslumped himself in his chair and was staring at me with watery eyes from under his tattered white eyebrows. His stare was so fixed that I became slightly unnerved. Conscious of my duties as host, however, I offered him a box full of cigarettes. He peered into it, as though it were a well, his jaw moving to and fro like a ventriloquist's dummy.

"Death!" he shouted so suddenly and so vigorously that I almost dropped the cigarettes. He lay back in his chair and fixed me with his blue eyes.

"Cigarettes are death, boyo," he said. He felt in the pocket of his white ducks and produced a stubby pipe as blackened and as gnarled as a piece of charcoal. He stuck it between his teeth, which made his jaw look even more lop-sided than ever.

"Never forget," he said, "a man's best friend is his pipe."

He laughed uproariously at his own joke and dutifully I laughed too. He got up and spat copiously over the veranda rail and then flopped back into his chair. I searched my mind for a topic of conversation. Nothing seemed to present itself. He would surely not be interested in the fact that today I had heard the first cicada, nor that Agathi's chicken laid six eggs the size of hazel-nuts. Since he was nautically inclined, I wondered whether the exciting news that Taki, who could not afford a boat, had been night-fishing (holding a light above his head with one hand and a trident in the other) and had successfully driven the trident through his own foot, imagining it was an exotic form of fish? But Captain Creech, peering at me from behind the oily fumes of his pipe, started the conversation himself.

"You're wondering about my face, aren't you boyo?" he said accusingly, and I noticed that the skin on his cheeks became pinker and more shiny, like satin, as he said it. Before I could voice a denial, he went on.

"Wind-jammers. That's what did it. Wind-jammers. Going round the Horn. Tearing wind, straight out of the arsehole of the earth. I fell, see? The canvas flapping and roaring like God's thunder. The rope slipped through my fingers like an oiled snake. Straight onto the deck. They did what they could with it . . . of course, we hadn't a doctor on board." He paused and felt his jaw meditatively. I sat riveted in my chair, fascinated. "By the time we got round to Chile the whole thing had set as hard as Portland," he said, still fondling his jaw. "I was sixteen years old."

I wondered whether to commiserate with him or not, but he had fallen into a reverie, his blue eyes blank. Mother came onto the veranda and paused, struck by our immobility.

"Chile," said the Captain with relish. "Chile. That was the first time I got gonorrhoea."

Mother started and then cleared her throat loudly.

"Gerry, come and help me bring out the tea," she said.

Together we brought out the teapot, milk jug and cups, and the plates with golden-yellow scones and toast Mother had prepared.

"Tucker," said Captain Creech, filling his mouth with scone. "Stops your belly rumbling."

"Are you, um, staying here long?" asked Mother, obviously hoping that he was not.

"Might retire here," said Captain Creech indistinctly, wiping scone crumbs off his moustache. "Looks a pretty little place. Might go to anchor here."

He was forced, because of his jaw, to slurp his tea noisily. I could see Mother getting increasingly alarmed.

"Don't you, um, have a ship?" she asked.

"No bloody fear," said Captain Creech, seizing another scone. "Retired, that's me. Got time now to look a little more closely at the wenches."

He eyed Mother meditatively as he spoke, masticating his scone with great vigour.

"A bed without a woman is like a ship without a hold," he observed.

Mercifully Mother was saved from having to reply to this remark by the arrival of the car containing the rest of the family and Donald and Max.

"Muzzer, we have come," announced Max, beaming at her and embracing her tenderly. "And I see we are in time for tea. Strumpets! How lovely! Donald, we have strumpets for tea!"

"Crumpets," corrected Donald.

"They're scones," said Mother.

"I remember a strumpet in Montevideo," said Captain Creech. "Marvellous bitch. Kept the whole ship entertained for two days. They don't breed them with stamina like that nowadays."

"Who is this disgusting old man?" asked Mother as soon as she had an opportunity of backing Larry into a corner away from the tea-party, which was now in full swing.

"He's called Creech," said Larry.

"I know *that*," said Mother, "but what did you bring him here for?"

"He's an interesting old boy," said Larry, "and I don't think he's got a lot of money. He's come here to retire on a minute pension, I think."

"Well, he's not going to retire on *us*," said Mother firmly. "Don't invite him again."

"I thought you'd like him," said Larry. "He's travelled all over the world. He's even been to India. He's full of the most fascinating stories."

"As far as I am concerned he can go on travelling," said Mother. "The stories he's been telling up to now aren't what *I* call fascinating."

Captain Creech, once having discovered our "anchorage," as he put it, became a frequent visitor. He would arrive generally, we noticed, just in time for a meal, shouting, "Ahoy there! Can I come aboard and have a chin-wag?" As he had obviously walked two and a half miles through the olive groves to reach us, it was difficult to deny him this privilege, and so Mother, muttering evilly, would rush into the kitchen and water the soup and bisect the sausages so that Captain Creech could join us. He would regale us with tales of his life at sea and the names of the places that he had visited. Names that I knew only from maps would slide enticingly out of his disjointed mouth. Trincomalee, Darwin and Durban, Buenos Aires, Wellington and Calcutta, the Galapagos, the Seychelles and the Friendly Islands. It seemed that there was no corner of the globe that he had not penetrated. He would intersperse these stories with prolonged and exceptionally vulgar sea-shanties and limericks of such biological complexity that, fortunately, Mother could not understand them.

Then came the never-to-be-forgotten day when Captain Creech arrived, uninvited, for tea as we were entertaining the local English minister and his wife, more out of a sense of duty than of religion. To our amazement, Captain Creech behaved remarkably well. He exchanged views on sea-serpents and the height of tidal waves with the padre and explained the difference between longitude and latitude to the padre's wife. His manners were exemplary and we were quite proud of him, but towards the end of tea the padre's wife had, with extreme cunning, managed to steer the conversation on to her children. This subject was all-absorbing to her. You would have thought that not only was she the only woman in the world to have given birth, but that they had been immaculately conceived as well. Having treated us to a ten-minute monologue on the incredible perspicacity of her offspring, she paused momentarily to drink her tea.

"I'm a bit too old to have babies," said Captain Creech.

The padre's wife choked.

"But," he went on with satisfaction, "I have a lot of fun trying."

The tea-party was not a success.

Shortly after this, Donald and Max turned up one day at the villa.

"Muzzer," said Max, "we are going to carry you away."

"Yacht party," said Donald. "Fabulous idea. Max's idea, of course."

"Yacht party where?" inquired Mother.

"Round ze island," said Max, throwing out his long arms in an all-embracing gesture.

"But I thought you didn't know how to sail her," said Leslie.

"No, no. We don't sail her. Larry sails her," said Max.

"Larry?" said Leslie incredulously. "But Larry doesn't know the first thing about boats."

"Oh, no," said Donald earnestly. "Oh, no. He's quite an expert. He's been taking lessons from Captain Creech. The Captain's coming along too, as crew."

"Well, that settles it then," said Mother. "I'm not coming on a yacht with that disgusting old man, apart from the danger involved if Larry's going to sail it."

They tried their best to persuade her, but Mother was adamant. The most she would concede was that the rest of the family, with Theodore, would drive across the island and rendezvous with them at a certain bay where we could picnic and, if it was warm enough, bathe.

It was a bright, clean morning when we set off and it looked as though it were going to be ideal for both sailing and picnicking; but by the time we reached the other side of the island and had unpacked the picnic things, it began to look as though we were in for a sirocco. Theodore and I made our way down through the trees to the edge of the bay. The sea had turned a cold steel-grey and the wind had stretched and starched a number of white clouds across the blue sky. Suddenly, along the rim of the sea, three water-spouts appeared, loping along the horizon like the huge undulating necks of some prehistoric monsters. Bowing and swaying, graceful as swans they danced along the horizon and disappeared.

"Aha," said Theodore, who had been watching this phenomenon interestedly, "I have never seen *three* of them together. Very curious. Did you notice how they moved together, almost as if they were . . . er . . . you know, animals in a herd?"

I said that I wished they had been closer.

"Um," said Theodore rasping his beard with his thumb. "I don't think water-spouts are things one wants to get on . . . er . . . um . . . intimate terms with. I remember once I visited a place in Macedonia where one had . . . er . . . you know, come ashore. It had left a trail of damage about two hundred yards wide and a quarter of a mile long, that is to say *inland*. Even quite big olive trees had been, er, you know, damaged and the smaller ones were broken up like matchwood. And of course, at the point where the water-spout finally broke up, the ground was saturated by tons of salt water and so it was . . . you know . . . completely unsuitable for agriculture."

"I say, did you see those bloody great water-spouts?" asked Leslie, joining us.

"Yes, very curious," said Theodore.

"Mother's in a panic," said Leslie. "She's convinced they're heading straight for Larry."

"I don't think there's any danger of that," said Theodore, "they look too far out to me."

By the time we had installed ourselves in the olive groves at the edge of the bay, it was obvious that we were in for one of those sudden and exceedingly sharp siroccos which blew up at that time of the year. The wind lashed the olive trees and churned up the bay to white-capped rollers.

"We might as well go home," said Leslie. "It isn't going to be much fun picnicking in this."

"We can't, dear," said Mother. "We promised to meet Larry here."

"If they've got any sense, they'll have put in somewhere else," said Leslie.

"I can't say I envy them being out in this," said Theodore, gazing at the waves pounding the rocks.

"Oh, dear, I do hope they will be all right," said Mother. "Larry really is foolish."

We waited an hour, with Mother getting increasingly panicky with each passing moment. Then Leslie, who had climbed to a neighbouring headland, came back with the news that he could see them.

"I must say I think it's surprising they got this far," said Leslie. "The boom's swinging about all over the place and they're tacking practically in circles."

Presently the yacht headed into the narrow mouth of the bay and we could see Donald and Max dodging about, pulling at ropes and canvas while Larry and Captain Creech clung to the tiller and were obviously shouting instructions. We watched their progress interestedly.

"I hope they remember that reef," said Leslie.

"What reef?" said Mother in alarm.

"There's a damn great reef just there where that white water is," said Leslie.

Spiro had been standing gazing out to sea like a brown gargoyle, his face scowling.

"I don't likes it, Master Leslies," he said in a hoarse whisper. "They don't looks as though they knows how to sails."

"Oh, dear," said Mother. "Why ever did I agree to this?"

At that moment (owing to the fact, we discovered later, that Donald and Max misinterpreted their instructions and had hauled up a length of canvas instead of taking it down) several things happened simultaneously. The yacht's sails were suddenly caught by an errant gust of wind. They puffed out. The boom came over with a splintering crash that one could hear quite clearly on shore and knocked Max overboard. The yacht turned almost on her side and, propelled by the gust of wind, ran with a remarkably loud scrunching noise straight onto the reef, where she remained upright for a brief moment and then, as if despairing of the yachtsmen on board, she lay down languidly on her side. Immediately all was confusion.

Mother shouting "Oh, my God! Oh, my God!" had to sit down hurriedly on an olive root. Margaret burst into tears, waving her hands and screaming, "They'll drown! They'll drown!" Spiro, Leslie, and I made our way to the edge of the bay. There was not much we could do as there was no boat available to launch as a rescue vessel. But presently we saw the four expert sailors swimming away from the wreck of the yacht, Larry and Donald apparently propelling Captain Creech through the water. Leslie and I and Spiro stripped off our clothes hurriedly and plunged into the sea. The water was icy cold and the waves had considerably more force in them than I gave them credit for.

"Are you all right?" shouted Leslie as the flotilla of shipwrecked mariners came towards us.

"Yes," said Max. "Right as rain."

He had a four-inch gash on his forehead and the blood was running down his face and into his moustache. Larry had one eye bruised and scraped and rapidly swelling. Captain Creech's face, bobbing between Larry's and Donald's, had achieved an extraordinary mauve colour, rather like the bloom of a plum.

"Give us a hand with the Captain," said Larry. "Silly old bastard only told me as we went over that he couldn't swim."

Spiro, Leslie, and I laid hands upon Captain Creech and relieved the panting Donald and Larry of their rescue work. We must have made an arresting tableau as we staggered, gasping, through the shallows and out onto the shore. Leslie and Spiro were supporting Captain Creech, one on each side of him, as his legs seemed in imminent danger of buckling.

"Ahoy there!" he called to Mother. "Ahoy there, my wench."

"Look at Max's head!" screamed Margo. "He'll bleed to death!"

We staggered up into the shelter of the olive groves, and while Mother, Margo, and Theodore did hasty first-aid on Max's head and Larry's eye, we laid Captain Creech under an olive tree, since he seemed incapable of standing up.

"Port at last," he said with satisfaction. "Port at last. I'll make sailors of you lads yet."

It became obvious, now that we had time to concentrate, that Captain Creech was extremely drunk.

"Really, Larry, you do make me cross," said Mother. "You might all have been drowned."

"It wasn't my fault," said Larry aggrievedly. "We were doing what the Captain told us to do. Donald and Max went and pulled the wrong ropes."

"How can you take instructions from him?" said Mother. "He's drunk."

"He wasn't drunk when he started," said Larry. "He must have had a secret supply somewhere on board. He did seem to pop down to the cabin rather a lot, now I come to think about it."

"Do not trust him, gentle maiden," sang Captain Creech in a wavering baritone. "Though his heart be pure as gold, He'll leave you one fine morning, With a cargo in your hold."

"Disgusting old brute," said Mother. "Really, Larry, I'm extremely cross with you."

"A drink, me boyos," called Captain Creech hoarsely, gesturing at the dishevelled Max and Donald. "You can't sail without a drink."

At length we had dried ourselves as best we could and wrung the water out of everybody's clothes; then we made our way, shivering, up the hill to the car.

"What are we going to do about the yacht?" said Leslie,

since Donald and Max, as the owners, appeared to be unperturbed by her fate.

"We'll stops at the next village," said Spiro. "I knows a fishermans there. He'll fix it."

"I think, you know," said Theodore, "if we've got any stimulant with us, it would be an idea to give some to Max. He may possibly suffer from concussion after a blow like that."

"Yes, we've got some brandy," said Mother, delving into the car.

She produced a bottle and a cup.

"Darling girl," said Captain Creech, fixing his wavering eye upon the bottle. "Just what the doctor ordered."

"You're not having any of this," said Mother firmly. "This is for Max."

We had to dispose ourselves in the car as best we could, sitting on each other's laps, trying to give as much space as possible to Max, who had now gone a very nasty leaden colour and was shivering violently in spite of the brandy. To Mother's annoyance, she found herself, willy-nilly, having to be wedged in alongside Captain Creech.

"Sit on my lap," said the Captain hospitably. "Sit on my lap and we can have a little cuddle to keep warm."

"Certainly not," said Mother primly. "I'd rather sit on Donald's lap."

As we drove back across the island to town, the Captain regaled us with his version of some sea-shanties. The family argued acrimoniously.

"I do wish you'd stop him singing these songs, Larry," said Mother.

"How can I stop him? *You're* in the back. *You* stop him."

"He's *your* friend," said Mother.

"Ain't it a pity, she's only one titty to feed the baby on. The poor little bugger will never play rugger and grow up big and strong."

"Might have killed you all, filthy old brute," said Mother.

"Actually, most of it was Larry's fault," said Leslie.

"It was not," said Larry indignantly. "You weren't there, so you don't know. It's extremely difficult when someone shouts at you to luff your helm, or whatever it is, when there's a howling gale blowing."

"There was a young lady from Chichester," observed Captain Creech with relish, "who made all the saints in their niches stir."

"The one I'm sorry for is poor Max," said Margo, looking at him commiseratingly.

"I don't know why he should get the sympathy," said Larry, whose eye had now almost completely disappeared and was a rich shiny black. "He's the fool who caused it all. I had the boat under perfect control till he hauled up that sail."

"Well, I don't call you a sailor," said Margo. "If you'd been a sailor you wouldn't have told him to haul it up."

"That's just the point," snarled Larry. "I didn't tell him to haul it up. He hauled it up on his own."

"It was the good ship Venus," began the Captain, whose repertoire appeared to be inexhaustible.

"Don't argue about it, dear," said Mother. "I've got a severe headache. The sooner we get into town, the better."

We got to town eventually and dropped Donald and Max at their hotel and the still caroling Captain Creech at his and drove home, wet and cold and acrimonious.

The following morning we were sitting, all feeling slightly wilted, finishing our breakfast on the veranda. Larry's eye had now achieved sunset hues which could only have been captured by the brush of Turner. Spiro drove up honking his horn, the dogs racing in front of the car, snarling and trying to bite the wheels.

"I do wish Spiro wouldn't make quite so much noise when he arrives," said Larry.

Spiro stumped up onto the veranda and went through his normal morning routine.

"Morning, Mrs. Durrells, morning Missy Margo, morning

Master Larrys, morning Master Leslies, morning Master Gerrys. How's your eyes, Master Larrys?" he said, screwing up his face into a commiserating scowl.

"At the moment I feel as if I shall probably be going round with a white stick for the rest of my days," said Larry.

"I've got a letters for yous," said Spiro to Mother.

Mother put on her glasses and opened it. We waited expectantly. Her face went red.

"The impertinence! The insolence! Disgusting old *brute!* Really, I have never heard anything like it."

"What on earth's the matter?" asked Larry.

"That revolting old Creech creature," said Mother, waving the letter at him.

"It's *your* fault, *you* introduced him to the house."

"What have I done now?" asked Larry, bewildered.

"That filthy old brute has written and proposed to me," said Mother.

There was a moment's stunned silence while we took in this remarkable information.

"Proposal?" said Larry cautiously. "An indecent proposal, I presume?"

"No, no," said Mother. "He says he wants to marry me. What a fine little woman I am and a lot of sentimental twaddle like that."

The family, united for once, sat back and laughed until tears came.

"It's no laughing matter," said Mother, stamping about the veranda. "You've got to *do* something about it."

"Oh," said Larry, mopping his eyes. "Oh, this is the best thing that's happened for ages. I suppose he thinks since he took his trousers off in front of you yesterday to wring them out, he must make an honest woman of you."

"Do stop laughing," said Mother angrily. "It isn't *funny.*"

"I can see it all," said Larry unctuously. "You in white muslin, Leslie and me in toppers to give you away, Margo as your bridesmaid, and Gerry as your page. It will be very affecting scene. I expect the church will be full of jaded ladies of pleasure, all waiting to forbid the bans."

Mother glared at him. "When there's a *real* crisis," she said angrily, "you children are of absolutely no use whatsoever."

"But I think you would look lovely in white," said Margo, giggling.

"Where have you decided on for your honeymoon?" asked Larry. "They say Capri is awfully nice at this time of year."

But Mother was not listening. She turned to Spiro, registering determination from top to toe.

"Spiro, you are to tell the Captain the answer is *no*, and that I never want him to set foot in this house again."

"Oh, come now, Mother," protested Larry. "What we children *want* is a father."

"And you all," said Mother, rounding on us in a fury, "are not to tell anybody about this. I will not have my name linked with that disgusting . . . disgusting *reprobate*."

And so that was the last we saw of Captain Creech. But what we all referred to as Mother's great romance made an auspicious start to the year.

THE TALKING HEAD

Summer gaped upon the island like the mouth of a great oven. Even in the shade of the olive groves it was not cool and the incessant, penetrating cries of the cicadas seemed to swell and become more insistent with each hot, blue noon. The water in the ponds and ditches shrank and the mud at the edges became jigsawed, cracked and curled by the sun. The sea lay as breathless and still as a bale of silk, the shallow waters too warm to be refreshing. You had to row the boat out into deep water, you and your reflection the only moving things, and dive over the side to get cool. It was like diving into the sky.

Now was the time for butterflies and moths. In the day, on the hillsides, which seemed sucked free of every drop of moisture by the beating sun, you would get the great languid swallow-tails, flapping elegantly and erratically from bush to bush; fritillaries, glowing almost as hot and angry an orange as a live coal, skittered quickly and efficiently from flower to flower; cabbage whites; clouded yellows; and the lemon-yellow-and-orange brimstones bumbled to and fro on untidy wings. Among the grasses the skippers, like little brown furry aeroplanes, would skim and purr, and on glittering slabs of gypsum the red admirals, as flamboyant as a cluster of Woolworth jewellery, would sit opening and closing their wings as though expiring from the heat. At night the lamps would become a teeming metropolis of moths, and the pink geckos on the ceiling, big-eyed and splay-footed, would gorge until they could hardly move. Oleander hawk-moths, green and silver, would zoom into the room suddenly, from nowhere, and in a frenzy of love, dive at the lamp, hitting it with such force that the glass shattered. Death's-head hawk-moths, mottled ginger and black, with the macabre skull and cross-bones embroidered on the plush fur of their thoraxes, would come tumbling down the chimney to lie fluttering and twitching in the grate, squeaking like mice.

Up on the hillsides where the great beds of heather were burnt crisp and warm by the sun, the tortoises, lizards, and snakes would prowl, and praying mantises would hang among the green leaves of the myrtle, swaying slowly and evilly from side to side. The afternoon was the best time to investigate life on the hills, but it was also the hottest. The sun played a tattoo on your skull, and the baked ground was as hot as a griddle under your sandalled feet. Widdle and Puke were cowards about the sun and would never accompany me in the afternoons, but Roger, that indefatigable student of natural history, would always be with me, panting vigorously, swallowing his drooling saliva in great gulps.

Together we shared many adventures. There was the time when we watched, entranced, two hedgehogs, drunk as lords on the fallen and semi-fermented grapes they had eaten from under the vines, staggering in circles, snapping at each other belligerently, uttering high-pitched screams and hiccups. There was a time we watched a fox cub, red as an autumn leaf, discover his first tortoise among the heather. The tortoise, in the phlegmatic way they have, folded himself up in his shell, tightly closed as a portmanteau. But the fox had seen a movement and, prick-eared, it moved round him cautiously. Then, for it was still only a puppy, it dabbed quickly at the tortoise's shell with its paw and then jumped away, expecting retaliation. Then it lay down and examined the tortoise for several minutes, its head between its paws. Finally it went forward rather gingerly and after several unsuccessful attempts managed to pick the tortoise up with its jaws, and with head held high, trotted off proudly through the heather. It was on these hills that we watched the baby tortoises hatching out of their papery-shelled eggs, each one looking as wizened and as crinkled as though it were a thousand years old at the moment of birth, and it was here that I witnessed for the first time the mating dance of the snakes.

Roger and I were sitting under a large clump of myrtles that offered a small patch of shade and some concealment. We had disturbed a hawk in a cypress tree near by and were waiting patiently for him to return so that we could identify him. Suddenly, some ten feet from where we had crouched, I saw two snakes weaving their way out of a brown web of heather stalks. Roger, who for some obscure reason was frightened of snakes, uttered an uneasy little whine and put his ears back. I shushed him violently and watched to see what the snakes would do. One appeared to be following close on the heels of the other. Was he, I wondered, perhaps in pursuit of it in order to eat it? They slid out of the heather and into some clumps of sun-whitened grass and I lost sight of them. Cursing my luck, I was just about to shift my position in the hopes of seeing them again when they reappeared on a comparatively open piece of ground.

Here the one that was leading paused and the one that had been following it slid up alongside. They lay like this for a moment or so and then the pursuer started to nose tentatively at the other one's head. I decided that the first snake was a female and that her follower was her mate. He continued butting his head at her throat until eventually he had raised her head and neck slightly off the ground. She froze in that position and the male, backing away a few inches, raised his head also and they stayed like that, immobile, staring at each other for some considerable time. Then slowly the male slid forward and twined himself round the female's body and they both rose as high as they could without overbalancing, as entwined together as two convolvulus. Again they remained motionless for a time and then started to sway like two wrestlers pushing against each other in the ring, their tails curling and grasping at the grass roots around them to give themselves better purchase. Suddenly they flopped sideways, the hinder ends of their bodies met and they mated lying there in the sun, as entangled as streamers at a carnival.

At this moment Roger, who had viewed with increasing distress my interest in the snakes, got to his feet and shook himself before I could stop him, indicating that, as far as he was concerned, it would be far better if we moved on. The snakes unfortunately saw his movement. They convulsed in a tangled heap for a moment, their skins gleaming in the sun, and then the female disentangled herself and sped rapidly towards the sanctuary of the heather, dragging the male, still fastened to her, helplessly behind her. Roger looked at me, gave a small sneeze of pleasure, and wagged his stumpy tail. But I was annoyed with him and told him so in no uncertain terms. After all, as I pointed out to him, on the numerous occasions when he was latched to a bitch how would *he* like to be overtaken by some danger and dragged so ignominiously from the field of love?

With the summer came the bands of gypsies to the island to help harvest the crops and to steal what they could while they were there. Sloe-eyed, their dusky skins burnt almost black by the sun, their hair unkempt and their clothing in rags, you would see them moving in family groups along the white, dusty roads, riding on donkeys or on lithe little ponies, shiny as chestnuts. Their encampments were always a squalid enchantment, with a dozen pots bubbling with different ingredients over the fires, the old women squatting in the shadow of their grubby lean-tos with the heads of the younger children in their laps, carefully searching them for lice, while the older children, tattered as dandelion leaves, rolled and screamed and played in the dust. Those of the men who had a side-line would be busy with it, one twisting and tying multi-coloured balloons together, so that they screeched in protest, making strange animal shapes. Another, perhaps, who was the proud possessor of a Karaghiozi shadow show, would be refurbishing the highly coloured cut-out figures and practising some of Karaghiozi's vulgarities and innuendoes to the giggling delight of the handsome young women who stirred the cooking pots or knitted in the shade.

I had always wanted to get on intimate terms with the gypsies, but they were a shy and hostile people, barely tolerating the Greeks. So that my mop of hair, bleached almost white by the sun, and my blue eyes made me automatically suspect, and although they would allow me to visit their camps, they were never forthcoming, in the way that the peasants were in telling me about their private lives and their aspirations. But it was, nevertheless, the gypsies who were indirectly responsible for an uproar in the family. For once I was entirely innocent.

It was the tail-end of an exceptionally hot summer's afternoon. Roger and I had been having an exhausting time pursuing a large and indignant king snake along a length of dry stone wall. No sooner had we dismantled one section of it than the snake would ease himself fluidly along into the next section, and by the time we had rebuilt the section we had pulled down, it would take half an hour or so to locate him again in the jigsaw of rocks. Finally we had to concede defeat and we were now making our way home to tea, thirsty, sweating, and covered with dust. As we rounded an elbow of the road, I glanced into the olive grove that sloped down the hillside into a small valley, and saw what, at first glance, I took to be a man with an exceptionally large dog. A closer look, however, and I realized, incredulously, that it was a man with a bear. I was so astonished that I cried out involuntarily. The bear stood up on its hind legs and turned to look up at me, as did the man. They stared at me for a moment and then the man waved his hand in casual greeting and turned back to the task of spreading his belongings under the olive tree while the bear got down again on its haunches and squatted, watching him with interest. I made my way hurriedly down the hillside, filled with excitement. I had heard that there were dancing bears in Greece, but I had never actually seen one. This was an opportunity too good to be missed. As I drew near, I called a greeting to the man and he turned from his jumble of possessions and replied courteously enough. I saw that he was indeed a gypsy, with the dark, wild eyes and the blue-black hair, but he was infinitely more prosperous-looking than most of them, for his suit was in good repair and he wore shoes, a mark of distinction in those days, even among the landed peasantry of the island.

I asked whether it was safe to approach, for the bear, although wearing a leather muzzle, was untethered.

"Yes, come," called the man. "Pavlo won't hurt you, but leave your dog."

I turned to Roger and I could see that, brave though he was, he did not like the look of the bear and was staying by me only out of a sense of duty. When I told him to go home, he gave me a grateful look and trotted off up the hillside, trying to pretend that he was ignorant of the whole scene. In spite of the man's assurances that Pavlo was harmless, I approached with caution, for although it was only a youngster, the bear, when it reared on its hind legs, was a good foot or so taller than I was and possessed on each broad, furry paw a formidable and very serviceable array of glittering claws. It squatted on its haunches and peered at me out of tiny, twinkling brown eyes, panting gently. It looked like a large pile of animated, unkempt seaweed. To me it was the most desirable animal I had ever set eyes on and I walked round it, viewing its excellence from every possible vantage point.

I plied the man with eager questions. How old was it? Where did he get it? What was he doing with it?

"He dances for his living and for my living," said the man, obviously amused by my enthusiasm over the bear. "Here, I'll show you."

He picked up a stick with a small hook at the end and slid it into a ring set into the leather muzzle the bear wore.

"Come, dance with your papa."

In one swift movement the bear rose on its hind legs. The man clicked his fingers and whistled a plaintive tune, starting to shuffle his feet in time to the music and the bear followed suit. Together they shuffled in a slow, stately minuet among the electric blue thistles and the dried asphodel stalks. I could have watched them forever. When the man reached the end of his tune, the bear, as of habit, got down on all fours again and sneezed.

"Bravo!" said the man softly. "Bravo!"

I clapped enthusiastically. Never, I said earnestly, had I seen such a fine dance, nor such an accomplished performer as Pavlo. Could I, perhaps, pat him?

"You can do what you like with him," said the man, chuckling, as he unhooked his stick from the bear's muzzle. "He's a fool, this one. He wouldn't even hurt a bandit who was robbing him of his food."

To prove it he started scratching the bear's back and the bear, pointing its head up into the sky, uttered throaty, wheezy murmurings of pleasure and sank gradually down onto the ground in ecstasy, until he was spread out looking almost, I thought, like a bearskin rug.

"He likes to be tickled," said the man. "Come and tickle him."

The next half hour was pure delight for me. I tickled the bear while he crooned with delight. I examined his great claws and his ears and his tiny bright eyes and he lay there and suffered me as though he were asleep. Then I leaned against his warm bulk and talked to his owner. A plan was forming in my mind. The bear, I decided, had got to become mine. The dogs and my other animals would soon get used to it and together we could go waltzing over the hillsides. I convinced myself that the family would be overjoyed at my acquisition of such an intelligent pet. But first I had to get the man into a suitable frame of mind for bargaining. With the peasants, bargaining was a loud, protracted, and difficult business. But this man was a gypsy and what they did not know about bargaining would fit conveniently into an acorn cup. The man seemed much less taciturn and reticent than the other gypsies I had come into contact with, and I took this as a good sign. I asked him where he had come from.

"Way beyond, way beyond," he said, covering his possessions with a shabby tarpaulin and shaking out some threadbare blankets which were obviously going to serve as his bed. "Landed at Lefkimi last night and we've been walking ever since, Pavlo, the Head, and I. You see, they wouldn't take Pavlo on the buses; they were frightened of him. So we got no sleep last night, but tonight we'll sleep here and then tomorrow we'll reach the town."

Intrigued, I asked him what he meant by "he, Pavlo, and the Head" walking up from Lefkimi?

"My Head, of course," he said. "My little talking Head." And he picked up the bear stick and slapped it on a pile of goods under the tarpaulin, grinning at me.

I had unearthed the battered remains of a bar of chocolate from the pocket of my shorts and I was busy feeding this to the bear, who received each fragment with great moans and slobberings of satisfaction. I said to the man that I did not understand what he was talking about. He squatted on his haunches in front of me and lit a cigarette, peering at me out of dark eyes, as enigmatic as a lizard's.

"I have a Head," he said, jerking his thumb towards his pile of belongings, "a living Head. It talks and answers questions. It is without doubt the most remarkable thing in the world."

I was puzzled. Did he mean, I asked, a head without a body?

"Of course without a body. Just a head," and he cupped his hands in front of him, as though holding a coconut.

"It sits on a little stick and talks to you. Nothing like it has ever been seen in the world."

But how, I inquired, if the head were a disembodied head, could it live?

"Magic," said the man solemnly. "Magic that my great-great-grandfather passed down to me."

I felt sure that he was pulling my leg, but intriguing though the discussion on talking heads was, I felt we were wandering away from my main objective, which was to acquire the immediate freehold of Pavlo, now sucking in through his muzzle, with wheezy sighs of satisfaction, my very last bit of chocolate. I studied the man carefully as he squatted, dreamy-eyed, his head enveloped in a cloud of smoke. I decided that with him the bold approach was the best. I asked him bluntly whether he would consider selling the bear and for how much.

"Sell Pavlo?" he said. "Never! He's like my own son."

Surely, I said, if he went to a good home? Somewhere where he was loved and allowed to dance, surely then he might be tempted to sell? The man looked at me, meditatively puffing on his cigarette.

"Twenty million drachmas?" he inquired, and then laughed at my look of consternation. "Men who have fields must have donkeys to work them," he said. "They don't part with them easily. Pavlo is my donkey. He dances for his living and he dances for mine, and until he is too old to dance, I will not part with him."

I was bitterly disappointed, but I could see that he was adamant. I rose from my recumbent position on the broad, warm, faintly snoring back of Pavlo and dusted myself down. Well, I said, there was nothing more I could do. I understood his wanting to keep the bear, but if he changed his mind, would he get in touch with me? He nodded gravely. And if he was performing in town, could he possibly let me know where, so that I could attend?

"Of course," he said, "but I think people will tell you where I am, for my Head is extraordinary."

I nodded and shook his hand. Pavlo got to his feet and I patted his head.

When I reached the top of the valley I looked back. They were both standing side by side. The man waved briefly and Pavlo, swaying on his hind legs, had his muzzle in the air, questing after me with his nose. I liked to feel it was a gesture of farewell.

I walked slowly home thinking about the man and his talking head and the wonderful Pavlo. Would it be possible, I wondered, for me to get a bear cub from somewhere and rear it? Perhaps if I advertised in a newspaper in Athens it might bring results.

The family were in the drawing-room having tea and I decided to put my problem to them. As I entered the room, however, a startling change came over what had been a placid scene. Margo uttered a piercing scream, Larry dropped a cup full of tea into his lap and then leaped up and took refuge behind the table, while Leslie picked up a chair and Mother gaped at me with a look of horror on her face. I had never known my presence to provoke quite such a positive reaction on the part of the family.

"Get it out of here," roared Larry.

"Yes, get the bloody thing out," said Leslie.

"It'll kill us all!" screamed Margo.

"Get a gun," said Mother faintly. "Get a gun and save Gerry."

I couldn't, for the life of me, think what was the matter with them. They were all staring at something behind me. I turned and looked and there, standing in the doorway, sniffing hopefully towards the tea-table, was Pavlo. I went up to him and caught hold of his muzzle. He nuzzled at me affectionately. I explained to the family that it was only Pavlo.

"I am not *having* it," said Larry throatily. "I am not *having* it. Birds and dogs and hedgehogs all over the house and now a bear. What does he think this is, for Christ's sake? A bloody Roman arena?"

"Gerry, dear, do be careful," said Mother quaveringly. "It looks rather fierce."

"It will kill us all," quavered Margo with conviction.

"I can't get past it to get to my guns," said Leslie.

"You are *not* going to have it. I forbid it," said Larry. "I will *not* have the place turned into a bear pit."

"Where did you get it, dear?" asked Mother.

"I don't care *where* he got it," said Larry. "He's to take it back this instant, quickly, before it rips us to pieces. The boy's got no sense of responsibility. I am not going to be turned into an early Christian martyr at my time of life."

Pavlo got up on his hind legs and uttered a long wheezing moan which I took to mean that he desired to join us in partaking of whatever delicacies there were on the tea-table. The family interpreted it differently.

"Ow!" screeched Margo, as though she had been bitten. "It's attacking."

"Gerry, *do* be careful," said Mother.

"I'll not be responsible for what I do to that boy," said Larry.

"If you survive," said Leslie. "Do shut up, Margo, you're only making matters worse. You'll provoke the bloody thing."

"I can scream if I want to," said Margaret indignantly.

So raucous in their fear were the family that they had not given me a chance to explain. Now I attempted to. I said that, first of all, Pavlo was not mine, and secondly, he was as tame as a dog and would not hurt a fly.

"Two statements I refuse to believe," said Larry. "You pinched it from some flaming circus. Not only are we to be disembowelled, but arrested for harbouring stolen goods as well."

"Now, now, dear," said Mother, "let Gerry explain."

"Explain?" said Larry. "Explain? How do you explain a bloody great bear in the drawing-room?"

I said that the bear belonged to a gypsy who had a talking head.

"What do you mean, a talking head?" asked Margo.

I said that it was a disembodied head that talked.

"The boy's mad," said Larry with conviction. "The sooner we have him certified the better."

The family had now all backed away to the farthest corner of the room in a trembling group. I said, indignantly, that my story was perfectly true and that, to prove it, I'd make Pavlo dance. I seized a piece of cake from the table, hooked my finger into the ring on his muzzle, and uttered the same commands as his master had done. His eyes fixed greedily on the cake, Pavlo roared up and danced with me.

"Oo, look!" said Margo. "Look! It's dancing!"

"I don't care if it's behaving like a whole *corps de ballet*," said Larry. "I want the damn thing out of here."

I shovelled the cake in through Pavlo's muzzle and he sucked it down greedily.

"He really is rather sweet," said Mother, adjusting her spectacles and staring at him with interest. "I remember my brother had a bear in India once. She was a very nice pet."

"No!" said Larry and Leslie simultaneously. "He's not having it."

I said I could not have it anyway, because the man did not want to sell it.

"A jolly good thing, too," said Larry.

"Why don't you now return it to him, if you have quite finished doing a cabaret act all over the tea-table?"

Getting another slice of cake as a bribe, I hooked my finger once more in the ring on Pavlo's muzzle and led him out of the house. Half-way back to the olive grove, I met the distraught owner.

"There he is! There he is! The wicked one. I couldn't think where he had got to. He never leaves my side normally, that's why I don't keep him tied up. He must have taken a great fancy to you."

Honesty made me admit that I thought the only reason Pavlo had followed me was because he viewed me in the light of a purveyor of chocolates.

"Phew!" said the man. "It is a relief to me. I thought he might have gone down to the village and that would have got me into trouble with the police."

Reluctantly, I handed Pavlo over to his owner and watched them make their way back to their camp under the trees. And then, in some trepidation, I went back to face the family. Although it had not been my fault that Pavlo had followed me, I'm afraid that my activities in the past stood against me, and the family took a lot of convincing that, on this occasion, the guilt was not mine.

The following morning, my head still filled with thoughts of Pavlo, I dutifully went into town—as I did every morning—to the house of my tutor, Richard Kralefsky. Kralefsky was a little gnome of a man with a slightly humped back and great, earnest, amber eyes, who suffered from real tortures in his unsuccessful attempts to educate me. He had two most endearing qualities: one was a deep love for natural history (the whole attic of his house was devoted to an enormous variety of canaries and other birds); the other was the fact that, for at least a part of the time, he lived in a dream-world where he was always the hero. These adventures he would relate to me. He was inevitably accompanied in them by a heroine who was never named, but known simply as "a lady."

The first half of the morning was devoted to mathematics, and with my head full of thoughts of Pavlo, I proved to be even duller than usual, to the consternation of Kralefsky, who had hitherto been under the impression that he had plumbed the depths of my ignorance.

"My dear boy, you simply aren't concentrating this morning," he said earnestly. "You don't seem able to grasp the simplest fact. Perhaps you are a trifle overtired? We'll have a short rest from it, shall we?"

Kralefsky enjoyed these short rests as much as I did. He would potter about in the kitchen and bring back two cups of coffee and some biscuits, and we would sit companionably while he told me highly coloured stories of his imaginary adventures. But this particular morning he did not get a chance. As soon as we were sitting comfortably, sipping our coffee, I told him all about Pavlo and the man with the talking head and the bear.

"Quite extraordinary!" he said. "Not the sort of thing one expects to find in an olive grove. It must have surprised you, I'll be bound."

Then his eyes glazed and he fell into a reverie, staring at the ceiling, tipping his cup of coffee so that it slopped into the saucer. It was obvious that my interest in the bear had set off a train of thought in his mind. It had been several days since I had had an instalment of his memoirs, and so I waited eagerly to see what the result would be.

"When I was a *young* man," began Kralefsky, glancing at me earnestly to see whether I was listening, "when I was a young man, I'm afraid I was a bit of a harum-scarum. Always getting into trouble, you know."

He chuckled reminiscently and brushed a few biscuit crumbs from his waistcoat. With his delicately manicured hands and his large, gentle eyes it was difficult to imagine him as a harum-scarum, but I tried dutifully.

"I thought at one time I would even join a *circus*," he said, with the air of one confessing to infanticide. "I remember a large circus came to the village where we were living and I attended every performance. Every single performance. I got to know the circus folk quite well, and they even taught me some of their tricks. They said I was *excellent* on the trapeze." He glanced at me, shyly, to see how I would take this. I nodded seriously, as though there were nothing ludicrous in the thought of Kralefsky, in a pair of spangled tights, on a trapeze.

"Have another biscuit?" he inquired. "Yes? That's the ticket! I think I'll have one, too."

Munching my biscuit I waited patiently for him to resume.

"Well," he continued, "the week simply flew past and the

evening came for the final performance. I wouldn't have missed it for the world. I was accompanied by a lady, a young friend of mine, who was desirous of seeing the performance. How she laughed at the clowns! *And* admired the horses. She little knew of the horror that was soon to strike."

He took out his delicately scented handkerchief and patted his moist brow with it. He always tended to get a trifle over-excited as he reached the climax of a story.

"The final act," he said, "was the lion-tamer." He paused so that the full portent of this statement could sink in. "Five beasts he had. Huge Nubian lions with black manes, fresh from the jungle, so he told me. The lady and I were sitting in the front row where we could obtain the best possible view of the ring. You know the sort of cage affair that they put up in the ring for the lion act? Well, in the middle of the act, one of the sections, which had not been securely bolted, fell inwards. To our horror, we saw it fall on the lion-tamer, knocking him unconscious instantly." He paused, took a nervous sip of coffee and then wiped his brow once more.

"What was to be done?" he inquired rhetorically. "There were five huge, snarling lions and I had a lady by my side. My thoughts worked fast. If the lady was to be saved, there was only one thing I could think of. Seizing my walking-stick, I leaped into the ring and marched into the cage."

I made just audible sounds, indicative of admiration.

"During the week when I had been visiting the circus, I had studied the lion-tamer's method with great care, and now I thanked my lucky stars for it. The snarling beasts on their pedestals towered over me, but I looked them straight in the eye. The human eye, you know, has great power over the animal world. Slowly, fixing them with a piercing gaze and pointing my walking-stick at them, I got them under control and drove them inch by inch out of the ring and back into their cage. A dreadful tragedy had been averted."

I said that the lady must have been grateful to him.

"She was indeed. She was indeed," said Kralefsky, pleased. "She even went so far as to say that I gave a better performance than the lion-tamer himself."

Had he, I wondered, during his circus days, ever had anything to do with dancing bears?

"All sorts of animals," said Kralefsky lavishly. "Elephants, seals, performing dogs, bears. They were all there."

In that case, I said tentatively, would he not like to come and see the dancing bear. It was only just down the road, and although it was not exactly a circus, I felt it might interest him.

"By Jove, that's an idea," said Kralefsky. He pulled his watch out of his waistcoat pocket and consulted it. "Ten minutes, eh? It'll help blow the cobwebs away."

He got his hat and stick and together we made our way eagerly through the narrow, crowded streets of the town, redolent with the smell of fruits and vegetables, drains, and freshly baked bread. By dint of questioning several small boys, we discovered where Pavlo's owner was holding his show. It was a large, dim barn at the back of a shop in the centre of town. On the way there I had borrowed some money of Kralefsky and purchased a bar of sticky nougat, for I felt I could not go to see Pavlo without taking him a present.

"Ah, Pavlo's friend! Welcome," said the gypsy as we appeared in the doorway of the barn.

To my delight, Pavlo recognized me and came shuffling forward, uttering little grunts, and then reared up on his hind legs in front of me. Kralefsky backed away, rather hurriedly, I thought, for one of his circus training, and took a firmer grip on his stick.

"Do be careful, my boy," he said.

I fed the nougat to Pavlo and when finally he had squelched the last sticky lump off his back teeth and swallowed it, he gave a contented sigh and lay down with his head between his paws.

"Do you want to see the Head?" asked the gypsy. He

gestured towards the back of the barn where there was a plain deal table on which was a square box, apparently made out of cloth.

"Wait," he said, "and I'll light the candles."

He had a dozen or so large candles soldered to the top of a box in their own wax, and these he now lit so they flickered and quivered and made the shadows dance. Then he went forward to the table and rapped on it with his bear stick.

"Head, are you ready?" he asked.

I waited with a delicate prickle of apprehension in my spine. Then from the interior of the cloth box a clear treble voice said, "Yes, I'm ready."

The man lifted the cloth at one side of the box and I saw that the box was formed of slender lathes on which thin cloth had been loosely tacked. The box was about three feet square. In the centre of it was a small pedestal with a flattened top and on it, looking macabre in the flickering light of the candles, was the head of a seven-year-old boy.

"By Jove!" said Kralefsky in admiration. "That is clever!"

What astonished me was that the head was *alive*. It was obviously the head of a young gypsy lad, made up rather crudely with black grease paint to look like a Negro. It stared at us and blinked its eyes.

"Are you ready to answer questions now?" asked the gypsy, looking, with obvious satisfaction, at the entranced Kralefsky. The Head licked its lips and then said, "Yes, I am ready."

"How old are you?" asked the gypsy.

"Over a thousand years old," said the Head.

"Where do you come from?"

"I come from Africa and my name is Ngo."

The gypsy droned on with his questions and the Head answered them, but I was not interested in that. What I wanted to know was *how* the trick was done. When he first told me about the Head, I had expected something carved out of wood or plaster which, by ventriloquism, could be made to speak, but this was a living head perched on a little wooden pedestal, the circumference of a candle. I had no doubt that the Head was alive for its eyes wandered to and fro as it answered the questions automatically, and once, when Pavlo got up and shook himself, a look of apprehension came over its face.

"There," said the gypsy proudly when he had finished his questioning. "I told you, didn't I? It's the most remarkable thing in the world."

I asked him whether I could examine the whole thing more closely. I had suddenly remembered that Theodore had told me of a similar illusion which was created with the aid of mirrors. I did not see where it was possible to conceal the body that obviously belonged to the Head, but I felt that the table and the box needed investigation.

"Certainly," said the gypsy, somewhat to my surprise. "Here, take my stick. But all I ask is that you don't touch the Head itself."

Carefully, with the aid of the stick, I poked all round the pedestal to see if there were any concealed mirrors or wires, and the Head watched me with a slightly amused expression in its black eyes. The sides of the box were definitely only of cloth and the floor of the box was, in fact, the top of the table on which it stood. I walked round the back of it and I could see nothing. I even crawled under the table, but there was nothing there and certainly no room to conceal a body. I was completely mystified.

"Ah," said the gypsy in triumph. "You didn't expect that, did you? You thought I had a boy concealed in there, didn't you?"

I admitted the charge humbly and begged him to tell me how it was done.

"Oh, no. I can't tell you," he said. "It's magic. If I told you, the head would disappear in a puff of smoke."

I examined both the box and the table for a second time, but, even bringing a candle closer to aid my investigations, I still could not see how it was possible.

"Come," said the gypsy. "Enough of the Head. Come and dance with Pavlo."

He hooked the stick into the bear's muzzle and Pavlo rose on his hind legs. The gypsy handed the stick to me and then picked up a small wooden flute and started to play, and Pavlo and I did a solemn dance together.

"Excellent, by Jove! Excellent!" said Kralefsky, clapping his hands with enthusiasm. I suggested that he might like to dance with Pavlo too, since he had such vast circus experience.

"Well, now," said Kralefsky. "I wonder whether it would be altogether wise? The animal, you see, is not familiar with me."

"Oh, he'll be all right," said the gypsy. "He's tame with anyone."

"Well," said Kralefsky reluctantly, "if you're sure. If you insist."

He took the bear stick gingerly from me and stood facing Pavlo, looking extremely apprehensive.

"And now," said the gypsy, "you will dance."

And he started to play a lilting little tune on his pipe.

I stood enchanted by the sight. The yellow, flickering light of the candles showed the shadows of Kralefsky's little hump-backed figure and the shaggy form of the bear on the wall as they pirouetted round and round, and squatting on its pedestal in the box, the Head watched them, grinning and chuckling to itself.

10

THE ANGRY BARRELS

At the tail-end of the summer came the grape harvest. Throughout the year you had been aware of the vineyards as part of the scenery, but it was only when the grape harvest came that you remembered the sequence of events that led up to it: the vineyards in winter, when the vines looked dead, like so many pieces of driftwood stuck in lines in the soil; and then the day in spring when you first noticed a green sheen on each vine as the delicate, frilly little leaves uncurled. And then the leaves grew larger and hung on the vines, like green hands warming themselves in the heat of the sun. After that the grapes started to appear, tiny nodules on a branched stem, which gradually grew and plumped themselves in the sunlight until they looked like the jade eggs of some strange sea-monster. Then was the time for the washing of the vines. The lime and copper sulphate in big barrels would be dragged to the vineyards in little wooden carts pulled by the ever-patient donkeys. The sprayers would appear in their uniforms that made them look like visitors from another planet: goggles and masks, a great canister strapped on their backs from which led a rubber pipe, as mobile as an elephant's trunk, through which the liquid would run. This mixture was of a blue that put the sky and the sea to shame. It was the distilled blueness of everything blue in the world. Tanks would be filled and the sprayers would move through the frilly groves of vine, covering each leaf, wrapping each bunch of green grapes in a delicate web of Madonna blue. Under this protective blue mantle, the grapes swelled and ripened until at last, in the hot dog-days of summer, they were ready to be plucked and eased of their juice.

The grape harvest was so important that it naturally became a time of visiting, a time of picnics and of celebrations, a time when you brought out last year's wine and mused over it.

We had been invited to attend a wine harvest by a Mr. Stavrodakis, a tiny, kindly, wizened little man with a face like that of a half-starved tortoise, who owned a villa and some big vineyards towards the north of the island. He was a man who lived for his wine, who thought that was the most important thing in the world; and so his invitation was delivered with all the solemnity befitting such an occasion and was received with equal solemnity by the family. In his note of invitation, written in bold copper plate, embellished with little frills and flourishes so that it looked like a wrought-iron tracery, he had said, "Do please feel free to bring those of your friends that you think might enjoy this."

"Wonderful," said Larry. "He's supposed to have the best cellar in Corfu."

"Well, I suppose we can go if you want to," said Mother doubtfully.

"Of course I want to," said Larry. "Think of all that wine. I tell you what, we'll hire a benzina and make up a party."

"Oh, yes," said Margo eagerly. "He's got that marvellous beach on his estate. We must get in some more swimming before the summer ends."

"We can invite Sven," said Larry. "He should be back by then. And we'll ask Donald and Max to come along."

"And Theodore," said Leslie.

"Larry dear," said Mother, "the man's only invited us to watch his grapes being pressed or whatever it is they do; you can't take a whole assortment of people along with you."

"He says in his letter to bring any of our friends we want to," said Larry.

"Yes, but you can't take a whole circus," said Mother. "How's the poor man going to feed us all?"

"Well, that's easily solved," said Larry. "Write and tell him that we'll bring our own food."

"I suppose that means I'll have to cook it," said Mother.

"Nonsense," said Larry vaguely. "We'll just take a few chops or something and grill them over an open fire."

"I know what *that* means," said Mother.

"Well, surely you can organize it somehow," said Larry. "After all, it seems to me a perfectly simple thing to do."

"Well," said Mother reluctantly, "I'll have a word with Spiro in the morning and see what can be done."

The result was that Mother penned a careful note to Mr. Stavrodakis saying that we would be delighted to accept his invitation and bring a few friends. We would bring our own food and picnic on the beach, if we might. Mr. Stavrodakis sent back another piece of copper-plate topiary expressing himself overwhelmed at our kindness in accepting his invitation and saying that he looked forward to seeing us. He added, "Do please come undressed as we are in the family way." The phrase puzzled us all considerably—since he was a bachelor of long standing—until we realized he had translated it literally from the French.

The party finally consisted of Donald and Max, Theodore, Kralefsky, Sven, who had turned up in the nick of time from Athens, Spiro, and the family. We assembled at six thirty in the morning at the sunken steps behind the king's palace in the town, where a dumpy, freshly painted benzina waited, bobbing a greeting to us on the tiny ripples. Getting on board took us quite some time. There were the numerous hampers of food and wine, the cooking utensils, and Mother's enormous umbrella which she refused to travel without during the summer months. Then Kralefsky, bowing and beaming, had to go through the performance of handing Mother and Margo on board.

"Gently now. Don't stumble. That's the ticket!" he said as he escorted them both onto the boat with all the courtesy of a doge handing his latest mistress into a gondola.

"Fortunately," said Theodore, peering up at the blue sky penetratingly from under the brim of his Homburg, "fortunately it looks as though it's going to be er . . . um . . . you know, a fine day. I'm glad of that, for, as you know, the slightest motion upsets me."

Sven missed his footing as he was getting on board and almost dropped his precious accordion into the sea, but it was retrieved from a watery death by Max's long arm. Eventually we were all on board. The benzina was pushed out, the engine was started, and we were off. In the pale, pearly, early morning haze, the town looked like a child's town, built of toppling bricks. The façades of tall, elderly Venetian houses of the town, crumbling gently, coloured in pale shades of cream and brown and white and cyclamen pink, were blurred by the haze so they looked like a smudged pastel drawing.

"A life on the ocean wave!" said Kralefsky, inhaling the warm, still air dramatically. "That's the ticket!"

"Although the sea *looks* so calm," observed Theodore, "there is, I think, a slight—almost imperceptible—motion."

"What rubbish, Theodore," said Larry. "You could lay a spirit level on this sea and you wouldn't get a wink out of the bubble."

"Is Muzzer comfortable?" inquired Max lovingly of Mother.

"Oh, yes, dear, thank you, quite comfortable," she said, "but I'm a little bit worried. I'm not sure whether Spiro remembered the garlic."

"Don't you worries Mrs. Durrells," said Spiro, who had overheard the remark. "I gots all the things that you tells me to get."

Sven, having examined his accordion with the utmost care to make sure that it had come to no harm, now lashed it round himself and ran an experimental series of fingers up its keyboard.

"A rousing sea-shanty," said Donald. "That's what we need. Yo, ho, ho, and a bottle of rum."

I left them and made my way up into the bow of the benzina where I lay, staring down over the prow as it sheared its way through the glassy blue sea. Occasionally little flocks of flying fish would break the surface ahead of us, glittering blue and moon silver in the sun, as they burst from the water and skimmed along the surface, like insect-gleaning summer swallows across a blue meadow.

At eight o'clock we reached our destination, a half-mile-long beach that lay under the flanks of Pandokrator. Here the olive grove came almost to the sea, separated from it only by a wide strip of shingle. As we approached the shore, the engine was switched off and we drifted in gently under our own momentum. Now that there was no engine noise we could hear the cries of the cicadas welcoming us to land. The benzina, with an enormous sigh, pressed its bow into the pebbles of the shallows. The lithe, brown boy, whose boat it was, came forward from the engine and leaped from the bow with the anchor, which he lodged firmly in the shingle. Then he piled a collection of boxes alongside the bow of the benzina in a sort of tottering staircase down which Mother and Margo were escorted by Kralefsky, who bowed elegantly as each reached the shingle, but somewhat marred the effect by inadvertently stepping backwards into six inches of seawater and irretrievably ruining the crease of his elegant trousering. Eventually we and all our goods and chattels were ashore, and leaving our possessions under the olive trees, strewn haphazardly like something from a wrecked ship that had been disgorged by the sea, we made our way up the hill to Stavrodakis' villa.

The villa was large and square, faded red with green shutters and built up high so that the lower floor formed a spacious cellar. Streams of peasant girls were walking up the drive carrying baskets of grapes on their heads, moving with the lithe gracefulness of cats. Stavrodakis came scuttling among them to greet us.

"So kind, so kind! Really so kind!" he kept repeating as each introduction was made.

He seated us all on his veranda under a great carnival-red wig of bougainvillæa and opened several bottles of his best wine. It was heavy and sharp and glowed a sullen red as though he were pouring garnets into our glasses. When we were fortified and slightly light-headed with this brew, he led us, skittering ahead like an amiable black beetle, down to his cellars.

The cellars were so big that their dimmest recesses had to be lit by oil lamps, little flickering wicks floating in pots of amber oil. The cellar was divided into two parts, and he led us first to where the treading was taking place. Looming over everything else in the dim light were three gigantic barrels. One of them was being filled with grapes by a constant procession of peasant women. The other two were occupied by the treaders. In the corner, seated on an upturned keg, was a grey, fragile-looking old man who, with great solemnity, was playing on a fiddle.

"That's Taki and that's Yani," said Stavrodakis, pointing to the two wine-treaders.

Taki's head could only just be seen above the rim of the barrel, whereas Yani's head and shoulders were still visible.

"Taki's been treading since last night," said Stavrodakis, glancing nervously at Mother and Margo, "so I'm afraid he's a little bit inebriated."

Indeed, from where we stood we could smell the heady fumes of the grape pulp and they were intoxicating enough, so their force must have been trebled when concentrated in the warm depths of the barrel. From the base of the barrel the crude young wine dribbled out into a trough, where it lay smouldering with patches of froth on top as pink as almond blossom. From here it was syphoned off into barrels.

"This is, of course, the end of the harvest," Stavrodakis was explaining. "These are the last of the red grapes. They come from a little vineyard high up and produce, I venture to think, one of the better wines of Corfu."

Taki momentarily stopped his jig on the grapes, hooked arms over the side of the barrel and hung there like a drunken swallow on its nest, his arms and hands stained with wine and covered with a crust of grape skins and seeds.

"It's time I came out," he said thickly, "or I shall be as drunk as a lord."

"Yes, yes, in a minute, my Taki," said Stavrodakis, looking round him nervously. "In a minute Costos will be here to relieve you."

"One must pee," Taki explained aggrievedly. "A man can't work unless he pees."

The old man put down his fiddle, and presumably by way of compensation, handed Taki a lump of coarse bread, which he ate wolfishly.

Theodore was giving Sven an erudite lecture on wines, pointing at both treaders and the barrels with his walking-stick as though they had been objects in a museum.

"Who was it?" said Max to Larry, "that drownded in a butt of malmsey?"

"One of Shakespeare's more sensible heroes," said Larry.

"I remember once," Kralefsky said to Donald, "taking a lady round one of the biggest cellars in France. Half-way round the cellar I began to feel uneasy. I had a premonition of danger and so I escorted the lady out and at that moment fourteen of the barrels burst with a roar like cannons . . ."

"Here, as you have seen, we do the treading," said Stavrodakis. "Now if you will just follow me this way, I'll show you where the wine is stored."

He led us through an archway into the other gloomy section of the cellar. Here rank after rank of barrels lay on their sides and the noise was incredible. At first I thought it must have some outside source, until I realized that it emanated from the barrels. As the wine fermented in their brown bellies, the barrels gurgled and squeaked and growled at each other like an angry mob. The sound was fascinating, but slightly horrific. It was as though in each barrel there were incarcerated some frightful demon mouthing incomprehensible abuse.

"The peasants say," said Theodore with macabre relish, tapping one of the barrels lightly with his stick, "the peasants say that it sounds like a drowning man."

"Malmsey!" said Max excitedly. "Barrels and barrels of malmsey! Larry, we'll get drownded together!"

"Drowned," said Donald.

"Most interesting," Mother was saying insincerely to Stavrodakis, "but if you will excuse us, I think Margo and I had better go back to the beach and see about lunch."

"I wonder what force it generates in there," said Leslie, glancing round moodily. "I mean, if it generated sufficient force to push one of those bungs out, I wonder what power it would have?"

"Quite considerable," said Theodore. "I remember once seeing a man who was quite badly injured by the bung from a barrel." As if to demonstrate this, he tapped a barrel sharply with his stick and we all jumped.

"Yes, well, if you will excuse us," said Mother nervously, "I think Margo and I had better be going."

"But the rest of you, the rest of you will come up to the house and have some wine?" pleaded Stavrodakis.

"Of course we will," said Larry, as though he were doing him a favour.

"Malmsey!" said Max, rolling his eyes in ecstasy. "We will have malmsey!"

So while Margo and Mother went back to the beach to help Spiro in the preparations for lunch, Stavrodakis fussily hurried us back onto the veranda and plied us with wine, so that when it was time for us to go back to the beach, we were mellow, warm, and flushed.

" 'I dreamt,' " carolled Max as we walked through the olives, taking a delighted Stavrodakis with us to share our lunch, " 'I dreamt that I dwelt in marble halls' with vessels and turfs by my side."

"He just does it to annoy me," Donald confided to Theodore. "He knows that song perfectly well."

Under the trees at the edge of the sea, three charcoal fires had been lighted and they glowed, shuddered, and smoked gently, and over them popped and sizzled a variety of foods. Margo had laid a great cloth in the shade and was putting cutlery and glasses on it, singing untunefully to herself while Mother and Spiro crouched like witches over the fires, larding the brown sizzling carcass of a kid with oil and squeezed garlic and anointing the great body of a fish—its skin bubbled and crisped enticingly by the heat—with lemon juice.

Lunch we ate in a leisurely fashion, sprawled round the bright cloth, the glasses glowing with wine. The mouthfuls of kid were rich and succulent, woven with herbs, and the sections of fish melted like snow-flakes in your mouth. The conversation drifted and sprang up and then coiled languidly again, like the smoke from the fires.

"You have to be in love with a piece of stone," said Sven solemnly. "You see a dozen pieces of stone. You say, 'Pah! That's not for me,' and then you see a piece, delicate and elegant, and you fall in love with it. It's like women. But then comes the marriage and that can be terrible. You fight with it and you find that the stone is hard. You are in despair, then suddenly, like wax, it melts under your hands and you create a shape."

"I remember," said Theodore, "being asked by Berlincourt —you know, that French painter who lives over at Paleocastritsa—being asked by him to go and look at his work. He said, er, you know, quite distinctly, 'come and see my *paintings*.' So I went one afternoon and he was most hospitable. He gave me, um, you know, little cakes and tea and then I said I would like to see his paintings, and he pointed to one large canvas which was on the, um, what is it, that thing that painters use? Ah, yes, *easel*. It was quite a pretty painting, really. It showed the bay at Paleocastritsa with the monastery quite clearly and when I had admired it, I looked round to see where the rest of his work was, but there didn't appear to be any. So I, um, asked him where the *rest* of his paintings were and he pointed to the easel and said, um, "under there." It appeared that he couldn't afford canvases and so he painted one picture on top of another."

"Great artists have to suffer," said Sven lugubriously.

"When winter comes, I'll take you over to the Butrinto marshes," said Leslie with enthusiasm. "Masses of duck there and damned great wild boars up in the hills."

"Ducks I like, but vild boars I think are a bit big for me," said Max, with the conviction of one who knows his limitations.

"I don't think Max is up to it," said Donald. "He'd probably cut and run at a crucial moment. A foreigner, you know."

"And then," said Mother to Kralefsky, "you put your bay leaf and sorrel in just *before* it starts to simmer."

"So I says to him, Misses Margos, I says, I don't care if he is the French Ambassador, he's a bastard."

"Then, at the edge of the marsh—it's a bit difficult walking, of course, because the ground's so mushy—you can get woodcock and snipe."

"I remember once I visited a village in Macedonia where they did very curious, um, you know, wood sculptures."

"I knew a lady once who used to make it without the bay leaf, but with a pinch of mint."

It was the hottest hour of the day when even the cicadas seem to slow down and falter occasionally in their song. The black ants moved busily across the cloth, gathering the crumbs of our food. A horse-fly, its eyes gleaming like malevolent emeralds, settled for a brief moment on Theodore's beard and then zoomed away.

Slowly, full of food and wine, I got up and made my way

down to the sea. "And sometimes," I could hear Stavrodakis say to Margo, "sometimes the barrels really *shout*. They make a noise as if they were fighting. It keeps me awake."

"Oh, don't," said Margo, shuddering. "It makes me creepy just to think of it."

The sea was still and warm, looking as though it had been varnished, with just a tiny ripple patting languidly at the shore. The shingle scrunched and shifted, hot under my bare feet. The rocks and pebbles that made up this beach were incredible in shape and colour, moulded by the waves and the gentle rubbing and polishing one against the other. They had been sculptured into a million shapes. Arrow-heads, sickles, cockerels, horses, dragons, and starfish. Their colouring was as bizarre as their shapes, for they had been patterned by the earth's juices millions of years before and now their decorations had been buffed and polished by the sea. White with gold or red filigree, blood-red with white spots, green, blue, and pale fawn, hen's-egg, brown with a deep rusty-red pattern like a fern sprawled across them, pink as a peony with white Egyptian hieroglyphics forming a mysterious, undecipherable message across them. It was like a vast treasure trove of jewels spread along the rim of the sea.

I waded into the warm shallows and then dived and swam out to cooler water. Here, if you held your breath and let yourself sink to the bottom, the soft velvety blanket of the sea momentarily stunned and crippled your ears. Then, after a moment, they became attuned to the underwater symphony. The distant throb of a boat engine, soft as a heart-beat, the gentle whisper of the sand as the sea's movement shuffled and rearranged it and, above all, the musical clink of the pebbles on the shore's edge. To hear the sea at work on its great store of pebbles, rubbing and polishing them lovingly, I swam from the deep waters into the shallows. I anchored myself with a handful of multi-coloured stones, then, ducking my head below the surface, listened to the beach singing under the gentle touch of the small waves. If walnuts could sing,

I reflected, they would sound like this. Scrunch, tinkle, squeak, mumble, cough (silence while the wave retreats) and then the whole thing in different keys repeated with the next wave. The sea played on the beach as though it were an instrument. I lay and dozed for a time in the warm shallows and then, feeling heavy with sleep, I made my way back into the olive groves.

Everyone lay about disjointedly, sleeping round the ruins of our meal. It looked like the aftermath of some terrible battle. I curled up like a dormouse in the protective roots of a great olive and drifted off to sleep myself.

I woke to the gentle clinking of tea-cups as Margo and Mother laid the cloth for tea. Spiro brooded with immense concentration over a fire on which he had set a kettle. As I watched drowsily, the kettle lifted its lid and waved pertly at him, hissing steam. He seized it in one massive hand and poured the contents into a teapot, then, turning, he scowled at our recumbent bodies.

"Teas," he roared thunderously. "Teas is readys."

Everybody started and woke.

"Dear God! Must you yell like that, Spiro?" asked Larry plaintively, his voice thickened by sleep.

"Tea," said Kralefsky, waking up and glancing round him, looking like a dishevelled moth. "Tea, by Jove. Excellent."

"God, my head aches," said Leslie. "It must be that wine. It's got a kick like a mule."

"Yes, I'm feeling a bit fragile myself," said Larry, yawning and stretching.

"I feel as though I've been drowned," said Max with conviction. "Drowned in malmsey and then brought back by artificial inspiration."

"Must you always massacre the English tongue?" said Donald irritably. "God knows it's bad enough having thousands of Englishmen doing it, without you foreigners starting."

"I remember reading somewhere"—began Theodore, who had awakened instantly, like a cat, and who, having slept like one, looked as immaculate as though he had not been to sleep at all—"I remember reading once that there's a tribe up in the mountains of Ceylon that speaks a language that nobody can understand. I mean to say, not even expert linguists have been able to understand it."

"It sounds just like Max's English," said Donald.

Under the influence of tea, buttered toast, salt biscuits, watercress sandwiches, and an enormous fruit-cake as damp and as fragile and as rich-smelling as loam, we started to wake up. Presently we went down to the sea and swam in the warm waters until the sun sank and pushed the mountain's shadow over the beach suddenly, making it look cold and drained of colour. Then we went up to Stavrodakis' villa and sat under the bougainvillæa watching the sunset colours blur and mingle over the sea. We left Stavrodakis, who insisted on giving us a dozen great jars of his best wine to commemorate our visit, and made our way back to the benzina.

As we headed out to sea we left the shadow of the mountain and came into the warm glow of the sun again, which was sinking, smudged blood-red behind the bulk of Pandokrator, casting a shimmering reflection across the water like a flaming cypress tree. A few tiny clouds turned pink and vine-yellow, then the sun dipped behind the mountain and the sky turned from blue to pale green and the smooth surface of the sea became for a brief moment all the magical colours of a fire-opal. The engine throbbed as we edged our way back towards the town, unrolling a white bale of lace wake behind us. Sven played the opening of "The Almond Tree" very softly and everyone started to sing.

> "She shook the flowering almond tree one sunny day
>   With her soft little hands,
>   The snowy blossoms on her breast and shoulders lay
>   And in her hair's dark strands
>   The snowy blossoms on her breast and shoulders lay
>   And in her hair's dark strands . . ."

Spiro's voice, deep, rich, and smooth as black velvet, harmonizing with Theodore's pleasant baritone and Larry's tenor. Two flying fish skimmed up from the blue depths beneath our bow, skittered along the water, and were lost in the twilight sea.

Now it was getting dark enough to see the tiny green coruscations of phosphorus as our bow slid through the water. The dark wine glugged pleasantly from the earthenware pitchers into the glasses, the red wine that, last year, had lain snarling to itself in the brown barrels. A tiny wind, warm and soft as a kitten's paw, stroked the boat. Kralefsky, his head thrown back, his large eyes full of tears, sang at the velvet blue sky, shuddering with stars. The sea crisped itself along the sides of the boat with the sound of winter leaves, wind-lifted, rubbing themselves affectionately against the trunks of the trees that gave them birth.

> "But when I saw my darling thus in snow
>   arrayed,
>   To her sweet side I sped
> I brushed the gleaming petals from each
>   lock and braid,
> I kissed her and I said:
> I brushed the gleaming petals from each
>   lock and braid,
> I kissed her and I said . . ."

Far out in the channel between Corfu and the mainland, the darkness was freckled and picked out with the lights of the fishing boats. It was as though a small section of the Milky Way had fallen into the sea. Slowly the moon edged up over the carapace of the Albanian mountains, at first red like the sun, then fading to copper, to yellow, and at last to white. The tiny wind-shimmers on the sea glittered like a thousand fish scales.

The warm air, the wine, and the melancholy beauty of the night filled me with a delicious sadness. It would always be like this, I thought. The brilliant, friendly island, full of secrets, my family and my animals round me and, for good measure, our friends. Theodore's bearded head outlined against the moon wanting only horns to make him Pan; Kralefsky crying unashamedly now like a black gnome weeping over his banishment from fairyland; Spiro with his scowling brown face, his voice becoming as richly vibrant as a million summer bees; Donald and Max, frowning as they endeavoured to remember the words of the song and harmonize at the same time. Sven, like a great ugly white baby, gently squeezing the soulful music from his ungainly instrument.

> "Oh, foolish one, to deck your hair so soon
>   with snow,
> Long may you have to wait;
> The dreary winter days when chilling north
>   winds blow
> Do not anticipate!
> The dreary winter days when chilling north
>   winds blow
> Do not anticipate!"

Now, I thought, we were edging into winter, but soon it would be spring again, burnished, glittering, bright as a goldfinch; and then it would be summer, the long, hot, daffodil-yellow days.

> "Oh, foolish one, to deck your hair so soon
>   with snow,
> Long may you have to wait;
> The dreary winter days when chilling north
>   winds blow
> Do not anticipate!
> The dreary winter days when chilling north
>   winds blow
> Do not anticipate!"

Lulled by the wine and the throbbing heart of the boat's engine, lulled by the warm night and the singing, I fell asleep while the boat carried us back across the warm, smooth waters to our island and the brilliant days that were not to be.

Epilogue

Corfu is of such importance to me that its loss would deal a fatal blow to my projects. Remember this: in the present state of Europe, the greatest misfortune which could befall me is the loss of Corfu.

—Napoleon

≈

MAIL

Letter

Dear Mrs. Durrell,

It seems at last war can no longer be avoided and I think perhaps you were wise to leave Corfu. One can only hope that we can all meet in happier times when mankind has regained its senses. I will look forward to that.

Should you wish to reach me, my address is c/o The Ionian Bank, Athens.

I wish you and your family the very best of luck in the future.

Love to you all,
Yours,
Theodore

Postcard

Mother,

Have moved to Athens, so keep in touch. Place marvellous. Acropolis like pink flesh in the sun. Have sent my things to you. In a trunk marked "3" you will find book called *An Evaluation of Marlowe*. Can you send it to me? Everyone here wearing tin hats and looking like war. Am buying myself large spear.

Love,
Larry

Letter

Dear Mother,

I have had all my travellers' cheques pinched by some bloody Italian. They nearly arrested me because I punched him in the snoot. Give me the Greeks any day.

Can you send some more money to me at the Magnifica Hotel, Plaza de Contina, Milan? Will be home soon. Don't worry.

Love,
Les

P.S. It looks like war, doesn't it?

Letter

Darling Mother,

Just a hurried note to tell you I'm leaving on the boat on Monday so I should be in England in about three weeks.

Things here are rather hectic, but what can you expect? It never rains but it snows. I think it's simply disgusting the way the Germans are carrying on. If I had my way I'd tell them.

Will see you soon.
Love to you,
Margo

P.S. I enclose a letter from Spiro. Most odd.

Letter

Dear Missy Margo,

This is to tell you that war has been declared. Don't tell a soul.

Spiro

The Secret Island
OF
EDGAR DEWITT

FERRILL GIBBS
Amberjack Publishing
New York, New York

Amberjack
PUBLISHING

Amberjack Publishing
228 Park Avenue S #89611
New York, NY 10003-1502
http://amberjackpublishing.com

Publisher's Cataloging-in-Publication data
Names: Gibbs, Ferrill, author.
Title: The Secret island of Edgar Dewitt / Ferrill Gibbs.
Description: New York, NY: Amberjack Publishing, 2017.
Identifiers: ISBN 978-1-944995-21-8 (pbk. | 978-1-944995-35-5 (ebook) | LCCN 2017931881
Subjects: LCSH Friendship--Fiction. | Fathers and sons--Fiction. | Survival--Fiction. | Washington (State)--Fiction. | Forest fires--Fiction. | Indian Ocean--Fiction. | Fantasy fiction. | BISAC YOUNG ADULT FICTION / Fantasy / Contemporary
Classification: LCC PZ7.G339218 Se 2017 | DCC [Fic]--dc23

Cover Design: Emma Graves

For Anna

ONE

EDGAR DEWITT FOUND a hole through the Earth two weeks after his fourteenth birthday. It was late summer then, and the sun was blistering with no clouds in the sky and no rain in the forecast.

On his first day in Mount Lanier, Edgar and his family walked downtown, window shopping in the strange mountainside village. It was nothing like back home in Bon Secour, Alabama.

"It's so . . ." mused Edgar's dad, straining for the right word.

"*Grizzly Adams*," blurted his mom, snorting, then abruptly quieting herself lest someone nearby hear her disparage their town.

It was true, though. Even the McDonald's was basically a log cabin. Edgar stared at the big golden "M" towering in front and wondered if they used moose meat.

Behind the McDonald's sat a string of mountains.

Edgar stared at them as they walked. He studied them top to bottom same as he'd done the whole ride up from Denver. They were angular against the Western sky, and in the dusk seemed like black, jagged fangs. They were magnificent. Majestic. He had never seen a mountain before, not outside of a textbook, anyway.

"Let's get milkshakes," said his mother.

She grabbed him by the back of the neck and began to veer him toward the ice cream parlor. The parlor, also something out of an old western, was dead for a Saturday afternoon.

The antique bell on the door of the parlor announced their arrival.

"How do ya do?" asked the shopkeeper, a large man with silvery hair. He studied the Dewitts as they corralled around the display.

"Y'all have good malts here?" asked Edgar's father, completely lost in the selection of ice creams. Edgar's dad was a non-reformed chocaholic. The old shopkeeper nodded sternly.

Edgar heard the distinct sounds of an arcade through the parlor walls.

"Mom," he whispered. "Can I go next door really quick?"

"But . . . what about the milkshakes?"

"Just order me something."

"OK," she said, sending him rushing for the door. "But don't be gone long!"

Once outside, Edgar stepped toward the adjacent shop. The place was called Al Capone's, a weird name for sure, but then again, everything in this town was weird.

He slipped his hands into his pockets to feel around for money. There were a lot of games through the window that he recognized, a lot of the same ones they had back in Alabama, but no Nitro Streak.

"Nice jeans," muttered a voice just down the way.

"Huh?" said Edgar, turning. Somehow he hadn't seen a group of kids about his age huddling at the front door of the arcade. Edgar nodded nervously and blew off the remark, then turned back to the window. He was suddenly self-conscious as they giggled and murmured about him. Hot blood rushed to his cheeks. Nerves danced in his gut.

"Nice jeans," repeated the voice, this time a little louder.

"I heard you the first time," said Edgar.

"Nice jeans!" the voice hollered.

Edgar looked over and squinted, straining to see past the glare of the streetlight. Emerging from the group was a rail thin kid, whose hollowed-out eyes were shaded from two bony, protruding cheekbones. He glared at Edgar. Edgar shrugged back.

"I really," the angry kid continued, "*really* like the way you roll them up at the bottom. It looks *super cool*." He pointed at Edgar's jean rolls as the crowd of kids at the arcade door exploded into hysterics.

"Yeah, thanks," said Edgar, shrugging again. The boy continued to glare at Edgar with clear, aqua blue eyes. Edgar looked beyond him. He surveyed the kid's group. There were a lot of them, maybe eight. A few guys, a few girls, one of whom stood at the back of the pack and peered at Edgar with a set of gorgeous brown eyes.

She was not laughing like the others.

For a moment, he was so captivated by her that he was almost unable to look away, suddenly forgetting the bully who stood before him. The girl's waist-length hair was mocha in color, and her lip gloss sparkled in the light like gold flakes in the Arkansas River.

"I just wanted to tell you about your jeans," continued the bully. Edgar snapped out of it and focused his gaze on the kid again. The guy's fists were clenching and unclenching, painting the picture of a total psycho. "The rolls, I mean. That's real, *real niiice.*" He blurted the last part through half laughter, half very bad southern accent—apparently mocking Edgar's Alabamian drawl.

"Got it," said Edgar, shrugging for a third time, "if you say so." He turned and went back to fake-staring through the window of the arcade. "Thanks for letting me know," he added.

"You're welcome, pussy bitch," said the boy.

"Edgar?" Ever so fortunately, Edgar's mother stuck her head out of the ice cream parlor at just the right time, except all the kids giggled when she called his name.

All except for the mocha-haired girl.

"Coming," he answered, and as he walked up the stairs to join her, he tried to hold his head high.

"Coming, Mommy!" sang the thin boy behind him, just loud enough for everyone to hear. At that, everyone giggled once more.

Everyone but the mocha-haired girl.

"SURE IS," said the shopkeeper, apparently in deep conversation with Edgar's dad. It was typical. Edgar's father was a terribly sociable person.

"The longest drought *ever*?" asked Mr. Dewitt.

"You bet," nodded the man. Edgar walked up to the counter and joined them. "It's killing the crops," the man added, "depleting the water supply. The worst drought we've ever seen. Everyone's miserable here if you haven't noticed. Been forever since a good rain."

"Hmm," said Edgar's father, looking down, noticing Edgar. "Hey man!" he smiled. "How's the arcade?"

"Sucky," he muttered.

"Fantastic!" said his father, winking at the shopkeeper. "All the more time to study, then."

Edgar's mom reached over and tousled Edgar's hair. She gazed down at him warmly. "I haven't ordered for you yet."

"Can I get a mocha shake?" he asked the shopkeeper, unable to get the girl out of his mind. As the shopkeeper made his shake, he bent and unrolled his jeans, and as he did, he thought of his friends back home, the older boys who'd taken him under his wing and shown him how to do everything: to roll cords, to pull in a massive tuna without breaking the line, and how to roll his jeans the way they did, in tightly bound folds, as was the style over there.

Unrolling them now, each unraveling felt like a betrayal. It was an assault to the very warm memories he held for all of them. Tears came to his eyes. He blinked them away.

He was in for a rough time here in Mount Lanier, it seemed.

"You know," said Edgar's father, addressing the shop-keeper, "I thought it was supposed to rain all the time here in Washington. Isn't it one of the rainiest places in America?"

"Climate change," frowned the man.

"Yeah?"

"Sure. How else does a drought happen so late in September, here in Washington, of all places? Same thing's been going on everywhere—hurricanes, tornadoes, droughts. You noticed that? Why, I'll bet you know a little something about hurricanes, too. Didn't you say you all were from Alabama?"

"Yes and yes," said Edgar's dad, frowning. "We've seen enough storms for a lifetime." He glanced at Edgar and then his wife. She took a big, thoughtful sip of her green mint shake.

"Like I said," continued the shopkeeper, still wiping.

"I'll take a hurricane by now if the rain doesn't come soon. We've got big trouble a-brewing. They'll extend the wildfire season an extra month if we don't get rain soon, and that's the last thing we need around here. Another wildfire."

Once Edgar and his parents had collected their plastic spoons and straws and said their goodbyes to the shopkeeper, they exited the shop. Edgar's heart raced as he prepared to face the mean kids again, but, fortunately, they were gone. He breathed a deep sigh of relief and calmed his thudding heart, following his parents up the road toward their new home on the north side of the town. As they strolled through the dry, late-summer air, he kicked the last of his jean rolls straight and looked over his shoulder to glimpse the dark, stark, jagged Cascades to the west. They sure were something.

TWO

THE WOODS BEHIND the new house were dry and crackly and, stepping through them, Edgar turned down a slight hillside in a direction he had not yet explored. Using his arms for balance, he zigzagged down a decline into a greenish, wooded valley below, where he suddenly found before him a babbling brook partly hidden by trees and shrubs. Clear, cool mountain water bubbled and gurgled over miniature falls that trickled sweetly through the trees, pooling up around a few mountain rocks every few feet or so. Edgar could tell by the deep cuts in the valley how wide the brook normally was, and how much higher, and noticed that tree roots had emerged in the valley walls like stairs.

The drought had certainly taken its toll.

He hopped across the rocks through the center of the valley, when suddenly, a few skittish fish darted beneath his feet.

Rainbow trout! He'd never caught a rainbow trout before. The next day, when he came back, that would surely change.

Then, from the corner of his eye, something brown came into view through a patch of alder leaves to his right. Just as a hot gust blew through, the leaves revealed the structure like a theater curtain. Keeping his balance on the rocks, he slowly peeled back the leafy partition and squinted through the leaves. There, in a slight clearing, was an old, broken-down cabin that looked like a slaughter-house from *The Texas Chainsaw Massacre*, only smaller and less threatening. Ever so cautiously, he stepped from the rocks and began to move through the branches toward the building, motivated now by abject curiosity.

Out in the sunshine, free of the thicket, he beheld the cabin with a hand shielding his eyes from the sun.

"Hello?" he said loudly, but no one answered. *Of course no one's gonna answer. What the heck would anyone be doing way out here?* He looked around the clearing, scanning for signs of movement. He moved closer in, entranced. The windows on either side of the door were practically glass-less with a few foggy shards remaining like dangling teeth in a rotten mouth. The hot wind whistled through the gaps in the wood where termite holes had turned everything into a honeycomb.

"Hello?" he said again, but received no response. *OK, just had to make sure. This might just make an adequate hangout if it's not too rotten on the inside.*

He paused with his hand on the ancient, rusty door-knob, and thought of the backwoods cabins back home in Alabama. Back home you sometimes came upon a structure while out exploring but you *never* went in since there were just too many stories of crazy old men with shotguns and mean, ferocious dogs, or just plain old copperhead snakes. Not to mention ghosts.

Finally, when he mustered his courage enough, Edgar turned the rusty knob and the door groaned open. He ducked into the dark, creepy opening, and before his eyes could even acclimate, a strange smell hit his nose. The smell took his breath away, not that it was bad, but it was just *strange*, unidentifiable—like something musty and warm. It definitely didn't fit the setting.

Rubbing his eyes to focus, a strong, hot gust from the valley slammed the door shut, and he nearly soiled himself. Once his thundering heart calmed, he surveyed the dark room again and took a timid step forward. Beneath his feet, the floorboards creaked and moaned. Once again, just like a horror movie.

The building was bare except for loads and loads of cobwebs, all draped across the wooden rafters above. There was no furniture, no pots, no pans, and no stove. Just a plain, old, funky room.

The decay of the logs and the strong, weird smell indicated that nobody had lived there for quite some time. Which was great.

Edgar turned a few circles and smiled big. *Yes, this would make a great hangout.*

Suddenly, something made him stop spinning. *What was that?* He cocked his head sideways to listen. It was a strange, eerie sound—something faint, constant, and nearby. Something *below.*

Listening as deeply as he could, concentrating hard enough to drown out the distant screech of two red-tailed hawks in an argument above, he closed his eyes tight and cocked his head further sideways until, finally, there it was. He looked down. From beneath the floorboards emerged a faint, strange sound. A strange whistling.

It was air. Whistling air.

Hot air, his ankles told him, and that's when he realized the gust had been licking at his ankles all along. He took another big sniff.

The rising air was definitely responsible for the strange, unidentifiable smell.

"Is there a basement down there?" he asked aloud, squatting to the floor. He squinted through the cracks and rubbed his chin but could see nothing. It was far too dark between the cracks to see.

Closing an eye, he peered deeper into the crack but to no avail. He stretched his hand to the floor and could feel the draft of air coming up. His cell phone rang violently in his pants pocket, almost giving him a heart attack. He nearly toppled over sideways.

"Hey Mom," he said breathlessly into the phone. "No ma'am," he muttered, "I haven't died yet." He decided not to mention the cabin. *There's no way she'd ever let me come back here.*

As he listened to her go on about how she registered him for school the next day—how she was holding his new schedule of advanced classes in hand (and consequently, he better get ready to study his butt off)—he rose from the floor and yanked a pack of Big League Chew from his back pocket and stuffed an oversized wad into his mouth.

"Mom," he said, smacking, "please. Can we not talk about school today? This is the last day of summer. I just want to check out the Indian Hills behind that old-timey McDonald's. Yeah, the one with the moose meat."

Holding the phone against his ear with a shoulder, he lowered himself to a knee and waved a palm over the floorboards. *Where is that air coming from?* He slumped to both knees and, with one hand, stuffed the rest of the pouch into his mouth and nodded.

"Yes ma'am," he said. "I swear to God on your future grave I won't get killed in the woods. Not by drifters or bears or swarms of hornets. Just let me . . ." He flicked the empty Big League Chew wrapper across the room and it did the most amazing thing: it played air hockey . . . with *itself.*

Instantly it was caught upon the uprising air and floated all the way across the room, then bumped into the opposite wall and bounced back, returning to Edgar's outstretched hands. It never even touched the floor.

"Yes ma'am," he muttered into the phone. "I'm still here." He stood and dusted off his knees and stuffed the wrapper back into his pocket. "Just let me check out a few more things, OK?" he asked. "I promise I'll be home for dinner. Just a couple more hours."

He hung up the phone and shoved it back into his pocket, then inhaled deeply, experiencing the musty, warm odor again. So strange. It was salty, like the sea. Which didn't make sense. There was no ocean around Mount Lanier—not for hundreds and hundreds of miles. Edgar knew the smell of the sea, though; it was an unmistakable smell. It was something that made him miss home terribly.

He studied the floorboards and wondered how well they were nailed down. Reaching out, he took one and gripped it by its edge, then gave it a good, upward tug, but it didn't budge.

Then he stood, kicking the corner of the plank with the back of his foot, trying to bend and tug as hard as he could to see if it would loosen. *Yes.* It wiggled. *Finally!* He kicked it once more, this time more vigorously than before, then bent and tugged again, rising and kicking and bending and tugging and it budged even more. After one more good kick and another violent yank, he could dig his fingers beneath the loosened board. With an angry growl, the plank surrendered its grip on the ancient, rusty nails, rising up from the floor with a scream.

"Yes!" he grunted triumphantly, tossing the board aside. Kneeling, he stuck his entire face into the dark hole and looked in.

But there was nothing—nothing but darkness. Only the earthy draft of air flowing freely that lifted his brown, stringy bangs and cooled the sweat on his forehead.

"Ugh," he groaned. "It's too dark!"

For a moment he paused, trying not to think of tarantulas and snakes, or fangy rodents that could be lurking down there. Mustering every bit of courage he had in him, he reached his hand down anyway and felt around in the creepy darkness.

"Dang!" he shuddered, shutting his eyes tight, thoroughly expecting to get bitten. Ultimately, he felt nothing. No bugs, no fangs, no snakes and, strangest of all, no ground beneath the cabin.

Slowly he opened his eyes. With renewed confidence he reached even deeper into the hole—all the way down to his shoulder—so far down that his cheek pressed against the adjacent plank on the floor. Still, his fingers reached no foundation below. No brick, no cement, no rock. Not even dirt from the hillside that Edgar knew must be down there. There was only air, a non-stop supply of the warm, salty breeze.

He stood. He scratched his head and studied the crack in the floor, then picked up the plank he'd uprooted from the floor. Holding it firmly in his hands, he slid it beneath the dark gap and, using leverage from an adjacent board, leaned on the plank with all his weight and suddenly up it popped from the floor like a weed from the dirt.

With a triumphant smile, Edgar snatched the loose floorboard from the floor and tossed it aside, hovering over a now even *larger* gap in the floor.

"Dang!" he said. He still couldn't see a thing.

He wiped the sweat from his brow and renewed his grip on the plank, then, using the wood as leverage, popped another floorboard from its nails. And then another. And yet another. And as they came up from the floor, he tossed them from the glassless windows into the meadow outside, until, before he knew it, most of the boards in the room had been removed.

Breathless and sweaty, he turned to survey what remained. It was unreal. He had never seen anything like it.

A massive hole, obviously man-made, existed beneath the floorboards. *That's where the salty air had been coming from!*

Energized by the mystery, he was now even more frantic in removing the remaining boards. The more he studied the vast depth of the hole in the room's center, the faster he worked and the quicker he was forced to the outskirts of the room in order to not fall in.

When finally he stood on the last few remaining boards, he leaned over the edge. How far down the hole went, he did not know.

It was eerie and beautiful and lined with bricks around the top—something like an old-fashioned water well, except much, much bigger. He guessed it was around eighteen feet in diameter.

Edgar kneeled to inspect the bricks that shaped the hole. They had each been smoothed and decorated with ornate, inscrutable markings. The markings weren't in English, but rather something like the dot-dot-dash of Morse code combined with some other type of writing.

Maybe alien!

Edgar inspected deeper into the hole and saw an occasional stick figure intertwined with more of the indecipherable words, all drawings of people hunting animals, utilizing ancient vehicles and tools. Edgar reached down and traced a pinkie over what seemed to be a picture of a dark cloud with a yellow bolt of lightning shooting through it.

"This is really old," he estimated. *Maybe cavemen drew this.* The whole world would want to see this, he suddenly realized. It could even make him rich.

With that money maybe we could move back to Alabama, he thought. He was going to be famous, that was for sure, but he didn't want to tell anybody just yet.

"Hello!" he yelled into the hole.

"Hello!" he screamed again, but this time he noticed the lack of echo.

"HELLO!" he yelled once more.

What kind of deep hole has no echo?

Perhaps it was full of moss at the bottom. Maybe the moss was absorbing the sound.

"HELLLOOOOOOO!" he yelled one last time. Still no answer, and still no echo. Then, leaning over the hole, he did what any ninth-grader might do when standing before a dark, deep hole: he spat. And as the mound of spit darted into the depths, he listened intently for the splat, but strangely, there came none.

Weird!

Vexed, but armed with an idea, he carefully skirted the edges of the hole and slipped from the cabin, out to the piles of wooden planks sitting outside the window. There, he selected a plank and checked it for rot. When satisfied, he walked it back to the hole's edge and tossed it down, standing still as a statue as the board disappeared from view.

He listened intently for a loud *thud* or *clank* or *clap*, but no such sound emerged. He scowled into the darkness.

This thing's deep, he thought.

He cast his eyes upward to study the roof. There, thin beams of sunshine streamed faintly down through rotting logs. *Of course,* he thought, *sunlight.* It was exactly what he needed.

Returning to the woodpile outside, he snatched up

another floorboard and carried it inside. Then, in a corner of the room, he leaned the plank against the wall and gave it a bit of weight with his foot to make sure it didn't snap in two. Satisfied, using the board as a ramp, he skirted right up toward the rafters, and just as he neared the top, straining to reach the closest rafter, the plank snapped violently beneath him.

"Ah!" he grunted, shooting his hands upward. At the last moment, he snagged a rafter and hung above the floor. The pieces of the broken plank thudded flatly beneath his two dangling feet.

Groaning and grunting, he yanked himself up onto the rafters, then teetered precariously in the attic on squatted legs. Above, he took a moment to find his balance and studied the hole from this new, elevated perspective. Then, slowly, he stood and placed his palms on the V-shaped roof overhead.

This is nuts, he thought, trying not to fall.

Slowly, carefully, he began to make his way across the rafters, and each step brought him ever closer to the dark, yawning hole below his feet. Each board growled threateningly as he stepped, but still he pressed forward, placing one shaky foot in front of the other, his lips moving in silent concentration and counting the steps, his heart beating wildly in his ears. Despite his fear he carried on. He just couldn't stop himself. He had to know what was down in the hole and his curiosity wouldn't let up until he did. He knew it was a Dewittian thing, that deep sense of curiosity handed down by his studious, investigative parents, that raged like a monster in him.

Inch by inch, step by step, he carefully navigated the rafters until the center of the hole was entirely beneath his feet like the mouth of a kraken. Cold sweat emerged all across his body, dampening his clothes.

"Why," he asked the empty room. "Why do I do

this kind of stuff?" Beneath his tennis shoes a sure death awaited.

With each foot firmly planted on a rafter, he slowly, *carefully* raised his right hand over his head and, maintaining a wobbly balance, began to claw at the disintegrating wood above.

"C'mon," he muttered, his lips pursed tight. Not daring to look up, he continued to claw and claw, peeling away at the rotten wood, until suddenly, just as he thought it would, something moved. The wood, spongy with age, began to give way.

"BLAH," he spat as debris began to fall, some of it onto his face. For several endless minutes, he held tight to the rafters and clawed and picked at the roof, jabbing and prodding, poking and punching at the rotten wood that soon began to surrender a bit of sunlight.

Then, magnificently, a massive chunk of the mushy stuff began to give way.

Yes, c'mon, he thought, willing the chunk to fall. When it did, it came down with violence, finally raining down in a cloud of debris so large that he was unable to breathe for half a minute. His grip on the rafters remained, however, as he brushed the pulp and rot off his body with his other hand. Slowly, he looked up and beheld his work. There, just above, was bright, blazing sun. It beamed gloriously down through the hole.

As the dust settled and sunlight filled the room, he looked down, a huge smile on his face. Beneath his feet, the tunnel had been illuminated with a brilliant flood of sunshine. It was like a spotlight.

Edgar kneeled carefully on the creaky beams, gazing headlong into the hole, studying its walls that seemed to stretch countless yards into the earth, how far down he didn't know. Another thing he noticed: the walls had been decorated with more of the same sorts of writings he'd seen on the bricks at the top.

Still, there was no sign of the bottom—just a shroud of darkness in the earth far below where the last beams of sunlight could stretch.

Investigating the hole, mesmerized, he almost didn't notice the large insect that was slowly crawling across the base of his neck. When he did finally feel it, though, the creature had traveled almost halfway around to his throat. Edgar's hand shot instinctively to the creature, and for a split second he could feel its twitchy legs in his fingers: a crawly, fuzzy body convulsing threateningly against his throat.

In one violent motion he snatched the spider and hurled it across the room, but when he did, he lost his grip on the rafters and immediately began to fall. *Wham!* His shoulders slammed against the rotting beams and then his head nailed them, too.

For a moment all he saw was the blinding blitz of sunlight above, coupled with stars in his eyes. Suddenly, he was slipping—falling into the hole through the beams.

Pain flashed through his head like lightning, the reddish sparkles storming his vision, but Edgar clung to consciousness long enough to flail his arms around and reach for the rafters. And, in the last possible moment, just as he was through the beams and in midair, by some sort of miracle, he snagged a rafter and hung tight. With all his remaining strength, he reached his other hand upward and grabbed a hold, then dangled dangerously above a certain, grizzly death.

"Oh . . . my . . . God," he muttered, swaying slightly side-to-side like a pendulum. He closed his eyes tight and tried to steady himself, but very quickly he began to feel his grip loosening on the rafters.

He would have to act fast.

Mustering all his strength, summoning his old

monkey bar skills he'd mastered back in Alabama, he began to swing his legs forward for momentum, letting go of the rafters at the very last second, and flung himself to the next rafter, snatching hold. Then he did it again—*whoosh*, onto the next rafter. Each move strained his screaming fingertips to the breaking point; splinters from the wood began digging into his flesh. But Edgar ignored it. With every moment, with every swing to the next rafter, all the strength leaving his hands, as hot, salty air from below shot up his pants legs like the hot breath from a dragon's mouth, he swung.

Please, God, he prayed in his mind. *Please get me out of this.*

The beams groaned like rocking chairs as he continued to swing across the room, making his way over the threatening hole, and finally neared safety. His shoulders screamed in pain. Hot sweat stung his eyes, blinding him.

And that's when he remembered what he'd told his mother earlier.

I won't get killed today.

No, he wouldn't.

Remembering it gave him a new wave of strength. With gritted teeth, he swung to the next rafter, and the next, clinging to each with all he had left, swinging like a wounded gymnast across the room, snorting and grunting, ignoring the howling cramps in his stomach and in his chest until finally, he was there. He looked down and thanked God. He'd made it past the hole. He was safe. Below his feet, a thin stretch of flooring awaited.

Counting to three, he let go of the rafters and dropped ten feet to the ground, collapsing on the remaining floorboards, rolling upon impact. He groaned in pain as tears filled his eyes, but he was safe. He brought his burning hands to his thighs and felt around, seeing if his ankle was broken, but it didn't seem to be. He lay on the remaining floorboards heaving, gasping for breath, staring blankly at the afternoon sun through the brand new hole in the roof.

As the burning in his muscles finally subsided, he rolled over and checked his wristwatch. It was 3:43 pm. His mother would be worried soon.

On wobbly legs, he stood and brushed himself off, then stepped to the edge of the hole to look down once more. He gazed into the murky depths and marveled at how completely it swallowed up the brilliant sunshine.

The tunnel, now aglow with symbols and pictures that stretched down into the depths, had been constructed with an endless expanse of golden bricks reaching as far as the eye could see. He stood massaging the last persistent pain in his shoulder, gazing down at the writings when suddenly, inexplicably, something strange began to emerge down there. It came shooting up from the depths with great speed.

What the heck?

Something was there, something was definitely coming up, careening up the tunnel with such velocity he wondered if he should get himself out of the way.

With each second, the thing streaked up like a blur, spinning around like a helicopter blade, slicing up through the air and twirling all around, like a rail-thin gymnast. Suddenly it was before him, springing up from the hole and freezing in midair.

Edgar, mystified, reached out and plucked it from its arc, just as it began to fall back down.

"What the . . .?" he said, studying it.

In his hands was the same floor plank he'd tossed into the hole an hour earlier—the first plank he'd pulled from the floor—the one he'd thrown down to make a SPLAT.

Somehow, it had come back up.

THREE

THE DEWITTS RETURNED TO town for a few things on Sunday evening. Edgar's shoulders still burned from all the rafter dangling. He massaged them deeply as the three strolled along.

"What's with you?" his mother asked.

"A bunch of pushups, nothing really," he said, dropping his hands.

"Great!" she said. "It's good to be in shape." She surveyed the sleepy downtown and elbowed him. "Didn't I see some kids your age at that arcade the other night? Why don't you go find them? Go on and make some new friends. You can't be hanging out all the time with us old people you know."

He gave his mom a one-armed hug and drew her in close, squeezing until she cackled.

"Thanks, Mom," he said, as she tousled his hair. Then he was off to Al Capone's. Not to meet up with those kids though, but just to play a few games. If he never saw those kids again, it would be too soon.

Though, as terrible luck would have it, those were the first kids he ran into. "This sucks," he said. The good news was, Al Capone's had Nitro Streak. But the bad news was, the skinny kid from the night before who'd made fun of his jean rolls was currently sitting on top of it, addressing his crowd of friends, the same group from the night before. Edgar looked down to make sure his jeans weren't rolled.

"Idiots," the boy laughed. "I can't believe nobody will even play me."

Nitro Streak was the game with four drivers' seats situated side by side, with four steering wheels and four sets of pedals. The point was, if you had three friends to play with, you could race each other, which was why it was so popular. Apparently the bully was the Nitro Streak king since nobody wanted to play him.

Edgar wondered how good he was.

"I'll play," said one kid, emerging from the crowd with a chili dog in his hand. He was tall with short, dark, almost greasy looking hair, and his mouth was full of the chili dog. He strolled from the air hockey machine to the Nitro Streak king and looked up at the bully, chewing all the while.

"Oh, fantastic. Kevin," said the curly-headed kid. "Kevin, you're too slow to play this game. Mentally, I mean." He rolled his eyes and snickered, waving Kevin into one of the seats.

Kevin plopped into a driver's seat and shoved the rest of his chili dog into his very messy mouth, smiling with satisfaction before placing his sticky fingers all over the steering wheel. It made the bully wince in disgust.

"So," the tyrant barked, addressing the crowd once more. Edgar ducked slightly to the side to avoid being seen. "Who else is playing?"

The bully gazed into the back of the crowd and spotted another potential player. He pointed and waved her on. It was the mocha-haired girl from the night before, the one with the sparkly lip gloss.

She mystified Edgar.

"How about it, Shay?" the bully called.

"What are you babbling about, Weedy ?"

Shay stood by the dance machine, mingling with her friends, and when he waved her on she slightly rolled her beautiful, sapphire-like eyes. Weedy softened as she did, probably because of how beautiful she was . . .

"C'mon," he said, now cordial all of the sudden. "Come play Nitro with us. Put those years of driving daddy's golf cart to some use." For a moment she seemed to think it over, then, biting her lip, she sashayed toward the game and took a seat beside the chili-covered Kevin.

Once there, she turned to Kevin and smiled sympathetically. "Kev," she said, pointing to her own chin. "You've got some right here."

"Yeah?" chewed Kevin, opening his mouth wide to reveal a pasty wad of chili dog.

She winced. "You're so gross," she muttered, turning away.

"One more!" Weedy yelled. "Who's it gonna be?!"

"I'll play," said Edgar, stepping forward.

The crowd turned to him and murmured as Weedy glared down from above, like a judge. When he recognized Edgar, he grinned. "Hey! It's Jean Rolls!"

Everybody laughed.

"Yeah," shrugged Edgar. "You got me."

He walked over and took a seat beside Shay.

"Hey," he said, taking the wheel. "I'm Edgar."

"Hey Edgar," she whispered.

Weedy dropped from the top of the game and plopped

into the fourth and final seat, and Edgar noticed the boy was gripping the wheel so tight, his two knottily knuckled, bruised fists turned snow white. Massaging it in a sort of uninhibited, unquenchable rage, he glared at Edgar and fumed.

Dude, thought Edgar, *you are definitely a psycho*.

"So, Jean Rolls. Mama's Boy," Weedy said loud enough that everyone could hear, all of them now congregating around the game to watch.

When Edgar looked around him he realized he was suddenly surrounded by bodies.

"Listen, redneck," Weedy added, as scattered chuckles erupted behind them. "We play 'Next Game' around here. Do you know what that means: *Next Game?*"

"Yeah," said Edgar. "We play like that back in Alabama. It means if you come in last, you pay for the winner's next game."

"Incredible!" said Weedy, imitating Edgar's southern drawl. "Did you hear that, Kevin? This redneck says they have extra dollars down there in Alabamer . . ."

Laughter again, always laughter with this guy. It was like he traveled with a studio audience.

The older boys who'd taught Edgar to play played that way back in Alabama, just like he'd explained. However, currently, for Edgar, he had one major problem: there was only one dollar in his pocket, the only redneck in Washington without an extra bill.

"Not a problem," said Edgar. "I'm down for Next Game."

Edgar watched Weedy, Shay, and Kevin select their cars, and was surprised about Weedy's choice; he'd selected the BMW, not even close to the best car in Nitro Streak.

Shay had chosen a convertible: the red Miata, not a very good choice for Nitro Streak, but then again, he could overhear her telling Kevin that she wanted a convertible for her sixteenth birthday. *Rich girl, huh?* Finally, he peered at Kevin's screen and discovered the sloppy eater had chosen the worst car of all, the Mazda 626.

He was a mess.

Delighted, Edgar spun the wheel to the best car in the game: the thunderous, rapturous, Nissan 370Z. How people in Washington did not know about the 370Z, Edgar did not know. Triumphantly, he smashed the gas pedal and selected the car, and the race began.

As the cars lurched from the starting line, all four screens were filled with smoke and debris, and the tire screeches echoed throughout the arcade.

For a moment the pack stayed together, with Weedy's car directly in front, but when the appropriate sidewalk came along, Edgar tapped the brake and swerved to the right, then smashed a particular trashcan on the side of the road. It burst into about a million pieces, revealing a Nitro Canister, which Edgar's Nissan gobbled up. It sent the fiery, red car surging forward like a rocket, and instantly he left Weedy's BMW far behind, along with the others.

"Whoa!" someone shouted. "I didn't know a Nitro canister was there!"

When his Nissan rocketed into another canister—this one hidden atop a building Edgar had ramped up onto—the car turned molten orange, and Edgar could feel Weedy glaring at him from the adjacent driver's seat. The crowd began to cheer him on.

"No way!" someone yelled. "You can drive on the *roof*?!"

Not many people knew about that, but the older boys back in Alabama did.

"Shut up!" snapped Weedy, glaring back at the crowd. "It's distracting!"

At the last turn, with the race easily in hand, Edgar

downshifted coolly and coasted toward the finish line, taking the car into fourth gear and then to third, weaving in between a few remaining orange barrels and cones just to mess around. Triumphantly, he glanced up at the lap time and nodded: just as he thought. It would be his fastest lap ever.

It might be *anybody's* fastest lap ever.

"Nope!" he heard Weedy say. Glancing over, Edgar realized that he was talking to Shay. They were battling it out for second. Weedy's car was just nearing hers from behind and he was shouting at her.

"No way, Shay," he growled. "You're not beating me."

Shay was beating Weedy straight up, even with a mediocre car. Her driving was impressive, Edgar noted. As he coasted his own car down the final stretch, he watched from the corner of his eye as she smoothly shifted up and down and took the curves like a good driver should, her palms sliding along the wheel smoothly and cleanly, all-in-all kicking Weedy's ass.

Yet, since her car was so inferior—a frumpy convertible without any open road speed—Weedy got her on the straightaway. He came up alongside her and, for good measure, swerved right into her with one quick and vicious motion. Suddenly, Shay's car was flipping off the road like litter in a sandstorm.

The crowd behind them erupted in protest.

"Asshole!" Shay's friends screamed. "What a jerk!"

Shay was shocked and sat defeated with her mouth wide open. She turned to Weedy and said, "Naturally!" as a bitter anger flashed in her eyes. "That's so . . . *you.*"

The crowd continued to groan at Weedy. What he had done was clearly against the unwritten rules of Nitro Streak: you never wreck another car on purpose. It was an honor thing. That's how it was back in Alabama, and Edgar was glad to see that in this weird, awful town, at least they had standards here, too. Not that Weedy was good enough to abide by them.

"Oh, shut up!" he shouted, cackling, a huge grin on his face. He sped ahead of Shay and laughed maniacally as he left her behind. Her car was left to spin helplessly against a curb where it finally conked out to a complete stop, steaming pathetically by the highway.

"Real classy, Weedy," she muttered, steering her battered Miata back onto the highway. "You ask me to play this stupid game," she said, fighting against the now out-of-alignment tires, "and then you wreck me. How many issues do you have? Jesus. Too many to list I'm sure."

"Yeah, whatever," he grinned. "It was an accident."

Weedy then downshifted and took the last turn, that was when Edgar—who had been stationed all along by the side of the road with the finish line still in sight—waited like a snake in the grass.

As Weedy drove unsuspectingly up the backstretch, Edgar smashed the gas and crashed Weedy's car off the road. With a violent surge, both cars went crashing and banging, instantly mangled and tumbling into the desert.

The crowd fell silent as they watched in awe. Then, suddenly, as they realized what Edgar had done, they burst into wild applause and cheered him even more.

"You . . ." said Weedy, whipping around in his seat, glaring at Edgar with two evil, smoldering eyes. "You inbred son of a *bitch*."

As Weedy cursed at Edgar, Shay—who'd recovered from her wreck, came sputtering around the last bend and passed them. She grinned as her car crossed the finish line uncontested, making her the winner. Again the crowd went wild.

"Serves you RIGHT!" her friends screamed into Weedy's ear, who winced at the sound and turned and glared at them all.

"Shut up, you skanks!" he yelled.

"Thanks, Edgar!" laughed Shay, leaning toward him. They locked eyes for a moment and he could smell her wonderful, sweet perfume.

"Anytime," he smiled.

"Yeah!" shouted Kevin, whose car suddenly crossed the finish line as well. "I didn't lose! Finally!"

Weedy's eyes widened. He glared at Edgar then whirled back around in his seat to slam on the gas. His smoking, demolished BMW whined as he slowly rumbled back onto the highway. And immediately Edgar knew: he was screwed. His heart sank. He'd been so preoccupied with helping Shay he was caught idling. Suddenly Weedy was off toward the finish line and Edgar had no chance to catch him. He was clearly too far away for Edgar's limping Nissan to challenge.

Edgar, it appeared, was going to lose.

Game Over flashed on the screen. The crowd fell silent.

"Oh no," muttered Shay. After an expert display of Nitro Streak, the room suddenly realized that Edgar had come in last place, and owed Next Game.

"That's RIGHT!" shouted Weedy, pounding the wheel with a fist. Then he pounded it again, with *both* fists, still glaring at the screen, as if Edgar's finishing in last place was still not enough to make him happy. "You owe next GAME, *hick*!"

Shay walked over to them. "I don't want the dollar, Weedy," she said. "Edgar doesn't owe me anything."

"Fine," Weedy growled. "Since Shay doesn't want her dollar," he announced to the crowd. "Jean Rolls will pay Kevin's Next Game since Kevin came in second."

At that, Kevin, who was busy tearing into a Snicker's bar, perked up.

"Yeah," he chirped. "Pay me, Jean Rolls."

"No problem," Edgar said. "I'll get Kevin a dollar. I just have to go ask my mom."

"Your *who*?" asked Weedy, enraged. "You mean you played Next Game and didn't have the money to pay for it?!"

"I . . ." Edgar answered, and just then, as if on cue, his mom stuck her head through the door.

"Edgar?" she hollered.

"Over here," he said meekly, rising from the Nitro Streak cockpit.

The crowd parted for him as he crossed the arcade and neared her. When he arrived, he said softly, "Mom, please don't embarrass me right now. I really need a favor."

"What kind of a 'favor?'" she asked far too loudly.

"Oh my God," he said softly, waving his palms down. "Just . . . OK, I need a dollar. OK?"

"For what?" she shouted above the arcade noise, as if trying to make him go insane on purpose.

"I owe that guy a dollar." He pointed to Kevin across the arcade.

Her eyes became fiery slits.

"Have you," she asked, her voice suddenly stern, "have you been . . . *gambling*?"

"No!" Edgar said defensively, his hands upraised in defense. "We were just playing loser pays 'Next Game,' that's all."

"Oh," she sighed, "what a relief. I was sure you were gambling, but it turns out, you were . . . *gambling*!"

With a frown, she withdrew a dollar from her purse and walked it over to the silent group of kids. They all looked up at her with wide eyes. Edgar felt like melting into the arcade carpet. Standing before them, she waved the dollar in the air, disgustedly, as if it was dirty underwear.

"Whose is this?" she asked softly.

Timidly, from the back of the crowd, Kevin raised a hand.

"Um," he said. "It's *mine*?"

"*Yours*," she said, then walked it over to him.

On her way back to Edgar, who she took by the arm to usher from the arcade, the word, "Douche!" resounded throughout the arcade. It was Weedy who'd shouted it. He slumped back into the Nitro Streak seat to hide from Mrs. Dewitt. All the kids gasped in horror. Slowly, Edgar's mother turned and scanned the crowd for the guilty party with laser eyes.

When she couldn't determine the guilty kid, she shrugged and looked down at Edgar. "You should be ashamed of yourself," she announced, scanning the crowd. "You lost to a bunch of clowns at Nitro Streak."

The crowd burst into wild laughter again, and there were even some shouts for Mrs. Dewitt. Edgar's mother led him to McDonald's where his father waited.

"Please," Edgar said. "*Please*. Just let me make a few friends before I get run out of Washington."

She draped a lazy arm over his shoulder, jerking him along toward the restaurant, swaying him back and forth even though he was making himself stiff and rigid. Together they strolled in silence throughout the warm, dry evening of central Washington, when suddenly she leaned down close to him.

"*You love me*," she whispered in his ear.

"No, I don't," he said dryly, trying not to smile.

"It's a *good* school you're attending tomorrow," she said quietly. "Much better than your old one back home."

They studied the townspeople as they strolled, the rhythm of their steps never syncing. He could not believe he was about to start a new school—it made him so sad. He could not have missed home more. He missed all his friends. He missed the guys at the charter who knew how to play Nitro Streak, who didn't wreck other people's cars.

When they reached the McDonald's parking lot, Edgar asked, "Are you going to tell dad what I did back there?"

"You're off the hook."

FOUR

On Edgar's first day at his new school, he ate alone at lunchtime.

He pulled a sandwich from his green Bass Pro Shops lunchbox and watched the JV football players catcalling the nearby girls. He looked down and peered through the straw of his thermos, thinking about the hole in the ground. Why had the plank come flying back up? Was there was a geyser at the bottom of the hole?

That couldn't be it. The wood wasn't hot or wet.

Maybe there was a trampoline down there.

Ugh. I'm an idiot.

After school, he grabbed some rope from his father's tool shed and an empty paint can. *Let's see how deep this thing really is,* he thought.

Even after lying on his stomach and lowering his arm as deep into the hole as he could stretch, the paint can stayed suspended in mid-air, banging on the tunnel walls.

Unbelievable. The rope was one hundred and fifty yards long, and it still wasn't long enough to reach the bottom.

One and a half football fields, he marveled.

He pulled the can back up to the surface and untied it from the rope, then placed it beside him. Sitting with his legs dangling over the side, he suddenly had an idea. Slowly, he pushed the can to the edge and let it fall over the side wall, leaning over to watch it drop like an anvil.

He rubbed his chin and waited.

After one hour and twenty-four minutes went by, the paint can shot up from the darkness, same as the floor plank had done the day before. He caught the can in midair and marveled.

"Hello?!?" he screamed into the hole.

After checking his Pathfinder watch to make sure he wouldn't be late for dinner, he tossed the can back into the hole once again.

After another hour and twenty-four minutes exactly, the paint can arrived on schedule, shooting up from the darkness like clockwork.

"This is *insane!!*" he howled into the hole.

But still. No echo returned.

THE NEXT day, on his way to fifth period, Edgar saw his Earth Sciences teacher. The wily-looking man, Dr. Van Rossum, stood in the crispy brown grass of the designated smoking area puffing on a Marlboro red and mumbling to himself as students walked by.

"What's up, Van Rossum?" a student yelled. "Toss me one of those!" A herd of testosterone-ridden young men erupted in laughter.

The teacher exhaled a thick, bluish cloud and squinted into the crowd of students, halfheartedly looking for the rascal then shrugged drowsily.

Dr. Van Rossum caught Edgar's eye. "Good morning, kid," he sang, throwing up a two-fingered salute.

Timidly, Edgar waved back.

In the Earth Sciences classroom, Edgar took a seat near the back of the room, doing his best to steer clear of the group of kids he'd encountered at the arcade the day before—especially the raging Chris Weedy.

For the second straight day, Chris Weedy seemed capable of only one thing: glaring at Edgar from the moment he entered the room.

Edgar leaned forward in his seat and doodled, trying not to look at anyone. He also tried not to stare at Shay who sat two rows over—looking great as always—but it was impossible.

"What is that SMELL?" barked Weedy, suddenly. "Flounder? Is that you? God!" The room fell silent as all turned to look.

Flounder was a kid who sat one row over, hunkered in his desk much like Edgar was, like a turtle inside his shell.

Edgar watched him from the corner of his eye. Flounder kept his hands folded in front, palms-down on the desk in a display of calm, eyes forward to the front of the room, and didn't dare turn around to look at Weedy.

Edgar knew *exactly* how he felt.

"Flounder," hissed Weedy, "it's called 'soap.' Jesus Christ, man! Don't you have any respect for yourself?"

"And while we're on the subject," continued Weedy, turning to Edgar, flashing a bright, over-the-top, far-too-happy smile. "What's with this new guy? The *Nitro King*?" His smile melted into a snarl. "Who's this big, dumb hick from *Jawja*?"

Edgar's face flushed bright red. His gut churned with anger and humiliation. He could feel every eye on him now.

"Alabama, actually," corrected Edgar, matter-of-factly.

"Not Georgia."

"Oh. Pardon me. That's fascinating," said Weedy, pretending to nod off to sleep. And then, as he awakened, his bright smile returned and he said, "Hey! Nice lunchbox!" That's when he pointed to the green Bass Pro Shops lunchbox beneath Edgar's desk, and cackled loudly. Suddenly Weedy's friends were joining in, falling into hysterics, all the JV football players and a few nearby girls, and even a few bookworms chimed in. Edgar tried to keep his cool. He let them laugh as he stared at his desk.

"Yeah," he said, as the laughter finally died down. "It *is* decent. My dad used it on his oil rig back home in Alabama. I always thought it was pretty cool, especially since he left it to me after he died."

The room quieted immediately and a heavy silence hung in the air.

"Cancer," added Edgar, his voice overcome with sadness as he allowed his head to droop and continued to stare at his desktop, trying to muster every sad thought he could possibly think of. He even gave the lunchbox a slight tap with his heel for good measure. "Lung cancer," he whispered. "And he didn't even smoke."

All eyes were now on Chris Weedy. The curly-headed tyrant leaned back in his seat, studying Edgar. He put two hands behind his head and nervously ran them through his golden, curly hair. Then he began to chuckle. Softly at first, testing the waters, then increased in volume.

"What a *redneck*," he blurted. "He's such a liar. You don't believe him, do you?" he asked the room. "His dad didn't die of cancer! He's lying."

Chris surveyed his friends faces. "Come on. Don't let this fool trick you."

Dr. Van Rossum, who came shuffling in, was seemingly oblivious to the strong tension in the room.

"Good morning, ya little rascals!" he sang, dropping

his lunch box clumsily on his desk at the front of the room.

He rummaged absent-mindedly through his cluttered desk for reading glasses and slipped them on. Upon looking up, he found Edgar Dewitt's hand raised high in the air.

"A question? So soon?" the teacher marveled, his brows climbing to an arch. "I haven't even taught anything yet! What can I do for you, Mr . . .?"

"Dewitt," said Edgar, clearing his throat. "How do I calculate the distance of a falling object using time?"

Snickers rang through the rows.

"What a *nerd*," whispered Weedy.

Dr. Van Rossum motioned for quiet. "Cool accent you have, Mr. Dewitt." He blinked at Edgar expectantly.

"Yes sir, I'm from Alabama."

"Ah!" said Dr. Van Rossum. "The Deep South!" He then whirled around and, with both hands, began measuring the distance between Alabama and Washington on a world map that hung beside the dry erase board. He pulled his hands away and demonstrated it to the class.

"It's almost two feet of map!" he said excitedly. "What a long way you've come!" He nodded enthusiastically to his outstretched hands. "What brings you *this* far from Alabama, Edgar?"

Edgar glanced at Weedy and smiled. If he was about to enrage the biggest bully in school, he might as well go down taunting him. "My dad got a job at the Department of Transportation here in Mount Lanier. So we had to move."

Murmurs and muted laughter trickled throughout the class.

"I told you he was a liar," said Weedy. "What did I tell you?"

"Christopher," interrupted Dr. Van Rossum, waving a hand in the air, dismissing Weedy's remark. "Don't interrupt."

"Oh, Christopher, is it?" Edgar whispered, grinning wide. Weedy opened his mouth to speak then snapped it shut and gave Edgar the finger.

Dr. Van Rossum popped the cap from a dry erase marker and turned his body to the board.

"Now," he said, "Edgar, from Alabama, let me ask you *this*: if I were to drop a piano and a baseball off a roof, which do you think would hit the ground first?"

"The piano," guessed Edgar.

"Wrong! They would both hit the ground *simultaneously*."

Edgar frowned in confusion. "So . . . how does that help me?"

"What a dumbass," snorted Weedy, sending ripples of laughter throughout the room.

"Christopher, can you try not to be a complete and utter buffoon for once in your life? See me after class," Dr. Van Rossum barked at Weedy, then turned his attention to Edgar once again. "So, Edgar," said Van Rossum, "since you seem to be the only person in class today who is passionate about learning something new, I'll indulge you for five minutes or so, but just this one time, as we need to get started on other assignments. Here's the formula you're looking for."

At that, Dr. Van Rossum turned and filled the dry erase board with a string of numbers and letters and formulas so indecipherable that Edgar hopped up and moved two seats closer so he could get it all down.

$F = Gm_1m_2/r^2$, it began.

With a scowl of concentration, Edgar scribbled furiously.

FIVE

AFTER SCHOOL, ON the way home, Edgar noticed Shay Sinclair walking through town.

OK, fine. He was following her.

She was a good distance in front of him, strolling casually down the opposite side of the street, saying hello to all the shop owners as she passed. They all smiled back, each of them greeting her warmly. Some even called her by her name.

As she reached town center, she came upon a little girl who was sitting criss-cross-applesauce in the grass, fretting over a giant mess of kite string. The girl, about six or seven years old, wore a blue ribbon in her hair. Her mother sat nearby rocking a baby carriage and waved at Shay as she approached.

The little girl folded her arms and huffed at the mess of string.

"Hello, Liz'beth," said Shay. "What have you got

there?"

"A mess," moaned the girl, who lifted the string to Shay for help.

Shay smiled and dropped to her knees, gathering it up. As Edgar lingered behind a light pole, totally not trying to be creepy, but probably appearing so anyway, he listened to Shay's soft laugh carry on the breeze. He ran a nervous hand through his sandy brown hair and knew it was now or never. Mustering up his courage, he finally moved out from behind the pole and walked over to them.

"Hi there. I'm Edgar," he said to the little girl, holding his arms out toward the kite. "Can I try?"

Shay looked up and smiled. She blocked the sun from her eyes with a forearm and studied him for a long, lingering moment.

"Sure," she said, her eyes squinty. "You can *try*."

The little girl giggled again, looking up at Edgar.

He kneeled down and took the jumbled mess of string from Shay's arms. Then, combing through the knots, he began to work. He tied a loop around the spool to prevent more unwinding and massaged one clump of string through a gap in the tangles.

"I used to work for my uncle at Gulf Shores," he explained through pursed, unmoving lips. He closed an eye to study a particular tangle. "He had a fishing charter and we went out every Saturday." Edgar navigated the spool through a tricky loop, then allowed it to dangle free for a moment so that gravity could do its work.

"The biggest part of my job," he continued thoughtfully, "was untangling lines for stupid tourists who drank more beer than caught fish."

The girls giggled.

Suddenly, the ball of string fell free as the spool danced and spun in the air before the little girl's eyes, like a wound-up yoyo. She leapt to her feet and squealed, snatching the kite from Shay's lap and running off across the square.

"Thank you, thank you, *thank you!*" she shouted, as the kite bounced violently behind her on the grass.

"Whoa, little girl," muttered Shay to Edgar. "Bet that kite doesn't last the day?"

"Yeah," Edgar laughed, who stood and reached out a hand to her to help her up.

Shay smiled, clasped her hand in his, and pulled herself up. For a moment, as they stood face to face, he totally forgot to let her hand go. It was the most wonderful, electrifying thing he'd ever touched in his life.

"Pretty nifty lying back there in Van Rossum's class," she said, turning toward the south of town. He released her and cursed himself for being an idiot, and together they walked for a while. "I was beginning to feel sorry for you for a minute, with that stuff about your dad."

"Yeah, well, Weedy and his goons have been on my ass ever since I got here. I had to do something."

"Well, yeah. That's what they do."

Together the two walked up the road to the edge of town, and as they did, she asked about his life back in Alabama. He talked about his old fishing job and the heat, and how the last month was the rainiest month they'd ever had.

"Bon Secour was the name of my hometown," he explained. "It's way different than this place."

"Yeah? Different how?"

"Well, for starters, it has beaches and bays and an ocean. The beach is . . . man, I really miss it. It's packed with fine, white sand and has a gentle surf that's good for boarding." Edgar paused. "The fishing is great, and it's warm all the time. Southern people are known for being very nice, too, you know."

Shay studied him.

"I've been trying to figure out how to get back home," he said softly, studying the mountains to the west. "To help my family get back home, you know."

"Oh Edguh," she teased, suddenly poking him on the shoulder. "Edguh with ya Suuuthen accent n'all! Y'all'l fit in round he-ah, '*ventually!*"

"Ugh," Edgar muttered, slapping a hand to his face. He smiled at her and shook his head. "Never do that again. That's the worst Southern accent I've ever heard."

She giggled. "Where," she asked, smiling wide as she poked him again, "is your 'Bass Pro Shops' lunchbox from earlier? I don't see it with you."

"Oh, yeah, that," Edgar replied, sheepishly. "Well, lunchboxes are for kids, and Bass Pro Shops lunchboxes, in particular, are for chicken-brain-eating, redneck hicks, didn't you know?"

"Oh, are they?" she laughed. "Well, just to let you know, my dad took me once to a Bass Pro Shops in Calgary and you know what happened? Later that afternoon, I caught a twenty-two-inch brownie."

"You caught . . . what?"

"A brown trout," she explained.

Amazing. Shay Sinclair knows how to fish. Can she get any hotter?

When they arrived at her street, she pointed to her house, which was as big as a governor's mansion. Maybe even bigger.

"That's mine," she said, sort of embarrassed. The house was truly gigantic. Shay, it appeared, was super rich.

"Dang . . . That's somethin' alright."

She turned, blushing. "Hey, I've been wanting to thank you for helping me beat that jerk Weedy yesterday in Nitro Streak. It was awesome."

Edgar shrugged. "Well, you could've beat him by yourself, you know. You're a much better driver than he is. Just don't pick the Miata, even though you like it. Never pick a convertible in that game. Bad wind resistance, you know."

"Yeah?" she asked playfully, nudging him with a shoulder. "So which one should I choose?"

"You should always pick the Nissan 370Z, if you want to win."

"But isn't that *your* car, Edgar?"

"Yeah," he said. "But you can have it, if we ever play again." Edgar smiled shyly, hoping his flirtation tactics weren't too obvious.

"Goodbye, Edgar," Shay said, turning toward her driveway.

"Goodbye," he said, entranced as he watched her. Her long, flowing brown hair dusted the top of her jeans as she ascended the porch steps. Her small, narrow waist and shapely legs made her look older, more mature. She was the most beautiful girl he'd ever seen.

On the walk home through the hills of Mount Lanier, Edgar almost seemed to float on air.

Maybe this place won't suck so much, after all.

SIX

AFTER SCHOOL THE next day, Edgar was back at the hole, this time with a small box in his hands, as well as a notebook filled with calculations. He placed the box at the edge of the hole and popped it open. Inside was a small turtle he'd caught down by the brook. He lifted it into the air and inspected it.

"If I'm wrong about this," he muttered, "it will suck to be you."

He hoisted the turtle over the hole and, with a bit of hesitation, dropped it into the vastness. The turtle's head seemed to retreat as it fell from view. *Poor little guy. Please let me be right.*

"It'll be OK," he said, more to himself as he started the stopwatch on his Pathfinder.

Then he ducked outside and chose a large boulder to sit on. He yanked out his notebook and, on a clean sheet of paper, wrote the number "8000."

This was the diameter of the Earth in miles, as Dr. Van Rossum had told him earlier when Edgar lingered around after class.

"Why don't you just Google this stuff, Edgar?" the teacher had asked. "I know a lot, but I'm not the physics teacher."

"Because it's complicated," Edgar explained. "Yeah, they have formulas online, but you can teach it in a way I can sort of understand. Also, Mr. Norman is totally weird and not as cool as you."

Van Rossum reclined in his chair and folded his hands behind his half-shiny, balding head. He smiled slyly at Edgar and rocked a bit. "Alright, alright. You don't have to suck up. What's this all about, boy?" he asked.

"What do you mean?"

"Oh come on, Edgar. What's with all these formulas and calculations and the constant preoccupation with gravity and falling?"

The professor's big, white bushy eyebrows rose in expectation.

Edgar shrugged, then exhaled in surrender.

"It's for extra credit. It's for the Science Fair."

Van Rossum rolled his eyes and howled.

"Science Fair?" he said, finally composing himself. "Man, Christopher Weedy is right. You *are* a big liar." He shook his head. "Just know," added the teacher with sincerity, "if you're building a time machine, I'd like a lift back to the seventies."

Out on the boulder, in the hot baking sun, just below the number eight thousand, Edgar scribbled his first formula:

$F=Gm_1m_2/r^2$

Using a conversion scale in the back of textbook he

found in the library, along with his cell phone calculator for calculating, Edgar discovered that 8000 miles is actually 12,755,660 meters.

He wrote it all down.

From there, he tapped four other formulas into the phone: Newton's Gravitational Law, the Density and Volume of a Sphere, Knowledge of Gravity Inside a Spherical Mass, and the Simple Harmonic Oscillator Equation.

The Harmonic Oscillator he'd taken to his father the night before, since it involved square roots. Edgar wasn't very good with them, but his dad was pretty much a math genius.

"Physics?" his father had asked, sliding on his glasses.

"Yeah. It's for extra credit."

"Yes, *sir*," corrected his dad.

Mr. Dewitt withdrew his glasses and wiped them on his sleeve, then slid them back onto his face before squinting at the complicated equations before him. "Isn't this stuff a little advanced for a freshman?"

"Dad," sighed Edgar, "this is Washington, remember? It's like mom's been saying. It's two and a half times more advanced than Alabama."

"*More* than two and a half," his father corrected him with a smile, submerging himself in the numbers.

"So what is the Simple Harmonic Oscillator?" Edgar prodded.

"Well, if you take a spring and compress it, the harder you push the spring together, the more it pushes against your fingers. It always wants to return to its original state. I guess you can think of it as a clock, or a pendulum. It's the principle that explains how a pendulum swings back and forth, see?"

OUT ON the hot hillside, with the red-tailed hawks spinning above in tight circles, Edgar tapped furiously into his calculator. One by one, he entered the calculations. Then, suddenly, when all the numbers had been crunched, Edgar hit the equals button. The number "42" stared back at him.

He recalculated everything one more time, *very carefully*, since his life might depend on it, just to be sure.

"42."

Edgar walked back into the cabin and sat next to the hole, waiting nervously as he munched on broken pretzel sticks that he'd stowed away in his backpack.

"*Where's your lunchbox?*" his mom had asked earlier that day.

"I've outgrown lunchboxes, Mom," he'd told her. "I'm in high school now. I'm making my own lunch from now on, too. No more peanut butter and chocolate chip sandwiches."

"But you love peanut butter and chocolate chip!" she cried.

"Not anymore I don't."

He waited by the hole for what seemed an eternity, but suddenly, exactly eighty-four minutes after he dropped the turtle to its death, it suddenly shot back up, rising high over the hole and then dropping rapidly. Edgar reached out and grabbed the frightened creature just in time.

Holy crap. It actually worked?! He clutched the turtle in his hands, cackling like a mad scientist. "Buddy, you're alive!" He danced around the dusty room, careful not to get too close to the hole.

"You've been to China, haven't you?" Edgar asked as the turtle peered out through its shell with two shiny, fearful, black eyes.

"And you're still alive," Edgar mused. "You're *still* alive." He inspected the turtle's shell, looking for signs of injury, but found none. The little guy was scared but otherwise unharmed. Edgar took him outside and placed him near the brook once again.

After walking back into the cabin, Edgar stared down the hole, thoughtfully. *Well, I've got eighty-four minutes to spare. Here goes nothing.*

And with that, he jumped.

SEVEN

For the first several seconds of freefall, Edgar's body clenched in defense. His stomach rose to his throat, threatening to release everything he'd eaten that day.

He opened his mouth to scream but no sound emerged. He could only grind his molars and slam his eyes shut and pray that he wasn't about to die.

This is probably not the best idea I ever had, he thought, regretting his impulsive decision. *Holy crap, how deep is this thing?*

After all the flailing and kicking, his limbs began to tire and he stilled, surrendering to the fall. In the pitch blackness, seconds led to minutes and minutes to *dozens* of minutes, and somewhere deep in the Earth, Edgar curled up into a ball and, just like a fishing lead, plunged through the depths of the world.

"Please don't let me die," he prayed.

The loud rush of air was deafening. It screamed in his

ears like blasting radio static. Each second the expectation of hard earth arriving to smash him like a pancake kept all his muscles tight and alert.

But the hard earth never came.

As he fell, he began to reflect on the floor planks—how they'd all popped back up, same as the paint can, same as the turtle. And none of them had come back damaged. Wasn't that why he'd jumped in the first place? Everything that had gone down had *always* come back up in the same condition as it dropped!

Dang it, he would too. *Right?*

A bit more confident now, he opened an eye and peeked around. He saw nothing but abject darkness—darkness so stark and unrelenting that he might as well have kept his eyes shut.

But when he thought to bring his Pathfinder watch to his face and tap the glow function, instantly the walls of the speeding hole were lit with a dull, murky, yellow-green light.

Immediately he discovered that the writings and drawings were down here too, way deep into the Earth. But they were speeding by so fast that they were only a blur.

Fully acclimated to the freefall now, his stomach not revolting so much anymore, Edgar, like a skydiver, began to spread his arms and legs a little and attempted to control his falling. He reached for the nearby walls and held the glowing watch out, shining it against the bricks for bearings. When he neared them, he reached out and lightly touched the wall with his fingertips.

When approximately twenty minutes had passed, the atmosphere of the tunnel seemed to change. The smell of the hole became overwhelming—that salty smell, like fermented dough, the same smell he first detected back in the cabin. That's when he knew: it was the smell of the deep Earth, the salty, Sulphurous nature of the core.

Also, in conjunction with the smell, the temperature seemed to be rising as well. The exponential rush of freefalling didn't stop the sweat beads from beginning to form on his brow. His head was suddenly pounding like a bass drum, probably from all the pressure in the world, and he could feel his body decompressing.

He checked his watch again. *Certainly*. It all made perfect sense.

I'm falling through the center of the Earth.

When his ears finally popped and he was sure he'd fallen past the core, he was halfway through the Earth and suddenly traveling upward at great speed. The sensation was very different, but similarly alarming.

He'd never even traveled outside of United States and now he was shooting hundreds of miles an hour up to God knew where.

When, according to the Pathfinder, he had fallen for *forty* minutes, he readied himself for the other side of the world. He turned his body in midair and, peering up the tunnel, scanned the darkness ahead for signs of any oncoming light.

Sure enough, at around forty-two minutes, Edgar noticed a faint speck of light coming up the way, maybe five hundred yards or so now, but falling as fast as he was, five hundred yards would surely come *fast*.

He flailed his arms and clumsily swam through the air, grasping at the walls. In a flash he was there, hovering in midair at the top of a hole, somewhere on the opposite side of the globe.

He reached out and snatched the hole's edge and, clinging desperately to it, he dangled there for a moment and steadied himself. He looked up from the hole and blinked at the night sky, beholding a perfectly clear, brilliant dome full of stars and satellites and the moon, all large and yellow and craterous.

"Night here?" he whispered.

Oh yes! Of course it was night!

Climbing from the hole, he stood, taking in the full moon just off the horizon. It was the biggest, most breathtaking moon he'd ever seen. He inhaled deeply and exhaled with laughter, shaking off the last of the trembles that remained from the gut-wrenching fall. The air in his lungs was crisp, cool, and, strangely enough, tasted of salt.

Sea salt.

"Where am I?" he said, looking down at the sand beneath his feat.

Sand?

Then he realized: replacing the wild roar of wind in his ears was the unmistakable crash of nearby waves, and the incessant chop of rippling water.

A shore! Once his eyes acclimated to the surroundings, he found he was gazing across an unknown sea, one that seemed to stretch before him to the horizon. The moon's reflection danced across its waters like a wavering yellow brick road, illuminating the end of the world.

"Awesome!" he said.

Definitely not China. Not unless China was actually the size of a baseball diamond.

It was an island—a deserted one—that was very small and surrounded by water on all sides. There seemed to be no sign of life anywhere—besides one sparse palm tree that could barely be considered a tree, no birds, no lights—*nothing.*

It was just a tiny plateau in the middle of a watery nowhere, it seemed, and the hole through which he arrived was perfectly placed in the island's center.

"Unbelievable," he whispered, grinning, walking down a slight slope to the churning waters. Once there, he took in more of the marvelous ocean air. The way the sparkly, moonlit waves licked the bubble-laden beach intoxicated him.

God, he had missed the beach.

He ripped off his shoes and rolled up his pants, and then, cautiously, tiptoed out onto the shore, letting his toes touch the incoming water.

"Dang!" he said. "It's cold!"

Even still, it *might* be swimmable on a sunny day.

Slowly he waded a bit further, all the while staring at the glorious stars on display above in the marvelous night sky. The celestial theater was utterly gigantic, pitch black, and filled with more stars than he'd ever seen in his whole life.

He took yet another step into the cold, dark water, but this time he could feel the sand drop off quickly beneath his feet. One more step and it might mean waist deep water.

I don't know these waters, he thought, suddenly aware of whatever strange creatures might be lurking beyond. He turned for shore in retreat.

Back on the beach, as he slapped sand from his feet and pulled on his shoes, he heard a fish splashing loudly in the water. He whipped around and strained to see in the moonlight and there, just a few yards away, was the unmistakable shape of a large tailfin protruding from the sea, its fin about the size of his hand.

"*Big one!*" he grinned, as bubbles from the animal lingered in the shimmering surf. As quickly as it had surfaced, the fish darted away.

Once the fish was gone and his thoughts turned to home, he glanced at his watch. It was time to get back. Dinner was soon. He couldn't be late. His parents might start to worry.

He would have to be careful from now on. He stood over the hole and gazed into the blackness, pursing his lips in dreary anticipation. He hated losing his stomach *so much*, but this was his only way home. Counting to three, he faltered—then counted to three once more and faltered again. It was like trying to psych himself to dive into an icy swimming pool, but worse.

"OK man, this time for real," he said, poising himself to jump, for real this time.

He really hated the freefall.

Once he leapt clumsily into the darkness, he balled up immediately, and again slammed his eyes shut, trying to endure the unbearable feeling. But slowly, as he could relax his clenched muscles, he got curious. He settled down and began to experiment. He stretched out his body and tilted his hands to the right and left, and it made him spin clockwise and counterclockwise.

This must be what skydivers do to steer, he thought.

He ducked his head and shoulders and leaned backward and tried a clumsy flip. He felt the flip was probably a pretty ugly one, so he tried it again. Because why not? He had thirty-five minutes to kill, after all.

The second time he flipped felt much, much better. Not nearly so wobbly this time.

Yeah, he thought. *I could get pretty used to this*.

Once he fell to the Earth's core and felt that unmistakable heat once again, Edgar started to ponder ways that he might sneak out of the house late at night. It would be necessary if he ever wanted to visit the island during the daytime, since the opposite sides of the Earth experienced day and night at opposite times. Considering their new house in Mount Lanier, he had no idea which windows might be the least creaky ones. He'd need to check them out during the daytime when his parents were gone, maybe put some oil on the hinges to quiet them down.

Just thinking about getting busted made him uneasy. He'd never been in trouble before. He'd never really disobeyed before. His relationship with his parents had always been strong. They loved him dearly and trusted him. As much as his friends back home warred with their parents, he never had that problem with his.

If his mom caught him sneaking out it would definitely break her heart. And he didn't want to do that. It would be a risk, certainly, but given all the crap he'd endured that week at school—being the new guy, dodging that low-life, Weedy, he *deserved* a beach day, dang it!

His mom would understand if she only knew what he went through.

Thirty-five minutes later, Edgar shot up from the hole safe and sound, back in Mount Lanier, alive, well, and without a scratch. Once he pulled himself from the hole, he walked to the doorway of the cabin and leaned on the frame, gazing out into the beautiful forest, a huge smile on his face. He closed his eyes and basked triumphantly in the warmth of the evening sun. He savored the fact that he might be the first human on Earth to see the sun and the moon in two different skies and all within one hour's time.

Astronauts not included, of course.

THAT NIGHT, as Edgar sat at the kitchen table working on "homework," his mother flitted around the kitchen humming a song. Edgar dismantled his childhood globe, ripping it entirely from its metal base and semi meridian. Now the big green and blue ball wobbled around the kitchen table along its uneven mountain ranges.

It was also severely marked up with a Sharpie and had a big, red X denoting the town of Mount Lanier.

He took a protractor and walked it side-to-side, Frankenstein-like, across the lands and seas of the Earth, along a path he'd mapped out. It finally landed among the oceans of the southern hemisphere.

"School was . . .?" pressed his mom, suddenly not humming anymore. She stirred chili powder into the taco meat and glanced at him from the corner of an eye.

"It was *school*," he said flatly, marking a triumphant "X" in a distant watery locale. The X was sandwiched between the Indian and southern oceans and was about fifteen hundred miles southeast of the tip of Africa.

Smack dab in the middle of a vast, dangerous sea, it looked like. This was where he believed his island to be.

"Well, have you made any new friends?" she prodded, but Edgar didn't answer. Instead, he hammered two nails into the two X's using the blunt end of a butter knife.

"Edgar, that's your childhood globe . . ."

"It's OK, Mom. It's for the Science Fair. I'm just getting a head start," he lied.

"Science Fair? This early in the year?"

He traced a finger from the southern hemisphere's nail to a string of landmasses, due west. These unfriendly islands were called the "French Southern and Antarctic Islands" and as he ran his fingers across them—a bunch of brown, rugged mounds in a wide expanse of blue, their mountainous peaks capped with white—they seemed jagged and ominous.

This was the island's only nearby landmass, and it was a pretty long way away.

"Any girls yet?" she continued to pry.

"Mom!" said Edgar, dryly. He finally looked up after circling the islands with the Sharpie. "No."

"'*No ma'am*.' But not one single girl?"

"No *ma'am*," he said. "They don't have any girls in Washington."

She threw a balled up napkin at him but he batted it away, grinning.

Turning his concentration back to the globe, he tied a string to both nails to ensure it would circumnavigate the ball smoothly. It did, perfectly, which meant that the two points he'd marked with red Xs were indeed opposite each other in the world—that they were indeed *antipodes*, a term that, like so many others lately, he had learned from Dr. Van Rossum.

The conclusion? Mount Lanier was directly opposite of his newfound island in the middle of the Indian Ocean.

The hole through the Earth led to there.

A weary Mr. Dewitt came wobbling through the door, dangling a hardhat. He looked at his wife with absolute exhaustion, his eyes bloodshot and his body covered head to toe in soot and sweat.

"Dad," said Edgar.

His father planted a kiss on his wife's cheek and yanked a Coke from the refrigerator, then came to the table to gaze over Edgar's shoulder.

"What'cha doing, man?" he asked.

Edgar proudly presented the dismantled globe.

"Remember when you used to say, 'Dig a hole deep enough and go all the way to China?'"

"Yeah," his father nodded, scanning the destruction on the table.

"Well, you don't go to China," informed Edgar, "not from Mount Lanier you don't. You would go here."

He hovered a finger over the big red X in the Southern Hemisphere, adding, "You go to the *Indian Ocean*, about two thousand miles west of Australia. Right . . . *here*."

"Hmm," said his father, gulping down another massive gulp of Coke. "I guess you better have a snorkel for that last shovelful, huh?"

EIGHT

LATER THAT NIGHT, Edgar tossed in bed. The hole called to him. The freefall, the wind, the *speed*. He yearned to feel the sensation of flying once more. It wasn't so bad after you got over the initial feeling.

For a while he thought about ducking out his bedroom window, sprinting off into the warm night to the cabin that housed the hole, and popping up into the sunshine of the other side of the world. But it was just too much of a risk. Somehow he couldn't bring himself to sneak out. He was petrified of what his parents might do. He would probably be grounded for years.

ON HIS way to school the next day, Edgar meandered down a deserted mountain road through a chorus of angry insects inhabiting the brown hillsides. Wildflowers here crumpled with dryness, waving as warm gusts fanned them. The whole world was stiff and brown from the lack of rain. Everything crackled. Everything hissed.

When he neared the town and topped a long, sloping hill, he peered down at Mount Lanier, noticing the grid of intersecting streets. Cars in the distance crawling the roadways like multi-colored ants darted to and fro. He held out his hand to feel the last of the dry wildflowers as they swayed in the mountain breeze, then descended to the bottom of the hill.

The ensuing valley was essentially the town square, and once in town he walked along until he came upon an old, western-style saloon. Elk horns hanging over the door and everything. It was, like all other establishments in Mount Lanier, fashioned in the rancher's style: log cabins, unused horse hitches, statues of wooly pioneers. If not for the SUVs and an occasional airplane overhead, it might have just been the Old West.

Nearing the movie theater, he came upon a make-shift fish stand. It was just a display case, really, with four wheels on the bottom, and one side hitched to the back of an old, beat-up van. It was filled to the brim with an array of beautiful fish and crustaceans.

Behind the case scurried a family of what seemed to be Italian fish mongers: a mother, a father, a daughter, and a son. The father was shouting, "*Fresh Fish!*" to all who passed by. Edgar recognized the son immediately: the kid from school they called "Flounder," the one from Dr. Van Rossum's class who Weedy had been picking on.

Edgar neared the stand and watched Flounder fillet a salmon for an elderly woman.

Flounder, he quickly discovered, was awesome at it.

"How many?" Flounder asked the lady.

"Four fillets, thank you, Anthony," she smiled. Edgar marveled at Flounder's handiwork. The short, timid teen-ager, who had a haystack of black, curly hair, was an artist with a fillet knife. Like a surgeon he assaulted the fish with quick cuts using his razor-sharp, blood-darkened blade. He made the skin and meat come away from the bone in a matter of seconds. It was better cutting than anyone Edgar had ever seen—better than any captain on any charter boat back home in Bon Secour, hands down.

"What are you gonna do with those pliers?" Edgar spoke up. Flounder looked up and seemed to recognize him. He nodded and pointed the knife down at the fish.

"Those are pin bones," he explained. "I pull them out of the bottom of the fillet. I yank them out with these pliers." He smiled at the old lady. "Who wants to eat bones, am I right?"

"That's awesome," said Edgar, watching him work. "You're pretty good at this."

One by one, Flounder yanked the bones from the fish.

"So," said Flounder, without looking up, "you're the Gravity Man, right?" He smiled and flashed Edgar a glance. "I think it's funny how you always drive Dr. Van Rossum nuts."

"That's me," said Edgar.

"So, do I call you Flounder?" Edgar asked from behind the stand.

Anthony, busy cutting into another fish, suddenly froze. His cheeks went red and he glanced up from the salmon mid-slice, shooting a quick glance at his mother who was busy icing lobsters. Thankfully, she did not seem to hear. Relieved, he flashed a conspicuous frown at Edgar and shook his head *no*.

"Sorry," mouthed Edgar.

"Here you go, ma'am," said Flounder, his salesman's smile easy and natural. He handed the woman her salmon steaks all neatly wrapped in clean, white paper. Then he moved to the water cooler to wash up.

Edgar watched as Flounder approached a bucket of

fresh water and washed meticulously, slowly soaping up three or four times. He scrubbed slowly and carefully, then dried off with a white towel. Afterward, he squeezed fresh lemon juice on his hands and then rubbed them with vanilla extract to kill the smell, and when finished, sniffed deeply of his hands. Nodding with satisfaction, he turned to hug his mother goodbye and gave his little sister a push (who tried not to smile), then joined Edgar for the walk to school.

"Dude," he said, once clear of the fish stand. "You can't ever call me 'Flounder' in front of my mom, OK?"

"But, why?" said Edgar. "I thought that was your nick-name."

"Well, it's not," said Flounder. "My name is Anthony . . . Artese. They call me 'Flounder' at school, but that's not my name. They say I smell like fish. Get it? *Flounder?*" He looked at Edgar, then absently sniffed his hands. "They make me work all morning—my parents do—and all the time it's all I can do to just make it to school without being late. What am I supposed to do about the fish smell? My smock can only catch so many of the fish guts. Sometimes a drop gets on my shirt, and sometimes on my jeans. I can't help it." He turned away in disgust and kicked a rock down the dusty road. "We don't even *sell* flounder," he mumbled glumly.

"Well, I actually think it's pretty cool, if you ask me," said Edgar. He bent and scooped a handful of rocks and tossed them in a trickling stream.

"What is?" asked Anthony.

"Your nickname."

"Yeah? Whatever."

"I'm serious. Back in Alabama we'd kill to have a nick-name like that. Especially at the fish charter."

Flounder didn't seem too convinced, so Edgar continued.

"Look, man," he explained. "Just think of those good mafia nicknames: *Bagel Joe. Two Shoes. Little Eddie.* If *Flounder's* not as good as those mafia names, what is? It's like: 'Who whacked Don Amici?' 'Oh, *Flounder did!*' That's a cool nickname if you think about it."

"You're crazy," said Flounder, smiling.

As they made their way to school, Flounder began to tell Edgar all about the family business. Each week, the Arteses drove several hours to the shores of Washington State and purchased various types of fish from different fisheries—as much as the van could hold. Bringing it back to Mount Lanier, they put it on display outside their van, like Edgar had seen earlier.

Apparently, the fish sold like hotcakes. Everybody in the town bought from them.

"We mark it up pretty good, too," Flounder said proudly. "It's a pretty good living. Just a lot of work."

"Yeah, well, I'll catch my own," said Edgar, smiling. "Why would I pay so much money for something I can always catch for free?"

"Dude," laughed Flounder, "I don't know if you saw back there but our stuff comes from the *deep sea.* It's super fresh, too!"

"So?"

"*So?*"

"Yeah! Like I said. I can catch my own."

"Well, good luck," laughed Flounder. "You've got about six hours to any shore."

FIVE MINUTES before the first bell rang, Flounder and Edgar were spotted walking up to school by the worst person: Chris Weedy.

"Flounderrrrr!" he yelled through cupped hands, cackling as his jock friends chimed in. From nearby tables just off the common, several around them began to sniff the air in what seemed to be a well-worn ritual. All of them yelled, "Flounderrrrr!" and cackled, and Edgar watched as Anthony stiffened and tried to ignore it, but couldn't.

Watching Flounder endure it, suddenly, without realizing it, he was enraged. He stopped and turned and glared directly at Weedy just outside the doors of the school.

He didn't even think about it; he just did it. And when Weedy saw it—Edgar glaring at him like he was, his fist twisting like a storm— Weedy's evil grin suddenly evaporated and his face went wrinkly with rage.

"That's right, *Christopher*," muttered Edgar, enunciating every syllable. "I'm looking at you."

"*Dude*," said Flounder, "stop that! Don't mess with that guy! He's totally nuts. You just don't know how bad."

Edgar turned to Flounder and smiled.

"Who whacked Chris Weedy?" he said. "*Flounder did, that's who!*"

Just outside the double doors, Flounder held out a hand to Edgar, and just as the first bell rang, the two boys shook hands. It was Edgar's first friend in Washington: a fellow fisherman and a genuinely cool dude. Edgar would have to toughen him up, though.

NINE

THAT NIGHT EDGAR lay awake again, unable to drift off to sleep. All he could think of was the bright, glorious sun that must be hanging high above the ocean on the other side of the world, and all the fish that must be leaping from the surf, and the clear, blue water surrounding it all.

At two in the morning he could take it no more. He rose from the bed and crept across the floor, *slowly*, so that the hardwood floorboards wouldn't squeak. Then, he withdrew a pair of beach sandals and swim trunks from his closet and, moments later, was standing before the window, gulping down his wildly thumping heart. Slowly, carefully, he lifted the latch.

It was something he'd never done before, sneaking out. Suddenly he felt like an outlaw. He carefully climbed out of the open window and landed softly on the ground.

He darted across the lawn and soon reached the backyard shed. There, large hinges on the door creaked with low, rusty groans as he pulled it open. Grimacing at the noise, he glanced fearfully back at the house, and was glad to see that no lights had come on.

Next, he slipped quickly through the slightly opened door and, using the green glow of his Pathfinder watch, located his fishing pole. The Abu Garcia Ambassadeur, an open faced, golden-colored rod, was absolutely beautiful.

He fingered the reel and felt for oil. Perfectly lubed, as always. His dad always kept the poles in great shape.

Next he felt around for the tackle box, and when he found it, he thumbed carefully through the lures inside, searching for the only one that could work on the other side of the world: *The Spoon Spinner*. His prized lure *always* got strikes, no matter the waters.

Surely the Indian Ocean would be no different.

Carefully closing the shed door behind him, he bolted off down the driveway, making for the dirt road beyond, then off through the moonlit trail he'd come to know so well. As he ran he calculated the deadline he must follow for the night: about an hour and a half to fall—round trip—that gave him at least two hours of fishing on the island. And maybe half an hour remaining for swimming. Nothing more. He simply couldn't be late. His mother usually woke up at six, and if he wasn't home before that time, safely in bed, he would definitely be caught.

And *that* would really, really suck.

Sprinting through the darkness, surprisingly unafraid of any creatures that might be lurking in the woods, he felt so energized at the promise of a sunny beach that he didn't even care.

Standing over the hole in the darkened cabin, panting furiously and leaning over the edge, he finally dropped over into the chasm, speeding like a brick toward the center of the Earth. He grimaced and giggled and tightened his stomach in a war against his revolting stomach, falling torward the warmth of the island. The spoon spinner at the tip of his fishing rod buzzed wildly beside his ear, like a flittering dragonfly.

APPEARING AT the opening of the hole on the other side, Edgar found himself bathed in Southern Hemisphere sunlight.

The brightly lit, cloudless sky and the neon blue, shimmering sea below it were like something out of a painting. The world was bright, light, and refreshing. *And warm.*

Squinting, his eyes watering as they tried to adjust, he stood on the hole's edge and let his entire body take in the daylight.

"Faaaantastic!" he said, stretching his arms wide and taking a deep breath.

It's almost tropical, he mused.

Stepping to the shore, he dunked one foot into the water and found it just warm enough for a swim! Hastily, he ripped off his shirt, kicked away his sandals and rubbed his hands together, then went ahead and dove right in.

"Wooo!" he said aloud. The surf was a little cold, but swimmable, just as he thought.

The beautiful blue water was like a revelation to his skin, and it electrified him—the best feeling he'd felt since he moved to Mount Lanier. He shot down beneath the waves like an otter, plummeting into the immaculate blue ocean beneath, the expert swimmer that he was. Down below, he opened his eyes and took in a fascinating mosaic of beautiful coral stretching down into a cylindrical underwater mountain cocooned over the outside of the hole, stretching far deeper than Edgar could ever possibly see, off into an oceanic haze beneath him.

There were also fish—*millions* of them—ranging in

all sizes and colors and shapes—a veritable goldmine of aquatic life below. Beneath his flapping arms, they darted to and fro amongst the coral, feeding and rolling and warming themselves in the sun. Some were similar to the deep sea fish back in The Gulf of Mexico, their deep purples and aqua blues and neon yellows betraying the characteristics of most deep water animals.

And some of them, Edgar noted with giddy excitement, were very, *very* big.

He steadied himself and fanned against the churning currents, taking in all the beauty of the pristine water world beneath his feet, and just as he could hold his breath no more, he turned to the surface and came lurching from the surf, giggling at his wonderful luck. He'd found a place all his own—a wonderful place—only accessible by the most unique of ways: by falling through the center of the world like a skydiving daredevil.

He felt like the only person in the world with such an incredible, unbelievable secret. He idled in the surf, scanning the new island in the broad daylight that was barely visible from sea level where he was, low as it was to the water, and he knew that if it were not for the one small palm tree, he might just miss it.

He swam to shore, dried himself in the sun for a moment, and then got down to business. Making his way to the hole's edge and retrieving the Abu Garcia from where he'd left it, he returned to the shoreline and, with a skillful flick of the wrist, heaved the spoon spinner as far as he could into the sea, maybe thirty yards from shore. Reeling it briskly across the waters, pumping his arms from time to time like his father always showed him, he waited.

Before long, from the depths, a creature lunged for the lure. A splash erupted in front of the bait, and for a moment, Edgar thought he had missed. His squinty eyes remained affixed to the sea, waiting in grave anticipation, when all of a sudden, *another* watery eruption devoured his lure, making his rod lunge immediately toward the sea. He howled with surprise and yanked backward with all of his strength.

It was *huge*.

There was a straight-up monster on the other end of the line, he could tell. It was so big it even jerked him forward a couple of steps.

"Oh my God!" he cried, reeling furiously, the fish now locked onto the lure. Edgar had him squarely for better or worse.

"Huge," he shouted joyfully, and the splashing fish—a beauty now leaping from the water, showing to him its massive top fin—now tested the limits of Edgar's mighty Abu Garcia.

And then, suddenly, he knew it: this island was a fishing goldmine. It was a hot spot. A *honey hole*.

AT FIVE-THIRTY in the morning, as the sun peeked over the hills illuminating the dirt road Edgar walked upon, he neared his driveway with a rather large fish tail protruding from his backpack.

The glow of fishing shone upon his face and was hampered only by a touch of weariness around the eyes.

Bang! came a noise from the driveway, just as he approached the house.

What the hell was that?

He dove into the woods and peeked through a cluster of leaves at the adjacent property.

It was the car door!

Just outside the work shed stood his father. For some stupid reason, he was unloading boxes from the Jeep.

The hell is he doing up so early? thought Edgar, suddenly

limp with horror.

Oh my God!

Edgar was, in a word, screwed.

There was no way to sneak back into his bedroom now. Not without getting caught.

He frantically checked his watch. If he didn't think of something quick, he'd have even worse problems when his mother found him missing from his bed in a few minutes. He thumped his head with hard knuckles and strained for a plan, when suddenly an idea emerged. It wasn't the best plan ever, but it was a desperate situation and he just didn't have any other options.

Flinging his backpack and the fishing pole behind an evergreen tree, he kicked off his sandals and rubbed tree leaves all over his hands to kill any remaining fish smell. Then, after a deep breath to calm his hammering heart, he leapt from the woods and trotted breathlessly up the driveway, right toward his unsuspecting father.

"Yo!" he yelled. "Dad!"

It startled his father, who whipped around and gazed groggily at Edgar.

"Huh?" he said, visibly confused at the sudden appearance of his son. He looked back at the house and then at Edgar as if to decide whether he was witnessing the ghost of his son or not. Just as Edgar had hoped: he might be able to take advantage of his dad's morning haziness. Edgar now had the advantage of clarity.

"Hey!" he said breathlessly. "I'm in training, see?" Waving off the questioning stare of his father, he added, "You know, cross country tryouts. I didn't want to wake y'all up. Guess it worked! I tiptoed out earlier, about half an hour ago." He bent over and did some stretches for good measure, to add to the effect. Hopefully the pine needles were doing their job and covering up any lingering, suspicious aroma.

I hope I'm downwind.

"Son," replied his father, "you're *barefoot.*"

Edgar looked down and said, "Yeah! I know! That's how they do it nowadays. Strengthens the arches."

"Ah," mumbled his father, scratching his head. Taking a pensive, sideways sip from his big coffee mug, he eyed Edgar, then, after another moment's consideration, he flashed a big, goofy smile.

"I'll come see you run then!" he exclaimed. "That is, if you make the team."

"Don't worry, Dad! I'll make the team," assured Edgar, shooting him an extra wide smile.

His plan was working! His dad was totally buying it.

But then, somewhere inside, something ugly turned over: a pang of dull guilt mixed with shame for playing his father in such a way. The man trusted Edgar—fully and completely—and now Edgar had gotten his hopes up. Which was cruel.

"So," said Edgar, suddenly wanting to change the subject. "What's in the boxes?"

"These?" said his father, a sly grin emerging on his face. "Oh, these are just a bunch of *sticks of dynamite!*" He yanked one of the boxes from the jeep and turned to the shed, then kicked open the old, wooden door.

"Wow. Explosives? *Really??*" asked Edgar, following him in.

"Yeah. Turns out I get to keep a few of these boxes at the house because of my job at the Department of Transportation since we live on this side of the pass. It's so I can get through an avalanche if there's ever a big emergency."

Edgar couldn't even imagine it—*avalanches!* Snow! A real winter was coming! He'd only seen an inch of snow in his whole entire life down in Alabama.

At least this was one thing cool about Mount Lanier.

"It's against the rules for me to have dynamite at the

house," continued his father, "but hey, they let me have a few boxes anyway, since I'm so cool."

"You're ridiculous," laughed Edgar, shaking his head.

"Hey," asked his father, "wanna give me a hand?" Edgar nodded and happily followed him out, so thankful he had survived sneaking out without getting busted. He grabbed a box from the Jeep and turned to the shed.

Turns out, dynamite was *heavy*.

"Whoa," said Edgar. "It feels like a box of bricks."

"Just put them over here," said his father, "on *this* side of the shed, so we can put the blasting caps on the other side. It's probably best to keep them both separate. I mean, it's probably overkill, but I do want to be safe you know?"

"Should I be nervous about dropping it?" asked Edgar, nodding at the box.

"Nah. Without the blasting caps they're totally harmless. No more dangerous than a box of wet hotdogs—and only half the cholesterol."

Edgar stiffened as his father brushed by the pole rack, hoping his father wouldn't notice that the Abu Garcia was glaringly absent.

Once they were finished unloading the boxes, Mr. Dewitt slapped Edgar on the back and beamed at him with pride. "Cross country tryouts, huh? Well, I'm really proud." Fully awake now, his father's face was aglow in admiration.

It didn't make Edgar feel good one bit, even though he smiled back. Actually, it made him feel particularly terrible, like a complete and total jackass.

"Thanks, Dad," chirped Edgar, closing the shed door behind him.

Once his dad had left for work, Edgar waited until he rounded the bend and then bolted to the woods for his fish and Abu Garcia. He snatched them up and darted across the yard, heading for the shed while trying to stay behind the line of shrubs and underbrush in case his mother looked out the window and saw him carrying a bunch of stuff this early in the morning.

Back in the shed, he yanked open the deep freezer in which his dad kept smoked sausage and black-eyed peas. After he checked the fish for freshness—its gills still red with blood—he wrapped it in some newspaper and stuffed it in the freezer.

Looking at the fish, now secretly hidden from everyone but him, he marveled at its size. *It's gotta be twenty pounds, easy,* he thought.

It was beautiful, somewhat prehistoric-looking, and had fins on top and bottom with two rows of pointy, razor-sharp teeth. Its underbelly tender and pudgy, promised to yield a good portion of hopefully edible meat.

What if it's poisonous? Edgar thought. But he didn't have time to worry.

He would need to get back into the house and deal with his soon-to-be-awake mother.

Edgar washed his hands thoroughly three times in the faucet outside, which made him think of Flounder. Edgar couldn't afford to smell like fish this morning. Mrs. Dewitt had the nose of a bloodhound and the suspicion of a DEA cop.

When he could no longer detect the smell of the sea on his hands, he ripped off his shirt and ran extra loudly into the house, stomping his bare feet and making sure to be extra calamitous on the hardwood floor. He found his mother in the kitchen, in the middle of pouring a steaming cup of coffee. At the sight of him, she clutched her hand to her heart and gasped.

"Edgar!" she exclaimed breathlessly. "What in the world are you *doing*?"

"Who, me?" Edgar wheezed. "Just training for cross country tryouts, Mom."

This time the lie came more easily—the trying not to wake them, the tiptoeing out, the bare feet strengthening the arches—all of it.

This isn't so bad. Lying is easier than I thought.

At dinner that night, Edgar was so sleepy his eyes began to close right there at the table. He'd been awake for over twenty-four hours now—the longest amount he'd ever been without sleep. His parents seemed to notice it, too.

"What's wrong with you?" asked his mother.

"Oh, just a lot of homework, that's all," he said, yawning.

"So early in the year?"

"Yeah, Ma. Like you said, it's a good school."

"I see," she said thoughtfully. "Your father and I need to go out of town this weekend. Think you can handle staying by yourself until Sunday?"

"Sure," he said. "Where y'all going?"

"To Bon Secour," murmured his father.

"But, *why*?" said Edgar, instantly awake, his fork clanging as he dropped it. The sound cast even more of a somber mood upon the room than before.

"Edgar," she explained softly, "we have to finish selling the old house. What would you like us to do? *Not* sell it?" She dropped her fork and rubbed her temples. "If you need something you can knock on Mrs. Irving's door down the road," she mumbled. "She seems to be a nice lady."

"OK," said Edgar. "Whatever."

He slumped in his chair and the two of them stared at each other for a long time.

"What's with your attitude, Edgar? You've been real . . . testy lately."

"Oh, I don't know," he shrugged. "Maybe because they're gonna make you *cry* again, Mom, just like they always do! Everyone treats you like crap over there."

"Watch your mouth, Edgar." She glared at him as she stood to clear the table.

They were traveling back home to Bon Secour—a city in shambles, the city he loved, and somehow hated even more. The townsfolk there were angry with his father; they blamed him for the oil spill that had decimated their economy. But truthfully, nobody cared more for Bon Secour than his dad had—or his mom for that matter. They'd given everything to the little town they called "home." But still, at the end of the day, no one cared. The loss of money and resources had made them monsters.

"You can eat leftovers on Friday night," murmured his mother. "On Saturday you can order a pizza," she continued. "I'll leave you some money."

"Fine," Edgar nodded, but he'd save the pizza money.

There was fresh fish to be eaten.

TEN

THE WEEK WENT by without a hitch. Edgar had resisted the urge several times to sneak out and opted instead to rest up for the weekend, knowing that when his parents left for Bon Secour, he'd have all the time in the world to work on his new hobby: skydiving.

He'd also been perfecting the art of steering clear of Chris Weedy and his goons for the most part—keeping his head down, staying out of conversations, not lingering in the hallway and not engaging him in Van Rossum's class. It had all gone fairly smoothly, that was, until Friday at lunchtime, when Flounder was suddenly pegged in the face with an apple, hard.

Edgar sat across from him at the table, his jaw wide open, stunned by the violent impact. "Jesus!" cried Flounder, wincing in pain. The hard fruit had come whizzing across the lunch room, smashing Flounder's temple like a fist, and Edgar, staring in disbelief, turned to see the jocks across the way—led in riotous laughter by

Chris Weedy—and watched with an ensuing rage as they cackled like loons at what had been done.

"I was aiming at *you*, redneck," Weedy mouthed to Edgar, burning with hatred.

"Jeez, man, are you OK?" said Edgar, turning to face Flounder.

"Yeah. I'm fine," he muttered, wiping the pulp and juice from his reddening cheek.

A welt had begun to raise on Flounder's temple. Silently raging, Edgar looked down at the tabletop and began to crush a stray Cheeto with his thumb, imagining it as Weedy's face. *There's nothing we can do about the psychopath*, Edgar reasoned. If they told on him, Weedy's pack of meatheads would get them on the way home from school. And if they tried to fight him, well, same outcome.

When there was nothing left of the Cheeto but a fine orange powder, Edgar blew the dust from the tabletop and looked up.

"Look, man," he said. "There's just nothing we can do right now."

"I know," said Flounder. He nodded his hanging head. His sleek, black curls fell over his dark eyes.

With the insults and laughter dying down, lunch returned to normal.

"What're you doing tomorrow?" said Edgar, trying to change the subject. Flounder's red welt was growing insanely large.

"Nothing," Flounder shrugged. "I mean, working. But other than that, nothing." He lifted a hand and brushed the last bit of apple pulp from his shirt, then massaged the gnarly, red knot on his head forehead. Rage pulsed through Edgar's chest, but for both their sakes, he tried to swallow it down.

"OK then," said Edgar. "Fake a stomachache tomorrow and be at my house at nine o'clock. I need to show you something."

Out of the blue, like an angel materializing from heaven, Shay Sinclair appeared and stood over their table, her face contorted into an angry scowl.

Huffing, she shot a glare at the mystified Chris Weedy and seethed.

"Have any room for me?" she asked angrily, slapping her lunch bag down on the table. Without receiving a response from Edgar and Flounder, she sat down.

Flounder winked at Edgar and smiled. Edgar motioned for him to scoot down and give her more room.

"No more lunches with stupid people," she hissed, unpacking her lunch by slamming each item down on the table. Edgar and Flounder watched her in absolute awe.

"That's OK, Shay," Weedy yelled across the room, extra loud so that everyone could hear. Edgar turned and noticed an empty seat at the end of his table where Shay had been sitting, and it dawned on him that she'd left his table and her group of friends to join his and Flounder's table, in *defense* of Flounder.

She's on our side. Edgar could have asked for her hand in marriage right then and there.

"Nobody wants to sit with the daughter of a criminal, anyway." A few nearby girls placed hands over their mouths trying not to laugh. *What's he talking about? Is her father a criminal? They sure did have a big house.*

Shay closed her eyes and placed two balled fists on the table, squeezing them until her knuckles went white. Edgar and Flounder watched intently, and after a moment she finally composed herself, defiantly lifted a sandwich to her mouth, and took a large, angry bite.

"If anybody's a criminal," she proclaimed, "it's t*hat* guy." She chewed angrily and toasted him with a salute of her sandwich.

"You don't say," muttered Edgar.

"Oh, he's a psychopath!" she continued, popping the cap on her Diet Coke. "He blows up stuff. Did you know that? Makes bombs out of chlorine and brake fluid. He salts yards, breaks windows, starts fires—just a regular vandal of the grandest proportions. The police can't seem to catch him in the act, and here at school, everybody's so afraid of him that they don't ever tell, like right now, with Flounder." She leaned over and looked at Flounder's welt. "Oh my God—Flounder!" she said. "Are you OK?" He nodded at her, and her face became red with rage. "That's it," she hissed. "I'm telling on the jackass!" She rose from the table but the two boys reached desperately for her and urged her to sit.

"Please," Edgar said. "If you want to help us, just let us work it out. You'll just make matters worse if you tell on Weedy."

She gazed at Edgar, face still contorted with disgust. Then she sat back down and stuffed the rest of her sandwich into her crumpled paper bag. "Why are people so afraid of him?" she asked. "I'll never know. He's nothing! My big brother would rip him apart."

"Yeah?" said Edgar. "But could your brother beat up the whole JV football team? Because that's what it would take." She stared at him and considered this for a moment.

"All I'm saying is," she said, sighing in resignation, "one day, Chris Weedy's gonna get himself and the whole JV football team—which is a basketful of total idiots—placed right into Juvi. Mark my words."

"Juvi?" inquired Flounder.

"You know, juvenile detention," Edgar explained. "It's like a prison for kids, which, yeah, she's right. Just the sort of place Chris Weedy belongs."

"You know," Shay said, deep in thought, her voice now lowered to a whisper, "if you ever saw him vandalize something, you'd understand just how freaking nuts he is.

Like, the stuff he damages or destroys, he always takes a picture of what he vandalizes with his cell phone, like he's collecting a trophy or something. It's *psychotic*. No matter how many dogs are barking, no matter how many front porch lights are coming on, he always sticks around to get his picture, like he's addicted to terrorizing Mount Lanier. It's like he needs something to remember it by."

"Huh," said Edgar, "I guess it sounds like somebody we know has actually *been* there when he took one of those pictures."

She hung her head and nodded. "Yeah," she admitted, "I was there one night. I was with him, once." Her voice went soft with the grave admission that seemed to pain her. "It was a mistake, I admit it, but I went out with him and his friends without knowing what we were getting into. They just invited me out and I was bored, so I went. I mean, I wasn't *with* him—it was just a big group and all my friends were going, so I thought, OK, maybe we're just going to a movie or something, or maybe we end up playing spin the bottle or something down by the football fields."

Edgar gulped at the notion of her playing spin the bottle. Picturing her kissing someone other than him pissed him off more than it should have.

"But after they got me from my house, he led us all down to the suburbs and before anyone knew it, there he was, lighting a car tire on fire. Everybody freaked and scattered laughing and squealing and, I mean, I ran too—even though I hadn't done anything wrong because I didn't want to be the one who got caught." She placed a hand over Flounder's hand and added, "I didn't want to be the only one to go to *Juvi*, you know?"

Flounder stared at her with wide, fascinated eyes, entranced by her as she twirled the Diet Coke cap around her fingers.

"There he was," she said, lost in the recollection. "Chris Weedy, the last of us, unwilling to run away, wearing this evil little grin on his face while the rest of us scattered like cockroaches. We dove into the bushes and hid behind trash cans, some of us sprinting up the mountainside—whatever we could do to keep out of sight from oncoming cars or cops. But not Weedy. He just stood there with this demented look on his face, cell phone in hand, taking picture after picture of the burning tire as if he didn't even care—as if nothing in the world could pull him away. His friends called out to him. They told him to run, but like I said, he never even seemed to care."

"So no Juvi for Christopher," muttered Flounder, visibly disappointed.

"Nah," said Shay. "Not that it would matter for a guy like him. Apparently for Chris, Juvi would be no worse than home. Rumor has it his mom was a heavy alcoholic, and his dad is never around."

"*Was?*" asked Edgar.

"Yeah," Shay nodded. "His mother supposedly drank herself to death a few years back. And his dad works a lot."

"Whoa," said Edgar. "That kind of explains a little."

THAT AFTERNOON, with Edgar's parents safely en route to Bon Secour, Edgar finally retrieved the fish from the shed that had been thawing behind the lawnmower since he'd left for school that morning. Now, in the warmth of the fall afternoon, he took his electric knife and sat down on the deck.

He began at the front and cut to the bone, then moved back to the tail, keeping the blade even with the deck boards before flipping the loose meat from the carcass and cutting outwardly to the skin, skirting as close as he dared without cutting through. Then he slid the blade just beneath the tough membrane and cut backward toward himself.

He lifted the fillet up to his nose and took a big, victorious whiff. The hearty cutlet of fish smelled just like the sea . . . which was *good.*

He nicked a corner of the meat and, after a moment's hesitation, popped the raw morsel into his mouth. His dad had called this "sashimi"—a fancy name for eating raw fish—last summer on a trip to Louisiana.

Savoring the flavor, rolling the piece of fish around in his mouth, he noticed that even raw it was delicious. It was sweet and mild, with just a hint of remaining saltiness from the Indian Ocean.

He was excited now. He darted into the kitchen to fetch spices and sauces and marinated the fish in a pan. Outside, he fired up the grill and waved the flies away.

It wasn't strong like redfish—Edgar knew that by the taste on his tongue. His father had always said, "If you cover up fresh tasting fish with a bunch of tacky-tasting sauces, you might as well be eating chicken. Or pig's feet. And you're probably a redneck."

But Edgar loved marinade and this was *his* cookout, so sauce was necessary.

Standing over the coals, he listened to the fish sizzle and waited impatiently. His stomach growled ravenously.

Once the fish was cooked, Edgar removed it from the grill and blew on it in his fingers. It was almost too hot to touch, but he was starving, so he bore the pain and rolled it around to cool it, then took a small, prospective bite. With his lips scalding and mouth releasing wisps of steam, he tasted and knew: it was, without a doubt, the tastiest fish he'd ever eaten.

This fish most certainly did *not* suck. And it definitely wasn't poisonous . . . *hopefully.*

Retrieving a list from his pocket with one free hand,

he ate and reviewed:

-2 Chains
-2 Chain Hooks
-1 Steel pole (at least 17 feet long)
-Stringers
-1 Lantern
-1 Hook
-1 Release
-Tackle Box

AFTER HE finished eating, Edgar licked his fingers and mounted an old, leftover bike he'd found in the storage shed. Behind it was attached a small, two-wheeled lawnmower trailer he'd also uncovered from storage, both presumably the property of the previous owners.

Though they were in very bad shape, a few pumps of air into the back tire and a squirt of WD40 on the bike chain got the combo rolling along well enough.

He tapped his pocket to make sure the wad of money was there. It was. Soon he arrived at the hardware store and the old man behind the counter frowned grimly when Edgar presented his list.

"I'm looking for a hook release," said Edgar, uncertainly.

"What's a 'hook release'?" grunted the old man.

"Um, you know, a hook release is basically a broomstick with a hook on it? For fishing. You use them to get hooks out of a big fish's mouth. Like for tuna."

"Huh," said the man, shaking his head. "You ain't gonna need one of those around here. Ain't no tuna in the mountains!"

Softening, the prune-faced man pointed toward the outboard motors.

"Check there."

"Thank you!" said Edgar, and when he had gathered up the items he needed—including an old, almost hidden, dusty hook release buried deep in the netting section—he paid for the merchandise and loaded the trailer.

He spent all but one dollar and sixty-three cents of the pizza money.

It was necessary, however, and money well spent.

With the lawnmower trailer bogging down, he tied the twenty-foot-long steel pole to the very back of the gate. As he pedaled away from the hardware store, the pole dragged loudly across the asphalt and several cars slowed down to let him by.

LATER THAT night, at around ten o'clock, Edgar stood above the hole once again, equipped with all of the necessary supplies. In a final act of preparation, he carefully placed the long steel pipe over the mouth of the hole and was relieved to find it was long enough.

He tied several stringers and chains around his waist, then connected them to his mound of supplies. He lifted his fishing pole and cradled it to his chest, then fell headlong into the hole, deep into the darkness of the Earth, dragging all his equipment with him.

Above him, the steel pipe remained in place at the top of the hole, awaiting his return.

Eight hours later, as the morning sun broke over Mount Lanier, Edgar came shooting up from the hole with a humongous haul in tow.

If the fish were going to survive the trip, Edgar knew that everything would have to work perfectly.

As he reached the steel pipe at the top of the hole, he artfully snapped the end of a chain to it. Then, simultaneously, he grabbed hold of the pipe himself and kept himself from falling back down.

Attached to the other end of the chain was the huge mound of fish, connected with a series of stringers through the gills. They, too, were snapped tight to the steel pole and dangled there, hanging just below Edgar's swinging feet.

It had worked. He marveled at this ingenuity.

Secured to the pipe about twelve feet below hung around one hundred and twenty pounds of fresh, meaty fish—the same kind he'd caught before. The creatures stared blankly up at him with wide, yellow eyes.

With his catch secure, he began inching his way across the pipe, monkey-bar style, until he reached the edge of the hole. There, he pulled himself out and stood on the cabin floor, stretching and yawning. It was five-thirty in the morning, and he was exhausted.

His father would have been *so* proud.

If he hurried, the fish wouldn't go bad—but he would have to work fast.

Soon the trailer was packed with fish and the ice packs were readjusted, and he jumped on the bike, pedaling hard to the house, glancing occasionally behind him to check on the bouncing trailer. *Yeah*, he thought, *it's the biggest haul of fish I've ever seen.* Especially for a fisherman who fished from dry land with no boat.

He checked his watch again. Flounder would arrive soon so he'd need to hurry.

It was going to be a *long* morning.

ELEVEN

Flounder kneeled over the kiddy pool full of fresh, iced fish that Edgar presented to him.

"Wow," muttered Flounder. "Where did you get those?"

"From my uncle."

"Your uncle?" said Flounder, leaning down to inspect them. "And where did he get them?"

"He got them from the ocean, Flounder. What does it matter?"

"And what kind did you say they were again?"

"Jeezus, Flounder, what are you, the friggin' Health Department? They're called Ambercod." Maybe if Edgar was pushy enough, Flounder wouldn't ask too many unanswerable questions.

"Well, I've never heard of 'em," barked Flounder.

He bent and investigated one of them more closely, pressing a finger into the fish's belly.

Then, he frowned and cocked his head sideways.

"Look, Flounder," said Edgar. "It's simple. My uncle owns a charter. He had this big haul two days ago in the Pacific. He caught these—*hybrids,* he calls them—they spawn deep in the water offshore during the change of season. Now . . . No matter what you think of it, Flounder, I'm offering you *free fish.* You get that? Free fish!"

Edgar nudged him on the shoulder. "I told him you could sell his fish here in Mount Lanier at your fish stand. He said we could keep half the money—you and me!"

"Ugh, Edgar! You told your uncle we would sell it at our fish stand? And you didn't even ask?"

"Yeah!" said Edgar. "Of course I did! Because who doesn't like *free money?*"

"Look, Edgar. I don't know anything about these fish."

"What's to know? They're *free.* That's the only thing you should care about." Edgar playfully shook the boy's shoulders. "Stop arguing, dude. Just take these fish to your family and see what they think. Let's get them selling at the fish stand. If they don't sell, fine—y'all can toss 'em, but . . ." Edgar pulled out a match and struck it, then tossed it dramatically into a nearby grill that flared with a gust of flame. "If they *do* sell, y'all keep half the money, then give me half." With Flounder's gears fully in motion, Edgar bent and blew on the charcoal. As he stoked the flame, he added, "No matter how you cut it, Flounder, it's no risk to you or your family. It's *crazy* not to take the fish."

Flounder rubbed his chin and turned to the kiddie pool again, glaring at the weird, foreign fish glistening in the heat.

"They're ugly," he muttered before bending and wiggling one of their alligator-like teeth.

"Yeah, for sure," agreed Edgar. "But I swear to God, they taste just like grouper. No, even better, actually."

"What?" balked Flounder. "*Nothing* is better than grouper!"

"Wait and see."

Once the fire was ready, Edgar tossed a fillet on the grill and it sizzled immediately. Flounder watched the process keenly.

"What have you put on the fish?" he asked suspiciously.

"Just a little Tony's and a little lemon," Edgar explained. "Oh, and a bit of dill."

"Ha!" scolded Flounder. "You say the fish is as good as grouper! Well, why are you covering it up, Edgar?! It's not chicken."

"God, Flounder. You sound just like my dad."

Once the fish was cooked through, Edgar pulled a piece from the grill and handed it to his friend. Flounder blew on it until the morsel had cooled enough to pop into his mouth, and after just a couple of chews, his face lit up with the revelation.

Just as Edgar had promised, it was absolutely wonderful.

"Wow!" he said, smacking. "That's really, really good! It's tangy like amberjack, but tender as lump crab!"

"Yeah!" exclaimed Edgar. "That's what I'm saying! It's what I've been trying to tell you all along!" He patted Flounder on the back excitedly. "I'm glad you're on board. Now, will you please help me clean them?"

Edgar walked to the patio table and retrieved his electric knife. He turned and offered it to Flounder, who took one look at it and exploded into pious laughter.

"Dude!" he chuckled. "I use a *real* blade!"

Flounder went to the kitchen and rummaged for a knife, returning with the best one in the house.

"This'll do," he said thoughtfully, twisting around Mr. Dewitt's sleek Wüsthof knife, trying to make it glint in the midday sun.

The two then took to the back porch where, after dousing the deck planks with water from the hose, they spread the fish and got to work, Flounder with the Wüsthof blade and Edgar with the Electric Greenie. Together they cut and sliced happily for almost an hour, chatting about fishing and movies and who was probably better at filleting fish.

Edgar knew Flounder was better at it, but he couldn't help getting a rise out of the kid.

When they were finished, the two stood over a mound of fish heads and slimy innards and large swarm of flies. On the patio table sat their prize: a huge pile of immaculately cleaned, meticulously washed fish fillets currently soaking in four buckets of cold sink water.

The two clanked a couple of celebratory glasses of cold Coke together, and then gulped audibly, smiling broadly at their triumph.

"This is forty pounds of fillets," exclaimed Flounder. "That's a ton of meat."

"Yeah," nodded Edgar.

Once the bike trailer was loaded with the fresh, bagged fish—each one vacuum-sealed perfectly, with help from Mr. Dewitt's nifty vacuum sealer—the two boys bumped fists in the oncoming dusk and said goodbye.

"Good luck!" yelled Edgar, as Flounder pedaled the bike away. He rode proudly with shoulders high, saluting Edgar with the back of a hand as he rounded the bend.

THE NEXT evening, Edgar took another trip to his island—not for fishing this time, but just for fun. He felt the urge to get away for a swim and another freefall—just to relax.

Swimming around the island this time, he spotted a

few lobsters in the coral below. *Lobsters!* Lobsters would bring a pretty penny too, he thought.

Swimming on the island was fun, but falling had become Edgar's favorite part. Who would have known it? He'd always been afraid of heights but now had come to love losing himself in the drop.

In the warm, salty air that brushed by him as he fell, he flipped and pirouetted and contorted himself into a veritable array of aerial gymnastics, and it always, without exception, helped him to clear his racing mind.

And, when he wasn't trying to master his skydiving skills, he would lose himself in thought as he careened through the darkness.

He thought about his new school and about Shay, about Flounder's troubles, and even Chris Weedy, and what would make anyone become such a giant ass.

As always, though, he thought about how he'd have to continue to keep the island a secret from his parents.

It would be difficult to hide it, but the island was special, and it would be worth it.

"DUDE!" FLOUNDER exclaimed, approaching Edgar in the commons and seeing the dark circles that had made a permanent home beneath Edgar's eyes. "Why are you so tired lately? Get it together!"

Edgar came to, mumbling a bum explanation. He'd been at the island again the night before, and sleep was dead last on his priority list these days.

"Whatever man. Listen! Are you awake now?"

"Yeah," said Edgar.

Flounder smiled and yanked out a big wad of money from his pocket, slapping it on the table before Edgar. "Every bit of the Ambercod sold!" he whispered. "The customers love it!"

"Sold?" said Edgar, his bloodshot eyes trying to focus on the huge wad of money in the middle of the table. Suddenly, when he came to his senses, he snatched it away, hiding it in his lap below the table.

Flounder giggled. "Your uncle's fish is a hit!" he said, as Edgar frantically stuffed the wad into his pocket. He glanced around the commons to see if anyone had seen him receive the cash, and Flounder laughed even harder at this strange behavior.

"Edgar, you're a dork. Just tell your uncle we need more Ambercod. I think when word gets out, there's probably gonna be a run on the market."

AFTER SCHOOL that day, Edgar stood in the cabin by the hole's edge and yanked out the large wad of money. Even there, in the middle of nowhere, he caught himself glancing around to make sure he was truly alone.

He couldn't figure out why exactly, but he was paranoid. Maybe it was because of how the money had been acquired: with all the lying and sneaking out. But there, in the sunlight streaming down from the large hole in the roof, he counted the money and marveled, letting out a long exhale.

Five hundred dollars.

Five hundred dollars!

He'd never had so much money before.

He was rich.

The Ambercod had sold for nine dollars a pound, and Flounder told him the Arteses wanted to mark it up even more the next time, assuming Edgar's uncle could catch some more.

Edgar figured he could probably arrange such a thing.

The Arteses essentially wanted to charge the same price as yellowfin tuna or prime salmon, which was as expensive as fish fillets get, especially this far inland.

Back home, safe in his room with the door locked, Edgar dislodged a loose baseboard in the corner by his desk.

There, behind the wall, he hid his money.

He slumped against the baseboards and stared absently at the boxed up baseball trophies and rolled up posters of rock bands that were scattered across his room. He knew he should unpack from the move, but he really didn't want to.

Just days later, Edgar found himself forging his mother's signature on a lackluster paper.

It was a "D" on a history exam. He'd never forged anything in his life, and here he was, doing it.

Milly Dewitt, he signed carefully on the bottom of the paper. He lifted it up to inspect the signature. His eyes ventured to the top of the paper where the teacher's brutal statements glared at him:

> *Edgar has not been performing. He constantly falls asleep in class! He's missed two homework assignments. Edgar can do better than this!*

Yeah, he concluded. *Milly Dewitt could never read that.*

The worst part was, he was actually pretty great at history.

One week later, after two more large hauls of Ambercod that earned him 1,500 more dollars, Edgar decided he'd upgrade his fishing operation. He was quickly accumulating far more money than he could ever spend.

Gone were the days of dragging catches two-by-two

up and down the hill, laboring with them from the cabin to the bike. On Friday afternoon, he asked his parents if he could spend the night at Flounder's and when they said "yes," he went shopping.

"What kind of a name is Flounder?" his mother had inquired, and his father had chimed in.

Edgar rolled his eyes at them. "It's a cool nickname," he argued. "Like a mafia guy, you know?"

"Maybe I should meet his mom," she considered.

"You can," said Edgar, maintaining a poker face. "She works downtown. Stop by sometime. She's the one who sells fish."

"Oh, yes!" exclaimed his mom. "I've seen her and her family before. She's a pretty lady! Is it really OK with her that you spend the night? You've asked her permission?"

"Oh, no ma'am," said Edgar, holding back a smile. "We don't believe in asking our mothers' permission."

AT DUSK he rode the rusty bike to the Walmart Supercenter.

There, with a huge wad of money, he bought a brand new bike: a Mongoose, the All Terrain Mountain Rider. It was $250 worth of beautiful, red, shiny bike.

He also purchased a towable luggage trailer for one hundred and fifty dollars, that connected to the back of the bike perfectly. It was far more spacious than the old lawnmower trailer, and rolled along more smoothly too, with its thick, inflatable tires. It also came with a handy strap beneath which the cargo could be secured.

That cargo, of course, being humongous hauls of fresh, tasty Ambercod.

Edgar also bought a portable, battery-powered refrigerator, four feet deep and four feet wide, for three hundred and fifty dollars. It claimed to freeze on a single charge for up to forty-eight hours and was small enough to fit onto the luggage trailer.

A small generator was also obtained for $250 that even came with a gas can.

It was high time the cabin had a power source, reasoned Edgar.

He also bought a small cutting table for filleting the fish—stainless and sturdy, capable of holding up to two hundred pounds.

Along with everything else, he bought the best knife Walmart could offer, a box of large, plastic bags, a box of sturdy freezer bags, and several gallons of distilled, bottled water.

At checkout, he encountered a suspicious cashier, who studied his every move, eyeing the overflowing cart with an inquisitive frown.

"It's for camping," he explained

"You going for a month?" she asked dryly, then began to scan his cartful of supplies.

His OLD bike and trailer sat dejected atop the heap in the Walmart Supercenter's dumpster. Brushing his hands clean, he mounted his new bike and carted the huge stack of new supplies through town and into the woods. Finally, back at the cabin, he unloaded everything safely inside, arranging the items, powering up the freezer and getting things prepared.

Then, by the light of the lantern, he unboxed the stainless steel table and constructed it, sliding it into the corner by the generator. He then placed the sharp knife on its surface with the plastic bags and the distilled water and scooted the freezer adjacent to them. Placing the small, humming generator next to those, he stepped back to survey his new kitchen.

It would do nicely.

Now he could haul his catch directly from the hole and to the cutting table for immediate cleaning. Then he could bag it, freeze it, and, afterward, fill the cooler with frozen, filleted fish, then load the cooler directly onto the luggage rack and pedal the entire operation down to the Artese's fish stand.

It was perfect.

He was a *genius*.

He thought for a moment and a horrifying thought emerged. What would happen if his parents drove by while he pedaled a huge haul of Ambercod to town—on a brand spanking new red bicycle?

TWELVE

AFTER SCHOOL THE next Monday, he caught up with Shay and tapped her on the shoulder.

"Hey," he smiled.

"Hey!"

"You wanna see something cool?"

"Sure!"

"But it's a secret."

Shay studied him through narrowing eyes.

"Trust me," he said. "It's the coolest thing you'll ever see, I promise."

"Well," she said, allowing herself to be guided in the direction he was pointing her to. "How could I turn down the coolest thing I've ever seen?"

"You *can't!*" he laughed.

Together they strolled into the reddish peaks beyond, out past the dirt roads and onto the foot trails, then deep into the "Indian Hills," as Edgar liked to call them.

"Where are you taking me?" she asked after a while.

"Just through there," he said, pointing through a dense thicket.

When the meadow opened up, the cabin emerged, and she stood before it with wide, investigative eyes.

"Edgar," she asked, "whose is this?" She stood before the structure, and seemed to wilt at the whistle of air streaming through the termite holes.

Edgar stepped forward and pushed the door open, then turned and waved her inside.

"C'mon," he said, "don't worry. I've been here a million times. There's nothing bad in here except maybe the occasional spider."

"You're not making things any better," she said fearfully, pausing halfway through the door.

He giggled and took her by the arm, leading her in, escorting her to the hole's edge where together they looked down in awed silence.

"Uh, that's crazy," she said, peering down. "What is this?"

"It's a hole," he said.

"Well. You don't say." She punched Edgar's shoulder playfully.

He let her gaze into the depths for a moment, her brown hair lifting from the rising air. Then she turned and walked to the make-shift kitchen where his fish-cleaning supplies were neatly arranged. She studied the workstation and the stainless steel table, the freezer, and the generator, and thoughtfully smudged a drop of dried blood on the cutting table with a pinky.

She frowned quizzically at the blood, then lifted Edgar's knife for inspection before placing it carefully back on the tabletop, frowning. From there, she moved to the generator and gave it an investigative tap of her shoe before opening the small freezer door to see what was inside.

For several moments, she studied the impressively organized packages of perfectly filleted fish, then slowly closed the door and turned to him.

"What *is* all of this?" she said, demanding an explanation.

He chuckled. "OK. How about I *show* you what it is?"

"Please," she said.

"Well, when do you have to be home?"

"Around seven-ish, I guess. Why?"

"Because. Just humor me. What time is it now?"

Shay yanked out her phone and checked the time. "3:27."

"OK," he said, walking around the hole, standing on the opposite side from her. "Toss me your cell phone for a second."

Hesitating for a moment, she tossed it across the hole to him. In return, he took off his watch and tossed it over to her.

"Hold on to that for a bit," he said.

"What are you doing, Edgar?" She was becoming more uncomfortable by the minute.

"So listen," he said. "Whatever happens, don't be afraid. Just remember that this cabin is perfectly safe. I should know, too—I spend all of my time here. I'm leaving for a little bit, but while I'm gone, please hang around 'til I get back, OK? Just don't go home."

He shot her a mischievous smile. "That is, if you want your cell phone back."

"What do you mean, when you 'get back?' Edgar?" she asked, her face darkened with worry. "Where are you going?"

"Down there," he said, pointing into the hole.

"What!"

"Shay, trust me. Can you look at my watch? Does it

say 3:39, exactly? That's what your cell phone says."

Shay absently looked down and checked it, nodding.

"OK. Listen. I will be back with your phone at *exactly* 5:03—*exactly on the dot*. Please don't leave. Please don't go home. At 5:03 I will come back up this hole."

"No! Edgar!" she said, running around the hole to stop him, but just as she came to him, he jumped.

She brought her hands up to her head and screamed.

"There're Cokes behind the freezer!" he yelled, falling rapidly.

As scared as she seemed, Edgar knew it would be a miracle if she stuck around.

EXACTLY ONE hour and twenty-four minutes later, Edgar popped back up.

"I'm back," he said, praying she would be there. As he yanked himself out of the hole, he looked around and there, in the corner, sat Shay. She rose to her feet at his arrival.

"You're still here!" he exclaimed, so relieved that she had stuck around. He walked over to her and offered her her cell phone.

"What kind of trick is this?" she said, snatching the phone from his outstretched hand.

"Hey!" he said. "Don't be mad! I had to show it to you this way. But trust me. Can I have my watch back?" She handed it to him, and he lifted it up to present it to her. "See?" he said. "It's exactly 5:03, just as I said. Remember that? It's important."

She looked at the watch and shook her head.

"Where did you go?" she demanded, her indignation flooding back in.

"Well," he said invitingly. "What if didn't *tell* you where I went. What if I *showed* you where I went?"

"What do you mean, '*show me?*'"

"Well, I mean that you're going to have to trust me—you gotta jump with me."

"No way!" she said, taking a quick step backward. "Are you *nuts?*"

"No!" he explained. "Just, please, Shay. I just jumped down, and I'm perfectly fine, right?" He spun a circle and showed her his perfectly intact body. "I'm telling you, there's no bottom, Shay. It's an island down there—on the other side of the world! Just *trust* me. I promise I would never hurt you. You've gotta see what I'm talking about. You've gotta come with me."

"Edgar, I said 'no,'" she said with finality, taking another retreating step backward.

"Shay," he said, waving a hand up and down his body to illustrate how he was still in one piece. "Again, take a look at me. There's not a scratch on me, you see? And I jumped down that hole over an hour ago."

He took a step toward her. "Not only did I jump down and come back safe, I also told you exactly when I would come back up and I came back up exactly when I said I would, didn't I?"

He let that sink in and noticed she was listening. "I came back at exactly 5:03," he repeated, "unharmed—not even a scratch—and ready to go again."

She studied him with two icy blue eyes.

"You know," he continued, "all the questions I've been asking in Van Rossum's class about gravity and falling and the Earth? Well, this is why." He pointed downward. "I want to show you what's down there—the most incredible thing you will ever see, I promise. If I'm wrong, I will never bother you again."

"Edgar, I just don't know . . ."

"*Please*," he said. "Just trust me. It will be the most amazing thing you've ever experienced. You'll remember it for the rest of your life. It's the most amazing thing *anyone's* ever experienced, undoubtedly. I've jumped down a million times before. There's really nothing to it, if you'll just trust me."

He held out a hand to her, and she gave it a long look.

Then, slowly, to Edgar's absolute surprise, she reached out and took it.

HER SCREAMS echoed for minutes after they jumped, one after the other, skull rattling and ear-drum piercing, all of them. He grabbed her by the shoulders as they fell and squeezed her tight, giving her body a gentle shake to bring her to. But, he also knew that nothing calms you the first time you fall.

Nothing can prepare you for that.

"AAAAAAHHHHH!!!!" she screamed, and even in the raging wind, it distorted in his eardrums.

If she keeps it up, he thought, *she'll hyperventilate. I've made a big mistake.*

"Shay!" he shouted, shaking her again. "Hey! Stop screaming! It's gonna be OK!"

He pulled a small flashlight from his pocket and shined her, then shined the walls around her.

"Look around!" he screamed. "Get your bearings! Remember how I jumped down first?!! Remember that? Well, I fell and came back up and I'm just *fine*, *REMEMBER?* You're gonna be OK, *too!*"

Then, suddenly, she stopped screaming, just like that. And when he put the light to her face and saw her crying, he was crushed. He had done this. He had, after all, convinced her to jump, but now there was no going back.

To show her everything was OK, he turned the flashlight onto himself and shined it on his own face. Then, he began to make a silly ghost noise.

"Oooooo!" he said, trying to lighten things up, but it wasn't working. Her teeth were still clenched in freefall.

"OK," he said. "Listen. I know you're feeling that 'lose-your-stomach' sensation in your gut, but that will fade soon. In just a few minutes, Shay, I promise you, you'll feel like you're flying—which is *amazing*!"

He kept the light on her and realized that his talking seemed to be putting her at ease. So he continued to talk, falling with her face-to-face, and chattered about whatever he could think of.

Once they were falling through the center of the Earth, he announced their arrival.

"You feel how hot it is?" he pointed out. "We are at the Earth's core now. Isn't that cool?"

She looked around, slightly overtaken by curiosity, and then nodded stiffly, her squinty eyes still stricken with fear.

"You're probably getting pretty thirsty right now, aren't you?" he continued.

She nodded again.

"Yeah, well, that's because it's a sauna down here! Outside this magical brick wall, it's probably about five million degrees."

He reminded her of a question he'd asked in Van Rossum's class just a few days before.

"Remember that? Van Rossum told me that no human could ever visit the Earth's core without gravity crushing him—or *her*? Well, here we are!"

When he noticed she was relaxing more by the minute, he released her and spun a circle in midair to demonstrate their surroundings. "You ever think you would visit the center of the Earth?" he shouted.

Her eyes widened at the thought. Then, wonderfully, her rigid body seemed to relax completely. She looked around and began to take it in, then spun and half-smiled at Edgar.

"Yes!" he grinned. "Yes! That's right! You're going to be OK!"

She loosened her rigid neck and twirled in a clumsy circle, checking out the walls around her, reaching for the bricks. Responsively, Edgar moved further from her to give her some space—to let her begin to enjoy falling. She floated over to the walls and touched the speeding blocks, then floated back to Edgar and smiled. He stretched his four limbs out wide and slowly rose above her, then brought them back in and quickly darted below her, flipping expertly in the air like an aeronautic daredevil.

He finished with a precise somersault.

"Wow," she mouthed. "You're good!"

In the white glow of the flashlight, she surrendered an uneven, sheepish grin.

As the other side of the world approached, he floated to her and took her gently by the arms.

"Up there," he said, pointing at the dim yellow light ahead, "when you get to the light, grab the side walls. And then hold on tight."

Shay looked ahead and nodded.

"When we arrive at the end of the hole, your body's gonna stop moving upward. That's when you grab hold of the bricks."

She nodded again and parted from him. He watched as she used her body to float to the edge—something she did very well—then, when the top of the hole came to her, she skillfully snatched the side and dangled safely.

"All right!" shouted Edgar. "You're a natural! Perfect!"

He dangled beside her on the ledge for a moment, then climbed out to help her up.

But when he turned to assist her, she was already climbing out on her own.

"Whoa," he said. "Do you do gymnastics or something?"

She stood and faced him for a moment, then, visibly distraught from the traumatic event that had just taken place, she bent over and placed her hands on her knees and stood very still, her mass of mocha hair hanging down over her face.

Oh no, I've scared her to death. She's having a psychological breakdown, he thought. He'd been so stupid to talk her into this.

She was deathly still for several moments, her body heaving along with each breath. Terrified, Edgar placed a clammy hand on her shoulder and bent down to her, to make sure she was OK.

"Dang, Shay," he said softly. "I'm so sorry I talked you into jumping. I sure didn't mean to . . ."

"Gotcha!" she said, shooting up, a wild smile on her face. She cackled at her marvelous revenge—scaring him half to death.

"You suck," he said, laughing, relieved that she wasn't hurt or sick.

"But, oh!" she exclaimed. "The falling was *awful!*"

"Yeah?" he chuckled. "Well, you totally get used to it."

Then they turned, and when she looked out over the beautiful, expansive ocean, he presented it to her with the wide sweep of his hand.

"This," he said, "is mine."

She peered at the horizon and turned slightly to the west, facing the big, yellow moon. As she did, the two of them fell silent and stared at it for a long, lingering moment.

"Where is this?" she whispered. "Where have you brought me?"

He turned and watched her beautiful brown hair drift in all directions.

"It's where the constellations are upside down," he said, pointing her to Orion. Orion sat directly on his head, like he was doing some sort of celestial handstand. From there, Edgar sat her down on the island's top and, over-looking the sea, he told her everything.

THIRTEEN

With the North American moon high in the sky, Edgar texted Shay:

Look outside.

He was standing breathless beside the street lamp on her street corner, waiting for a bedroom light to come on. Then, suddenly, a curtain fluttered in one of the windows upstairs. Shay's face appeared for a moment, but then it vanished.

"Ugh," he said, smashing a palm to his face. "I'm such an idiot."

Turning forlornly, he headed for home but not before shooting one last glance over his shoulder.

There, on the balcony beneath her window, was Shay! He squinted to see her, but yes, she was weaving expertly through the limbs of a sycamore tree that was adjacent to her bedroom sliding effortlessly down to the bottom of the tree trunk like a fireman's pole.

"Whoa," he whispered as she approached. "Sneak out much?" She giggled quietly and looked up at him.

"I used to do gymnastics," she explained, a wild, invigorated smile on her face. Then she followed him into the night, and together they made off for the Indian Hills.

Escorting her into the cabin, Edgar quickly lit the lantern for her and asked her to wait by the hole.

"I just need to get a few things together," he said, dashing to the worktable, where there, several items had been arranged for the trip: a soft cooler with ice, two flash lights, two beach towels, and two backpacks, complete with sunscreen, drinks, baseball caps, bagged lunches, and even a music player.

All the essentials for a day at the beach.

"You ready?" he said, and when she nodded, he added, "I sure hope it's not raining when we get there. Hard to check the weather for an island in the middle of a strange sea on the opposite side of the world and you don't even know where it is . . . you know?"

He handed her a backpack to carry and took her by the arm, readying for liftoff.

"Oh, I hate this part," she said, scrunching her nose and grinning.

"Yeah, but you get used to it," he said, and on the count of three, together they went whooshing through the planet Earth.

Two hours later, as Shay was sprawled on the island, sun tanning, Edgar fished hard for Ambercod.

"It's been so long since I've had a beach day!" she cooed, rubbing a glob of suntan lotion on her light brown shoulders.

It was a really beautiful day.

"Me too," he said, grunting as he hooked a humongous fish.

"What are you even talking about?" she laughed. "You've been a walking zombie at school every day! I bet you come here every night!"

"Not *every* night," he insisted.

She was a fabulous addition to his island. Her being there made him notice how quiet the island always was, and how often he talked to himself aloud there, or got lost in his dreary thoughts with nobody else around.

But Shay's presence made the island feel like an actual beach resort or something—like the two were on a vacation in the Caribbean.

"You hungry?" he asked, as the hooked fish came flopping to shore. Edgar bent and unhooked it, then placed it on a stringer along with the other fish. "I'm starving if you ask me."

She nodded and laughed, then joined him as the two walked down to the shore, their backpacks slung over their shoulders. Edgar spread a towel out across the course surface and they distributed the food for each other, then ate with their sun-soaked feet in the sea.

"This is great, huh?" he chewed happily.

She smiled and nodded, leaning into him for a moment.

"So," he said.

"So?"

"Well, I guess you're pretty rich, huh?"

At that, she ceased to chew. Her face darkened immediately. She dropped her head and began to stare at the sand beneath her legs, shaking her head.

"So?" she asked defensively.

"It's just that," he said, clamoring to fix the wrong he'd just committed, "I just thought, you know, you live on Japonica Street. With all the big houses." He painfully swallowed a dry mouthful of sandwich and cursed himself. "That's the richest neighborhood in town, so I guess I was just pointing that out."

Shay shrugged again and looked into the sea. "We don't have as much as some do, I guess."

He scolded himself again and shrugged.

"Look," he muttered. "I'm just an idiot. I'm sorry. I shouldn't have brought it up."

She nodded and took another small bite of her sandwich.

"I guess while I'm being a jerk," he continued, "maybe I could ask you another personal question. That is, if you're game?" He leaned over and bumped her shoulder playfully with his own.

She nodded and flashed a downcast smile. "Fine. What do you want to know?"

"Well," he said, "the other day, Weedy mentioned something about your dad being a 'criminal?'"

"Oh, yeah," she said grimly, "*that.*"

She tossed a bit of uneaten crust into the swarming pool of Ambercod offshore. "Well, a couple of years back, my dad was charged with embezzlement," she said softly. "This was back when he was mayor."

"Whoa! Your dad was mayor? That's pretty cool." After a moment, he asked the obvious question. "Well? Did he do it? Embezzle, I mean?"

"I'm not sure," she answered, quite candidly. "Although he swears he didn't do it."

"Well, then he *didn't*," Edgar confirmed.

She picked up a tiny mollusk shell and inspected the inside.

"He's the county commissioner nowadays," she explained. "He's never been convicted of anything."

"Well, good," said Edgar. "I'm glad nothing ever came

of it."

"Not *yet*," she corrected him.

He joined her in looking thoughtfully out to sea, the air whipping around them crisp, and the sunshine bright, and the western breeze cooling their faces.

"I'm sorry for prying," he mumbled, terribly sorry that he'd bummed her out.

"Oh, Edgar. I don't mind."

Then she brightened and elbowed *him*. "Now you've gotta tell me one of *your* skeletons."

"A . . . *what*?" he asked. "What 'skeleton'?"

"You know, a 'skeleton from your closet.'"

"I showed you this island, didn't I? I showed you a hole that goes all the way through the Earth! If you told anybody my secret, I'd lose it all. That's not '*skeleton*' enough for you?"

"Nope," she said playfully. "You've gotta give me something you're *ashamed* of. Not *proud* of."

"Oh, I see," he said, taking a large, thoughtful gulp of Coke. Then, pausing for a moment, he took a deep breath and looked at her, then told her about Bon Secour.

"Two years back," he began, "I was eating lunch at a marina when suddenly I looked up and there was Dad on national TV—or a picture of him anyway. Below the picture they were showing his rig on fire.

"*An oil rig has exploded off the coast today,*" continued Edgar, mimicking a reporter's voice. "*The base of the oil rig has been completely engulfed in flames, as you can see on your screen. Crude oil is spewing unabated into the Gulf of Mexico now . . .*"

"I remember that," Shay said.

"Well, remember how a bunch of those people were killed?"

She nodded somberly.

"I totally freaked out at first," said Edgar, "thinking

my dad was dead, too. All the guys I worked with who were eating with me tried to calm me down, but for about an hour I didn't know if he was alive or dead and I just couldn't get it together. Then, finally, when my mom—who was even more hysterical than I was—got ahold of me, she gave me the news."

"He was OK, right?" Shay said.

"Yeah, for the moment," explained Edgar. "He was shell-shocked, for sure, but he was OK. You've got to understand, Shay, that day he lost several good friends, close ones. But afterward was the worst. Suddenly he was facing press conferences and court appearances and testifying for days on end, defending himself for the oil spill. Everyone was blaming the whole thing on him.

"So he was at court defending himself, and we went every day to support him. Every night on the news, there he was, my Dad, the most hated man in Bon Secour."

Edgar's mind flashed back to that horrible day, when the judge had questioned his father on trial.

"Were you, Mr. DeWitt, responsible for attaching the safety valves to the bottom of the rig?"

"Yes ma'am, I was."

"Did you, Mr. DeWitt, do so according to the safety regulations required of you by the guidelines of the EPA?"

"Yes ma'am, I did."

"Were you, Mr. DeWitt, aware that the equipment in question—the C18-35 Containment Valve—particularly the part you were commissioned to inspect—was eight days beyond its annual safety check up on the day it failed?"

"No ma'am, I was not."

"So you were responsible for the Deepwater Horizon oil spill?"

"If you need to hold someone accountable, ma'am, for this terrible thing that has happened, I suppose it can be me."

Edgar disgustedly tossed the remainder of his sandwich to the Ambercod. "Dad got choked up twice on the stand," he muttered, "he tried not to cry constantly, actually. It was so awful to see. You've got to know: he *never* cries. He never has a reason to! He's the happiest guy I know. We sat in the courtroom and watched them hammer him all day long, every day, for *weeks.*

"It wasn't long after they went ahead and fired him too. He had to endure all that BS just to get fired in the end. Well, even still, he made us stay in Bon Secour for weeks afterward. We didn't just flee to Washington. He dragged us to town meetings every week and kept telling us that any decent person helps others even when their help is not wanted. Which is *exactly* the way it was in Bon Secour: they hated him and they hated us because we were his people, but still, he stayed and did all he could to help Bon Secour. They didn't deserve him."

"Why?" she asked. "Why did they hate him so much? Wasn't it an accident? They sound like terrible people."

"Yeah, but you see, what you don't understand is how badly the town was *devastated.* Its tourism industry dried up like *that.*" He snapped his fingers. "All the fishing, all the swimming, all was lost. Nobody came around anymore. I even lost my job on the charter boat that year because nobody was fishing. The ocean was sludge. My uncle—my Dad's brother—eventually lost his fishing charter. He lost his boat, too. And my dad was the one to blame. All because of a stupid regulation that screwed him because he was as much behind on his work—and really, even less so—than any other city worker going around doing all their tasks. Hell, he was busy working on all the other crap they were piling on him! My dad is the hardest worker I know. He was the hardest worker in Bon Secour. He loved his job. He loved that place."

"How terrible," she whispered.

"Yeah, it was. It *is.*"

"So that's why you all moved up here?" she asked. "To Mount Lanier? To get away from those angry people back in your hometown?"

"Yeah," he nodded. "Dad got a job up here with the Department of Transportation. It's a pretty crappy job, considering he's a really smart guy, you know. PhD in Engineering. Master's in Chemistry. He should be building nuclear bombs and stuff, but you know, *this* had to happen."

Shay sighed softly and placed a hand on his shoulder. "Me and my family watched that oil spill on TV. We watched it every day for weeks."

"We did too," he said grimly, then reclined beside her on the sand.

Shay straightened and flicked her hair.

"So tell me, Edgar. Why does Flounder not know about this island?"

"Well," he said, shaking his head. "Flounder's my good friend, but I'm not sure how calm he is under pressure. There's a lot of people asking about the Ambercod lately, and his parents probably are, too, so I just can't risk him knowing the truth right now, not when we're making so much money."

"Why do you call it Ambercod?" she asked.

"Well," he said, nodding proudly at the stringer currently splashing by the shore, "because they're flaky like Amberjack, but buttery like cod. When Flounder asked me what they were called, 'Ambercod' was the first thing that came to mind."

"I see. So do you have any plans for all this money, Edgar? Besides giving it all to Walmart, I suppose?"

"Yeah," he said, brightening. "I'm using it to get us back home."

"To . . . where? *Alabama*?"

"Yeah," he nodded.

"But . . . *why?* What about all those angry people down there in Bon Secour? The ones who treated your family so terribly?"

"Yeah, well," said Edgar, "you can fix things like that. You can make them like they once were, even a town. Even *people.*"

"No you can't!" she said. "You can't fix a whole town, not if they're dead-set against you!"

He thought for a moment. "Yeah, you can. I can fix everything now. I can fix everything with the Ambercod."

As THE sun dipped in the sky and the two collected their things, Shay calculated aloud what time they should arrive back at her house.

"I need to jump before it gets any later," she urged him. "I can't get caught sneaking out."

He certainly knew how she felt.

"OK," he said, "let's go." He yanked the stringer of fish from the water and joined her at the hole's edge.

Before they jumped, she turned to him.

"I asked you before. What's so good about Alabama?" She looked up at him with big, beautiful eyes.

He could stare at them for days.

"Lots of things," he explained. "You've got hunting and fishing, and the boating's great, and there's water-skiing too, and the weather's just perfect down there: five million degrees in the shade." He smiled slyly. "Also, it rains occasionally there, which is different than *some* places I know . . ."

He looked down into the hole and his smile faded.

"It's just home," he said finally, contemplatively. He hoisted his backpack and looked at her. "You know, like, *home?*"

"Yes, Edgar, I understand," she said, slipping her feet

over the hole's edge. "But you know what they *don't* have in Alabama?" She smiled and leaned out further. "*Me!*"

And then she leapt over the hole, dropping like a brick into the darkness, and in seconds was gone.

He stared after her in shock, his mouth wide open.

He was *thrilled!*

He laughed and leapt down, yanking the stringer of fish behind him as he went whooshing after her. In freefall, he pointed his body straight, like a pencil, as he'd learned to do, then careened headfirst at a blazing speed, blitzing after her while dragging behind him all the flopping, wiggling fish.

Ahead in the darkness, he could see her flashlight flickering. Giggling, he straightened his body even more and accumulated speed, and within seconds he was there, joining up with her. Upon his arrival she twirled to greet him, laughing loudly, her beautiful hair lifted high in the wind.

He gestured above with a thumb and she looked up to see the mass of flopping fish above, floating over him like a bunch of strange balloons. She looked back down and grinned at him, then suddenly, wonderfully, she stopped smiling.

He noticed this and released the stringer, then allowed them to float freely, before flipping and twirling around her with some artful somersaults and crisp, tight spins.

She was laughing again, until he eventually curled around her like a snake, twisting up and down her body, which made her smile even more.

"You're so stupid," she said flatly. Then, when he stilled in midair, she placed her hands on his shoulders and brought him to her. Her lips were suddenly dangerously close.

Then, wonderfully, *magnificently*, just on the outskirts of the center of the Earth, Edgar and Shay Sinclair kissed deeply.

It was warm and soft and left him unable to discern the heat of her breath and the heat of the core. He could taste her tongue and suddenly, even when falling, somehow, he was dizzy.

When they parted Shay smiled sleepily. Edgar's whole body pulsed with lust, and yearning.

It was his first kiss.

FOURTEEN

OCTOBER CAME, AND as the leaves turned orange and shriveled in the trees, the drought remained. Cloudless skies continued the assault on Mount Lanier as the epidemic stretched regionally: the second-worst drought in Northwestern history.

Still, the money flowed for Edgar and the Arteses. Ambercod sold as fast as Edgar could reel it in. Hard thighs and biceps had begun to develop on his overly-tanned body from all the hefting and pulling and lifting.

One day, his mother plopped two packages of Ambercod down on the kitchen counter, like two pieces of evidence from a murder trial. He saw it and froze, and for a moment, his heart skipped a beat.

"What's . . . *Ambercod?*" he gulped, noticing Flounder's handwriting conspicuously scrawled across the white wax paper like the signature on a death sentence.

114

"I thought you might know," she said, "since you're pretty close to that Flounder guy."

"Yeah, well, we're *kinda* close."

She looked at him suspiciously. "Kinda? I talked to his mother for a while today and apparently this *Ambercod* is the greatest fish known to man."

When he heard that, his chest swelled with pride, but he couldn't let on.

"Better than bass?" he objected. "I doubt that."

"Apparently it's a lot like Amberjack."

"Oh. Cool."

She put the fish in the fridge and then poured a glass of water. "They seem to be very nice people, Edgar. I think your friend is a talented fish monger."

"He's alright," muttered Edgar, limp with relief that she hadn't seemed to gather anything on him. The Arteses must not have asked her about her fake brother too—Edgar's "uncle," the fantastical supplier of Ambercod.

"Hey," said Edgar, "please tell me you didn't call him 'Flounder' in front of his mother. Did you?"

She looked at him disdainfully. "Edgar. Do I look like the type to call people by their *street* names?"

At dinner that night, Mr. Dewitt chewed thoughtfully on the "Ambercod." He rolled it around on his tongue and squinted, a self-professed connoisseur of everything seafood.

"Yeah, well, I guess this Yankee fish tastes pretty good," he declared, flashing a smile at Edgar. Edgar was enthralled and watched his father eat a piece of fish that he, himself, had caught the day before.

"Henry, we don't call people *Yankees*," said his wife. Edgar's mother was always trying to keep them civil.

"But what if they deserve it?" said Mr. Dewitt, as Edgar tried not to laugh.

AT SCHOOL the next day, Flounder came walking up in a fit. "People are asking questions, man," he said, nervously.

"What kind of questions. *Which* people?"

"The customers, Ed. They're wanting to know about the Ambercod and what *exactly* it is. Like, they want to know about calories, nutritional information, mercury content—stuff like that, and they're looking it up on the internet, too, trying to figure it out. What do I tell them? Some of them are refusing to buy any more until they know. What do we say?"

Edgar ran a hand through his stringy hair and tried to think.

It wasn't good.

"Just—um—tell them it's new," he said. "Tell them that the fish is listed under its—uh—official name."

"Well, what's its official name?" Flounder asked.

"It's . . ." muttered Edgar, looking around, searching for an idea, but he realized that he was suddenly out of ideas. He was tired. He didn't have the energy to be brilliant anymore. "Man, Flounder, I don't know what to tell you. Just sell the dang fish. Figure it out! Be a *salesman*."

AT HOME, Edgar was running out of explanations for the fact that his skin grew darker and darker every other day.

"Flounder and I went hiking," Edgar explained one afternoon. "We like to hike up on the hills."

Mrs. Dewitt frowned. "Wasn't Flounder at the fish stand after school today?" She studied him, closely.

"No," shrugged Edgar. "Like I said, we went hiking. We hike a lot these days."

Mrs. Dewitt sighed. "Well don't get yourself a

sunburn. And what happened to cross country training?" she asked.

"Oh that," Edgar replied, panicking slightly. *Think of a lie, quick!* "Flounder said only dweebs do cross-country at my school. It would kill my image." He waited quietly for her reaction.

"Huh. And what image is that, Edgar?" He could tell she was suspicious, but he'd already committed to the lie.

"Oh you know, the coolest kid in school. Obviously," he laughed, hoping she'd take his joke and drop the subject. Mrs. Dewitt chuckled and turned back to the dishes, shaking her head.

Phew! That was close.

Things were getting worse and worse at school each day. Edgar and Flounder were currently the sole targets of Chris Weedy and his gang, especially at lunchtime.

Food splattered across their table every day at lunchtime, always followed by laughs from across the commons.

When Flounder would turn around to look, Weedy would shout, "Turn around, jackass! Eat your lunch! Don't look at us!" In surrender, Flounder would do as he was told.

Day after day it was the same. Food raining down on them, and subsequent cackling. As soon as they were seated—before they could even take a bite of their lunches—in came objects hurtling through the air, ricocheting across the table: food, drinks, even pinecones and textbooks. Edgar and Flounder quietly brushed the food from their clothing, waiting for the thunderous applause and laughter to subside, then tried to take a bite of their sandwiches.

"That guy is a douchebag. I *hate* him," grumbled Flounder.

"Man, why don't we just move somewhere else?" pleaded Edgar in a whisper. "This is stupid, Flounder! When Shay sits with us, it's all good, but when she has Driver's Ed, like today, we sit here and endure this? Why?! Let's just go eat in a classroom or something. We could even go to Van Rossum's room. He wouldn't care."

"No," said Flounder, who flashed the jocks a glare from the corner of his eye. "To hell with that."

And at just that moment, before Edgar could even launch a counterargument, a carton of cold milk sailed through the air and hit him directly at the base of his neck.

"OOOOOOOHHHHH!!!!!!!!" exploded the table of jocks across the walkway.

It was freezing. Edgar winced and thrust a hand to his back, and there, frigid milk streamed beneath his shirt. He tried to shake it away, but it was too late: his shirt was soaked.

Suddenly, uncontrollably, his face grew flush with rage, and humiliation seized through him. The lack of sleep lit sparks in his extremities and suddenly he felt like the Hulk. He looked up at Flounder and Flounder stared back, and in Flounder's eyes Edgar saw something that made him finally, irreversibly, irretrievably, lose his cool; he saw *pity*.

The howling laughter from Weedy's table continued. It began to somehow climb up Edgar's spine and ultimately burrow uncomfortably in the nape of his neck, like feeding worms. It reverberated through the channels of his ears like fingernails down a sidewalk, and with his eyes reduced to two angry, instantly ferocious slits, he slowly turned around in his seat and glared at the whole gang behind him

At one moment they had been barking like dogs. Now, they were silenced by his insubordination.

It made Weedy beside himself with rage.

"You better watch yourself, redneck," he hissed, pointing a crooked finger at Edgar. Undeterred, Edgar stood and faced him. The students at all the tables around them suddenly fell silent.

Deep inside, the sensation of hatred continued to pulse through Edgar, lighting his belly on fire, like habanero chili. It trickled to his feet, stretched outward to his fingertips, and throbbed in his forehead: a rage so strong that he balled his fists without knowing it.

Losing control, with molten lava in his veins, and dark, delirious circles under his eyes, he squinted at Weedy with a blazing fury, squeezing and releasing his fists over and over.

"Calm down, man," whispered Flounder, who half-stood to reason with his friend.

As if in response, Edgar lowered his arm down to the tabletop. Edgar swiped all the food away, sending it all tumbling across the commons with a quick slip of his forearm. Flounder jerked backward. Food and plates and cups and cans whirled into the air, ricocheting like buckshot, dancing among the feet of the upperclassmen of Mount Lanier High, most especially, Chris Weedy and his cohorts. As Edgar continued to glare at them, forks and spoons clanked across the polished brick and the students of Mount Lanier High fell to an even quieter hush.

Chris and his gang bristled and stood, glaring at Edgar. They studied him with mouths pursed in rage as plastic pudding cups and Coke cans halted at their feet. Like a gunfight in the old west, all eyes turned to Edgar.

Politely, he leaned down to a girl who sat at an adjacent table.

"Hey," he said. "Can I have your apple?" She looked up at him for a moment, then shrugged at her friends and smiled, then lifted the green apple to him.

"Thank you," he said, then polished the apple dramatically on his shirt sleeve. Then, to Flounder's absolute dismay, he stepped forward and climbed on top of the girl's table.

Standing above them all, he turned and squared up to Chris Weedy's table, glaring down at him.

"You!" screamed Weedy. "Sit down, Dewitt!" He rose from his seat and pointed a threatening finger.

"Christopher," said Edgar. "You will never tell me what to do again. Your time is *over*."

And then Edgar bent and selected a few items from the table to go with the apple: a half-full carton of milk, an aqua-blue lunch tray, a half-eaten hamburger, an orange, a whole candy bar. Then, targeting with a licked thumb the terribly angry Chris Weedy, when Edgar was ready, he did his best baseball-windup routine and aimed the apple at Chris's face.

"You better not," hissed Chris, standing firm. "We'll kill you, Dewitt."

"There's that word," said Edgar, pausing his warmup. "*We*." He grinned tauntingly at Weedy. "That's the only word you know."

Then, letting his rage consume him, Edgar wound up and hurled the apple directly at Weedy's face, launching it with everything he had.

The apple whizzed through the air like a blur, missing Weedy's face but knocking him thunderously in the chest with a violent, hollow thud. Weedy crumpled over in pain and withered to his seat, as the commons erupted in outright jubilation.

"Oops!" called Edgar. "I *missed*. I was aiming for your face!" But he was drowned out by the thunderous laughter.

"Edgar!" pleaded Flounder. "Please! You're gonna get us both killed!" But Edgar ignored him, and fitfully—with Weedy on the ropes—began to launch other things:

a lunch tray, that he slung through the air like a Frisbee, that just buzzed Weedy's head but slammed into one of his goons, right in the neck. Edgar laughed.

It felt so, so *good* to see them scurry.

Then he hurled an orange that smacked the side of Chris's head like a fist. Weedy ducked and placed his face in his hands, rubbing at the spot where he'd been hit.

"You bastard!" he screamed into his hands. "You're freaking dead!"

Edgar then called upon all his years of little league baseball. Revenge-crazed, he let all of the objects fly, one by one, as fast and as hard as he could throw them, striking Chris Weedy with most of it. And, once the objects were depleted, he strode briskly across the table and snatched up even more things—another tray, another fork, a book—anything he could get his hands on. With his mouth peeled back into an enraged snarl, as each object left his hand and sped across the commons with the greatest amount of force, he cackled as he realized the adjacent jocks were being peppered with food as well, who disdainfully shook food from their lettermen's jackets and cursed him violently, but he didn't care.

"You're dead!" one of them hissed, who pointed to a ketchup splotch on his Letterman's sleeve. "You dumbass, Dewitt!"

But Edgar didn't stop. He couldn't stop throwing for anything, especially because they deserved it. He *hated* them. It was for all they'd put him through since the first day he arrived—since the first day he saw them—when they'd made fun of his jean rolls and called him a redneck.

And plus, it felt really, *really* good.

As he threw, for just a brief moment, a small, reasonable voice inside told him to stop.

What are you doing Edgar? Stop it!

"Shut up," growled Edgar, who chucked another

unpeeled banana, and reached for a full can of Coke.

Calm down, said the voice, but Edgar wouldn't listen. He reared back to throw the can of Coke, and suddenly, he was yanked completely off his feet by two large hands, from behind.

Nothing but clear sky spun above as he was whisked away kicking and fighting.

It was Van Rossum beneath him.

The teacher had been the voice of reason talking to him from below.

"Calm down," grunted Van Rossum again, and suddenly Edgar was being carried across the commons. As they went, students from all the tables cheered for Edgar.

"Let me down!" cried Edgar, squirming with rage, but Van Rossum did not let him go. Instead, he thrust Edgar through the two large, red, double doors and into the locker well. As Edgar was being carried, he caught one last glimpse before the doors closed of Weedy and his boys.

"After school," shouted Chris, his white teeth snarling like a rabid dog. He shook a balled fist at Edgar as he rose from the ground where he had been ducking and behind him, his gang nodded with him in vigorous agreement.

Inside the hallway Dr. Van Rossum placed Edgar in front of the lockers and towered over him, glaring down from above until Edgar finally stilled.

"Are you crazy?" asked the teacher.

"No!'" said Edgar, his voice full of hurt. "They started it!"

"So?" said the man. "Who cares who started it?"

A moment of silence ensued. Van Rossum studied Edgar with a piercing glare, as Edgar lifted his hands to wipe away beads of sweat that formed on his brow.

"Let me ask you something, Edgar," said Van Rossum. "And please don't tell me any lies." He bent to Edgar's level and looked him in the eyes. "Why are you flunking my class?"

It made Edgar completely unravel. His tense muscles loosened and he slumped over. Van Rossum's question had sent the adrenaline flowing from him like a rushing tide. Suddenly he fought the urge to outright weep. His life had been falling apart—*he* was falling apart under the strain. Edgar looked up at the man and peered into his kind face, wishing he could go back to the beginning, to the day he found the hole.

Maybe he would have brought his mom and dad. Maybe he would have done everything differently.

"I'm not trying to flunk your class," he answered softly.

"Yeah, well," said the teacher, "you're doing it *anyway*."

Edgar continued to hang his head until Van Rossum leaned down and took him gently by the shoulders, then gave him a friendly shake.

"You must," said the teacher, "get control of your life, Edgar. You're *down-spiraling*, son. You're far too smart for stuff like this." He caught Edgar's gaze and smiled.

Edgar smiled back.

"Right?" said Van Rossum.

"Right," said Edgar.

"OK then," said the man, letting Edgar's shoulders go.

"Wonderful," he said, straightening. "Glad we had this talk." Then he turned and made for his classroom, just down the hall, but not before saying over his shoulder, "No more food fights, Edgar, you hear me?"

"Yes, sir," he answered.

"That's not your style, boy. Throwing food like a monkey. For shame!"

As Van Rossum strolled down the hall, he added one more thing. "I say fight with your brain, Edgar. I'm sure it wouldn't be too hard—not with guys like those."

Edgar grinned broadly and wiped the last of the milk from his neck. Then, he turned to the big double doors and gazed through the sliver of window in the metal.

There was Flounder, still getting nailed by the boys. It was their payback—their revenge for what he had done—and they were taking it out on Flounder. The food rained down on Flounder even worse than before, and Edgar was not around to help.

To Flounder's credit, he sat stoically with both hands gripping the edges of the table, enduring it.

Edgar felt the rage return. He grabbed the door with both hands and burst out into the commons, but just at that moment—right above his head—the bell rang, louder than a fire truck. It almost scared him half to death.

When it did, students came spilling through the doors around him. He looked back outside and saw that the bullies had suddenly stopped with Flounder and were rising to go to class.

He'd been spared. At least for the moment.

Flounder lingered afterward and cleaned himself. Edgar felt sorrow for him. It was absolutely pitiful to witness. He was a disaster, with fluids dripping from his hair and chin and from his cheeks—food everywhere on him. Flounder sat and wiped his dark brown eyes with many napkins, attempting to brush the rest off with his hands, but it was too much. What he really needed was a full change of clothes and a shower, but that was not possible. Edgar ran a hand through his own filthy hair, and wracked his brain for a plan.

He knew that on the walk home today, they'd try to catch him, knowing that he and Flounder always walked to the fish stand together. Should he get his mom to pick them up? Maybe.

"*You're a smart kid,*" said Van Rossum's voice, reverberating in his mind. "*You should learn to fight with your brain.*"

And that's when the crazy idea emerged. It was risky,

and it was complicated, but he figured it just might work.

He'd go over it with Flounder next period. They didn't have much time so they'd have to get it right the first time.

FIFTEEN

FLOUNDER STEPPED ACROSS the stones of the brook, peeling away the last partition of leaves that revealed, finally, the cabin in the woods.

"This is it, I think," muttered Flounder, as Weedy's gang lingered behind, forming a wall around him so that he couldn't escape.

"In that crap heap?" hissed Weedy, pointing at the cabin beyond.

Flounder nodded and stepped aside to let the boys through. The stains on their letterman jackets from Edgar's outburst at lunch had grown crusty and faded. One guy, Kevin, had a greasy splotch in his hair, which was hilarious to Flounder, but there was no way he dared stare at it.

"So, how deep is this hole?" probed Weedy, as they made their way toward the cabin.

"Uh, Edgar says it's about a hundred feet deep,"

answered Flounder. "That's what he thinks, anyway."

When they reached the cabin door, Chris whirled and got in Flounder's face, snarling at him from inches away. "And he told you he wants to throw me into it?"

"Yeah," confirmed Flounder, swallowing hard. Weedy's scowling face grew even more suspicious. "Well, why tell me all this, Flounder?" He leaned in even closer, almost touching Flounder's nose with his own. "Everybody knows you two rejects are friends."

"Yeah, well, to be honest," said Flounder, his voice cracking, "to be honest, I'm just tired of getting picked on every day. With all the stuff about how 'I stink' and all the food being thrown at me at lunch. I told you, if I give you Edgar in an isolated place, you agree to leave me alone. That's the deal, right?"

Weedy thought it over for a minute, and through a cruel, broken smile, he gave his answer. "Sure, Flounder. Whatever you want."

Weedy then stepped by him and pushed open the cabin door. It creaked loudly on its hinges as it swung open, and inside Edgar stood facing Weedy and his gang, before the large, gaping hole in the floor.

"Flounder!" called Edgar. "I hope you didn't rat me out!"

Flounder shrugged and looked down. Edgar laughed as Weedy escorted his gang inside, then closed the door behind them.

"You're trapped," informed Weedy.

"And with the entire football team, too, apparently," grinned Edgar. "What, do you think it takes this many guys to beat me up, Weedy? Besides yourself, of course?"

Weedy scowled. "We're here for what you did to us at lunch. We want to make sure you don't get away, idiot," he snarled.

"Dang Weedy, you sure use the word 'we' a lot," Edgar

grinned, egging him on.

"Block the door," instructed Weedy. "Nobody gets out of here unless I say."

Like a police force, his three big boys spread out and guarded the door, and one even sequestered Flounder, making sure he was contained. When Weedy was satisfied the cabin was on lockdown, he took a long look around the room.

"What *is* all this stuff?" he said, pointing to the fish cleaning station. "What's this—a refrigerator and generator? What, Edgar, is this where you host all your little parties?"

"You know it," grinned Edgar.

Suddenly Weedy's anger seemed to blossom and overflow and he darted across the room and got in Edgar's face. The boys at the door cackled in anticipation, cheering Weedy on. Weedy brought his fists to attention, standing ready, looking as if he might strike at any moment.

Edgar, meanwhile, kept his eyes on Weedy and tried to remember to breathe. If he only kept his wits about him, he could get himself and Flounder out of this. In the bright spotlight of sunshine pouring down from the roof, the two were like wiry prizefighters in the middle of a boxing ring.

"You gonna take a swing?" whispered Edgar. "Or, what? Do you need permission from your girlfriends over there?"

At that, in a rage, Weedy swung his fist. Deftly Edgar ducked it, bobbing to the left, dipping down low below Weedy's stomach. Then, aiming for Weedy's waist, he lunged and latched himself to the skinny boy, pinning his arms, and rendering him unable to strike.

Trapped by Edgar's hold, Weedy convulsed and jerked and wiggled, bucking like a bronco to get away.

"No!" screamed Edgar suddenly, and could feel Weedy

limpen. "Don't do it, Weedy!"

"What?" hissed Weedy. "What the hell are you talking about? Let me go, you freak!"

"No!" Edgar continued to shout, "please don't push me down there, Chris! PLEASE DON'T PUSH ME DOWN!" And at that, Edgar launched himself off Chris Weedy, falling backward into the hole, flipping dramatically so that everyone could see, and as he did, he screamed as loud as he could for as long as he could, just for effect.

"NOOOOO!" his voice rang from the hole in the floor, until, finally, it faded into nothingness.

The boys walked to the hole and looked at Chris Weedy, then downward, crowding around the hole to see.

Weedy's face, pale with horror, was stoic as he gazed into the hole alongside his clan, his mouth wide open in shock.

"I . . . I didn't push him," he said softly, a long moment passing. Then, he turned to his friends and repeated himself. "Guys, I didn't push him," he insisted. "The redneck jumped."

The boys said nothing, but continued to stare downward into the darkness. "He grabbed my arms, and then he jumped backward on purpose like an idiot, I swear to God. You guys saw it, right?"

Their three frightened, gloomy faces could only stare back at his. Even Flounder could tell that nobody believed him.

"OK, then," he said, an angry snarl emerging on his face. "Just so you know, I'm not going down alone. You're all accessories to murder *with* me. Everybody's as guilty as I am. What do you think of *that*?"

The boys burst into a rowdy protest and crowded around him, yelling in his face.

"It was you!" they yelled. "Not us!" and then like a pack

of dumb animals they began arguing amongst themselves, which, to Flounder, was absolutely delightful.

But he'd never let them know that.

"This is how it's gonna be," said Weedy, silencing them, his hand upraised. "We're in this together, so let's figure it out together." The boys became silent at that, gazing down the hole, searching for ideas.

And then they all turned to Flounder who stood innocently behind them, near the door. With Weedy leading the way, they moved from the hole, approaching him.

"Anthony," Weedy purred.

"Yes."

Weedy gave Flounder a friendly pat on the back.

"You know I didn't push Edgar into that hole, right?"

Flounder bit his fingernails and stared at Weedy. "It sure looked like you pushed him down, to me at least."

That sent Weedy's gang into an absolute frenzy.

"Oh my God!" they shouted. "This dork is gonna rat on us! We're screwed!"

"No, no," said Weedy, waving his hand downward. "Anthony is not a dork." Then, a peaceful, almost benevolent look came upon Weedy's face. "Shut up, you morons," he said to them softly, and obediently, the group quieted.

"Now," he cooed to Flounder. "Flound—I mean *Anthony*. Didn't you say you wanted me to call you that?"

Flounder nodded enthusiastically.

"How then, Anthony, can I convince you that I didn't push Edgar in the hole?"

"Uh, well, I have no idea," said Flounder. "I already told you. It looked to me like you pushed him."

"Well, I didn't," answered Weedy, softly. "Look, Anthony. There has to be something—some way I can convince you that I didn't do it, right? You don't want me to push you down the hole, too, do you?" Then, reconsidering that, he shook his head and said, "Wait, I'm sorry.

I shouldn't have said that. There's no need for that. But you see, the other guys here don't think I pushed him and they're acting a bit intense, and didn't you say you didn't want us to bully you anymore? Well, how about meeting us halfway. We will definitely and *once and for all* stop throwing food at you *forever*, and we will stop talking about how you smell. How about that? Wouldn't that be good?"

Flounder nodded. "I guess that would be pretty good."

"You *guess*?" laughed Weedy. "C'mon Anthony! It's a good deal! This is a big moment for you! Don't you want us to leave you alone?"

"Yeah," said Flounder, scratching his head, "but I also want . . ."

"Oh? What's that? What do you want, Anthony?"

"I guess I want money," said Flounder, flatly.

Weedy's jaw fell open, and so did the other boys'. For a long time, Weedy was unable to respond.

"What do you mean, *money*?" asked Weedy.

"Well, you know. Cash."

Chris flashed his crew a quick smile and they all burst out into laughter. "Sure," chuckled Weedy, turning back to Flounder. "We can certainly do that."

"That's cold, Flounder!" laughed one of the boys, and another slapped Flounder on the back. "You're not such a dork after all!"

"Remember," Flounder corrected him. "I'm *Anthony*."

"Oh, yes," said Weedy, his hands upheld to his crew. "He's right, it's *Anthony*." Then, addressing Flounder, he said, "So how much should we give you?"

"Oh, I don't know," said Flounder, rubbing his chin. "Let's see. I guess give me everything you have."

Weedy's smile vanished in an instant, and he glared at Flounder as the jocks murmured to one another behind him. Overcoming his rage, Weedy swallowed it down and withdrew the cash from his wallet, offering it to Flounder.

"No," said Flounder, "I meant to say, I want everything you have on you. Could you empty your pockets?"

Christopher began to snarl at Flounder, but then resisted, reaching into his pockets and emptying their contents onto the floor. One by one the items plopped onto the planks beside the hole—a bill fold, a set of car keys, a cell phone. Flounder bent and scooped everything up, nodding his thanks to the bully.

"I guess I'll take everything," he said thoughtfully, "but not the car keys. I don't need a car. I'm not even fifteen."

"Christ," muttered Weedy, visibly trying to keep it together. "That never stopped me before. OK, Flounder, you win today. Are we good now? You've got my wallet and phone, for God's sake."

Flounder thumbed through the money in the wallet and, satisfied, he nodded.

"My name is Anthony, remember?" he reminded Weedy, and feeling just like one of those mob bosses that Edgar always talked about, he extended the car keys to Weedy and nodded toward the door.

"You know," said Weedy, snatching the car keys away, "I half-respect you right now. But only *half*."

Weedy ushered his gang out of the cabin and they scurried out the door, leaving Flounder all alone in the cabin. In a breathless mess, he collapsed in the corner and pulled his knees to his chest and tried to get his thundering heart under control.

Then he waited, just like Edgar had told him to do.

Every once in a while, he'd rise from the floor and walk around the hole, staring at it, investigating it. *Who dug this?* he wondered. *Where did it come from?* Interested as he was, he stayed a good distance away from the ledge, since Flounder was deathly afraid of heights.

Eventually he returned to the corner and withdrew

Chris's cell phone and turned it on. He scrolled through the pictures on the SIM card and the videos that Shay had told them would be there.

Sure enough, Flounder found shot after shot of incriminating photographic evidence of vandalism. There were street addresses, license plates, even pictures of unsuspecting victims.

What a dummy.

His phone offered an immaculate folder of evidence of all the crimes he'd committed against the community of Mount Lanier. Most of them were dark, to be certain—due to the fact they were taken at night—and the ones involving fire were almost always too bright to see details. But there were so many that had been captured *just right*. Chris Weedy could get years in Juvi for this.

As the sun began to fade, and as the insects of twilight began to call out, Flounder could hear something coming up from down in the hole. It was the faint, but instantly recognizable, hollering of his friend. Edgar was coming. And he was singing!

Flounder mustered up the courage to lean over the edge and watch him come up, and suddenly, Edgar appeared right in front of him. He had a huge smile on his face.

"What's up, man? I see you survived Chris Weedy!"

Edgar snatched the side wall and climbed out from the hole, standing before his friend. "Ta daaa!" he sang, like a magician.

"What in the Sam hell is going on around here?" said Flounder, pointing into the hole. "Dude, where have you been?"

"Never mind, Flounder," said Edgar. "First thing's first. Did you get it?"

"Oh, yeah," grinned Flounder, pulling the cell phone out of his pocket. "It worked just like we planned." He dangled the phone in front of Edgar's face.

"Oh! My man!" said Edgar, punching Flounder playfully on the arm. Flounder looked down at the hole again and his face darkened with curiosity.

"OK dude," chuckled Edgar. "Let's get out of here and I'll tell you everything."

ON THE way home, he did tell Flounder everything. He hadn't had time in seventh period when they'd commiserated to trap Weedy and his gang, but now, strolling home in the warm, Autumn sun, Edgar painted Flounder a picture.

As they walked, he described the island and the fishing and the Ambercod, and how beautiful the water was on the shores at night on the Indian Ocean.

"So *that's* where the Ambercod has been coming from!" exclaimed Flounder.

"Yeah, dude, it's crazy fishing," said Edgar. "They *always* bite."

Edgar also described what it felt like to fall weightlessly through the Earth, and how hot the Earth's core was, and how much fun it was to spin and flip around in the middle of the world. "You've gotta come with me sometime!" he said.

"No way, guy," insisted Flounder. "I don't do heights. I'd have a heart attack in midair."

"Shay's been," smiled Edgar.

"What?" said Flounder, incredulously. "You dog!" He grinned broadly and wiggled his big, black eyebrows.

THE NEXT morning, when Edgar and Flounder reached the commons outside the school—the place where the students always waited for the opening bell—

Edgar noticed Weedy sitting with his crew, who were in their usual spot.

"OK," he said to Flounder. "Let's go. But be cool."

They approached the table of jocks and when Weedy saw Edgar—who was obviously alive and well—he grinned evilly and hung his head. Behind him, the jocks exploded into wild protestations, but Edgar could also tell that some of them were quite relieved.

After all, they'd probably stayed up all night scared half to death they might get busted for murder.

However, Weedy's face remained stony. If he was relieved Edgar was still alive, he sure didn't show it. He showed no emotion other than smiling that bitter, sinister, angry smile.

"I must say," sang Weedy as they approached, "I liked you much better dead, redneck." He leaned back on the table and folded his hands behind his head. He squinted up at the bright sunshine of Mount Lanier. Then he looked down his nose at Edgar and Flounder.

"We've got something of yours," explained Edgar.

"It's your wallet," added Flounder. "You want it back?"

Weedy's evil smile dissipated. He shrugged his shoulders nonchalantly, as if he didn't care about the wallet. "Whatever," he said.

Flounder retrieved the leather wallet anyway and handed it to the bully who sat up and snatched it from his grasp.

"This wallet," Weedy growled, "is worth more than your . . . *everything*." Then he opened it and counted the money. As Edgar waited, he said, "It's all there, Weedy. We don't want your money, dumbass."

Satisfied, Weedy stuffed the wallet into his back pocket and glared at Edgar.

"Here's the deal," Edgar continued, positive that he had Chris and his gang's undivided attention. "We've got your cell phone now. Do you know what that means?" He let it sink in for a moment.

Weedy massaged his chin and shrugged.

"It means we have a *lot* of pictures of you committing various acts of vandalism around town, you catch my drift?"

A dark look emerged on Weedy's face, and at that moment, when he knew that the ramifications had successfully sunk in to the bully's thick skull, Edgar knew that things were going to be different. He knew they had all the power now, him and Flounder.

Weedy glared and fumed, but there wasn't a single thing he could do about it now.

"And you guys," said Edgar, pointing at the jocks sitting behind him. "You are all in the pictures, too."

Immediately the jocks rose into hysterics, cursing Weedy and cursing amongst themselves, furious that they had been incriminated by Weedy's recklessness.

"Don't worry!" shouted Edgar, motioning for calm, as they all stopped and looked at him—their stupid faces contorted in anguish. "Don't sweat this, because we—me and Flounder—we're not going to tell on any of you, so long as you leave us alone. That's all we want." He paused for a moment and let it sink in. "For the next four years," he added, "until graduation day, we demand to be left alone. And, after that, we will give back the phone. Is everyone agreed?"

Nobody said a word, they just looked at him and Flounder.

"I said," he hissed, his angry eyes turning to slits, "*are we agreed?*" Slowly, in unison, they all began to nod like a bunch of powerless, pecking chickens. But Chris Weedy didn't. His face remained hard as a stone.

"You'll get your phone back at graduation," Edgar growled at him, and then he and Flounder walked away.

"This isn't over!" said Weedy from behind.

"Yeah, it is," muttered Edgar, then stopped and turned. "By the way, I forgot to tell you. If I catch any of you going to my cabin in the woods, I will go straight to the cops with the pictures. Stay away from my cabin."

And suddenly the jocks were protesting again, quietly this time, to Weedy, to each other, as they walked away. From the other side of the commons, Edgar turned and looked one last time at the snookered bully, who was still glaring at him, oblivious to his gang's own disintegration.

"*This isn't over,*" mouthed Chris Weedy.

But surely it was.

LATER ON that day at lunch, Edgar and Flounder ate their food in absolute peace. It was incredible.

The jocks sat quietly across the courtyard and chewed on their food in a sort of moody surrender. Their expressions were painfully subdued as they ate and studied Edgar and Flounder, like a pack of bears who must, for some unnatural reason, allow a couple of helpless fish to swim by.

The following morning, Edgar and Flounder strolled up to the school without any yelling or insults raining down on them—no "Redneck," or "Flounder, you stink!"

No one called them anything. Nobody threw any pinecones. Nobody did a single thing to them, which was wonderful. Things got so quiet at school the two boys almost began to forget that the bullies were even there. It was enough to make Edgar sleep well again, if he ever found time to sleep at all.

SIXTEEN

WITH THE BULLIES fresh off their backs, Edgar felt like celebrating.

He shot Shay a text: *Wanna go swimming tonight?*

Across the classroom, Shay nodded and smiled.

That night they snuck out together and made for the other side of the world. Back on the island, they raced, laughing, down to the shore as the sun hung high and wonderful. They plunged breathlessly into the chilly water, where finally they surfaced and shrieked, convulsing with laughter.

"Whoa!" she exclaimed. "It's way warmer than last time!"

"Yeah, you're not lying," Edgar nodded, who suddenly stilled. His smile fading, he cupped his hands over the surface of the water and peered through the window of his palms, squinting into the blue depths.

"What are you doing?" she asked, her voice suddenly

worried.

"Nothing," he said. "Let's get those bags."

So they swam to the shore and collected the backpacks they brought. Inside were two pairs of snorkels, two pairs of flippers, two collapsible prods, and two wadded-up burlap sacks.

"My dad showed me how to do this at the Florida Keys one time," she explained. "It's kind of freaky at first, but you'll get the hang of it. Just keep your fingers away from the pincers."

Hopping back into the surf, she led him down to the reef below, kicking deep into the clear blue water. Once down, she approached a hiding hole in some coral and began to pry a red crustacean from its bunker. As the lobster scooted backward into her burlap sack, she turned and gave Edgar a wild thumb's up, her eyes sparkling with excitement inside her mask.

He took another quick glance around. The truth was, the night before, while fishing, he'd seen something absolutely terrible on the island's shore: the unmistakable sight of a shark's fin breaking the surface.

Still no sharks, he thought. *Thank God.*

After several trips back and forth to the surface, with two bags overflowing with ruby red pincers, Edgar and Shay finally made for shore.

"We're rich!" she exclaimed, ripping off her mask, holding up her fat sack. Kicking in the ocean, she marveled at the catch. "I must have ten lobsters in here, *easy!*"

THAT NIGHT, with the lobsters bagged and stored in the cabin freezer, they walked to her house, strolling slowly, giggling in the waning moonlight.

"What are you going to do with your profits?" he

asked.

"Buy a new Bass Pro Shops lunchbox," she giggled. "And give it to you."

There, at the base of the sycamore tree, just below her bedroom, Shay kissed him. It was nearly dawn and their faces were as red as the lobsters they'd caught.

"Goodnight," she whispered, kissing him again, her hands still wrapped behind his neck, drunken with fatigue. She closed her eyes and pressed a third warm and wonderful kiss onto his lips, and he drank in her lips, utterly overcome with passion.

He wished it would never end.

Afterward, she climbed up the tree and lingered for a moment, then waved to him and slipped inside.

He turned and, with a delirious smile, made for home.

AT FIVE-FIFTEEN in the morning, he arrived at his driveway. No suspicious activity seemed to be occurring, luckily. No lights were on, and nobody seemed to be up. He seemed to be safe.

With a sigh of relief, he made his way to the bedroom window, then wearily lifted the glass.

"What are you *doing*?"

Edgar froze. The voice had come from inside his room. His knees nearly buckled from the shock.

He was *busted*.

"What?" he asked into the darkness, frozen halfway inside his window.

"I asked you, *what are you doing, Edgar?* Where have you been?" It was the angry, incredibly wounded voice of his mother.

"I," he began, sitting frozen on the wooden windowsill, utterly paralyzed with fear, unable to breathe, his sweaty heart thundering in his shirt. "I was out for a bit," he admitted.

He climbed inside and there, in the corner of his room, sat Mrs. Dewitt on his chest of drawers. How long she'd been there, he had no idea. Currently she was holding a balled-up tissue in a clenched-up fist, that was obviously used for wiping away worried tears. Immediately he knew without question: he was in big, *big* trouble.

"Mom," he began. "I . . ."

"No!" she interrupted, closing her weepy eyes. "I do *not* want to hear any more of your lies, Edgar." She lifted a trembling hand and massaged her forehead, then opened her eyes and glared again. "All you do is lie nowadays, over and over again."

"What?" he croaked, his throat suddenly dry. "What do you mean, 'lie?'"

She laughed angrily. "Edgar, come on! Your father and I—we are not stupid. You've been lying to us for weeks!"

"No I haven't!"

"*Speaking* of your father," she said, talking over him, "he came to say goodbye to you in the middle of the night, but unfortunately you couldn't find it in your busy schedule to *be at home* in the middle of the night—so he said to tell you that you've really let him down, and when he gets back home, you are in serious, serious trouble."

Edgar had a front row seat to the collapse of his entire operation. Piece by agonizing piece it was falling away, every bit as terrible as he thought it might be when he considered it all those times when falling through the Earth, wondering what might happen if his parents ever found him gone in the middle of the night.

"Dad came to say goodbye?" Edgar muttered. "Where did he go?"

She blew her nose on the ratty tissue and balled it up again. "He left for Yakima two hours ago."

" . . . Why?"

"To fight a fire."

"But Dad's not a fireman."

"You know he volunteered. He told you last week. Or were you not listening? Anyway, stop trying to change the subject, Edgar," she said grimly.

He ran a nervous hand through his hair and nodded.

"So now," she continued, "you were saying? About sneaking out to God knows where?"

"I—" he began, defensively, but she held up a hand and cut him off again.

"You know, I can just feel another lie coming," she said disgustedly, shaking her head. "I just don't think I want to hear it."

"OK," he said. "*OK*, Mom. So we went catfishing last night."

"Catfishing?" she chuckled. "And where exactly did this *catfishing* occur?"

He gulped audibly and tried to keep his cool. "Out at the Coulee Dam. I didn't tell you because I knew you wouldn't let me go, since it was a school night."

She glared at him, searching his face. "Coulee?" she said. "How did you get all the way out to Coulee?"

"Well, my friend Flounder has a car."

He anguished as she thoughtfully scooped up an old picture from the top of the chest of drawers. She gently caressed Edgar's photographed face—a photo she'd always liked from back in little league, but one he always hated since it embarrassed him how chubby he'd been as a kid, from baby fat, and how he looked like a beaver with his two huge, buck teeth.

"You know," she said softly, smudging a speck of dust from his photographed face, probably wishing she still had him—the *young* Edgar—instead of the grown-up Edgar she seemed so disgusted with who stood before her. "You remember the science fair project you mentioned a few weeks back? You remember how you sat at the table and destroyed your childhood globe? Well, I know they didn't assign you that project on the first week of school."

Edgar dropped his head and stared at his sandaled feet.

"Even then I knew you were lying, Edgar."

She placed the picture back on the chest of drawers and looked up at him, gazing at him. "The way I could tell, Edgar, was that I knew it in your *voice*. You were lying. You've never been a good liar, son, which is a *good* thing, but tonight with all this 'catfishing' business, I just know I've caught you in a bigger lie—I've caught you doing something worse—but you just continue to dig a hole for yourself."

She shook her head and shrugged. "I just don't think I even *know* you anymore."

She rose from the chest of drawers and walked across the room to him, glaring down.

"Cross country tryouts?" she muttered at him. "Running into the house at five in the morning with no shoes on? What a fool you have made of me! Of *us!*" That stung Edgar deeply.

"Where are all your progress reports, Edgar?" she probed, lifting her palms to her hips, making his already petrified heart skip another beat. "I guess you'll tell me they haven't been sent home yet, huh? Or what, they don't do progress reports in Washington? Which lie do you have ready for me this time?"

Breathlessly attempting to maintain his composure, he looked her in the eye and said, "Mom, we haven't gotten any progress reports. Not yet."

"Oh, is that right? Are you sure?" she asked, a bitter, angry smile emerging on her face. "Wow. You must think I'm really dumb, Edgar."

The jig was up. She was onto him and would never let

up now. Edgar was screwed. He was also suddenly so very tired, and so overwhelmed by the horrible confrontation that he just wished he could go to sleep—to lie down and sleep the sleep of a clean conscience again, to start over again. Nothing was worth this terrible moment of seeing his own mother fall apart like this. Edgar knew he had ruptured something between them, and that their relationship had been shaken to the point that he didn't even know if it could be made whole again. She was looking at him differently now, standing in the oncoming dawn of his room, a woman who, until now, had always been just as much a friend to him as a mother. He thought about her guiding him by the neck through town, leading him to the ice cream parlor.

But now, he could tell in her eyes: their friendship was jeopardized. She was in survival mode now. He had hurt her very deeply.

None of this was worth the island or the hole through the Earth or the fishing business or the money or the freedom.

None of it was worth a dang thing to him. He just wanted his Mom to trust him again, but the way she was looking at him now, it might not ever happen again.

"Please," she asked, "just tell me the *truth*, Edgar, and I promise things will get better for you. That's how the truth works. It heals. It's like medicine."

Which sounded good. But for some weird, inexplicable reason, when Edgar opened his mouth to tell the truth, terribly, inconceivably, the lies continued to come.

"We went *catfishing*," he said with finality, his shoulders slumping from the confrontation. "Over at the Coulee Dam, like I said."

He couldn't stop thinking about Shay and the times they'd had together, swimming and laughing and catching lobster and how they'd kissed freefalling through the

Earth, and commiserated in the middle of the night walking home. How could he possibly give that up? He gazed at the floor in misery unable to bring himself to look at his mother. "I'm very sorry I snuck out," he added. "I will never do it again."

"Oh, finally," she said. "That's the truest statement you've made yet: you certainly are *not* going to sneak out again." Freshly enraged at his unwillingness to come clean, Milly Dewitt leaned down to him. "Is there anything else you'd like to tell me?" she asked threateningly.

"No!" he said, a fresh sheen of sweat breaking out upon his forehead. Something was wrong. Things were getting worse. She knew something, but what?

"This is your last chance, Edgar," she said, her voice fraught with danger.

"I'm super positive," he nodded, his voice rising an octave. "Just that stuff about going catfishing, that's all. Nothing else has been going on."

She nodded grimly, then brushed past him and walked to the corner of his room, where she bent to the floor and to the baseboards.

Then, terribly, *unbearably*, she began to wiggle the same exact baseboard that he used to hide all his money!

"Whoa, Mom!" he shouted, lifting his hands in surrender. "*Please*! What are you doing!"

"What's the matter, Edgar?" she asked loudly, turning to glare at him. "Nothing's '*going on*,' remember?"

"Yeah, but, Mom!" he cried, yet she ignored him, yanking away at the baseboard.

With each pull, the awful baseboard began to loosen; and, each time it did the cry of the small nails were to him like a gang of cackling demons.

When suddenly the baseboard popped loose, there, behind the wall, sat his Bass Pro Shops lunchbox, and on top of it sat an obscene stack of progress reports and forged test scores.

He had stupidly failed to throw them away.

And beneath those, the lunchbox sat open to reveal a stash of stacked money so thick, it spewed out like a pirate's chest. Mrs. Dewitt turned and looked fearfully at her son, then jerked a thumb to the evidence.

"I thought you said you'd outgrown your lunchbox," she said, matter-of-factly.

"*Mom*," he said, his trembling voice hoarse with fear, his whole world collapsing now, "I can explain."

She reached for a stray progress report and studied it with disgust, turning the paper to him for him to see, but he looked away. Before she stood, she reached behind the wall and snatched the progress reports and the money-dripping lunchbox and tossed it all onto the bed.

"Go ahead!" she shouted, pointing to the lunchbox. "Explain it! Explain why you have exactly *one thousand dollars* in a Bass Pro Shops lunchbox that you've hidden behind the wall!"

He opened his mouth to speak, but there was just nothing to say. He was simply plain old *busted*, and he knew it, and she knew it, too. As he stared at her he knew that there was no way out for him, so why make things worse?

Do what they do when they take you to jail. Say nothing.

Nothing could repair this. There was no lie he could ever use to cover this up, and so, completely boxed in, he simply stood and waited, his mouth pursed shut, his shoulders hanging. He would hunker down and weather her storm.

"So . . . nothing?" she probed. "You're done? That's *it*?"

He sat down on the bed beside the money—which made several bills poof outward and waft to the ground like green confetti. She stared down at him with moist, shimmering eyes.

"I'm asking you one last time, son. Where did all this money come from?"

To that, he said nothing.

"Where were you all night, Edgar? Out . . . *making* this money?"

He stared at the ground and gritted his teeth. His entire island, his fishing business, the only special things he had in his whole godforsaken life—being stuck as he was in the godforsaken *town*—everything was at stake now. Saying anything more to his mother might only jeopardize it further.

Besides, he didn't have to speak. There was no law against it.

He didn't have to give the island up to her.

"OK, then," she said, straightening, dotting her eyes again with the obliterated Kleenex. "We'll just get you a drug test then, when your father comes home from the fire."

"What?" said Edgar, as she darted from the room, well before his tears could fall.

"Drugs?" he yelled at the door. "DRUGS? Yeah, well, I WISH I HAD SOME DRUGS FOR ALL THIS—" unable to find the right word, he looked around his room and bit his lip and yelled, "—SHIT! YOU'VE BROUGHT ME TO A TOWN AND TOSSED ME INTO A WORLD OF *SHIT!* YOU MADE ME FIGHT FOR MY LIFE EVERY DAY LIKE SOME KIND OF PRISONER! MOUNT LANIER IS LITERAL SHIT! MY LIFE SUCKS! SO YEAH, I WISH I HAD SOME DRUGS!"

He collapsed onto the bed and curled up into a ball as more money spilt over onto the floor. Disgusted, he kicked the money away in a sweeping motion, like making a green snow angel.

AT TEN o'clock in the morning he woke up from a restless sleep—a feverish state full of nightmares and turmoil. Wiping drool from his face and coming to, at first he thought it had all been a nightmare but then, he realized his nightmare was real.

Oh man, was his life ever terrible now.

For a while he just lay in bed, trying to work up the courage to join his mother in the kitchen, to maybe figure out a way to make peace with her. She was out in the kitchen right now, making coffee. He could hear her.

When he did amass the courage to stand and turn the doorknob, he made his way out into the kitchen and faced her.

She sat at the table and did not look up, stirring her cup of coffee while reading the newspaper. Only when he sat down beside her did she look up from the paper and speak.

"Where did the money come from?" she said. "I want to know, Edgar."

He wiped a puffy eye and shrugged. To that, she nodded grimly and returned to her newspaper.

"OK, then," she said coldly. "Fine."

Reaching out, he dragged the front page slowly to him.

"WILDFIRE BREAKS OUT IN YAKIMA," the headline read. "Teams of engineers and city workers from neighboring counties have assembled to fight the blaze."

His dad was there fighting a fire and must be worried sick about his son.

"I called your father this morning to let him know you are fine," she said, as if reading his mind. "And boy . . ." she said, looking up with an angry smile, "is he *pissed*."

Yes, Edgar imagined that this might be the case.

"Also," she added, "we talked it over. We are taking your little pile of fun money away from you." She eyed him for a response, but there was none. "We are giving it to charity, Edgar—every *cent*. What do you think about that?"

"That's fine," he said, because it was. Besides, there was another thousand dollars stashed away inside the back of his TV that she didn't know was there, so it wasn't like he was out of money.

"Oh, and one more thing. You are grounded, for like, e*ver.*"

Yeah, he thought. *No shocker there.*

"So, now. If maybe you want to tell me where the money came from, we could possibly work out a reduction in your sentence. How about that? Would you like to cooperate?"

"Sure," he said, sitting up. *What the hell*, he thought. "Fine, Mom. I will tell you *exactly* how I got the money. The way I got it was, I fell through a hole in the Earth that goes to an island in the Indian Ocean, not down to China like they always say when you're a kid. And on that island, I went fishing. I brought back the fish to Flounder's fish stand where we sold it for about twenty dollars a pound. I had to tell the Arteses that it came from your imaginary brother that I made up, my fake Uncle Louis. Sometimes my new girlfriend goes with me to the island to help me catch lobsters, which I also sell at Flounder's fish stand."

She stiffened and huffed at his explanation. "You," she said angrily, "are *so* disrespectful! This is not a joke. Have it your way, Edgar. Don't tell me how you really got the money. God knows and I will too, someday. The truth always comes out."

He shook his head and pushed the newspaper away. It was the worst day of his life, hands down.

SEVENTEEN

His mom stayed on his case all week and when she wasn't on his case, she barely spoke to him, while his father—still deeply ingrained in the Yakuma firefight—had not been home for days.

Life at home sucked immensely.

As the fire spread in Yakima, and with his father calling for fresh clothes, a phone charger, and other essentials, Mrs. Dewitt had been forced to leave and bring him the supplies.

"Swear to me," she said, cornering Edgar, "that you will honor your restriction while I'm gone. That you will go to school and come home and do all your homework and just go to bed."

"I swear," he said.

"No . . . catfishing. Or whatever it is you do."

"Mom, I swear."

Later that evening, Edgar broke his promise and fell

through the Earth deep in thought, wondering why his life was so out of control.

It had to be the hole.

At all times he could feel it calling to him, burning in his blood like desire—to feel the wonderful whir of hot air whizzing through his hair as he plummeted through the Earth, of feeling his weight diminishing to absolute zero. This was his calling. To fall. No matter how bad things ever got—no matter how stressed out he felt—falling would always bring him back. It was the one thing that could bring him peace.

Two MINUTES out from the other side of the world, he knew something was different this time around. Water droplets began to sting his skin and as each moment passed, the drops became thicker than before, peppering his whole body and making him wet.

Finally, as the opening on the island came into view, he saw only a dim light through the hole—no bright moon or stars, just a swirl of rain and angry, twirling clouds.

When he surfaced on the island and climbed out, immediately staggering backward from a violent gale, he leaned forward and braced himself, digging into the island crust.

Immediately he realized: it was a *hurricane!*

He spun a circle with arms outstretched and took in the raw power of the swirling monster. Waves crashed the shore and winds screamed from the heavens, and it was all wonderful against his skin. The roar of the world mirrored the roar that raged inside his conscience, of the tempest of guilt that made him an outcast in his own home.

Facing the storm now, it was the best he'd felt in days.

He laughed at its fierceness.

"*I caawi!*" a strange voice called through the night. It was a *human* voice, and Edgar's knees almost buckled from shock.

"*I caawi!*" the voice called again, this time a bit louder. It was hoarse, weak, and barely audible over the roaring winds, but Edgar could clearly hear it. Though petrified, Edgar reached for his flashlight and shined toward the voice—which was coming from the sea.

At the appearance of the light, the voice began to scream wildly.

"*I caawi! I caawi!*" it shouted.

That's when Edgar spotted him. There, drifting quickly by, was a man clinging desperately to a life ring, obviously lost at sea. He must have heard Edgar laughing at the hurricane and now, he was screaming uncontrollably at Edgar to save him. He was shaking his fist at the flashlight and weeping, calling for Edgar in a strange tongue.

"*Fadlan!*" the man cried.

As the current swept him by, Edgar realized that he was too far from shore to be grabbed. Edgar knew that if he, himself, tried to step into the churning waters he too would be swept away along with the man.

"Hold on!" he screamed, then dashed for his fishing pole. As the man paddled uselessly but frantically toward the island, he drifted even further away. The current was much too strong. Still, the man clamored for shore, screaming and gurgling and flailing his arms.

Edgar pocketed the flashlight and took the pole in his hands, then marched to shore and spread his legs, bracing himself against the hurricane. Then, digging his feet into the wet, rocky sand, he skillfully cast the spoon spinner out into the blackness.

Reeling violently, he yanked the spinner across the seas until its treble hooks snagged true.

"ARRGHH!" howled the man. The hooks were

digging into his skin, but he was surely caught.

"*I know!*" yelled Edgar.

Mumbling a prayer that the eighty-pound test would hold, he slowly and carefully reeled the man in, giving only the occasional slack as the current demanded.

"AHAGA!!" the man gurgled. "ARGGGGHH!"

"Calm down!" shouted Edgar, knowing that if the man kept flailing the line would certainly not hold. If that happened, the drowning man would surely be lost.

The string was tightened to its limits, and it was just about to snap.

"JUST GO LIMP, MAN!" yelled Edgar. It was pointless to yell. He continued to reel gingerly.

Then, suddenly, the line went limp—but not in a good way. Horrified, Edgar dropped the pole and whipped out the flashlight. Shining it on the shore, there, just out of the water, Edgar saw the man, safe and sound. He was weeping bitterly and clinging to the thin beach, collapsing on his stomach, coughing with his face in the sand.

Edgar had done it. He had brought the man to shore.

Braving the gales, Edgar staggered down to the seaside and bent over, giving the muscular man a timid pat on the shoulder.

"Man?" he said. "Are you OK?"

Edgar shined the light on the man's shoulder and discovered the fish hooks. They were dug in deep by now, and looked gnarly.

"Man," Edgar explained over the storm. "We've got to get those out." He pointed to the barbs and nodded. Then, from his pocket he withdrew a small a pair of fishing pliers and waved them before the man's eyes. "See? I've got to pull those out, man. Don't hit me when I do! It's gonna hurt!"

The man glanced at the pliers and the realization of what Edgar was asking seemed to dawn on him. Wearily, he nodded and turned his muscular back to Edgar, presenting his shoulder.

"ARRGH!" he shouted as Edgar began to twist the hooks around.

"Just be still!" shouted Edgar as the man jerked slightly away. Stabilizing himself, the man nodded and invited Edgar to continue, so he pulled at the shiny hooks some more as the man moaned in pain. Digging into the man's flesh, he could almost feel the pain himself. He had never had to de-hook a human being before.

The man had velvety-dark skin and a huge, wooly beard. His hair was disheveled and poked out from beneath a sea-washed, camo-green military cap. His eyes were bloodshot and lips deeply cracked from the onslaught of the ocean, like chasms in his flesh. The man's muscles pulsated with absolute tension as Edgar worked, his soldier's uniform holding on loosely to his famished frame by mere threads, seeming to suggest he'd probably been suffering from many days lost at sea.

Finally, *thankfully*, the last of the treble hooks came free from his skin. He slumped on the shore and heaved in the storm, grunting aloud, then nodded his appreciation at Edgar.

"*Mahadsanid,*" the man said breathlessly.

"Yeah, gotcha," said Edgar. "But look. We've gotta get out of here, man. If we hang out any longer, we're gonna get blown out to sea! The water's never been this high!" He pulled on the man's shoulder and urged him up toward the center of the island. "C'mon man!" he yelled. "We've gotta go!"

The man nodded and rose to his wobbly legs, then limped with Edgar to the edge of the hole.

"Look," said Edgar, explaining their situation. "I know you don't understand this, but we've got to jump down this hole. Right now. It's the only way out."

The man's eyes followed Edgar's finger and he looked down into the hole, where Edgar was shining the light.

"Yes!" yelled Edgar. "That's right! Down there! We must go!" He took a demonstrative step toward the edge and pulled gently on the man's arm to urge him to jump.

"Hey!" he said, feeling something unnatural. "What's that?"

Edgar's hand had touched something metallic dangling beneath the man's shirt.

"Is that a . . . a machine gun?"

Edgar shined the light on the object and, just above the bottom of the green camo shirt, there hung a black, menacing-looking UZI, connected to a strap around the man's shoulder.

"No," shouted Edgar, "absolutely not! You can't bring a gun to Mount Lanier."

He pointed to the gun and mimicked shooting a machine gun in his hands.

"*Qoriga!*" the man shouted.

"No!" argued Edgar. "*No qoriga!*"

The muscles in the man's face tightened as he glared at Edgar, but Edgar stared back just as fiercely, pursing his lips at the man. For a long moment they glared at one another before the man was pushed slightly backward from a tremendous gale.

The storm was getting worse. Suddenly it seemed to change the man's mind.

With a slight nod, he reluctantly unslung the machine gun from around his shoulder and dropped it to the wet, crusty ground.

It plopped unceremoniously to the island like a brick.

"Thank you!" shouted Edgar, relief cascading through him. "Now. Let's go to Washington!"

Edgar pushed the gun slightly away with his foot for good measure, then shined the hole again before giving the man a slight push toward it. The man gazed into it and suddenly, when it occurred to him what Edgar was truly asking, a look of horror came upon his face. He looked up at Edgar and shook his head violently.

"*Maya!*" he screamed, shaking his head.

"Yes!" shouted Edgar. "You've *got* to! If you don't jump, the storm is gonna kill you! You don't have a choice!"

Adamantly the man continued to shake his head.

"It's the only way out, man!" shouted Edgar, pointing into the hole. He made an "A" with his arms that demonstrated a fake dive into the blackness, but suddenly, the man was stepping backward—away from the hole. He continued to shake his head, arguing with Edgar in the foreign language. "*Maya! Maya!*" he shouted.

Knowing the situation was quickly deteriorating, Edgar darted toward the man and snatched him by the hand, yanking him backward with everything he had in him. Lucky for Edgar, the man was slow to react, weary as he was. But as Edgar dragged him backward toward the hole, he dug his feet into the ground and bucked wildly.

Even still, Edgar did not let go. He clamped down on the man's stony hand and yanked and pulled and heaved with everything he had, and after a few moments, he could feel the weight of the weary man budge. As he strained and pulled, caught in this strange tug of war, that's when the man hit him in the back of his head, his boulder-like fist rocking Edgar like a car crash, and for a moment, Edgar could only see stars.

"What the hell are you *doing*?" screamed Edgar. "Stop that, dude! I'm trying to save your danged life!"

Wrestling the man to the hole's edge, Edgar discovered that with each hard-fought step, the man was finding strength. He'd stiffened and planted his feet in the wet sand like an oak, screaming wildly in Edgar's ear, lifting his strong back in order to obtain balance and not be dragged down into the hole.

But Edgar, like a ball of super glue, refused to let go of him.

That's when the man heaved and screamed and, nearing the hole's edge, lifted Edgar out over the surface to toss him in.

"Yeah!" shouted Edgar, "just like that!"

Once the realization that Edgar was not afraid to be thrown into the hole struck the man, a look of abject horror came across his face. Edgar knew he was probably thinking, *what kind of crazy kid am I dealing with?*

"Just let yourself fall!" shouted Edgar. "You can't stay here, man! If you do, you'll be blown back to the sea! You'll drown or starve, man!"

The man continued slapping at the dangling Edgar with his free hand, kneeing him in the ribs as well. Edgar yelped as the blows crashed against him, but still, he did not let go.

Finally, when there seemed to be nothing remaining in the man's tank, with one massive, wounded howl, he glared into Edgar's face and roared like a lion.

"YOU ARE COMING WITH ME!" shouted Edgar, kicking his feet wildly over the hole to topple the man. Just then, a furious wave came sweeping across the sea and the man was plummeted over the edge. Instantly Edgar felt himself dropping with the man into the Earth, and thought to himself, *finally. Thank God.*

"AAAAAAHHHHH!" screamed the man. *Loudly.*

The screams did not subside for several minutes. Together they fell in the darkness until the man went hoarse. Then, falling in the sweet silence Edgar floated nearby and rubbed his aching ribs. The man had done some damage, kneeing him several times, *hard.*

When Edgar rubbed the pain away, he floated to the man. "Sir?" he said, shining the flashlight on him.

The man was unconscious. Edgar hoped he wasn't dead. He reached out and took the man's limp hand, then felt for his pulse.

"You're still alive," said Edgar, relieved. Then, for good measure, he reached into the man's pockets and felt for any more weapons.

He just couldn't bring an armed man up to Mount Lanier.

"You can't go to Mount Lanier with weapons on you," he explained to the sleeping man, patting him down further. The search rendered nothing but a silver coin and a crumpled-up picture, all blurry from the salty sea.

"Hey!" shouted Edgar, slapping the man's face. "Man! Can you hear me? You've got to wake up, sir!"

But it was useless. He was out like a light.

"Please!" begged Edgar, quickly becoming frantic, considering the consequences of what might loom ahead. He began to slap the man even harder. "You've got to wake up, man! I can't lift you out of the hole alone!"

But the man continued to sleep all the way through the Earth, that was, until about five minutes out from the cabin. Using a last ditch effort to wake the man, Edgar grabbed a fistful of his camo shirt and slapped him across the face as hard as he could.

The man erupted into consciousness. He gaped at Edgar with wide, wild eyes, both full of fear and bloodshot in the glow of Edgar's bright flashlight.

"Hey!" said Edgar, the man beginning to look around in horror at the speeding walls. He thrust his hands outward for balance, but Edgar patted him on the shoulder to reassure him.

"I know," he explained. "You're still falling. But it will be OK, see?" He floated a bit from the man and shrugged to demonstrated how calm and unafraid he was. He could see the muscles on the man's body began to soften as he studied Edgar—as he seemed to understand that maybe they weren't going to hit the ground.

Was the man beginning to trust him?

The man stared at Edgar deeply. Then, he seemed to give a slight nod.

"*Mahadsanid*," said the man.

Edgar pointed the flashlight up the hole to demonstrate with his right hand a clawing gesture.

"You'll have to grab to the side wall when it comes, alright?" he said. Edgar took the man's arm and drifted them both to the side wall, then placed the man's hands flat against the speeding, glassy bricks. "See?" he yelled. "You just grab the side wall when you get to the top. Got it?"

The man stared at Edgar, the puzzled look returning.

But when the cabin came, Edgar continued to hold the man's wrists to the wall until suddenly, they landed on the edge of the hole. Instinctively, the man grabbed the bricks and held tight.

"Yes!" cried Edgar, snatching the ledge as well. Together they dangled at the cabin floor, grunting.

"Good!" said Edgar. "You're gonna make it!"

It was a calm afternoon outside the cabin, and an incredibly wild transformation from the rocky, stormy trip that had preceded it. Edgar climbed out and stood before the man.

"You've got to help me pull you out now," he explained. Edgar took one of his hands and together they heaved until the man climbed entirely out of the hole, then, slumping wearily beside it, safe on solid ground, he wept terribly into his hands.

There were cuts on his face and heavy burns on his skin and a tongue so heavily swelled from thirst Edgar thought it might burst. Instantly Edgar stepped to the ice cooler to snatch a bottle of water, and the man looked up and saw what Edgar was offering and snatched it from his hands. Frantically, he uncapped it and greedily slurped the whole bottle down, finishing it in one continuous pull. As he did, Edgar walked to the cooler and got another, then two more.

"Wow," said Edgar. Six empty bottles lay scattered at his feet. "You're in *bad* shape." The man, finishing his seventh bottle of water, crushed it and smiled, then nearly tossed it into the hole.

"No, man!" shouted Edgar, throwing up both hands to stop him. "You can't throw it down there!"

This startled the man, who had begun to finally appear comfortable with his surroundings. Wounded, the man slowly pulled the bottle back toward his chest and stared up at Edgar, with a dose of hurt in his eyes.

"I'm sorry," explained Edgar, "but if you throw that bottle down, it'll eventually end up hanging in midair in the center of the Earth. So, the next time I jump down, I might hit it going a million miles an hour, which could hurt me pretty good. I go so fast, you know. If I hit a bottle at a speed like that, who knows what it could do."

Edgar peeled the bottle from the man's hands and walked it over to a wastebasket. Then, he visited a small pantry by the freezer and withdrew a bag of potato chips, tossing it to the man, who ripped it open in one frantic yank and stuffed mounds of the chips into his mouth, crunching with audible moans.

"Hungry?" marveled Edgar.

The man ate and ate, staring around the room, then back at Edgar.

"*Mahadsanid,*" crunched the man, nodding at Edgar.

"Mahad . . . na . . . sand? Oh, wait, I see what you're trying to say. You're *welcome.*"

Eventually the man's gaze returned to the ominous hole in the floor beside him. He looked over the edge and stared down intently, chewing thoughtfully, tracing his fingers over the designs in the bricks.

"Yeah," agreed Edgar. "It's quite incredible."

Edgar rose and returned to his stash at the pantry, returning to the man and dumping everything he had onto the floor: Twinkies, beef jerky, pizza flavored Combos, Doritos, and even a half-eaten burrito from Taco Bell.

The man ripped into the food and stuffed every morsel into his mouth. With each swallow and each audible smack, he groaned with intense pleasure. Finally, once the snacks were gone and the packages licked clean of crumbs, the man wiped his hands on his holy green shirt and burped loudly, chuckling.

"I hope that fills you up," said Edgar. "Because all I have left is frozen lobster."

Edgar studied the man and tried to come up with a plan, but there was nothing more he could do. If he took the man to town, the people there would ask questions like "where did he come from?" Then they would surely trace his steps back to the hole, and that would be *it*. No more fishing, no more falling, and no more island. Just plain old Mount Lanier with his unremarkable, bland old life.

The man was so strong, considered Edgar, and seemed resourceful. He was a soldier! He'd do fine. At least he wasn't still lost at sea.

He watched the man pick the last crumbs off his shirt and put them into his mouth.

"You're a good guy, aren't you?" he asked, fretting about turning an unknown man loose on the unsuspecting nearby towns.

The newly-full and happy man nodded at Edgar as if he understood.

"You can't hurt people, OK? You're not a soldier here."

The man stared intently back.

Standing, Edgar walked to the man and reached out his hand, helping him stand. Then, he led him outside the cabin and across the brook, and together they stood looking down the trail.

Edgar pointed through the trees toward the town of Ellensburg—the opposite direction of Mount Lanier.

"*Indian Ocean*," said Edgar, tapping a finger into the man's chest. "You tell them you came from the *Indian Ocean*, OK? They'll help you get back home." He tapped the man on the chest and looked him in the face so that he would understand. "You tell them you're from the *Indian Ocean*."

"Imdiam Otshean," repeated the man.

"Yeah! That's right."

Edgar then yanked out his wallet and paused for a moment, looking up into the man's bloodshot eyes, then gave him everything he had. It was about eight hundred dollars.

Of all the places in the world, his mother had never thought to check his wallet.

"*Mahadsanid*," said the man, nodding. Apparently he understood American money. He took it from Edgar and nodded respectfully.

"Cool, yes, Mahatma Sand," said Edgar.

Edgar then extended a hand to him. The man looked down at it.

"It's to *shake*," said Edgar. "You do it in America when you want to say goodbye to someone. You *shake*."

Instead, the man dug into his pockets. He retrieved the old coin that Edgar had found earlier, and placed it into Edgar's hand. Edgar looked down at it: a silver disk, reading: REPUBLIC OF SOMALIA, 10 SHILLINGS.

The man also presented Edgar with the sea-washed photograph, and Edgar studied this, too, in the sunlight.

The photo seemed to reveal a much younger version of the man—a more rested and a better fed one, who wrestled with a young boy in a grove, presumably his son. A beautiful woman looked on and laughed. Probably the man's wife, deduced Edgar. They all seemed to be very happy.

It made Edgar instantly miss his father.

"Cool, man," said Edgar, pocketing the picture. "Thank you very much."

Then the man turned and staggered away, eastward toward the town where Edgar was pointing, down the trail a piece. Then he turned to wave, his face awash in contemplation, as if processing the strange events that had just occurred over the past hour or so: one moment lost at sea, the next fighting a young boy who wouldn't let go, who dragged him down through the center of the earth and clear to the other side.

Saving him from the tempestuous sea.

Edgar gave the man a short salute, and the man, with a grave look of thankfulness on his face, nodded at Edgar, then turned into the thick brush and disappeared.

With the man on his way, Edgar glanced down at his watch. Oh no! He was late! His mother would be home soon!

He shot up the trail like a rocket. If he wasn't there when she got home, he was *dead*.

EIGHTEEN

EDGAR RODE FRANTICALLY, praying his mother had not beaten him home, and was relieved to find the Jeep still missing from the driveway when he finally got there.

Thank you god, he thought. She was still in Yakima.

Stashing the bike in the shed, he dashed into the house for dry clothes. Then, for good measure, he ran to the kitchen to splay across the table all his homework, just to give the impression he'd been studying all afternoon. All was well.

IT WAS four hours later, at ten o'clock that evening, when his worry turned to outright dread.

He had not heard from either of them. Not even so much as a text.

It was certainly not like them, especially his mom. He'd called her multiple times but all he got was voicemail. Same with his father. Pacing the house, fretting, he knew she would never be this late without calling to let him know.

Another message was left on her voicemail. "Mom? Where are you? Call me back!" His heart sank deeper by the minute. As it neared eleven o'clock, his dread gave way to panic.

Something was terribly, terribly wrong.

Taking the remote in his clammy hands, he flipped the living room TV to the local news, and immediately the screen was awash in wildfire, the newscasters from Yakima speaking with electric intensity, indicating behind them a wall of raging fire so prolific it seemed like a flaming waterfall. Firemen and service people scurried to and fro in a swarm, the broadcasters displaying footage of houses in flames and countless fortunes going up with them, and pet owners weeping for abandoned pets.

It was terrible.

But worse than anything, they reported that the winds had pushed the fire northerly now. Which meant it was pointed *directly* at Mount Lanier. Apparently, wildfires could turn on a dime, just like hurricanes.

Great, he thought. *Wonderful*. Was Edgar cursed? He wondered what other catastrophes could possibly chase him down.

He stepped forward and traced a finger across the screen, scanning the onlookers in search of his mother's face, but he did not see her.

A frozen pizza burned to ashes in the next room. Breathlessly, he pulled out his cell phone and hit redial. Still no answer—only her voicemail for the millionth time. He glanced nervously at the clock. It was nearing midnight now. She was five hours late. His nervous heart thudded in his throat.

Suddenly, his cell phone buzzed. Snatching it to his

ear, he nearly shouted, "Mom?"

He waited breathlessly for an answer, but there was none—not at first. It was only her tragic, muted whimpers. It made him so weak with fear, he was dizzy.

"Mom!" he asked, grasping for breath. "What's wrong? Are you OK? Is Dad OK?" He was feeling déjà vu again, like the day she called about the Deepwater Horizon. Trembling with fear, he slumped to a stool at the kitchen counter and prodded her again.

"Mom, please. Talk to me." He ran a hand through his hair and swallowed hard, placing his elbows on the cold granite counter. "What happened?"

"Your dad," she whimpered softly. "Your dad is gone. He's missing."

"What," said Edgar, "do you *mean*, 'missing?'" He gulped. "What do you mean?'"

"Your father is out on a hillside, and he's trapped," she said, breaking like a levee into waves of bitter weeping.

"Mom," he said, straining to understand. "Tell me what happened."

"He got trapped on all sides by the fire. No way to communicate with him now. Cell phones are down. They didn't have their walkie-talkies with them. He's helpless right now. Until they can get in and save him."

Then she broke into even louder sobs, and as Edgar took in the news along with her abject desperation, sitting numbly at the counter, he looked up with searching eyes. They landed directly on his father's yellow raincoat hanging neatly on the back door, like a floppy, rubber ghost.

"They are doing all they can," she continued, trying to get it together. "He has seven team members with him. They are all trapped together, when they fell behind the fire wall trying to save a little boy."

"Well," asked Edgar, "did they save him?"

"Nobody knows," she said, bursting into fresh waves of tearful agony. Edgar put his forehead down on the hard counter and closed his eyes.

"The fire, the smoke, the winds are so out of control," she whimpered, "they tell me they can't get a helicopter in there to save any of them—not right now. It will only be until things clear up. *If* they clear up."

"A hill?" probed Edgar. "How big is this hill?"

"It's huge," she said. "Looks like a mountain to me. You can see it from the road, even. You know the people out here—what they call 'hills' are obnoxiously huge. That's where they've set up the blockade, in front of the hill. I've been watching the hill all night, looking for him. It's covered in tall trees and that's one of the reasons it's hard to get a helicopter in there."

Overcome with fear and dread, Edgar let the receiver droop from his ear, and hot tears flowed down his cheeks as he peered up again at that big, stupid, yellow raincoat that hadn't seen the first drop of rain here in the idiotic, stupid, useless state of Washington.

For a moment, he tried to picture his father's face staring back from underneath the hood, but to his sadness, he couldn't quite conjure the image.

The night his father had left, he had been away at the island. Selfishly, without regard to their feelings, he had done what he wanted to do. That's all he could think of now: how the last thing his father might ever know of him was how he was a liar, and a sneak, and a selfish, childish ass.

"They've got a perimeter of firemen and policemen down at the fire line," she was saying, "and I've been yelling at them all night to get in there and . . . well, to go *do* something! But they just won't, and though I understand, I will still push, you know? Apparently it's too dangerous at the moment, but they arrived with fresh firetrucks about an hour ago and currently are trying to bust through the fire line to get your dad. The flames are awful and everything is out of control—they're four stories high in some places! It's like staring into the city of hell." Her voice softened. "I'm giving them a lot of grief. I know that. I'm just so scared. They're actually very nice men who are trying to do their jobs. I've driven up the road to get a hotel room in Meridian, just so I could have a basecamp and drop off our stuff, and also to get phone reception to call you since all the towers have burned in Yakima. So in a minute I'll be heading back to the fire line. I just wanted to call and say, I'm safe, and that I'm not coming home without your father."

The two of them shared a moment of grim silence.

"Edgar," she said, "your dad is the most resourceful man I've ever known. I love that about him. He'll be using the wildfire to roast a wild pig before it's over with, you know he will."

Edgar nodded, and then, freely and without restriction, he broke down into silent waves of weeping: hard, unrestrained, draining, maintaining just enough control to keep it quiet, so as to not let her know his deep sadness. Yet, she must have known, because immediately, she called him to order.

"Now, Edgar," she said, drying up with a resilient sniffle, "it's time we must be strong. Both of us I mean. I want you to get to school tomorrow and come back home, then do your homework, and if I'm not home early enough, I want you to eat something and get to bed. I called Mrs. Snead to see if she will come check in on you, but I had to leave a message. So you can expect a visit from her."

"Yes, Mom," said Edgar, drying up himself.

"I have to go now," she informed him. "I'm trying to get back to the fire, so I'm counting on you to be strong.

Do you think you can manage that?"

"For sure," he confirmed, and for a moment, the line went silent again. He wondered if maybe the wildfire had disconnected them.

"I'll be back when I'm back," she said, finally eliminating the silence.

"I'll be here, Mom," he said.

"I love you, Eddie."

"I love you, too."

RESTLESS, UNABLE to fall sleep, he tried his dad again. By now it was three in the morning. And just like all the other calls, this one went to voicemail, too.

"*You've reached Henry Dewitt,*" the cheery voice said. "*Please leave a message!*"

"Dad," said Edgar, trying to muster his most conversational voice. "I just wanted to call and say, I'm real worried. I really hope you are OK out there." He paused for a moment, composing himself, since it was all he could do not to cry. "The reason I've been calling you is, I was thinking tonight how there is something I've really been wanting to show you for a long time now—a secret place I found in the woods that has a . . . remember that hole down to China you always used to tell me about when I was a kid? Well, I guess you could say, I found that hole, except it actually leads to a small island that has the best fishing *ever*. The fish are *huge*, Dad, not a single one under twenty pounds or so. It's like deep sea fishing on dry land—you wouldn't believe it! They hit the line hard like mahi-mahi. You reel 'em in as fast as you can cast. It's the best fishing I've ever seen."

Thinking about his lost dad, somewhere out in the blaze, his voice was beginning to crack, his chin was beginning to tremble. But somehow he mustered the strength to add one more thing. "I was there in the middle of the night when you came to my room. I was fishing on the island. I'd been there for many nights before out fishing all night. Now that you are missing, I really wish I had done things differently. I would have taken you there and shown you the hole, no matter if y'all told me I could never go back . . . I wish I had . . ." He paused suddenly, then added, "I just want you to know, I love you very much. I know I must have scared you pretty bad. I've been lying a lot lately—I know—but when you get back home, if you ask me, I will tell you the truth every time from here on out. Just, please, whatever happens, get back home. *Please*, Dad."

And again, he added softly, "Please come home."

EDGAR DIDN'T sleep a bit after that. Instead, he sat on the couch flipping through the news channels, hanging on every word, scanning each bit of greenery behind every newscaster in hopes that any minute now, bold as day, his father might come leaping from the dry foliage like Tarzan, king of the apes.

The story of the "Missing Seven" was now the leading story—a national story with constant coverage on CNN, MSNBC, FOX, and every other channel there was.

At two in the morning, they finally showed his father's picture. It was one from the oil rig days back in Bon Secour. He had a slight, scruffy beard on his neck and a dark brown tan, brightened by a wide, happy smile.

As the local news shifted to reports on wind direction and trajectory of the blaze, there was suddenly a tiny knock at the door.

Frightened, he looked down at his watch. It was three thirty in the morning.

"Who is it?" he said softly, but no one answered.

Who could be knocking at this time of night? He crept to the door to look out the peephole, and there, staring back, was Shay Sinclair.

"Hey!" he said, fumbling against the latch. When he finally got it open, he stared at her and she back at him with a deep look of sympathy. Then, like a weary traveler, she fell into his arms.

"I've been watching all night," she whispered into his ear. "I just couldn't sleep. I feel so terrible for you and your mom!"

Quivering, feeling so in need of this moment, he surrendered his head to her shoulder and it felt wonderful. He squeezed her tight, breathing in the wonderful scent of her hair, and in that moment, he realized how utterly terrible this had been to endure, all alone, watching his family being taken from him by the wildfire over the course of a single night. He parted from her and escorted her in, locking the door behind them. Together, they made for the TV and watched silently as the news continued, scanning the screen for any signs of his parents.

"You know," mumbled Edgar, confessing to her, "they caught me sneaking out the other night, and while I was gone, she found all my money in the wall. I haven't even seen my dad since. It was awful. He came to tell me goodbye, to go fight the fire, and I wasn't here."

With a grave look of sympathy, she moved closer to him on the couch and he could feel the immediate heat of her body. She put a hand on his hand. She looked up and looked him in the eyes.

"He will forgive you," she said, a deep earnestness in her eyes. "Edgar, he knows you love him."

Edgar shook his head. "I just wanted the chance to tell him the truth, that's all. I just want one more chance, just to level with him."

"Well, you'll get it," she reassured him.

Then, suddenly, with her so close, he leaned in to her and kissed her glossy, red lips. As she reciprocated, she ran her soft hands through his hair.

"I'm just saying!" came a blaring voice from the TV, as jarring as any voice that has ever been uttered. "Are you saying you 'can't' or you 'won't' get in there and rescue him?!"

That's when Edgar shot up from the couch. He gazed at the TV and suddenly his own freshly-sparkled, glossy mouth fell open.

"Oh my God," he muttered. "It's Mom."

And sure enough, it was. She was giving the firemen and cops all sorts of hell on the fire line, just like she said she would.

"Please!" she urged them, their big, rugged arms folded at their chests. They were not budging a bit, Edgar could tell, but it was also obvious they had sympathy for her.

They were just doing their job.

"We're sorry, ma'am," one assured her. "The fire has to die down first and then we can get in there and get him."

"No it doesn't!" she argued, "you *can* go get him now! This is not a matter of 'can!' It's a matter of 'will!'"

The man folded his arms again and looked away.

Edgar knew *just* how he felt.

"They'll find him," said Shay, sitting up, corralling her freshly tussled hair behind an ear. She leaned in closer and said it again, patting his thigh. "They *will.*"

"Yeah," he said dryly, hoping that she was right.

"I have to go now," she whispered. "My father will be up soon." She rose from the couch and he stood to meet her. Facing one another, she leaned in and kissed him tenderly on the cheek.

"See you at school," she said, walking out the back door.

Immediately Edgar returned to the TV, continuing to

scan all of the greenery behind the newscasters, knowing that at any second, his father would come bursting right out of there.

He was *certain* of it.

THE NEXT morning, on his way to school, Edgar bypassed Flounder's fish stand and strayed away from Shay's street corner, hoping to walk alone. Big tears dangled from the bottoms of his eyelids, as fearful as he was. Things were worse today than the night before. With each passing minute, with no word from his mother or father, the terrible dread kept building. Each moment that slipped away meant things must be worse and worse on that fiery hill.

Finally, when the tears did drop, he lifted his eyes to the sky and scanned the hazy heavens for any sign of a cloud—but there was none. He was suddenly, profoundly aware just how much he much he had become a True Citizen of this crappy town of Mount Lanier: someone who walked around hopelessly all day, looking up in the sky for rain.

Like the shopkeeper they met on their first day in Mount Lanier said: everyone here was miserable from the drought.

"Rain better come soon, or they'll extend wildfire season . . ." he'd said.

For some strange reason, disasters seemed to follow him around.

Either it rains soon or the fire will most likely have to burn itself out. That's what the newscasters had said the night before.

"Burn itself out." And this with his father still trapped on the hill. What an absolutely unimaginable proposition.

They needed *rain.* Badly.

Still, like always, there was no rain projected in the forecast.

When he finally approached the school, he soon discovered that everyone knew about his dad. Some kids whispered to each other as he walked up, and *everyone* stared. Edgar tried to ignore them as he walked by, but as they parted for him, it was difficult.

Numbly, he moved to a corner of the commons and slumped in a corner waiting for the bell to ring. When he finally looked up, Shay and Flounder both stood over him, bending with hands on their knees, sympathy painted on their faces. Shay bent lower and hugged him. Flounder just leaned and awkwardly grabbed his shoulder, squeezing it gently. None of them said a word for a while.

"It will be alright," muttered Flounder, finally, looking around. "You said he's an Eagle scout, right, your dad? Well, he's probably roasting a pig by now. Like *Lord of the Flies.*"

"Huh," chuckled Edgar, trying to make a smile. "My mom said the same thing."

Over Shay's shoulder, he could see Weedy across the courtyard. Weedy stared back, a bored look upon his face.

Suddenly, fighting a rage, Edgar had a good mind to go slap it *off* his face.

"Hello, Ed," said Dr. Van Rossum, who materialized over Shay and Flounder's shoulders. Looming over them, he smiled as Shay and Flounder stepped aside to let him through. "How you holding up?" he asked.

"I'm good, Doc," said Edgar, nodding.

Van Rossum bent and squeezed Edgar's wrist. "Listen, son. I live on Cherry Blossom Lane. My house is last on the left. If your mom doesn't get back tonight, you come stay with me and my wife Loretta until things get back to normal. We would love to have you. My castle is your castle."

At that, with an encouraging smile, he rose and towered over them, the sun silhouetting his bald head like a halo.

"Thanks," said Edgar, and before Van Rossum could turn to walk away, he seemed pressed to reach down and pat Edgar's wrist again.

AT LUNCHTIME, school got canceled. Indefinitely. The fire had grown, and it was gaining speed. Worst of all, now it was headed their way—straight for Mount Lanier.

By two o'clock that afternoon, a full-scale, mandatory evacuation was issued for the town and its surrounding areas. With its unfavorable winds, the fire line was projected to arrive as early as forty-eight hours.

It was terrible news.

As he walked home from school—dazed by how quickly the world could fall apart—he meandered through town watching people flutter all about: the put-upon adults packing their most precious belongings; the high schoolers scrambling to say goodbye to one another before the imminent evacuation; and the younger kids scurrying excitedly to their homes, as if everything was one big party. He wasn't mad; he totally knew how they felt. This was just how he used to feel when hurricanes spun over the gulf and headed for town. It always felt like a vacation, like one big *party*. School was out, and unexpectedly! It was a break in the routine. Edgar remembered the days he would even pray that a hurricane might hit Bon Secour, so he could get out of school for a day or two, maybe surf on the beaches in the oncoming waves. But that changed after the *big one*. *Katrina*. After that, he didn't pray for hurricanes again.

The people of Mount Lanier emerged from their homes in masses, readied their cars and trucks, packed their lawn furniture, and caged their pets. All the while a newly arrived and ominous dark cloud pulsated in the sky, just south of the city, and everyone looked skyward.

So utterly bleak and lost inside—so totally unable to care—he watched it all unfold as he walked through the town square, unable to muster any more emotion, because he'd spent it all. He'd known so much disaster in his short life, watching cities and towns stripped to their very cores, ravaged by nature, ravaged by man—and as the people there stood to lose all they had—as the people *here* stood to lose all *they* had—*at least* they had each other—which was more than he could say for himself as he and his parents faced tragedy.

For him, it seemed, disaster was never-ending.

Hurricanes, oil spills, puberty, bullies. Was there even a safe place to be on the whole Earth? That was, besides the warm and wonderful hole that cocooned him as he fell?

If so, he had never been there.

When he found himself on the far side of town, absently turning down a road toward the woods, off in the distance, looming like salvation, were the reddish pointy hills he knew so well—home of the only place he knew that could make all this misery disappear, at least for an hour or two.

As if compelled, he walked toward the Indian Hills, almost absently, almost *automatically*, like a sleepwalking kid. Somewhere deep in him, he longed for the hole in the ground that was always there for him—that always offered some sort of hope and excitement. It had always, in a town of never ending dead ends, offered him an easy way out.

This was his safe haven. His happy place.

"To the sea," he said, marching forward, falling down.

NINETEEN

As HE FELL he thought about the town, scrolling through the dreary scenarios that flashed through his mind: the Arteses' fish stand, how it was all packed up and headed out of town in the morning, along with his good friend. They were towing it to California the next day and staying with relatives there until the wildfire subsided.

As for Shay, she was headed for Alaska with her family. They had a vacation home there by the sea.

As for him, his thoughts ranged from his father to his mother, to the cabin, the empire he built: the cutting table, the generator, the freezer full of Ambercod—this hidden hole had bestowed everything on him. But before the week would be up, it would burn, and with it, the planks of the cabin would turn to ash, revealing the hole for the entire world to see.

He closed his eyes and unclenched his hands, darting down, knowing this was surely his last trip through the

Earth. He spread his fingers and felt the hot rush of air on his face, pointing his body downward like an arrow.

Like *Superman*.

When he emerged from the hole on the other side, he stepped into the cool ocean air into a beautiful, serene night, and the first thing he noticed was the black man's machine gun still glimmering in the moonlight, just beside his foot. He gave it a nudge with his shoe, lifting it a tad from its burial in the coarse, crusty sand, studying it solemnly in the moonlight.

Why not?

He bent over and lifted it up, then pointed it at the sea. He'd never shot a machine gun before, let alone even held one. It was heavy, and it was sinister. Aiming it at the horizon, he closed his eyes and pulled the trigger, expecting all chaos to break loose.

Click

But nothing happened.

It didn't even work!

Must have been damaged by the sea, he thought, but then he checked by the trigger and noticed the safety was still on.

"Ah well," he muttered with a sigh. "Probably just the same." In a depressed haze, he dropped the gun to his feet and stepped over it, continuing his push down to the mesmerizing seashore.

Plopping down to the damp beach, he gazed into the darkness of afar and felt the continuous wind on his face. He kicked off his shoes and then lay back, staring absently at the beautiful, starry sky.

Was his father still alive? He hoped so. Where would he be hiding? What sort of quick thinking was he doing to keep everybody alive?

Tears formed. He tried to fight them off but there were too many to withstand. Waves of sadness rocked his body as a carousel of images paraded through his mind: his mother's, his father's, Shay's, Flounder's—all the people he loved and cared for, he tried not to weep for them all. He tried, but he failed.

As the tears streamed down his face, and as he closed his eyes, listening to the symphony of the rippling waves, he soon fell into a deep, sound sleep.

In moments, he was dreaming.

In the dream, his father drove a boat. It was a beautiful day at sea, and the two were anchored off some giant oil rig somewhere near the shores of South Louisiana, where they had fished before. His father was reeling in big fish after big fish, as Edgar cheered him on.

But then, suddenly, for some strange reason, Edgar noticed his father stop reeling. He looked over at him, and he appeared to be, in all of an instant, somewhat somber and downtrodden now, his eyes appearing glassy and dark, almost alien-like—almost possessed.

"Dad?" asked Edgar. "Are you OK?"

His dad suddenly didn't look anything like himself at *all*.

Suddenly the small boat was adrift in the heavy breeze as his father took his hands off the wheel. With each moment, it moved further away from the coral-covered legs of the rig.

Edgar's foot, dangling over the side of the boat, felt the warm water below. That's when his father began to stare up at the clear blue sky.

"What's wrong, Dad?" Edgar asked again. "Is everything OK?" His father said nothing, *did* nothing. He did not even look at Edgar.

Edgar put down his pole and stared worriedly at his father.

"Dad, is everything OK?"

"Son," sang his father, in a creepy, monk-like voice,

almost like the monotone drawl of a zombie. "I ask you to consider this sea before you." He nodded at the waters. "This is to be *burned*. I *must* burn it, for the *cleansing*."

"Burn? You must burn what?" said Edgar, terribly frightened, looking out to sea. When he did, to his horror, he realized the boat was drifting on a thick, smelly, sludgy dark sheen.

It was oil. An oil *spill*.

As far as Edgar could see, there was nothing but a corrosive oil, the blackness engulfing them. With it, all manner of dead Ambercod bobbed up everywhere—all of them belly up and rotting.

"Buuuurrrnnnn," chanted his father, lifting a large flare gun from his side, pointing it at the sea.

"No!!" Edgar screamed. "Dad! *Don't*!"

"We must," his father answered. "We must make a lake of fire. For the cleansing!"

"Noooo!" shouted Edgar, but suddenly, it was too late. His dad had pulled the trigger. The flare gun barked upward and a glowing, fiery thud dove into the sea. Instantly the ocean hissed and raged with a grand wall of fire, consuming Edgar's leg that was still dangling from the boat. Fire seared like acid all the way up to his thigh, scalding him, torturing him—and although he screamed no sound emerged. His breath had been taken away by the pain. He reached out and felt for his thigh, patting it down, trying to put out the fire, but the fire only burned his hands. He was only left to whimper in agony and let it burn.

"Dear Lord," prayed his father, oblivious to Edgar's suffering, his head upraised to the churning clouds, his inexplicable glowing red eyes turned skyward in demonic reverence, "Please bless this cleansing."

"Daaaaaad!" screamed Edgar. "You're hurting me!!"

Flopping on the bottom of the boat alongside a heap

of dead Ambercod, all covered in thick, black oil, Edgar squirmed in pain.

"It's just a leg," said the evil rendition of his father. "It is no sacrifice whatsoever in comparison to all the sins you've committed . . ."

That's when Edgar woke up in a fit, but safely back on the island. For a moment, he thought he was OK, gasping at the beach air convulsing with the horror of his dream. But then, reaching down to his absolute and vexing dismay, he realized his leg was still on fire.

And so were his hands!

Was it another dream? A *dream inside a dream*? Kicking his leg, lifting it frantically from shore, he leapt to his feet like a spring, screaming in pain. Each time he reached for his leg his hands were electrified by another blast of cool, strange, electrification. Shaking his leg like a seizure now, he screamed again, turning painful circles in the sand and trying to shake off the fire. Only when he looked down and forced himself to endure the pain did he realize what was hurting him: a large, foreign-looking jellyfish that had wrapped itself around him in the night as he slept, washed in by the high tide. Through blurry eyes, Edgar glanced out across the sea and in the bright moonlight he noticed a million of them congregated by the shore of his island: an army of huge, neon-glowing jellyfish, illuminated by the brilliant white light, all huddled around the island in a spawning session.

Dizzy with pain, groaning in abject agony, backing away from shore, he bent over and defied his throbbing hands, pulling the tentacle away from his leg until finally, *mercifully*, the blob jiggled off and fell to the sand. Edgar stared down at it, wide-eyed in the nocturnal glow staggering backward toward the hole with an injured whimper. His leg was now fiery red, covered in furious, sinister-looking white blisters that speckled across his thigh in a single tentacle's path. It did not look good. It was like a deadly tattoo.

After years on the ocean, Edgar knew that with such stings you had to get to the hospital quick, but being on the Indian Ocean as he was, there wasn't a hospital around. Groaning in pain, mustering up all the strength he had in him, he limped to the hole and toppled over like a wounded soldier, dropping to his death. Before he could even pass the Earth's crust, he slipped into an almost instant delirium from the venom that now coursed through his veins like battery acid.

At the Earth's core, still trying to keep himself above the tide of consciousness, he knew if he missed the other side of the world it would mean another long fall, which would probably mean his death, with a jellyfish sting this severe. Blasting through the earth, he shined the wound with the flashlight and noticed his thigh was swelling, the blisters rising now, bubbling sinisterly. Dying slowly from a jellyfish sting and from thirst floating in the middle of the world: this was no way to go. He must stay awake.

He must.

SURFACING IN the cabin, straining to climb out with his leg almost doubling in size, pulsating right along with his panicked heart, each throb a hammer into his thigh, he stumbled out and moved over to the workstation to retrieve a bottle of Bragg's Apple Cider Vinegar. It was something he used to clean the fishy smell off his hands after cleaning fish.

Back in Alabama, vinegar was readily available on beaches everywhere as the number one administrant for jellyfish stings. So, he looked down at the gnarly welt on his leg and whimpered. It looked something like being attacked by a wolverine. He closed his eyes and poured the entire bottle of vinegar onto the sting, which both cooled and burned him at the same time.

"Dang," he uttered, trembling.

Then, pulling the bike from the corner of the room, he walked it out to the hillside and down to the brook, then up the hill to the trail. On level ground, he lifted his injured leg up and tried to mount the bike. It hurt so bad, like it might just split in two.

With his aching leg draped over the bike, he rested his swelling foot upon the pedal and took a rest.

Then, skidding down the hills, moaning with each bump, he steadied himself and made for Mount Lanier, forcing his bum leg to keep pushing the pedal down, no matter how bad it screamed at him. After all, it was only his life that was at stake.

Occasionally, when his leg would brush the frame of the bike, he quavered with agony, nearly toppling over.

Halfway to town, he finally lost steam. His vision blurring and his systems malfunctioning, his head throbbing wildly and his heart thumping erratically, he toppled over a curbside in the late evening sun, his cargo trailer crashing down on him mercilessly. He was two miles from Sunnyslope Hospital. Just two miles.

He closed his eyes for a moment and almost gave in to the fainting, thinking it might be the end, but who cared?

"Hey, bud?" came a voice from the street. "You OK?"

Edgar, forcing open his eyelids, gazed out. In an idling red sportscar by the curb, there was an older boy watching him—Edgar recognized the guy from school—a senior.

"No, man," muttered Edgar, squinting. "I mean *yeah*, I'll be OK." Just above the sports car, the street sign said: *Whippoorwill Court.*

I live on Cherry Blossom Lane, Van Rossum had told him.

Cherry Blossom Lane was just two streets away.

"Thank you," said Edgar, struggling to his feet and lifting his bike. "I'm OK." The boy watched him with concern as Edgar gritted his teeth and climbed back on, forcing himself to pedal away and tackle the last remaining distance to Van Rossum's house, steering himself through one last neighborhood and street.

In the delirium, everything seemed like a dream now—like a cartoon or a video game—but a *terrible* one, like the one he'd had about his demonlike father. Objects doubled, cars honked and screeched, slamming on brakes.

"Sorry!" called Edgar, waving them around.

Somehow, he looked up and saw the sign: Cherry Blossom Lane. He had made it! There, at the end of the road, Edgar crashed the bike into the lawn of the last house on the left, landing with a massive grunt, toppling into the brittle shrubbery. Standing, *praying* somebody would be home, he limped to the door and pounded it with a fist, leaning on the doorframe for support while trying to maintain consciousness.

Miraculously, Dr. Van Rossum was there, looking down on him like an angel.

"Edgar?" exclaimed the man, yanking open the glass door. "What has happened?" Like jelly Edgar slumped inside the threshold of the house, then collapsed onto the hardwood floor like the dead. Turning, looking up at his teacher, he pointed to his leg.

"Jellyfish," he muttered.

"Loretta!" shouted Van Rossum over his shoulder. "Quick! Call an ambulance!"

Then, Van Rossum bent down to study Edgar's leg.

"Jellyfish . . ." repeated Edgar. "Indian Ocean. *Imdiam Oshtean* . . ." and suddenly, his eyes rolled back into his head and he was gone.

Back in the fishing boat, back near the oil rig in south Louisiana, deep in another dream, the murky black water still surrounded him and stretched all the way to the horizon. It was just as thick, and still full of drifting carcasses. Edgar noticed a few dolphins now and even a sperm whale, all belly up from the sludge; but this time, there was no fire, nor any signs of his demon father, which relieved him. This time, it was only him and the thick black sea, nothing more, as his boat drifted aimlessly among the carrion, with no type of paddle or rudder to move him around.

Feeling a sense of urgency, Edgar looked down and noticed a rather large hole in the bottom of the boat, a big one, actually, that was letting in all the sludge. He leapt to his feet and dove for it, fretting as the corrosive sludge leaked unabatedly in, the liquid rising quickly to his feet and then up to his calves.

He leapt to the side of the boat and began to paddle the vessel frantically with his bare hands, trying to make progress to the nearest oil rig, but quickly, he discovered that it was useless. The boat was too big and his hands were too small.

Out of reach from the barnacled legs of the rig, Edgar's tiny, wounded little vessel began to surrender itself to the rotting, oil-soaked sea.

And with it, he slipped down, too.

Into blackness.

TWENTY

THEY SPOKE IN hushed tones by his bedside when he awoke. His mother, mortified, was one of them. The other was a doctor.

Quickly he decided not to open his eyes to let them know he was awake.

Who knew what kind of trouble he was in?

"So," she asked quietly, but with an urgency to her voice, "you're telling me a *jellyfish* stung my son? Like, a jellyfish from the *sea*?" She chuckled bitterly. "We are hundreds of miles from shore!"

"To be honest, Mrs. Dewitt," explained the doctor, "I've been perplexed all afternoon, myself. Your son's science teacher—the man who saved his life—told me that in Edgar's delirium, he claimed the injury occurred in—well, this sounds totally ridiculous—but, in The Indian Ocean."

"You're right. That *is* ridiculous. My son was delirious,

didn't you say, Doctor?"

"Yes," he admitted. "But then, I saw *this*."

As Edgar tried to lay as still as possible, the doctor pulled back the sheets from his wound and pain shot up and down his leg. He almost cried out, but at the last moment, he was able to bite his tongue.

"Oh my God," whispered his mother. Whatever she saw, it did not look good.

"Yeah," the doctor agreed.

Now they were really freaking him out.

"Ma'am," said the doctor, turning to her, "I'm from the coast. Down there, we surf a lot. So, as a doctor *and* a surfer, I've come across many jellyfish stings, and I have treated them all. That being said, your son's here is a particularly fascinating sting, especially given our location inland, so many hundred miles from shore. This sting is totally consistent with a specimen frequently found in the Indian Ocean, called a 'Box jellyfish' sting. It is extremely poisonous. Actually, Mrs. Dewitt, it's the most venomous sting on the planet."

Together they stood over him, marveling at his gnarly wound.

"See?" he continued, tracing an outline around Edgar's thigh. "This is a perfect sihouette of a Box jelly-fish tentacle, right here." Ugh. With that guy poking and prodding around his wound he was about to come out of his skin. "This area here—it's all swollen and upraised, like a cattle brand, see? Mrs. Dewitt, this is a serious jellyfish sting."

The doctor then lowered the sheets.

"When he arrived," continued the doctor, "I called for vinegar to pour on the wound, which, as you know, being from the South, is how you usually treat jellyfish stings. Well, strangely, your son came in smelling of vinegar already. Dr. Van Rossum told me that in your son's delir-

ious state, he admitted to pouring the vinegar on himself
in a cabin in the woods—near your house. From there, I
removed the remaining barbs from his leg and studied the
size and pattern of the sting. That's how I deduced that
it does, in fact, belong to a 'box' jellyfish or a 'sea wasp.'"
After a pause, he added, "What you must understand,
Mrs. Dewitt, is that this is not possible—not for your son
to have been stung by a box jellyfish today, so far from
sea, so far from a sea that box jellyfish swim around in!
The only thing I can think of is he . . . well, I don't even
know . . . could he have fallen into an aquarium somewhere? Does he have any well-off friends—anyone who
might have access to a saltwater aquarium?"

"I don't think he has many friends," she said with
a dazed, contemplative note in her voice. Returning to
Edgar's bedside, he could feel her looking down and
standing over him.

When he finally stirred, as if rousing from sleep, she
bent slightly and brushed a bit of hair from his forehead,
giving him a slight smile. He squinted up at her and
blinked. She looked exhausted. She had ghoulish black
circles beneath her eyes, as if she hadn't slept in days.

"Doctor," she asked without looking away from Edgar.
"Will my son be OK?"

"I think so," said the doctor, to Edgar's relief. "I
contacted several hospitals in California today and
remarkably, there is one in Santa Cruz that has a single
vial of box jellyfish anti-venom, which is very lucky for
your son. In fact, they're flying it in as we speak, special
order for Edgar. It should be here in an hour or so. After
that? Well, I think Edgar will be just fine, although a
violent scar will remain on his leg for the rest of his life,
I'm afraid."

Edgar watched the doctor over her shoulder, who gave
his mother a reassuring squeeze on her shoulder.

"Thank you, Doctor," she said behind her, nodding. He nodded back and out the door, leaving the two alone.

Edgar returned his gaze to her, studying the circles beneath her eyes.

"You look real tired, Mom," he said. He had never seen her so exhausted or more troubled.

Frowning, she turned and reached for a stool, then scooted it close to his bedside and sat down. Then, placing her elbows on the railing, she rested her chin on her knuckles and studied him, sighing deeply.

"Well, Edgar," she said. "Look at us. Aren't we a mess?"

"Yeah," he smiled. "But we're still here."

Nodding, she said, "So tell me, *honestly*. It's the million-dollar question. How did you get that jellyfish sting on your leg?"

He rolled on his side and faced her, propping his head up with an elbow. He looked deep into her eyes and, at that very moment, decided to come clean once and for all about *everything*.

"Mom," he admitted, "I was on an island in the middle of the Indian Ocean. That's where I got stung." Suddenly, in the catharsis of telling the truth, he felt a sudden release of burden that had weighed on him so relentlessly. Something had loosened in his knotted gut that had been wound up tight, and instead of feeling terrible about revealing his secret, like he was compromising his happy place, or like he was giving up something that made him special and wonderful and unique, he knew he had never felt more free. In all of one moment, a realization washed over him: her love and faith in him meant so much more than a tiny little island in the Southern Hemishpere.

"Hmph," she said dryly, snatching her purse. "It's the same old stuff."

"Huh?" he said. His happiness had suddenly evaporated.

"When are the stories going to stop, Edgar? I don't have time for this."

"Mom, I swear I'm telling the truth."

"Well. You need to rest. We will sort this out when this is all over." She walked to the door and pulled it open. "I need to get back to the fire line," she said. "I need to make sure they're doing all they can do to save your father's life. You'll be OK," she assured him, composing herself. "The hospital will transfer you to Sunnyslope tonight. Until then, your teacher, Dr. Van Rossum, has said he will come stay with you until I get back." Then, with a worried, final nod, she closed the door behind her and was gone.

AT FIVE-THIRTY, a nurse finally arrived to administer the anti-venom. The medicine, which came in a little purple bottle, was drawn out by a needle that she inserted into it and sucked out the fluid. It made for a long, sinister-looking shot, but in this case, as bad as his leg was aching, he would have stuck it in his leg himself.

The fascinated doctor stood just behind her, studying his sting, watching everything. As she prepared the shot, she looked up at Edgar and gave him a warm smile. "You know what this particular medicine is made out of?"

Edgar shook his head no.

"Sheep's blood," she said, giving him a wink.

"Cool," he said, smiling at her. "Baaaa."

She chuckled and after the hideous prick in his skin, he could feel the mysterious liquid coursing through his leg. Icy tingles worked their way around his veins, cooling the wound, and soon it felt much better.

As she was packing her equipment, she asked, "Say. How'd you get stung by a jellyfish, anyway? We're four hundred miles from the beach!"

"Ma'am," said Edgar, looking her in the eye, "I couldn't even make my own mom believe me today. Sometimes I can't believe it myself. So how could I make you believe?"

ALONE IN his room once again, restless and tossing, he finally got up and limped to the sink. Staring into the mirror, he watched water droplets fall from his chin as he washed his face, which made him think of his dad.

Water.

That's all his dad needed, *water.*

As the sink drained, he looked down and caught a whirlpool, dancing just above the drain. It was sucking and gurgling and seemed kind of like a liquid tornado. For a while he watched it dreamily, wondering what makes whirlpools whirl: was it the water? Or maybe the pull of gravity, or the rotation of the Earth?

Or maybe it was something on a molecular level?

Just then, as if on cue, Dr. Van Rossum poked his head through the door, breaking the train of thought. Smiling, Edgar waved him in.

"You're alive," said the man, closing the door behind him. "Good! Because who else could I possibly teach the concepts of gravity to, if you up and croaked?"

Edgar beamed. "Thank God you're here," he said. "It just so happens I have a pressing science question for you."

"How surprising," the teacher quipped.

Edgar limped toward him and offered him the stool. "This one is a physics question, actually. You might need pen and paper."

Dr. Van Rossum took a seat and withdrew his thin eyeglasses, then crossed his legs and assumed a more professor-like position. In his most snobby, professor-like way, he gestured for Edgar to continue.

"Cool!" grinned Edgar, limping to a nearby desk.

"Now," he said, snatching up some pen and paper, placing both on Dr. Van Rossum's lap. "Suppose you had a hole through the Earth . . . you know, like the one that goes all the way down to China."

"Impossible," blurted Dr. Van Rossum, "but, fine. Just so you know, there's not any such thing and there could *never* be," which, to that, Edgar giggled heartily.

"Fair enough," said Edgar. "OK, then, let's say there *was a hole* through the Earth," he posited, taking a seat across from his teacher. "And at the other end of the world, let's say it wasn't China, but rather a big, vast ocean."

"OK," said Van Rossum. "So what do you want to know?"

"I want to know all about *whirlpools*," said Edgar, wiggling his own eyebrows.

"Edgar?" chuckled Dr. Van Rossum. "You are one strange kid."

TWENTY-ONE

Edgar crept barefoot across the cold hospital tile in search of supplies, knowing he would need a lot to reach his destination for this crazy plan to work. A cabinet by the bathroom surrendered a few.

Opening a tube of medicine for his jellyfish sting, he splotched it on liberally, using a tongue depressor to spread it. Then, he wrapped several gauze strips around his leg until it was mummified, and after that, just for good measure, he slipped on a neoprene leg brace that went all the way up to his thigh.

Placing weight on his freshly encased leg, he bent it and lifted it a few times, noticing it felt pretty good. Then he got dressed as quickly as he could, keeping an eye on the night nurse down the hall through a crack in the door. Wincing as he squeezed his swollen foot into a now undersized shoe, he gritted his teeth and pushed it forward until fire shot up his leg. He gulped in pain and eventually relaxed as the shoe reluctantly accepted his foot, then, after the pain settled, he took a deep breath and tied his laces.

Now he was ready.

Limping to the door, he peeked through the slit and took a deep breath.

This was *insane*.

In the quiet of the hospital, Edgar waited behind the door and spied through the crack until she finally slipped away for coffee. Then, when the coast was clear, he limped from the room and skirted his way down the darkened hallways, hobbling through the creepy halls amid foreign, sickly coughs, until finally he was there: standing before the big double doors of the hospital's back exit. He pushed them both outward and dashed into the dry, Washington air.

"Free," he said, standing in the glow of the parking lot lights.

From the hospital he headed west, limping painfully toward Cherry Blossom Lane, knowing it would be a grueling affair: his destination being at least two miles away.

As he wobbled through the side streets, he marveled at how dark and quiet the town was. There was nobody left anymore—only a stray car every ten minutes or so. This felt like a hurricane evacuation, he mused, but even more severe, because in a hurricane, you always had lots of people staying, no matter how strong the storm was— some because of their businesses, or their loved ones, their homes. Many were forced to risk the hurricane.

But in a wildfire, there was no such negotiation. Fire was fire, and there was no rolling the dice with that. And so, it had made Mount Lanier a ghost town. Finally, after two long hours of painful hobbling using the stick from a lawn sign as a cane, he limped wearily on to Dr. Van

Rossum's lawn, eyeing the windows from the curbside, trying to make sure nobody was watching. But when he saw the house was dark, he realized that the doctor had probably evacuated too.

So, slipping around back, he peered around in the darkness. There, leaning against some lawn furniture, was his trusty bike and trailer.

Doctor Van Rossum had kept it outside in case he returned, God bless him.

Edgar lifted it and rolled it around the side of the house, then mounted it on the curb and was off, down the dimly lit street, pedaling for home, using mostly his left leg for the heavy pushing.

Sure, it was very painful, especially when he hit big bumps, but the cast and medicine were providing great cushion.

Maybe if he ever got back to school and turned his grades around he would go into the medical field. He seemed to have a knack for it. After all, he *did* save his own life.

Finally back home, he turned the key and walked into the house. It was dark and quiet inside, and very creepy. With the glaring absence of his mom and dad it didn't seem much like a home anymore. He flipped the lights on and moved directly down the hall, straight to his room. There, he unscrewed the back of his television with a Phillip's head screwdriver, and from inside the box, took a large stack of money that had been hiding there for days—his emergency money. Money his mother never found, thankfully. It was folded and wrapped carefully with a thick rubber band and as he thumbed through it, he nodded. All fifteen hundred dollars were accounted for: everything that remained from his final hauls of Ambercod.

Pushing the money deep into his pockets, he then crossed the hallway to the bathroom and there, yanked open the medicine cabinet. Its contents were studied until he began to snatch items feverishly, especially medicines: Tylenol, Triple Antibiotic Ointment, Hydrocortisone Cream, Rubbing Alcohol, Peroxide, Band Aids, Gauzes, two bottles of Sunscreen, and a half bottle of painkillers. Surveying his throbbing leg, he popped open the bottle of painkillers and downed two for the miles he'd logged. Then, he snatched his favorite toothbrush, along with two tubes of toothpaste, and dumped everything into two large, empty duffle bags.

After that, he made his way to the kitchen.

There, he yanked open the pantry door and went for the MREs (Meals Ready to Eat) on the bottom shelf. They were square packages of food used just for emergencies, their stock compiled by his father for the hurricanes they used to have back in Bon Secour. Edgar checked the dates on the packages: *still good*. Of them he chose the Turkey Tetrazzini and the Hearty Beef Stew, both complete with sides, dessert, crackers, plastic utensils, and even moist towelettes for good measure.

He shoved it all into his duffle bags.

Then he snatched every chocolate bar and Hostess Ding Dong in the pantry, as well as the Pop Tarts and two big bags of chips. He also snatched as many canned goods as his duffle bag would hold, but only the stuff he liked: no English peas or carrots or yams, because they were gross.

Then he stacked the bags by the door, making his way solemnly to his father's office, where, inside, he powered up the computer and searched the internet for a world map, hovering his mouse above the Indian Ocean. There, he zoomed in and scribbled notes on his father's note pad.

Next he traced the water currents with an index finger, knowing that if out on the open sea, it would be critical to know which way the water flowed. Staring at the French Southern and Antarctic Islands on his father's Mac, he calculated the distance from his island. It was a long, long boat ride away.

About four hundred miles away, to be exact.

Realizing this, reclining back in his father's office chair, he began to second-guess his entire plan.

It really wasn't safe. It was suicide. But then again what choice did he have?

Sitting up, he ripped the top piece from a note pad on his dad's desk and set it aside, then, carefully, he detached another. On one sheet, he addressed the letter to "Mom." The other was addressed to Shay Sinclair.

Upon them he wrote slowly and legibly, printing, concentrating on forming each letter to its most eloquent curvature since his handwriting was fairly awful. He would have to be very careful here; these were only the most important letters he'd ever write in his life.

When they were written and he was satisfied, he slid them into two business envelopes and licked the flaps shut, then moved from the back office to the kitchen where he stood before his father's ultra heavy duty rain-coat: a high-grade piece of raingear that was worn during the strong Gulf storms out on the oil rig. It hung on the back door, yellower than a school bus. Yes, it could prob-ably withstand a hurricane.

Lifting it from the hook, he tried it on, stretching his arms out as far as he could reach. Even with his fingers barely poking through the cuffs, he nodded. It was big, but it would definitely do.

Just as he was about to leave, he turned around and beheld the empty house: a half-eaten loaf of bread, his father's humidor, his mother's knitting case. Their arti-facts. His heart was heavy now. There would be no saying goodbye. The ghosts of his family were there, haunting him through every object. Maybe tomorrow, before night-fall, it would even be burning to the ground. Scanning the kitchen through a blur of hot tears, he noticed a blinking red light on the answering machine. He readjusted the bags on his shoulders and walked over to hit play.

"Hello, this is Shay Sinclair. I'm calling for Edgar," Shay's soft voice uttered. "I just wanted to say that, Edgar, we're leaving tomorrow. I wanted to tell you—*him*—goodbye. We don't have cell reception any more. We're heading for Alaska tonight. If anybody gets this, would you tell him to call me?"

He hit save.

READJUSTING HIS packs once more, he kicked open the back door with his one good leg and hobbled out to the dark shed. Opening the door, with the aid of his keychain flashlight, he spotted his father's tackle box: the holy grail of all fishing. Opening it carefully, as if it was the Ark itself, he checked to make sure that the survival knife was there, along with the heavy tackle and the weatherproof lighter and the tiny burner—not to mention the flares and the can opener.

Nodding with satisfaction, he snapped the lid down and packed the tackle box in the duffle bag.

Then, finally, when he was all packed up, he turned to the back of the shed and took a deep, steadying breath, then eyed the latch on the floor. There, beneath the floor-boards, resided the last item he needed to take.

Standing over the hatch, he lifted it and peered nervously into the sinister blackness below. With a canvas bag slung around his shoulders, he took a deep whiff of the dank, musty earth, and lowered himself down into the sinister crawlspace.

It was time to pack the dynamite.

THE TRAILER scraped the asphalt as he pedaled his supplies back to town, a flapping blue tarp hanging loosely over the supplies, kind of reminding Edgar of a superhero's cape.

His leg felt much better at the moment, as the painkiller was settling in, which made him feel warm and tingly inside and made the tip of his nose feel itchy.

It was almost eight o'clock. It was getting late. With a new sense of urgency, he wheeled into the Walmart Supercenter and parked the bike by a cement pylon near the front, then chained up his bike. Suddenly, he could sense a large automobile encroaching upon him from behind.

He turned. It was a gigantic truck bearing down on him, with all its glass blackened as it pumped loud, blaring music into the parking lot.

As the roar of the loud engine quaked, he peered into the passenger-side window.

It was Chris Weedy and two friends. They all cackled hysterically at Edgar.

Weedy leaned to the window and locked eyes with Edgar.

"I'm so glad we found you!" he purred.

"Weedy," said Edgar. "A fire's coming, dumbass. Is there really time for this?"

Chris spat out the window. "Is there a better time for this, redneck?"

Edgar backed away from the bike and readied his good leg. As Chris continued edging the huge truck up to the curb, Edgar glanced at the front door of Walmart to measure the distance.

"I guess you've been following me?" Edgar shouted over the rap music, which sent the jocks into maniacal convulsions.

"For miles, redneck," smiled Chris. "And now, we've

got you."

Edgar nodded grimly. "I see. Well, I hope you haven't forgotten our little deal. I wouldn't want to go to the police with all your naughty pictures."

At that, Weedy let loose an evil laugh, tossing his head back and really howling. "The town is going to burn down. I'm not scared of the cops. Better run!" Suddenly his laughter ceased. His eyes narrowed and from his lap, he lifted his cellphone to show Edgar.

Somehow he'd gotten it from Flounder!

Edgar turned and made for the front doors of the store, limping like crazy. As he did, the three boys leapt from the truck and bolted after him. With his leg convulsing in pain, he hobbled as fast as he could, making for the automatic double doors just a few feet away.

"Punk!" Chris shouted, right behind him now, but just then Edgar made it inside.

"Hello sir!" he said loudly to the Walmart Greeter, then turned to the stacked-up boys and smirked, knowing he had made it to sanctuary.

Chris glared back like the devil.

"You're dead," he grumbled.

Then Chris and his boys backed away toward the double doors, retreating into the dry night. "We'll see you outside," he hissed, just before the doors closed.

Once they were gone, Edgar crept to the door to see what they were doing. Chris and his two boys were busy rummaging through his stuff! In a panic, Edgar limped over to the help desk and asked for security.

"What's wrong?" asked an associate.

"I am being robbed," said Edgar. "There are three boys—I mean *gang* members—stealing all my stuff."

"Oh dear!" exclaimed the lady.

Moments later Edgar was outside flanked by a uniformed guard. He had a stern, wrinkly face, and a shiny badge on his shirt.

"Are those the boys?" he asked Edgar.

"Yeah, that's them!" said Edgar loudly, and when Chris looked over, he summoned his goons and they bolted for the truck.

The night guard tried to get the tag number as they fled, but he wasn't fast enough. Squinting, he flopped his note pad shut in frustration and turned to Edgar.

"Did you say that kid is fourteen years old?" he asked, "and driving around parking lots like that?"

"Yes," said Edgar. "That's probably the safest thing he does."

"Well, he's gonna kill somebody if we don't get him off the road," said the guard. "I'm gonna go call the police, not that they'll be able to do anything tonight, what with everything else that's going on in town." He pointed to the red skyline. There, set against the dark sky, the glowing fire raged like hell itself. Finally, it had become visible, something no longer on the TV or to be talked about as if still far away, but it was here, in town: it had arrived.

Edgar and the guard stood in silence and, for a long moment, they watched the glowing flames against the backdrop of a night sky.

When the guard returned inside to call the police, Edgar returned to his trailer and retied the bungees on the tarp that Chris and his guys had undone, making sure that the dynamite was still there and perfectly strapped down.

Luckily they hadn't located the dynamite, probably because Edgar had buried it beneath his other supplies.

With the trailer secured, Edgar walked back into Walmart and marveled at the amount of people who were still there shopping. These were the last remaining people in Mount Lanier, he figured. All of them stood in long lines seeking last minute items: buying generators, coolers, tie downs, gas cans, food, water, and all other sorts of things. Edgar thought about the last minute shopping dashes of people back home in Bon Secour before a hurricane, and as he walked past all the waiting people on his way to the Sporting Goods section, he noticed that they were all looking at him. Forlornly, wearily, every single one of them gaped at him. For a moment he wondered why; but then, suddenly, he remembered.

He was wearing his father's yellow raincoat. He forgot he was still wearing it! It stretched comically down to his shins and engulfed his arms, and suddenly he realized how strange he probably looked, especially since there had not been a drop of rain in Mount Lanier for almost a half a year now.

AFTER FORTY-FIVE minutes of shopping, collecting all the other supplies he would eventually need, he emerged from the store with two heaping shopping carts full of stuff, then scanned the hazy lot for signs of Weedy's truck. Positive that Chris was gone, he quickly proceeded to the trailer where he unloaded the goods, piling them up, then strapping them down with caution.

Then, afterward, he pedaled off into the night, making a wild dash for the suburbs, and for Flounder.

He was almost home.

He was almost to the point of no return.

TWENTY-TWO

FROM THE DARKNESS beyond the glow of the street-lights, Edgar watched the Sinclairs pack up their house. The lights were on in every room, lighting up the whole yard outside. In one room, Shay's mother helped Shay wrap china. In another, Shay's father packed fancy guns into polished leather sheaths.

Edgar lingered a bit, trying to see if Shay might break away from her mother so he could tap on a window—maybe signal her to come outside, but soon he lost heart. They seemed sad and were moving along pretty slowly. It might take all night.

Glancing at the momentous inferno behind him that slowly crawled along over the hill—its smoke billowing forth like a coughing volcano—he could now see the red of the monster's simmering against the dark, bleak, polluted sky.

Creeping up the lawn of the Sinclairs, he slipped the

letter he wrote for her under the door, and once it was irretrievable, a sudden pang of fear shot through him.

This was suddenly real, now. What if they overlooked the letter in their dash to get out of town? The contents of the letter would be his only way back home. Without her seeing it his life might be in serious jeopardy.

He thought about that for a long moment, standing frozen on the Sinclair's porch, knowing that if he knocked on the door and told her his plan, outright, just explained it to her, she would certainly try and stop him because his plan was absolute insanity.

He couldn't let her talk him out of it.

So, backing away, hobbling in retreat across her lawn, he took one last, lingering look at her through the windows—the lip gloss girl, the *true* best thing about Washington State.

When he reached his bike—heartbroken and lonelier than ever—he pedaled away toward the suburbs so he could say goodbye to Flounder.

PARKING THE bike and its overloaded trailer on the sidewalk, he limped to the front door and rang the bell.

"Hello Mrs. Artese," he said when she answered the door. She immediately showed signs of sympathy and concern.

"*Hello, honey*," she said kindly. "Is everything OK?" He nodded. "I'm so sorry to hear about your father," she said, placing a hand over her heart.

"That's OK," Edgar said confidently, "they'll find him. Is Flounder home?"

She pursed her lips and asked, "Flounder?"

"Oh, I'm really sorry, Mrs. Artese," he said, correcting himself. "I meant to say 'Anthony.'"

As she stepped aside, Flounder emerged, and Edgar could only stare in absolute disbelief. His friend's lips were busted apart, and both eyes were blackened, like a raccoon. He wore two cotton balls in his nose and both were soaked through with fresh blood.

Flounder looked like he'd survived a wood chipper—*barely*.

"I crashed my bike," Flounder explained, flashing a glance up at his mother. He gave Edgar a sharp look to insist he ask no questions in front of her. Flounder's voice, muffled from the plugged up nose, hung heavy in the air like humidity.

He glanced up at his mother again. She looked down sorrowfully and caressed his thick, black hair.

"My poor Tony," she said, then, turning, she left the two alone.

Flounder closed the door behind her and stepped out onto the porch, saying,

"Weedy got the phone, man! My mom found it in my sock drawer and made me ride to Weedy's house on my bike and return it while they packed the house. It took no time for Weedy and his goons to catch me on the way home and rough me up."

"Oh man," said Edgar, shaking his head sorrowfully. "Weedy just came after me, too. I'm so sorry, Flounder."

"Don't be!" insisted Flounder. "Because we *fought back*. We kept them off of us for a good, long while, Edgar. We did what we had to do!" A wide smile unraveled across his busted lips and he nudged Edgar on the arm. "Besides, my mom went from being super pissed that I stole Weedy's phone to, you know, she feels sorry for me now. Besides, I proved I can take a beating like one of those mafia guys, right?"

"Flounder," he muttered, wishing he'd never introduced his friend to that mob boss stuff, "I've got to go. I came to tell you goodbye."

As if refusing to let him leave, Flounder pointed at

Edgar's cast. "What happened there?" he asked.

"Uh . . . that's a jellyfish sting. From the island. I'll tell you all about it later." Shifting his weight to his good leg, he asked, "So when do y'all leave?"

"As soon as we're finished packing." Flounder glanced over Edgar's shoulder and spotted the loaded trailer. "What's with all the stuff?" he asked, then a troubled look emerged on his face. "Wait," he said thoughtfully. "Edgar is that a load of fish? The fish stand's closed, you know."

"No, it's not fish. It's . . . nothing," he replied.

Flounder suddenly seemed to realize what he was up to. "Oh, no, Edgar—you can't go to the hole tonight, man! What's wrong with you? If the town starts burning and you come back up the hole while the cabin is on fire . . ."

"Flounder," he said reassuringly. "Don't worry. I will be fine. I promise."

Flounder could not persuade him, and hung his head in frustration. "You've got an addiction, you know that? To the hole. You're *addicted*."

"Yeah, well, maybe so," admitted Edgar. "But the island's been good to me. Listen, Flounder, California has a lot of earthquakes. So when you get out there, try not to fall into the sea."

He smiled and extended a hand to Flounder, who readily reached up and took it even as he stared over Edgar's shoulder at the ominously loaded trailer with all the stuff piled up.

"Edgar . . ." he said again.

"I'm telling you, Flounder," he said. "*Please.* Do not worry about me. I'm going to be perfectly fine, OK?"

"OK," said Flounder, squeezing Edgar's hand tight.

A lump rose in Edgar's throat. Before he cried in front of Flounder, he quickly swallowed it down and turned to the sidewalk, and to his supplies. Then, climbing up on his bike, he pedaled away into the night.

As he did, he lifted a hand to Flounder and held it high, as Flounder waved back, both their arms extended above them until the moment that Edgar made it beyond the streetlights and became completely engulfed in darkness.

Down the road, as he pedaled, he found it increasingly hard to shake the look he'd seen in Flounder's eyes: it wasn't worry. It was outright *fear*.

Things were about to get *insane*. There was a lot to carry, and it would take several trips and plenty of time to get all the supplies up the hill, Edgar knew, because even with two good legs, it would've taken a while.

In the faint light of the harvest moon, Edgar grabbed an armful of duffel bags and walked them up to the brook, then across the stepping stones and through the leaf partition to the clearing, then up the hill into the cabin. Once there, he dropped everything at the hole's edge and felt his way to the corner of the room where he lit the lantern, illuminating the cabin with a bright, warm glow. Pausing to catch his breath for a moment, he massaged his wildly throbbing leg, then began another grueling journey across the dark meadow and trickling brook.

He figured to himself as he walked along. It always helped him to keep his nerves under control—helped him forget about the dark, unseen forest around him. During this time, he cemented his plans, restating them, refiguring them, so that when the time came to act, he would have no time to think. Sometimes thinking could be deadly in a situation such as this.

Fall down the hole, he thought. *Get your supplies to the island. Unpack them. Prepare the island. DO what you need to DO.*

After several trips back and forth to the bike, he soon built a large pile of supplies at the hole's edge. Standing on the bricks, he unfurled a large net beside the pile—a net his father used to use for bait while fishing in Bon Secour. Edgar tossed the pile of supplies into the net and gathered up the other end, yanking everything into a large, tight, netted ball. On the other end of the rope, he tied a wrought iron plant hook, then yanked on this to make sure it would hold.

It felt nice and tight.

Then he made for the bike and trailer one last time to collect the one lone remaining duffle bag, the heaviest bag of them all.

Down by the bike, he slipped off the hot raincoat and slung the contents of the duffel around his shoulders. Then, replacing the raincoat over himself like a poncho, he nodded at the bike and told it, *so long*.

"Good bike," he said aloud. "Best money I ever spent."

Stepping carefully back across the stones, he headed for the cabin one last, final time. He looked down into shimmering water beneath his feet and wondered if the rainbow trout still swam around down there. He'd meant to go fishing for them so many times, but he'd been so distracted. Life had gotten so complicated lately. The stream was so low now. The drought had been so relentless.

"Let's fill you up," he said with a smile to the stream.

In the dark woods, as usual, he felt lonely and afraid. Fear reverberated through his chest almost painfully, but quickened his breath and heightened his senses, and yet, as he crossed the creek toward the shack, he also felt a certain peace. The peace came from his doing something now, from *acting*, from having a plan. He felt that, at the very least, he was *doing his part*, even though his act would be, at best, suicidal.

Putting one gimpy foot in front of the other, he was doing it all in the name of his father—and also, for his mother.

Moving up the hill toward the cabin now, he knew he would rather die falling *down* than lying in a hospital bed and falling *apart*.

Just waiting for his dad to die.

Yes, he was weary, and there were miles yet to go—many, many miles—*thousands* of them, and his head buzzed woozily from the lingering medicines and his leg throbbed angrily, but still, he rambled on.

"'Ha! Ha! Ha! Ha! Ha!' came a voice through the quiet forest."

TWENTY-THREE

Edgar froze, startled so tremendously by the strange laughter that he almost came out of his skin.

"I knew you'd be here," a voice called. "What a dumb redneck! Wearing that stupid raincoat all around town and everything. It's not even raining, you dumbass."

It was Weedy.

The bully's evil chuckle rang out into the night. Edgar strained in the moonlight to see, and there, in the doorway of the cabin, stood his dark silhouette against the warm glow of the lantern. His figure was skinny, angular, threatening, and totally unmistakable.

"Jesus," sighed Edgar. "I thought you were somebody. You scared me for a second!"

"Oh, Edgar," said Chris joyously. "Don't you know? I am somebody!"

Still yards away from the cabin, Edgar nodded and clenched his fists.

"Yep," he said in his best get-down-to-business voice. "I'm right here, Weed."

Edgar knew by the way Chris was blocking the doorway, with arms folded and chin high, that the kid had no intention of moving.

"You alone?" asked Edgar, glancing around the woods.

"Of course I am!" chuckled Weedy. "Who else would I need?" Edgar could see that Chris was clenching his fists, too.

"You do realize," said Edgar, taking a small step toward toward Chris, "that there's an evacuation going on around town, don't you, idiot?"

"Oh yes," said Chris. "Which is what made it easy to find you! And Flounder, too. Have you seen him? I have . . ."

"Weedy, I am going to say this just one time. I don't have time for this. You better get out of my way."

Silence ensued as they glared at each other. Edgar knew his injury was too much to sustain a fight—a fight that he couldn't survive, all half-exhausted and half-medicated as he was. He couldn't punch through wet parchment paper right now, let alone Chris Weedy. He only had one option left, and it would have to work, or else.

He would have to bluff.

He took another step towards Weedy and tried not to limp this time. He would have to keep his weakness a secret.

"Are you crazy?" hissed Weedy, his eyes widening. "I know your leg is hurt! I saw you limping through the door of the Wal Mart, you idiot." The bully departed the door frame and stood straight, taking a menacing step toward Edgar, but even so Edgar took a relentless step towards him.

A pissed Weedy shook his head angrily, like an obstinate grizzly being taunted by a badger, and raced toward

Edgar. Enraged, he marched into the night and stood before Edgar, who glared back at him.

Just as Edgar hoped, Chris raised his fist to strike, and as he reared back, Edgar grabbed both the flaps on his father's raincoat and thrust them open wide, revealing a terrible sight: there, dangling from his shoulders and all across his chest, was stick upon stick of red, interwoven dynamite, all roped together by long strands of black electrical tape.

Weedy shrieked and yanked his hand away from the wired-up Edgar.

"Are you . . . crazy?!?!" he squealed. "What is the matter with you?" Backing away from Edgar, he half-tripped across a tree root and almost lost his footing.

It was hilarious.

"Yes, I believe I am," admitted Edgar, limping past him towards the cabin door. Standing in the glow of the room, he turned and said to Weedy, "Now get out of here. For your own good."

Edgar watched hopefully as the bully glanced down the trail—even taking a step towards town. But, then, his heart sank. Chris Weedy turned around and had turned, seemingly seduced by second thoughts. His brow had suddenly ruffled. He massaged his chin and studied Edgar, just like he'd done back in Van Rossum's class when Edgar had told him his dad was dead.

Suddenly a look came over Weedy, an all too familiar one. There was that scowl on his face, his eyes churning, his brow wrinkled in contortions of rage. A scowl reverberated from his whole being. The kid scratched his curly blonde hair, and he smiled.

"Oh wow," Weedy said thoughtfully. "I almost forgot about you!"

"What did you forget?" asked Edgar, breathlessly, his heart beginning to pound again. And suddenly, Weedy was moving dangerously towards him again.

"You almost had me fooled!" the bully cackled. "But then I remembered: you're the biggest liar I've ever known."

Edgar stood in the doorway and thought about just turning to the hole and jumping in, escaping this idiocy, but he couldn't. He needed time to pack all his stuff for the trip, so he had to stay and see this through.

He opened his raincoat flaps again and waved them. He warned Weedy. "I'm telling you," he shouted. "If you attack me, you'll blow us both up. And at this point, I really don't care."

Undeterred, Weedy continued to step toward Edgar.

"Don't you remember?" Weedy said thoughtfully, moving slowly towards the cabin door, as if entranced. "All your lies? Well, I do. Like when you said your dad was 'dead.' Or when you faked your death and stole my phone. Well, that was another lie."

Edgar stiffened and readied himself as the boy approached. He wouldn't just let Weedy wail on him.

"And now," Chris continued triumphantly, "you expect me to believe that that is real dynamite? C'mon man! Ha ha!"

Face to face now, with Weedy's breath on Edgar's nose, the two glared at each other.

"This dynamite is armed," Edgar hissed. "If you knock me down, it will detonate. You can believe me or not."

"Blah blah blah," growled Chris. "What a truck load of shit."

Suddenly he lunged for Edgar, and Edgar deftly jerked backwards and fumbled at the dynamite, trying to unstrap it so he could fight. However, it was far too heavy and far too tightly wrapped wound around his body, and it was much too late. He was basically tied down, over-encumbered, and was suddenly at the mercy of the wild

Chris Weedy. The tape—stuck to his skin and to the red dynamite—was also sticking to the inside of the yellow raincoat. He was like a stuck fly on flypaper.

As Weedy rebounded and stepped to the threshold, snarling, looming with a raised fist, Edgar covered his head and braced for the brutal punch, but then, the most wonderful thing happened.

The punch never came.

Just as Weedy's fist came hurtling across the night, a wide open blur like a speeding train came out of nowhere and lifted Weedy off his feet, thudding him into the ground with the force of a jackhammer. Weedy was crushed by the weight of one hundred and twenty pounds of charging Anthony Artese and was driven to the forest floor like a big sack of rocks. With a satisfying squeal, he crashed to the dirt and rocks and rolled over in pain, clutching his gut.

Flounder! Flounder had been watching, and waiting, and miraculously, he'd saved Edgar's butt.

Then, with all the weight on his knees that pinned the awful Chris Weedy to the ground, Flounder hovered over the bully's limp frame like the grim reaper. Just as Weedy began to regain his breath—since it had been clearly knocked out of him—Flounder balled his fist and raised it over Weedy's face.

"Had enough?" shouted Flounder into Chris's contorted face, grabbing a hold of Chris's shirt and lifting him up. "I said, do you still want to fight?"

Coughing, Chris murmured, "No. Truce."

When it was clear that Weedy was finished, Flounder rose and stood over him and smiled, nodding at Edgar and pumping his bloody fist. Edgar, relieved, allowed himself to enjoy the moment. Behind him, Weedy rolled over and groaned in the pine straw, clutching his stomach and face.

Good for you, Flounder, he thought.

Instantly he turned back to the cabin. *Now that that's out of the way, I must get down to business.* He walked to the hole and gazed down into it, peering into the bitter darkness. Then he bent and yanked the hook-end of the rope from the floor—the one tied to all his supplies in the net—and slung it over his shoulder, readying himself.

"Hey!" called Flounder, who happily jogged to the doorway. "What are you doing, Edgar? Hey! Who whacked Weedy, remember? Don't leave me hanging, right?"

"Anthony did," said Edgar glumly, turning. He tried trying to manage a victorious smile.

"What are you doing?" asked Flounder, his voice softening, the realization coming to him. "Why are you running away? Don't go down there."

"I have to go," said Edgar.

"But . . . why?"

"Because, Flounder. I have to save my dad."

A puzzled look emerged on Flounder's face. "By going down there?"

"Yeah, listen," said Edgar, "I really don't have time to explain. Just . . . get him out of here, OK? It's really important. Y'all can't be here much longer." Edgar nodded at Weedy who was now whimpering audibly on the forest floor. "One more thing. Whatever you do, don't come back here tonight, OK? Promise that."

Then Edgar turned back to the hole. "I'll see you again when the fire is out," he said, over his shoulder.

Then shoving the big ball over the edge of the hole, Edgar held up a hand and saluted his friend.

"Thank you for saving my ass!" he said, then leapt down into the darkness after his ball of supplies. Flounder watched helplessly as the rope uncoiled, and just like that, Edgar was gone, off into the Earth.

As Edgar fell, tears rose, which squirted out and lifted

in freefall.

They continued all the way down to the core.

TWENTY-FOUR

EDGAR TRIED TO savor the fall, knowing that if everything worked as planned, he would never fall down the hole again.

Releasing the end of the rope attached to his supplies, he allowed the bundle to fall weightlessly beside him and then, twisting his body, he closed his eyes.

There, in the warm, salty air, he began to flip and pirouette and twist like an acrobat, letting the wind do the work, just like he had done so many times before.

I'm so going to miss this, he thought, *the falling.* There was nothing else like it in the world. This was the most beautiful thing he'd ever done. He would savor it to the very end.

As the other side neared, he stabilized himself and located the falling hook with a keychain flashlight. There, hovering slightly above him, he took the hook in his hands and turned his body, readying himself for arrival.

He would need to snap the hook to the top of the hole like a grapple, then pray the hook would hold his netted supplies and prevented them from falling back down into the Earth. He would only have one shot to do this.

As the hole arrived, he did just that: he artfully thrusted the wrought iron hook to the side wall and held his breath as the other end dropped back down the hole, snapping secure and saving the items.

In one violent jerk, his supplies—dangling on a stretch of rope below his feet—swung safely about ten yards down, just beyond the edge of the light.

Edgar emerged from the hole, beholding a beautiful, sunny day on the island. There were calm waters and blue skies stretching broadly across the world, like a painting. Turning grimly back to the hole, he sat on the fine sand with his legs spread slightly, then, using the upraised bricks of the hole's edge as leverage, he took hold of the rope and yanked.

Pulling on the rope as hard as he could, the rope and supplies did not budge.

Why am I not surprised? he thought. The supplies probably weighed about three hundred pounds or so.

Why hadn't he worked out more in PE?

Warding off a sinking feeling, he knew that if he didn't get the supplies out of the hole, then nobody else would. And then who would save his father?

His injured leg trembling beneath the strain, he ignored it and pulled even harder, finally feeling the bundle begin to give way and inch upward, braid by braid.

"AARRRGGGGHHHH!!!" he screamed, hefting with all that he had, when suddenly the big pile of supplies made it to the top and toppled over, spilling from the hole, rolling onto the sand.

With his supplies finally safe and sound, he lay back and massaged his fiery leg and freshly burning hands, and took a rest.

Finally, he stood and walked down to the sea, dipping his hands into the cool water. Blisters had already begun to swell on the palms of his hands.

He spread out the items across the seashore, taking inventory. Yes, everything was accounted for. All his precious supplies had made it safely to the island, all in one piece.

First was the large inflatable raft he'd bought at Walmart for three hundred bucks: the most expensive raft they had. He unboxed it, then spread it out across the shore. He glanced at the instructions: *This raft is impervious to sunlight, salt water, and gasoline. It can also carry four adults, or eight hundred pounds.*

Awesome, he thought. It was plenty strong enough to tote Edgar and his oversized load.

There was a small post script on the bottom of the page, that made his heart sink: *This raft is made only for ponds, lakes, rivers, and swimming pools.*

It didn't say anything about deep, vast, impossible oceans, with waves the size of office buildings.

Ah, well. What can I do now? This raft will have to do.

Tossing the instructions aside, he fished out an air pump from the box and connected the hose to the nipple of the raft, and within minutes, his big lifeboat was fully inflated and ready to go. He lay down in it and shifted his weight all around—violently—pushing against the side walls as hard as he could and even standing and stomping with his good leg, bouncing the floor of the raft until his shoe hit the ground through the rubber, *hard*.

Then, after that, he stilled and listened for leaks, but he heard nothing.

Thank God.

Next, he pushed the raft into the water and loaded all his supplies onto it. When finished, half the floor space of the raft was crammed with a massive, unorganized mound of stuff: food, medicine, a waterproof sleeping bag, a small bag of clothes, a battery powered radio, books, a Gameboy, a compass, a dismantled fishing pole, his father's awesome tackle box, two oars, a life vest, a life ring, binoculars, his dad's neatly folded raincoat, and one big group of gallon water bottles.

All the weight made the back of the raft dip dramatically toward the ocean, which made him curse.

"Why is everything working against me?" he grumbled.

The front end had begun to scrape the sand of the shore as the high tide began to roll in, which worried him immensely, but there was nothing he could do now.

Hastily, he tied a rope to an end of the raft and anchored it to a grounded spike on shore, even though the supplies did a pretty good job of anchoring it themselves. He just couldn't risk a wave carrying it all out to sea.

Then, with the boat packed, he turned and readied himself to wire up the island.

Separating the dynamite sticks one by one, he armed them with blasting caps by plunging a silvery tube into the top of each stick—like pushing shish kabob skewers through tender hunks of sirloin.

With his heart soundly in his throat, he then carried the armed dynamite as gingerly as possible—like fine china—around the island, tenderly wedging the sticks into any tiny cracks he could find on its rocky surface.

Anywhere there was an opening, he plugged it with a dynamite stick, then back to the pile for more sticks, then wedging more dynamite into cracks.

Finally, with all but four sticks scattered across the island, making it look like a warzone, he made for the island's center and placed the remaining four sticks into the cracks between the island and the hole's edge.

It pained him to do this, as good as the hole was to him.

But since there was only one chance for this to work, he was meticulous about where he placed the dynamite sticks. No use half-blowing the hole, stranding himself here, and failing to reach the goal that he intended. He could feel his father's deep grasp of engineering surging through him as he studied the cracks, despite the pain-killers still dulling his thoughts, still fuzzying up his mind.

"Slow that swing down," his dad often said when they'd go golfing. Edgar always hated it when he did this—trying to teach him fundamentals in the middle of a game, and *especially* in the middle of a swing. All he wanted to do was hit the dang ball.

"Huff all you want to," his dad would say, "but if you'll listen to me, I'll teach you how to hit the ball straight and long. Don't you want to hit it straight and long?"

"Yeah," surrendered Edgar begrudgingly, aloud on the island this time, lost in his thoughts all of a sudden as his dad stood right in front of him.

"OK then," said his father. "Swinging harder doesn't always matter. Most of the time, it makes you lose control more than anything else. Forget about power. Concentrate on hitting the ball *in the right place*, Edgar. I'm telling you, son, it's all about *where* you make contact, not how you make contact."

He looked across the sands and saw the ghost of his father pointing to a spot on the back of a ghost of a ball. "Just take a smooth, easy swing, boy. Nothing too hard. Just make steady contact with it. It's all about where you disperse the force. *It's all about where you disperse the force.*"

"And now," concluded his father, smiling down at him, "you know exactly where to place the dynamite."

"Distribute it evenly," whispered Edgar, still staring at the imaginary golf ball. Then, shaking the vision away, he bent down and stuffed the last dynamite stick into a small, crooked crevice, then stood and looked down the big hole beyond it.

All around him, the island was a warzone—red sticks and wire were scattered everywhere, like a Pacific beach in World War II, but down in the hole he knew there was a dark peace.

He could fall back home and abandon all this craziness if he wanted to—just choose to live and not strand himself, or starve himself or drown himself—if he would only just topple over.

He could join his Mom at the fire line the next day, and they could take their chances with the wildfire.

Or, he could put the wildfire out.

Solemnly, he unfastened his Pathfinder wristwatch and caressed it gently, tapping the buttons on the side and dialing up the tides and moons and the compass, as well as the fish indicator (which currently flashed Three Out Of Five Fishes. Not bad for that time of day). Checking the indicator, he looked out over the waters and noticed the Ambercod swarming.

"Great watch," he said, his heart returning home, not necessarily to Bon Secour and not necessarily to Mount Lanier, but to wherever his parents were. In the oncoming dusk he mashed the glow button. It lit his face alien green.

It was dusk now, and nearly dawn back in Mount Lanier.

Giving it one last, final squeeze, he tossed it down into the hole and watched it go. The green of the glow function streaked through the blackness like a falling star, and, turning from it, just before it could vanish, he hobbled a half-circle and then faced the great blue ocean once again.

"It's time to make rain," he said, mustering his courage one last time, initializing a final check of the dynamite as he made his way to shore.

The sun was half-dipping below the dark blue horizon now.

"Goodbye," he said to the island—and to his home back in America.

Down at the shore, he untied the rope fastened to the raft, then flopped himself clumsily onto the big orange thing and gave his swollen, throbbing leg a rub.

"I hope you stay afloat better than I think you will, you big piece of crap," he muttered to it, bouncing up on the sudden choppy waves that had begun to splash all around him.

High tide, he noticed, had definitely arrived.

Quickly, he crawled to the center of the boat and took the two oars in his blistered hands, then shoved them into the sands below and pushed off to sea.

Surprisingly, the raft floated extremely well—even with all his supplies on board. Encouraged, he embarked upon a tight, brisk circle around the small island.

Up and down the choppy waves he went, and immediately in his aching hands he felt the stinging of the rope burn blisters.

Ugh, he thought. *How far are the French Southern and Antarctic Islands again?*

He didn't know if his hands could take so much rowing but then again, what other choice did he have?

He would just have to suck it up.

Once the raft had completed a successful circle around the island, and he gave it an affirmative nod of satisfaction, he said, "Maybe you don't suck so much after all." Patting its orange, vinyl side wall, he gave the clumsy raft his blessing.

Glancing over the side, he noticed the Ambercod were out in numbers—as far down as he could see—feeding on darting bursts of smaller, silvery prey. It would have really been a great day to fish.

It would have been a great day for *anything*—anything other than this.

With the reality of his plan weighing heavily on him now, he paddled to shore once last time and with his heart beating wildly in his chest, he stilled, closed his eyes, and tried to calm himself by taking deep breaths in sync with the splashing, swishing tide.

H tried to gather his courage and remember what he was doing all this for—trying to remember *whom* he was doing all this for. With trembling fingers, he lifted his father's old Zippo lighter from the pocket of his yellow raincoat and struck it. A blue flame burst forth upon the wick, and, tipping it forward, he touched its orange tip to the master fuse coiled up upon the shore. Like a slithering fire snake, it jumped instantly into action and slithered toward the dynamite, sending sparks everywhere in its wake, forcing Edgar to frantically retreat, his arms rowing like blender whisks.

The fuse hissed wildly on the island behind him. Edgar lurched away from the dynamite sticks, breaking madly for the open sea and churned the two plastic oars with all he had in him.

How much time was there before the island exploded, he had no idea, but guessed about five minutes before the lit fuse reached its first stick of dynamite, based on the practice strips he'd lit back at the house and using simple mathematics. It would be just enough time to get himself clearly away from the impending blast—that was, if the blast wasn't bigger than what he estimated. Truth was, Edgar knew nothing about this sort of thing: he'd never been around any dynamite. The only thing he knew for sure was how much dynamite he'd used for that, and that was *all of it*.

Frantically he continued to paddle expecting at any moment to be shaken by the blast—the blast that he knew might either deafen him or even sink his boat—or both—and every now and again he glanced behind him to see just how much distance he'd covered and if he was safe. For the moment, the island was suddenly nothing more than a tiny yellow speck in a vast seascape of blue—he had really been moving!

This little orange raft is even swifter than I expected! he thought, realizing he might just survive this lunacy after all.

Suddenly, just when he thought he'd rowed far enough for the boat to be clear of the blast, he rested his tiny oars on the side wall and checked his watch to see how much time had passed. There, on his wrist, was nothing but a white, watch-shaped region where his Pathfinder watch used to be. He'd almost forgotten: he threw it down the hole.

Why had he done that again?

Because, he thought, *it was an offering—a good one*, too, *to the Earth. For good luck. For good sailing.*

And most importantly, for homecoming.

Any good seaman would have done just the same.

So just as he was studying his watch-less wrist, the world up and convulsed before him like Armageddon.

It was an explosion like nothing he'd ever seen or known, rocking the seas before him, shaking the wide expanse of waters as if Poseidon himself had stabbed the ocean with his mighty trident.

In a flash, Edgar was hurled to the back of the raft like a ragdoll and for a moment, he thought he was dead.

"Ugh," he muttered, coming to, his ears howling with pain—his temples throbbing and pulsing. In the bottom of the boat he remained curled into a ball, feeling about his ears and earlobes, checking for bleeding. *Am I deaf?* he thought, suddenly horrified at the possibility. He pulled his fingers from his ears and checked them for blood, but, thankfully, they were clean.

As he continued to stare at his fingers, his entire body numb from the blast, suddenly he began to feel the sting of hot rubble and ocean water falling from the sky splashing down all around his boat. At first he could only, marvel at the strange shrapnel pelting down, and was fascinated in his reverie by the shards bouncing off the rubber side walls of the raft. Then, in a panic, as the situation washed over him, he lunged across the raft and spread his arms open wide, sprawling outwardly as far as he could to absorb as many of the projectiles that he could. If his rubber raft was punctured, with no island remaining in the sea, he would slowly sink and drown. His raft was all he had left.

Jagged bits of the island mercilessly pelted his yellow raincoat which he flung across the uncovered remains of the raft. Then, stretching his body even further, he prayed silently that the material might hold.

Holding his breath as he absorbed the sting of the falling rubble, he waited. Soon, the horrible rock shower was over, and he sat up and blinked at the huge waves coming for him.

Why hadn't he brought a raft repair kit? He cursed himself for not doing so.

As he rose and fell upon the tall waves, he inspected the material for pinholes and felt of the vinyl, tuning his ringing ears to the surface to listen for escaping air.

Thankfully, the raft was intact. It didn't seem to be leaking. Relieved, he took a deep breath and turned to the island, squinting to see what had become of it.

"Holy . . ." he said, marveling at the destruction. He had sure blown the island to smithereens. There *was* no island anymore: *everything*—the hole, the shore—everything was gone. All that remained was a wide-open sea all the way to the horizon, and nothing more.

Reaching into the supplies, he withdrew a pair of binoculars and scanned the waters more closely, rising to his knees. When he finally saw it—the perfect circle of bricks that marked the top of the hole, that were just under the water now, he let out a big, cackling laugh. He thrust up a finger in celebration as he stared through the binoculars, like a sea-swept pirate just discovering land, bouncing up and down, hollering in the raft, he now saw in the last fading light of day what he'd hoped he would see at the end of all this.

A large, churning whirlpool spinning angrily in the sea.

The spout was spinning directly on top of the submerged bricks where the island used to be, and he totally knew why: because the hole was giving way to the Indian Ocean. The island was blown below the waterline, so it was nothing but a drain now—just like a drain in a hospital sink. The ocean was falling headlong into the hole, and it was then that Edgar knew he'd done all he could do.

There was no going back now. The center of the Earth was quickly filling with water, stranding him on this side of the world.

Dead bodies of Ambercod began surfacing all around the boat, belly up from the blast. It made Edgar sad to see them floating alongside, but as he studied their bobbing bodies, he discovered an extremely troubling fact: the more he rowed away from the whirlpool, the more the Ambercod bodies seemed to stay with him and the boat.

Meaning: he wasn't *moving forward* much at all.

Setting down his oars, he turned around and cupped a hand over his worried brow to scan the seas, and there, with panic in his chest, he realized that the remains of the hole had not moved at all. Soon, it became apparent that he was not *not* out-paddling the Ambercod; no, rather, it was much worse than that.

The whirlpool was getting closer to the back of his raft.

No, that wasn't it, either.

Actually, the hole was now sucking him *backward* into itself! He hadn't been strong enough to out-paddle its pull and now it was drawing him backward—threatening him with a watery death—like a tractor beam.

Diving to the front of the boat, he snatched up his oars and thrust them into the sea, rowing with a brand new fervor, heaving with all his might. He was rowing for his life now—rowing just to stay alive—and as he did, he looked behind him and let out a whimper, discovering that with each vigorous stroke, he got no closer to the falling seas, but also, he got no further away. Basically, if he rowed as hard as he could row, he would only maintain staying in one spot—like a hamster on a running wheel.

Meaning he'd have to row like mad for as long as he could maintain it just to not drown.

It was a terrible predicament to be in.

"God help me," he muttered, already feeling his shoulder muscles beginning to burn. "There's no way I can keep this up for long."

When the sun went down and the stars came out, every few minutes or so, Edgar would slow his rowing and turn the flashlight to the raging whirlpool. Each time he did, his heart sank knowing that he hadn't moved an inch from where he started earlier that day.

The current of the falling water seemed so strong there was no way he could outlast it. Even still, fueled by panic and the base desire just to stay alive, he kept rowing all night.

If he wanted to survive this, he knew one fact: he'd have to row until morning—until low tide.

He just didn't think he could do it. He didn't have

much strength anymore and it was all he could do to keep up the rowing. It had broken him down, knowing this, and in his misery, he tried not to cry as he kept going.

But still, he kept going.

His MOTHER sipped hot coffee at the barricade, rubbing her temples from weariness, unashamed that she was the last non-press member remaining at the fire line in probably the entire region of western Washington.

She was determined, though. Nobody would ever argue that.

Milly Dewitt knew the officers' names by now and they all knew hers. They'd long since brought her a stool to sit upon—the only person at the barricade who even *had* a stool.

They brought fresh cups of coffee, too, just like the one she was drinking now, and around the clock they made conversation with her, talking about how their wives had been praying for her and her husband, and for her son as well.

"Thank them for me," Milly said to them.

The reporters and journalists *themselves* had even begun to treat her as one of their own, sometimes bringing her slices of homemade chocolate chip pie from the local restaurant, or bottles of cold water.

And always, at dusk and dawn, they brought her coffee. Lots and lots of coffee.

And when it got chilly at night, they covered up Milly Dewitt with their own coats and sleeping bags and blankets.

They loved her, basically.

"Thanks, y'all," she'd say in her charming Southern drawl. "Any word on the next search party?"

At night, with her eyes beginning to shut, those at the

fire-line escorted her to various news vans where they'd offer her a pallet made of spare clothes or duffle bags or whatever else they could pile up together that was soft.

Drowsily, she nodded to them and said, "G'night, y'all."

As the reporters practiced their stories in the mornings outside of those vans, reporting on the wide swath of destruction that the wildfire had wrought, their voices tapered off she came to, and passed them by.

"Good morning, Mrs. Dewitt," they'd say, swallowing their lines out of respect. "Any word from last night's search party?"

At dawn the day, the miracle happened—the event that changed everything—in the soft morning light she sat by the barricade sipping from her cup, chatting warmly with Robert, the head ranger of the Mount Baker— Snoqualmie National Forest. They were fast friends by now, Bob, originally from the Mississippi Coast, which made Milly feel like she'd found herself a real Southern companion.

They'd both discovered they had a common love, too: the beautiful Gulf of Mexico, as well as deep fried crab claws. Bob had moved to Washington from the South many, many years back, but Milly told him she didn't hold that against him.

A half-white wooly beard stretched across his face, and hard lines around his eyes widened and grew when he smiled, kind of like Santa Claus, revealing to her a life lived out in the unblocked sunshine, with fresh air, and contemplation.

For now, though, they spoke of pleasant things as they waited for word from the fire line: about gardening, local restaurants, and animals he'd seen frequently in the area. Bob rattled on about all the species of the forest he'd encountered—about the time the grizzly who'd sired her cub near the road had drawn photographers from around the world that blocked the highway for days.

"If you ever had a Southern accent, Bob," said Milly, interjecting, "you've certainly lost it by now."

"Well," he said, "I think it's best not to have a Southern accent up here. The bears can sense it."

"Oh?" she asked. "And which do they think tastes better: a Southerner or a Yankee?"

"'Yankee?'" he chuckled. "Mrs. Dewitt, that is a very derogatory word. It also turns out that bears are also attracted to hateful talk, too, so I'd watch myself."

She grinned at him and sipped her coffee again, reminded of a similar conversation she'd had at her own dinner table with her long-lost husband and son: how they'd both giggled at the word "Yankee," and how the times were easier then, and how she'd give up everything to be back home at that moment, at that very same dinner table. All of a sudden, as she was thinking about these things, a boom shook the Earth and rattled the landscape like nothing she'd ever felt—or heard—before.

Everyone shouted in surprise, swaying from the Earth's lurching, as they reached for the nearest stationary objects to maintain balance.

"Earthquake?" somebody shouted, and in a way, it was. Turning to the north, the people began to point and shout and the others, who were lost for words, stood with mouths open beholding the sight.

Something due north of them—just south of Mount Lanier—was shooting out of the ground and stretching into the sky.

Milly turned to Bob and shouted, "What is that?" over all the thundering and shaking.

He was gazing at it, in awe. "I have absolutely no idea," he proclaimed, just as a small pebble avalanche came tumbling down the hillside near them. The sands and rocks across the mountain road were dancing wildly around their feet, first with slight vibrations, and then, like popcorn.

"WHOAAAA!!" cried the newsmen, as well as the firemen, the large crowd holding palms over their eyes to behold the unworldly sight in the faint light of dawn.

For many moments they all just gaped at it—nobody saying a thing as the translucent beam shot into the sky like a rocket—with wide eyes they scanned the valley and mountaintops, watching it, until suddenly, Bob turned and looked at his own arms, saying.

"What the—?"

Milly watched as he lifted his forearms to his face, and there, running down his tanned, leathery skin, were droplets of clear liquid.

"What is that, Bob?" asked Millie, trying to gulp down her fear.

"It's . . . well, Milly," he said, frowning at his arms. "It looks like . . . *rain.*"

And at that, many more droplets began to fall, covering them, and soon, the drops came bigger and fatter and they were a torrent, and before long, they were all at the barricade standing beneath a full-blown shower, looking at each other in confusion, trying to understand.

Only when the cameramen turned and began to frantically film the beam, and the newscasters began their wild chattering to report it—all of them squawking on their cell phones to collegues in Mount Lanier like a bunch of wild ducks—did the firefighters turn their faces to the falling moisture and begin to raise their hands in celebration, cheering on the onslaught of rain.

They turned to each other and hugged one another, laughing and cheering, jumping up and down with huge grins lifted to the sky, all of them shouting a wild and enthusiastic welcome to the first rain they'd seen in over half a year.

With arms around one another, pulling each other into themselves tightly, they began to dance.

As for her, surrounded by the chaos, she looked up into the sky with all humility, a sort of sudden peace upon her face.

Her face, which was very beautiful in the soft glow of the fresh morning light, filled with rain like big tears from the sky.

Finally, bravely, she decided to open her mouth and taste the water—trying not to be shocked at what she might find, because for the last eighteen hours, after trying to figure out how her son could have possibly been stung by a box jellyfish, trying to unravel the mystery of what he could have possibly been involved in that brought him so much monetary success—she was ready to believe in something.

She was ready to believe *anything*.

And, just as she figured, this, too, would turn out as strange as everything else.

As the rain finally dropped into her mouth, she knew that something fishy was going on.

It was salty.

"Edgar?" she whispered. "Is that *you*?"

TWENTY-FIVE

EDGAR ROWED FOR his life well into the night.

Just twenty hours before, he'd known the serenity and comfort of a hospital bed; but now, he wasn't even sure he could make it five more minutes.

Shirtless and broken, covered in sweat, his hands blistered and injured leg screaming—too scared to even look behind him now, to see how close his watery fate loomed—he rowed.

He could hear it, though, just as he had all night: swooshing just like Niagara Falls right behind him, like a water monster, with its wet jaws open wide.

How terrible it would be to die this way! To end up drowned, bloated, water-logged and consumed by sea creatures in the black depths of the water-filled Earth— that was no way to go. The dreary prospect scared him so badly, he continued to huff the pre-dawn air and, buckling down, he ignored the pain and rowed some more.

With each painful stroke, he thought about how good it would feel to simply give in, to stop rowing, just to let his muscles rest. He felt like a marathon runner, exhausted and ready to fall down.

As Edgar thought these things over, thinking about dying and his parents and how much his hands burned, or how thirsty he was—about Shay and Flounder and how they might be doing in their evacuation, about Weedy and how his threats paled in comparison to the evil waterfall behind him—suddenly, he realized something strange was happening.

What was it? What was *different*?

Hunched over the raft, his head down, his eyes closed, he suddenly opened them and looked up and realized that the sky was white with dawn. He looked around and surveyed the sea.

All the dead Ambercod had vanished—there wasn't a single one left, all of them having plunged down the hole into the Earth. The ocean was smooth as a countertop now.

Shaking with weariness, he struggled to raise himself up, then, turning in the raft, he beheld the sea behind him: there, many yards from where he first began, was the tip of the hole. It now protruded slightly from the sea, the result of the now incoming low tide. No longer was the seawater pouring down into the Earth. No longer was the whirlpool around to threaten him.

The whirlpool had been shut off, like a faucet.

Suddenly, as he realized this, he broke down into waves of weeping, crawling up into a ball on the raft floor and shaking.

He had done it. He had survived.

"Oh, thank you, God," he whispered.

The only bad thing was that his way back home was forever sealed.

He was in this for the long haul now. But, at least for the time being, he would not sleep forever in a watery grave.

It felt so good to lay, he almost allowed himself to drift off from the exhaustion; but then, just before he gave way to sleep, something told him to sit up and row.

If you sleep, you will die, the voice told him. *Get away from the hole. The whirlpool returns with the high tide!*

He pulled himself up from the raft and took the oars in his blistered hands then rowed like a madman for the current, discovering a newfound energy. Somehow, some way, he mustered the strength to row vigorously away, punishing his burning arms and blistered hands, making a wild dash toward the sun, hoping to catch the oceanic river he'd discovered on the map pictured on his father's Mac.

On that current, he knew he could almost coast to the French Southern and Antarctic Islands—the ones he'd found on his childhood globe—that landmass with the jagged peaks and a French seaport. From his calculations, he suspected it might be only a few hundred miles away.

He could do it. He could make it.

He could do anything.

Though his body begged for sleep, he denied it. Though his stomach begged for food, he overruled it. He would row until his arms fell off if he had to—anything to shake the horrible whirlpool that would soon reemerge behind him, and to attain safety at the port of the French Southern and Antarctic Lands many days before him.

If all there was to do was to be a seaman now, then no sweat, he decided: that's what he was born to do.

Almost as if fate had heard him thinking the thought, he noticed something flash in the water nearby—just beyond the raft in the light of the rising sun. Leaning the oars against the side wall of the raft, he looked over the ends and there, swarming in the deep water below him, like an oceanic nightmare, was a school of toothy sharks, tracking him as he rowed.

They were following him, obviously, congregating around his raft and ultimately lured here by all the bits of dead Ambercod that had been scattered across the ocean by the dynamite.

"Oh no," he whispered.

Inadvertently, he had chummed the waters.

He fretted as he rowed, but rowed even still, making his break for the French Southern and Antarctic Lands, pausing only now and again to take a greedy slurp from one of his water bottles or to check on his position by studying the rising sun.

Only hours later with the sun towering high in the sky did Edgar finally consider himself to be far enough from the whirlpool for a rest and a bite to eat. Dropping the oars on the raft, he collapsed into a heap of exhaustion and wild relief.

Then, once his hands stopped burning, he rolled over to the supplies and snatched out a thick bag of beef jerky and stuffed it into his mouth, chewing delightedly, then washed all the delicious meat down with a hefty slug of lukewarm water.

As he chewed, he leaned over the side and looked overboard. There, just below the raft, continued to lurk ten or twelve sinister, longish sharks, all meandering in circles, some large, some small. They must be attracted to the splash of his rowing, he decided, which made him tense with fear.

After he polished off the jerky, he rowed for a half hour more; but when he could not keep his swollen eyes open any longer, he surrendered to exhaustion and collapsed into the raft, falling into a deep, dreamless sleep.

The sharks will just have to wait, he thought.

WITH THE first blast of water erupting in Mount Lanier, Milly looked down at her phone. It was buzzing in her hand.

It was the hospital.

"Mrs. Dewitt?" the nurse said. "We really don't know how to tell you this, but your son fled from the hospital in the middle of the night." There was a pause on the other end. "We are so, so sorry. We know you have a lot on your shoulders right now."

"Fled?" she demanded. "What do you mean, '*fled?*'"

"Again," assured the nurse. "We are so, so sorry we failed to see him go. He snuck out between shifts. He stuffed his bed sheets with pillows."

"Yeah," muttered Milly. "He does that. Well, don't worry. I'll find him."

Hanging up the phone, she made for the Jeep and fired it up, then hit the gas and began the winding, mountainous trek to Mount Lanier.

As she drove, she studied the beam of salt water shooting up in the sky through the rhythmic swipes of her windshield wipers. It was an otherworldly sight, the alien water, leaving her yearning to know what it was, and if somehow it was related to the now-missing Edgar.

Reaching to the dash, she flipped on the radio to see what people were saying. Every station on the dial frantically covered it. The DJs' voices were frenzied.

"*The salty geyser,*" they said, "*is currently flooding all the low-lying lands of Mount Lanier!*" The reception suddenly vanished to static, so she flipped the dial to another station. "*. . . is turning the streams into rushing rapids right now, so please be advised.*" In the same breath, the reporter added, "*Fortunately, it can't be denied how wonderful this turn of events is for the firefighters fighting the wildfire! Somehow, some way, good people of Mount Lanier, it's* *raining! And we will take it!"*

Milly quickly learned that the fire had been snuffed in some places and was becoming more manageable by the minute in others.

Somehow, some way, it seemed as though Mount Lanier might find itself spared from the wildfire after all.

"The firefighters are totally energized now!" barked a DJ on WGDC. *"They're attacking it on all fronts now, with help from the strange underground rain. It's the first real progress that has been made in this fight."*

Stranger yet were reports that had begun to file in of large fish and marine life dropping from the sky.

Reportedly, in the middle of a trailer park, a shark had fallen on top of a Corvette. It smashed the hood and windshield and sent the entire surrounding neighborhood into an uproar.

Across the town in a small shopping mall, a box jelly-fish had landed in a wishing fountain.

A box jellyfish, she thought.

"What can I do to make you believe me?" she remembered Edgar had said, as she lost herself in recollection. *"I went fishing on the Indian Ocean. I sold the fish at the Arteses' fish stand . . . I caught lobsters with my new girlfriend, Shay."*

Oh my God, she thought as the words repeated in her mind, over and over. Squinting at the beam of water shooting out of the northwest, she raced the Jeep along the back roads of the mountains, disregarding the fact there were cliffs beyond the shoulder of the road.

By the time she skidded into her driveway—praying frantically that Edgar might be there, but for some reason doubting it—she dashed through the door and yelled his name.

"Edgar!" she screamed, but there was no answer. She scoured the house front to back, whimpering more and more each time as she walked into yet another empty room.

"Edgar!" she called again and again, from the doorway of each, but she did not find him.

Once the house had been scoured, she returned to the kitchen where she came upon a letter that sat on the granite countertop addressed to "*Mom.*"

How she missed it when she first came in, she did not know.

Frantically, she tore it open.

Mom,

I hope there wasn't too much flooding in Mount Lanier. Pretty sure there's a chance that something could have gone wrong. And I'm aware I might have drowned some animals and stuff, but I really hope not.

Dr. Van Rossum thinks it would just make it rain, because of the force of the Indian Ocean pushing the seawater up through the Earth like an untied water balloon. It should just shoot water out and fall back to the ground in drops, but we will see.

I'm trying to make it rain for dad. Also, I'm sorry you couldn't believe me, but I wouldn't have believed me either. I know I've been lying a lot. Please forgive me.

And also, call Shay.

Milly read the letter twice, placing her fists knuckle-down on the cold countertop, allowing the fearful tears to rise and then fall out of fear for her son. Hanging her head in worry and exhaustion, she suddenly began to weep.

Her stringy, unwashed hair draped entirely over her face.

Finally, after a long and helpless cry, she lifted her head in a show of strength to see that there, across the counter on the answering machine, was a blinking red light. She lunged for it, hoping that it would be from Edgar.

"Hello? Mrs. DeWitt?" a soft voice played on the machine. "It's Shay Sinclair again. I got a letter from Edgar, who says he wants me to get in touch with you. Can you please call me when you get this? It's really important."

Milly took down the number and then bolted for the door.

She moved faster than she ever had, jamming the stick shift into fifth gear and praying to God to save her son as she barreled down the road.

For all she knew, headed to the police station as she was, they were probably all out at the spewing geyser, or whatever it was, trying to figure out why it was erupting from the Earth and flowing through Mount Lanier.

As she sped toward downtown, she almost missed a strange story that was playing on the radio—a station out of the town of Ellensburg. When she heard the phrase, "*. . . jumped through a hole in the Earth . . .*" she turned the radio up and pulled the Jeep over to the side of the road, to listen in.

This was a piece on the strange arrival of an illegal alien who had an incredible story.

"*. . . The foreign man,*" said the reporter, "*who speaks no English, has claimed to be a citizen of Somalia. He has asked authorities in Ellensburg—through aid of a translator—to assist his return home, to Africa. The man, purported to be Captain Cali Ibrahim Warsame, has been questioned thoroughly on how he has arrived here in Central Washington, to which he continues to answer, 'I am Captain Warsame, Captain of the Somali Navy, shipwrecked in pursuit of pirates near Madagascar. I was pulled onto a small island by a young American boy, who then pushed me into a hole that went all the way through the world . . .*"

"Oh my God!' screamed Milly, pounding the gas, wheeling the jeep around and making a full, squealing circle in the middle of the road. As she did, she forced a horrified truck driver to swerve out of her way, almost crashing over the side of the road. When she saw he was OK, she waved apologetically as he shook his fist at her, then peeled off down the road at full speed, dialing the number that Edgar had given her as she drove.

"Hello?" came a girl's voice on the other end. "Mrs. Dewitt?"

"Shay?" said Milly. "Oh, thank God!"

"I'm so glad you called!" said Shay. "It's so good to hear from you. Edgar left a letter, Mrs. Dewitt."

"Yeah," muttered Milly, fresh tears sparkling in her eyes as she rounded a bend. "He left me one, too," she said.

"What did it say, Mrs. Dewitt?" asked Shay.

"It said, 'I did it for Dad.'" And then, trying not to cry, she added, "I guess I finally know the origin of all that 'Ambercod' everybody's been talking about, huh?"

"Yes ma'am," answered the girl softly. "My dad thinks it's Chilean Sea Bass."

"Have you been there, Shay?" Milly asked. "To the island? With my son?"

"Yes ma'am," she admitted. "I have. It's the most wonderful place I've ever seen."

Milly nodded and pushed the jeep up to seventy miles per hour.

"So, Shay," Milly asked. "Tell me. What does your letter say?"

"Oh, well, it says: 'Go find mom,' and then it gives coordinates." There was a slight pause. "He says he didn't want to put coordinates in your letter because he didn't want to freak you out."

"Well," said Milly, "mission not accomplished."

By the time she arrived in the small town of Ellensberg, the water had stopped spewing in Mount Lanier. She parked in a handicapped spot and ran frantically inside the police station, almost shouting at the front desk clerk.

"Please!" she cried. "I need to speak to *Captain Ibrahim Warsame*."

"Oh? Captain Cali you mean?" said the young officer. "What do you need with him?"

"Please," begged Millie. "You must know, my son is in trouble. I think Captain Cali can help him."

"OK," said the desk clerk. "In that case, I'll go get him for you."

Once the man was escorted to her—towering over Milly Dewitt like an oak tree—she looked up and gave him a polite, reassuring smile, then dug into her purse for Edgar's picture. He watched her keenly as she did. Then, withdrawing the only picture of Edgar she carried— his little league photo, the one he hated so much—she showed it to Captain Cali and awaited his reaction.

The man's eyes lit up, and he reached out and tapped the picture urgently.

"*Eu O Conheco!*" he shouted, looking down at her, a knowing look in his eyes. Repeating himself, he cried, "*Eu O Conheco!*"

"Yeah, Captain," she said, dryly, "that's what I thought. You and Edgar must be friends."

TWENTY-SIX

EDGAR WOKE IN the evening sunburned from sleeping the day away. He was groggy, bloodshot, and thoroughly weakened from thirst. After gulping down his first gallon of water, he almost drank another. But better sense prevailed.

Once his blazing thirst was finally under control, his stomach growled and told him how hungry he was. He hadn't had a bite to eat since the hospital room back in Mount Lanier—except for that bag of beef jerky on his retreat from the whirlpool—and boy, was he ravenous.

Greedily, he dug through the supplies, seizing a family-sized bag of Fiery Hot Habañero Doritos, which he decided would be his reward for escaping the horrible whirlpool. Stuffing a humongous handful in his mouth, he closed his eyes and chewed in ecstasy. The tasty chips were better than anything he'd ever put in his mouth. One after another he crunched the spicy triangles, leaning his head back against the cushiony sidewall of the raft with eyes closed in delight.

Suddenly, the thought occurred: *shouldn't I save a few Doritos for later*? *Nah*, he thought, disregarding the notion. He *deserved* a family-sized bag of Doritos, after all.

After he'd had his fill and one-fifth of the bag remained, he licked his fiery-red fingertips and belched, then stowed the rest of the bag away. And after a few more sips of water to wash all the food down, he leaned over the side wall and checked on the sharks he hoped weren't still lurking below.

Same as before, there they were, swimming beneath him and following his raft along the current. They'd been following him all day, actually, and maybe it was the heat he was emitting through the plastic that kept them around. Or maybe it was the splashing of the oars. Either way, the sharks were intent on following him for as long as it took, and he realized they were probably there to stay.

Shaking off the dreary thoughts, he dug into the medicine bag and retrieved sunscreen, Chapstick, and a bottle of ointment. The ointment he applied to the fresh blisters on his hands; the medicine he splotched all across the jellyfish sting, which seemed to be getting better by the moment. He wrapped it with a fresh bandage and then popped two Tylenol for pain.

Then, taking a pair of socks from the clothes bag, he slipped them over his hands for mittens, which he hoped would ease the pain of blistering from the handling of the oars.

Next, he propped the radio against the sidewall of the raft and turned it on for background noise, frowning when nothing came on over the dial. Sure, he didn't expect there to be anything smack dab in the middle of the Indian Ocean, but still, it would have been nice. All up and down the dial he searched, end-to-end, but there was nothing.

It was, after all, the third-largest ocean in the world.

He shrugged and hooked up his iPod to it instead, resuming his position in the back of the boat, taking the oars firmly in his freshly mitted hands and rowing to the sound of Coldplay's latest album, his oars rising and falling with the beat, propelling him due west, cruising along the current.

Something yanked on his oar.

"What the hell!"

In a rash act of aggression, one of the smaller sharks had gotten bold and nipped one of his oars, causing him to panic. Breathlessly, he rose to his knees and sliced the plastic blade into the water, swinging with everything he had, narrow side down, to show the sharks he wasn't to be messed with.

"You bastards!" he screamed, glaring into the sea.

In the surface of the water, he noticed his face—his reflection—all scrunched-up into a horrified, full-toothed scowl. His stringy brown hair was disheveled, and he looked like a crazy person. The sharks were making him crazy.

HE ROWED into the night as the fresh sleep, food, water, and medicine powered him on. As his muscles throbbed and burned with each stroke, the stars put on a heavenly show above, making him think about how his parents might be doing.

He hoped his dad was still alive. And that he, Edgar, hadn't drowned the whole town of Mount Lanier with ocean water. The thought of the destruction it was probably causing in Mount Lanier made him paddle even faster—it made his muscles burn even more.

He just couldn't die without knowing what had happened, could he?

In the light of the high-hanging moon, on the surface of the sea he noticed a glimmering shark fin surfacing near the raft. It made his heart sink in fear. Shining a light on the waters, he ran a trembling hand through his hair.

They were getting bolder now, apparently, swarming much closer to his raft and much closer to the surface. The fear of his oars was quickly diminishing.

What would he do? he thought.

That's when, pondering these things, he saw something just beyond the school of sharks rolling up from the deep, dark sea: a large, fleshy creature that, in the faint light of the night sky, surfaced like a behemoth. It splashed and groaned like a kraken.

"Oh my . . . God!" he whimpered, straining to see it in the dim light. He couldn't exactly tell what it was, but whatever it was it was monstrous—the size of maybe four eighteen wheelers side-to-side, its wet body glistening in the moonlight.

"A whale," he murmured, "it must be." And suddenly, in his tiny little rubber raft, he'd never felt smaller.

Whatever it was, the sharks were not afraid of it, and unconscionably continued to nip at the surface near him and at his oar, testing him, mortifying him. Terrifying him.

FINALLY, WHEN morning came, the sun popped itself up clearly above the horizon, and Edgar, rubbing his weary eyes, noticed a school of dolphins were darting toward the boat.

He rose to his knees and cheered.

"Hey! Yes!" he cried, pumping his oars into the air. "Come get these dang sharks away from me, you guys!"

But they didn't. He'd always heard dolphins chased sharks away from helpless human beings, but he watched forlornly as the school quickly darted away, weaving around him and the sharks—the sharks not even changing their trajectories the slightest bit.

They didn't even stop their menacing lurking for a single, godforsaken second to even acknowledge the dolphins had even come by.

He really hated the sharks.

Reclining helplessly in the raft, a wet oar on his lap, he wished he had saved a single stick of dynamite. How good it would feel to light it and blow these jokers up . . . As he stared behind the raft at the retreating dolphins—all of them leaping across the waters now, all happy and rambunctious and free—a sleek sensation ran across his butt below the raft, even lifting him several inches.

"Oh my . . . God!" he shouted.

One of the bastards had brushed the underside of his boat.

Petrified, he lunged to one side and peered over into the sea, trying to figure out which shark had just bumped him, but even as he glared at them, he could feel it happening again: this time, right across his knees went the slick body and fin below the raft, its blunt nose followed by a rigid tail.

He was panicked now. Whimpering with fear, he snatched up the oars and did the only thing left he could do: he paddled like a wild man—like the relentless pumping of an oil rig in Texas—hoping that maybe a few miles down the current might tire them out, maybe prevent them from getting too much bolder. After all, it would take only one bite for the raft to deflate and then, he'd be a goner.

Throughout the afternoon and late into the evening, he'd sometimes feel the raft lurch again and again from below. It began to dawn on him: his rowing had not deterred them one bit. Mercilessly, as if in the grip of frenzy now—or maybe it was hunger—they continued to bump and test the boat, and, as the bumps came more frequently, so did his desperate whimpers of anguish and prayers to above. His face was soon scrunched into a permanent, stone-like expression of misery, which turned side to side incessantly, looking for sharks, his oars slapped wildly at the waters each time they surfaced.

Even still, the sharks were not deterred.

"Please God," he muttered, rowing ever faster.

WHEN DAWN approached, Edgar found himself so delirious from all the rowing that his fear was unable to keep him awake any longer. Collapsing into the boat, lying flat in exhaustion, his eyelids so heavy they were like big slabs of lead, in no time he was asleep—sleeping a deep, black sleep, rocking slightly from the peaceful waves.

Suddenly, jolting from a peaceful dream, Edgar was lurched airborne above the raft, screaming as he rose above the sea.

The largest shark from the school had come shooting up, delivering a punishing blow to the underside of the raft, and sending him flying. The strike was violent and came with great velocity—obviously intended to knock him from the boat, which it did, halfway.

Just as Edgar was cast into the air several feet he twisted his body and reached for the bouncing raft— knowing that if he fell into the water he would instantly die a horrible, gruesome death.

As he slammed back onto the raft, the subsequent bounce flipped him over the side into the ocean. Half his body plunged into the sea as he grabbed to the side wall of the raft. A salty blast of water shot up his nose and went down his throat as he entered the cool water, and as it did, he screamed with horror into the vast blue. Knowing the sharks would strike at any moment, he scrambled backward out of the ocean and fell panicking into the bottom of the raft, balling up into a ball, trying not to hyperventilate.

He balled his fists and rose to his knees and quaked with anger, pointing a crooked and blistery finger down at the sea.

"*You!*" he screamed, hissing like a madman, glaring at the water as an insane snarl crept across his face. "I've got something *for you!*"

Standing there, his finger pointing in defiant anger, he suddenly noticed that, across the water, half of his stuff was launched overboard and scattered out to sea, some of it sinking, some of it floating. Floating in the sea were six water bottles currently being attacked by the frantic, swarming creatures, and the jugs with bite marks had quickly filled with undrinkable seawater and were submerging as he watched.

"Dangit!" he cried, coming to his senses, frantically grabbing the oars and paddling to them as fast as he could. When he got to them, he reached out the oars to corral them in, but even as he did, the emboldened and aggressive sharks struck at them, as well as his oars. One nearly ran off with one, and Edgar actually had to play tug-of-war for a moment. Edgar snatched it away and concentrated on bringing the bottles to the boat. Finally, he was able to bring one in. It had a few bite marks in it. He lifted it to his lips and took a taste. And then another. And then another.

When they were all back in the boat, five of the six bottles were ruined with salt water. They were undrinkable. Only one could be salvaged.

That left him with only three water bottles to get to the French Southern and Antarctic Lands.

Man, he thought. They had really screwed him this time.

Disgustedly, he tossed the salty jugs to the swarm and then attuned his fiery glare at the devil fish.

"You," he said, "you sons of bitches. You *all* die, now."

The fishing pole, his iPod, all of his medicine—he could still see them sinking in the deep blue below the swarm, all off to Davy Jones's locker. And, worst yet, his radio was sinking along with them: his last remaining life-line to another human voice. He watched it all fade into the depths, and it was enough to almost make him cry.

Almost.

The half bag of Doritos still floating in the center of the mayhem, he watched as it got snapped under, too, noticing the jagged teeth of a shark glistening in the sunlight beneath it, almost as if it was smiling—almost as if they were all *laughing.*

Then, unconscionably, *another* violent bump lifted him from the floor of his raft below—this one almost bounding him over the side wall again, just like the last one—well, this was the final straw.

He regained his composure and rebounded from the blow, then gritted his teeth and made for his stash.

A dark, desperate rage clouded his face. His mind was swirling like a hurricane. Hatred oozed from his pores, like acidy sweat.

"You want to bump me?" he asked to the monsters. "Well, this is what you get."

Reaching beneath the bottom of the pile he dug it from his supplies and cradled it in his lap, all cool to the touch and sinister. It was the last item he'd packed when back on the island, the very last thing he thought he would need while drifting alone on the sea: it was the black, sleek, Somalian instrument of death—the Somalian man's machine gun.

Rising to his feet, grinning with power, he leaned over the side wall with his jellyfish leg propped high, and, like a one-legged pirate, he pointed the snub nose down into the sea and, giggling like crazy, he pulled the trigger and expected to give them hell.

Click

He blinked blankly at the gun.

"Oh," he said, flipping it upside down. The safety was still on.

Flipping the safety off, he realigned his weapon at the sea and took aim at the largest shark among them: the one he suspected had bumped his boat and knocked him into the air.

"Hey!" Edgar shouted to it. "This *here* is the top of the food chain!"

Then he pulled the trigger and the gun was a fiery burst of violence. Instantly it danced upward with raw, shocking power and fury, making Edgar scramble to control it. But, then, he stabilized and re-aimed the gun back at the dastardly swarm of sharks, still grinning like a madman, and through the fire and smoke and lurching seawater he watched as big splotches of red blood began to spill out all over the sea like a bloody oil spill.

Blood. What a wonderful sight!

Spraying bullets everywhere, he tore into the flesh of the bully sharks like buckshot through paper, jerking the gun around and giving them all something for every bit of rage and fear that had built up in him over the past many hours. And oh, did it feel wonderful. Unleashing his fury, he glared at the sea, and with each spattering from the UZI, he realized that unbeknownst to him, he'd been screaming the entire time.

Click

What a bummer. He was finally out of bullets.

There, just beyond the boat, was a gang of large and small bodies floating at the top of the sea, all riddled with red, violent, jagged holes, all belly up—all of them deader than doornails.

He began to laugh for a long time—it was so wonderful to be free of those terrible creatures. With a hand, he wiped his sweaty forehead and with the other, he cradled the hot gun in his lap so it would not melt the plastic.

"Yeah," he said, looking over the side, trying to make sure that he got them all. "That's what you get, jerks."

LATER, WHEN the gun was cool and stowed and he'd resumed his rowing upon the current, he noticed at the south horizon a bunch of clouds had been accumulating there.

These were not just any old clouds: they were storm clouds. Haymakers.

Simply put, they didn't look good.

Reluctant and weary, he put his head down and thrust the oars once again into the sea, knowing that he probably couldn't outrun them, but also knowing he had to try. What else was he supposed to do? All he could do was row.

And row and row and row.

That's when, crushing him, he realized another terrible, terrible thing: he heard a familiar small splash occuring near the raft. Whipping around, he strained to see what it was.

There, just a few feet away, a small shark nipped the surface. Edgar rose to his feet and dropped the oars, staring wide-eyed into the sea.

There, just a few yards away, swam another one. And another one.

He looked beyond them. There, coming up from the deep below, was a *second* school of sharks, their occasionally visible white underbellies flashing like mirrors in the waning light.

"Oh, God, no," he whimpered, his heart sinking. The new school was much larger than the previous one— maybe thirty sharks—that no doubt had been attracted by all the gunfire and splashing, and especially, all the blood.

Once again, he'd chummed the waters.

With haste, he grasped the oars and frantically began to row, but after only an hour, more joined the school, and their numbers surged to maybe fifty. They were all keenly on his trail, just like the others had been, and before long, just like the others, they, too, began to circle the boat menacingly.

"What did I ever do to you?" he whimpered to God through the assembling storm clouds. He looked up for an answer, but there was none. God seemed intent on torturing and killing him, probably for lying to his parents, maybe for sneaking out at night, possibly for his "impure" thoughts about Shay—all of this, even though, to him, his crimes did not meet the punishment. Dying by way of a swarm of hungry sharks seemed incongruent, and cruel.

It was as if every time he made a bit of headway, something more awful swam up from below. Instead of fretting, however, knowing there would be no other way to fight the sharks as he was out of bullets, he did the only thing he knew of to do: he put his head down and rowed. He rowed like crazy.

He'd row all night if he had to.

TWENTY-SEVEN

THIS NEW SCHOOL of sharks wasn't bumping the boat like the other ones did, so at least there was that.

They hadn't *yet*, anyway. Maybe they just weren't hungry enough.

Yet.

While they were a real concern, what ultimately began to worry Edgar was the southern storm coming up on him. He just couldn't seem to outrun it, and it was a fully-formed storm now, a real rager, swirling above like a monster just due south, still many miles away, but getting closer all the time. Although he paddled furiously, he knew it was useless; it was indeed coming his way, and there would be nothing he could do about it.

Even still, as always, he rowed.

Capsizing now had become his greatest fear. Checking on the sharks, he rested the oars on the side walls and leaned across the boat, looking down at them.

They were still lurking. Always lurking.

And when the storm finally caught up to him, he tossed the remaining supplies evenly across the raft's bottom, for balance.

"This is called 'ballast,' son," said his father, who floated in an imaginary raft, just behind him.

"What?" asked Edgar. "Oh, yeah. I know what it's called. You've already told me like two times already."

He quickly realized he was hallucinating. He counted backward from one hundred as he prepared the raft bottom, hoping to make the hallucination disappear. When the apparition asked how many days he'd been adrift on the sea, Edgar inadvertently answered it.

"It's been, hmm . . . ten days I think," he said, figuring. "No, two weeks maybe?"

Of those days, however many there were, with the sharks pursuing him and the sun beating down, he'd probably slept a total of twelve hours. And that's why he knew he was having hallucinations.

Watching the storm take over the sky, he took a break from the useless rowing and stirred in the supplies, withdrawing a can of Vienna Sausages. Greedily, he wolfed them right down, then ate an entire MRE, as well as two king-sized candy bars.

But on the jug of water, he sipped lightly—even though the storm promised to bring him more. Using caution with his supply, he made himself stop just as the last of the caramel's saltiness was washed away.

"Who knows?" Edgar said to his dad, answering the previous question. "Who knows how long I've been floating in this boat?"

He bobbed gently up and down and lifted his nose to the air, beginning to feel the cool, electric vibe of the storm. He picked his teeth and watched the angry skies organizing overhead.

Death from above, death from below.

And then, like a bulldozer, the winds came surging in, and with them the rising swells. Like a rollercoaster, his tiny raft began to climb the multi-storied waves, as high as hills, and then plummeted down the other side. It was enough to make him instantly seasick.

As he clung to the raft's sides, his fear ramping up with each lightening stike, he tried to remember to stay in the middle of the raft, to keep it balanced. As the rain came spattering in, and then in torrents, he opened his mouth wide and campaigned for a free drink of water.

It was getting darker by the minute. He glanced over the side and used the lightning to see, and when it flashed, he saw clearly the entire school of evil sharks lurking underneath like a photo shoot—a virtual army of them.

Whimpering, he reached into his pile of supplies and yanked out the big yellow raincoat. There, in the center of the boat, he grabbed the plastic handles on the raft and zipped up the coat, laying back to stare at the swirling skies.

Soon, when he saw the power of the storm and the state of the angry sea, he wondered how he would ever survive the night.

When the swells got to thirty feet—far higher waters than he'd ever seen before—he finally relented and screamed to the clouds.

"PLEASE! LEAVE ME ALONE! *PLEASE!*"

But his voice was nothing to the chaos building around him. And, as if an answer from God, a bolt of lightning popped the ocean just yards from his vessel, lifting the hairs on his neck, like static. Immediately following was a loud, soul shrinking crash of thunder, making Edgar jerk his head away and scowl.

As if things weren't bad enough, terribly, his raft began to take on water. In moments the water was rising up the sides, so he scrambled to his knees and swept the water out frantically, using an empty water jug that he'd cut at the top with his Swiss Army knife.

He knew the raft wouldn't last the night: who was he kidding? A three-hundred-dollar raft from Walmart that was only meant for lakes and pools? The plaything was already overburdened to its limit, and now it was taking on too much water, and enduring far too many violent waves.

Regardless, all night he clung to the feeble thing, riding each wave up and down in the center of a merciless ocean, praying aloud often, twisting his body against the swirling sea to prevent the waves from toppling him. The ocean was pitch black from the stormy night, so much that he was unable to see his hand in front of him. It was darker than the center of the Earth. Leaning over the edge, he shined his flashlight on the sea, but in all the driving, sideways rain, he could not even see below the top of the surface.

It made him wonder if the sharks were still following him with all the calamity on the surface.

Yeah, probably.

ALL NIGHT he fought the storm and somehow stayed afloat.

The next morning, inexplicably, *impossibly*, the storm finally died down. Off in the gray distance there was a smudge of sunlight trying to break through the thick, black clouds, and as the rain slacked, so did the wind.

For once, Edgar began to believe that he might have just skirted death one more time. But just as he thought it, the terrible tempest unleashed one last, remaining blow, mercilessly launching him into a dire fight for his own survival.

A gargantuan wave—no less than forty feet high—came rolling like a bowling ball over the disrupted seas. Edgar, worn and beaten, watched it almost indifferently from the side of the raft as it came barreling forth. He knew he was in huge trouble because of the way the wave was cresting.

Suddenly, as if waking from a dream, he snapped to and fell to the raft floor, spreading out across the raft, distributing his weight, gripping the sides tightly and holding his breath, preparing for the blow.

It was going to be rough. This one was dangerous.

And then, as he looked up, it reached into the sky above him—like the watery hand of God Himself, then crashed down with the finality of a judge's gavel. Suddenly the wave was on him and like nothing the tiny raft was flipped headlong into the sea, casting Edgar and all his supplies into the cold, dark, shark-infested Indian Ocean.

As he hit the water, he screamed bloody murder as the wave plunged him into the deep, bracing himself for the shark teeth he knew would be upon him any second. With eyes tightly shut and arms flailing all around, he fought for the surface of the sea. Each stroke he made for the top, he expected to be his last—expected at any moment the bites to come furiously and all over, but for some strange, wonderful reason, none came.

Finally, he opened his eyes as he continued to fight for the surface, and took a good look around in the freshly brightening dawn, slowly straining to see.

The sharks were gone. *They were gone!*

The storm had dispersed them.

He was energized and felt gleeful his whole body over, making for the surface like an Olympian, bursting into the wet, open air and gasping for breath. Then, drifting atop the bouncy sea, he paddled around in a circle in search for his raft.

But he didn't see it anywhere. Where was his raft?! Had it sunk? Suddenly he began to think he'd come this far—surviving the whirlpool, the first group of sharks, the *second* group of sharks, the storm—just to drown. It didn't seem fair.

But then, through the mist of the storm, there was a bright speck of orange drifting aimlessly beyond another huge wave. It was there!

Mustering all his strength to make a break for it, he lost sight of it immediately as it summited another wave, then retreated down the backside. Again he spotted it as it climbed a wave again, and again it was gone. Gulping mouthfuls of splashing seawater, knowing that soon this might be it if he didn't make it to the raft and reel it in with muscles burning and chapped lips stinging—with all the feelings of futility swirling inside of him, like all his struggling had been for nothing, he fought.

When, suddenly, *miraculously*, a wonderful thing happened: from the opposite direction, out of nowhere, a counter-wave came spilling forth big as a tow boat, smashing against the wave currently lifting his raft twenty feet in the air, shifting the raft gloriously in his direction and, just for the moment, almost brought it within arm's reach.

"PLEASE!" he screamed, with all his might disregarding the burn in his muscles and lungs and blistery hands, and Edgar swam like he'd never swam before.

"This is called the breaststroke!" shouted his father over the churning waters, swimming beside him in the sea. "This is the reason why the Olympians do it this way, because it's the smartest way. It's *aerodynamic*."

"I know!" gurgled Edgar, as yet another wave plowed into him. And just when he thought he could swim no more, pausing to look up from the sea, there it was: his raft, only ten feet away now.

Kicking frantically in one final, frantic lunge, he somehow caught hold of the plastic and in his wrinkled, outstretched fingers. And, before another wave could take it from him, he desperately climbed aboard and hugged the side walls like a bear.

"Thank you, God," he panted.

Without a doubt, the raft had taken a grand beating. All its contents were long gone, tossed away into the sea: the water, the food, everything. Even the oars.

Once he'd caught his breath, he rose to his knees and scanned the ocean for any signs of them, and just a few feet away, he noticed the flash of something shiny on the surface.

It was one of the water bottles—its plastic was partially afloat, upheld by a small pocket of air at the top.

He scrambled for it, using his hands for paddles. It took a while to get himself there, fighting the still-raging sea, but finally he was there, leaning out over the choppy waters with a trembling hand. He stared down below the bottle as he reached for it, trying to see if the sharks were there, but it was just too murky and stirred up to see below. Finally, his trembling fingers touched the precious water bottle, but it slipped away, bouncing on the choppy waves. He tried again, this time straining even harder, reaching out as far as he possibly could, until finally, he snatched it by the handle, scooping it toward him, bringing it quickly to his chest, cradling it.

"Thank you, God," he murmured again.

ALL DAY, as the storm sputtered and spat and then died, he sat with the water bottle in his lap and tried to recover.

As weary as he felt, for some reason, he was still unable to sleep.

Later that afternoon, when the ocean had calmed and evened out to a slick sheen, he fell into a delirious sleep and awoke hours later, in the middle of the night, to a million, bright, twinkling stars that hung high in the sky above.

"The best skies are always after a storm," his father who floated just off the raft, right on top of the water, explained. "Remember the sky right after hurricane Katrina? Remember that night?" he prodded. "The lights were off in the city because the power was out, remember? That sky was like a real planetarium."

"Yeah," admitted Edgar. "That was definitely a good sky."

"Yes, *sir*," corrected his father.

"Yes, *sir*," said Edgar. "But this sky is better."

THE HARD sun returned the next morning beating down on him mercilessly, and soon his stomach began to growl, but what could he do?

"You can't get blood from a turnip," his floating dad informed.

Scanning all the horizons with wild, bloodshot eyes, he finally admitted to himself that if someone didn't come along pretty soon . . .

He sat in the center of his tattered little boat, continuing to cradle the water bottle like it was life itself. Taking stock of his situation, he admitted to himself that he had no oar and no compass, no radio, no food, and no *nothing*. He was undeniably, miserably, and dangerously lost at sea.

Without a doubt, he was dead in the water.

Even still, it would be days before the *real*, deep hunger set in—the most troubling, profound hunger that he'd ever known before—to which he could only respond with fretting, searching the water for anything edible, and then, with sleep.

Starving became an acute sort of all-encompassing sensation that made his jellyfish sting seem like an unpleasant, long ago dream.

Sleeping all he could, sometimes, when he awoke with puffy eyes and blistered lips, he would measure out a tiny capful of water and bring it to his lips, sucking out every drop. After the sip, food would become his hourly preoccupation as he dreamed of his mother's spaghetti, double bacon cheese burgers, steaks, potatoes—even the English peas and carrots and yams he'd turned his nose up to back in the pantry.

I'd tear a yam up, he admitted wearily, trying to be funny and light in his thoughts. But it didn't help a bit.

In the daytime, as the unrelenting sun punished his overly tanned skin, Edgar, with no way to block it, could only resign to sitting there and taking it.

After all, there was no way he was jumping underneath the raft for a bit of a shady reprieve; there was no way he was jumping in for any reason.

He'd swum in this sea for the absolute last time.

ONE AFTERNOON he heard a sound and listened intently. "Thunder?" he uttered hoarsely. "Is that another storm?"

Weakly, he rose to his knees and scanned the billowy clouds, hoping that it might actually be rain. If so, he could fill his almost-empty water bottle a little. But when he saw it, he realized it was far better than rain. It was the most wonderful sight he'd ever seen.

Gazing out over the sea with his empty, almost pupilless eyes, he discovered that just below the line of cloud cover, there circled a small, passenger-style airplane. Edgar watched it descend and fly very low to the sea, as if it were searching for someone.

As if it were searching for *him*.

"HEY!" he screamed wildly, leaping to his feet, bouncing up and down in the beaten raft and waving his arms like a lunatic.

"I'm HERE!" he screamed at the sky, but to his absolute heartbreak and interior deterioration, suddenly, mercilessly, the plane veered west. When it dawned on him that he had not been seen and he would *not* be saved, his eyes filled with demoralized, painful tears, and he was left only to watch as the plane flew away, toward the horizon, the hum of its engines silencing with the growing distance.

When it was finally gone, he collapsed onto the hot vessel and wept harder than he'd ever wept before.

BY THE end of the next day, his last sip of water was gone.

He tapped the last of the drops from it and then began to bite and claw through the top of the plastic, to make a container of it—just in case it rained again.

If it rained again, maybe he could catch some rainwater—*if* it rained again. He knew that the awful sea he battled and its propensity to give him exactly the opposite of what he actually needed would make water a rare commodity.

His new pastime became scanning the skies for signs of clouds around the clock—and, for airplanes. But there was always *nothing at all* in the brutal, continuous blue—nothing but relentless drought, same as it was back in Mount Lanier.

One merciless drought replaced by another.

When his tongue began to swell from thirst and heat, without saliva, his cracked lips split open and bled.

Around the clock, he began to hallucinate now, making him gaze out to sea several times and witness a spattering of oil rigs across in the Indian Ocean, and oil spills, and always, oily, dead animals.

"Have I ever told you," confessed his father, "that I'm so sorry about the oil spill? I know that must have been tough on you, son." Edgar was resting his head against the side wall and woozily waved it off, shaking his head forgivingly.

"Nah, Dad, it's not a problem," he whispered. "I got through it—I got *here*, didn't I?"

"Well," said his father, "I *am* sorry. I just wanted you to know. And another thing. You should know your mom is fine. Just know she misses you a lot."

"Man. I miss her too," he said, a big lump rising in his throat.

ONE DAY he woke with a strange sense of clarity. After so many days of deliriousness and fuzziness in his head, it felt weird to be so sober and alert—weird, but good.

He glanced to the back of the boat and expected to see his dad back there, but no. Which was good. It meant he wasn't loony for the moment.

Stirring from the bottom of the raft, he took advantage of his apparent second wind and began to paddle furiously with stinging, blistered hands toward the east— still ever-pressing for the French Southern and Antarctic Lands.

He paddled for hours—at first vigorously, then tiring out over time, until, eventually, he slumped to the side wall of the raft and collapsed. With bloodshot eyes and a thoroughly broken spirit, he leaned over the edge and vomited into the sea, but nothing came out. Through hot, straining tears, he stared deeply into the waters and horrorstruck, it occurred to him that he was floating once again on a sea of black oil.

Belly-up carcasses of so many animals of the deep bobbed around him, their dead eyes glazed over with rot.

"Help!" a voice screamed from nearby, and Edgar rose up to see who had said it

He just couldn't believe it. It was Flounder.

"Flounder?" whispered Edgar. "What are you doing here?"

"Edgar!" Flounder screamed again, from the back of a small boat just yards beyond Edgar's bow. In the boat with Flounder was Chris Weedy, who, obviously, like a pirate, was holding Flounder hostage.

Weedy beamed at Edgar as he manned the motor, drifting around Edgar's beaten raft.

"My boat has a motor," he bragged. "Isn't that fantastic? I bet you wish you had a motor, huh?"

"Weedy?" asked Edgar. "Don't you ever just *stop*?"

"Edgar," Weedy answered, a broad smile on his face. "Why did you always fight with me? You always felt like you had to put me down, didn't you? Like crashing me in Nitro Streak, or making me look like a fool in Van Rossum's class. You should have never come to Mount Lanier! You should have asked to stay in Bon Secour! Remember when your grandmother offered to take you in so you could finish high school back home? Where everything was familiar and you could have gone to that private high school where all your friends were, and joined the high school fraternity there, and you could have gone to college—and in all of that you could have played it safe, and had a normal life. You could have stuck with the familiar." Weedy beamed at him. "You wouldn't be where you are right now."

"What do you want with Flounder?" demanded Edgar, his voice weakening.

"Well," explained Weedy, "you see, Flounder cheap-shotted me, back at the cabin. So now, I'm going to sink him to the bottom of the ocean. I'm gonna make him walk the plank!" He giggled at his clever plan. "See? Edgar? Isn't it great, Edgar? Nobody knows we're out here, and I will never get caught actually killing a kid. Man, seafaring is so much fun."

Weedy then lifted a cinder block from his small boat so that Edgar could see, and on one end was tied a rope, and on the other end, Flounder's bound hands.

"Oh no," muttered Edgar. "Don't do that."

Weedy cackled as Edgar took a wobbly step toward the front of the raft and fell, paddling himself over.

"No use, redneck," taunted Weedy. "You're done. And Flounder's crab meat now."

"No!" pleaded Edgar. "Please stop, Weedy! I'll give you anything you want! You win! What is it you want? *What is it you want?*"

But Weedy still lifted the cinder block into the air anyway, dangling it threateningly over the side, for Edgar to see.

"There's nothing I want but this," he growled, lowering the weight into the sea. "I want to see you beg. I want to see you miserable. That makes me happy."

"OK," said Edgar. "Well, you got me. I'm miserable, see? You win. I'm very sorry I crossed you, Weedy."

Just as Flounder was about to be drowned, Edgar noticed something horrible. There, from the bottom of Weedy's boat, emerged Shay. She stood, her own wrists bound with cord, and her mouth bound with a tight gag.

She wept profusely and fearfully, staring at Edgar.

"Shay!" he shouted, then reached over into the sea and began paddling with all the fury that remained in him. But, even as he did, Weedy cackled delightedly, touching the gas on the motor, backing easily away from his raft.

"I thought they had oars in Alabama, you hick." Weedy giggled at this, then turned and commanded Shay, "Get up front with Flounder."

Edgar watched them helplessly as Weedy took hold of her hair and yanked it violently, urging her along.

"You!" shouted Edgar, pointing at Weedy. "You're dead!"

"How?" laughed Weedy, yanking Shay's head side to side again, to demonstrate his power over the situation.

In a fit, Edgar tried to stand on his wobbly legs but his knees gave way and he flopped back to the raft again, which made Weedy howl even louder.

"Ha! Ha!" the bully cried. "What are you going to do, Edgar?" Are you gonna blow me up with some fake dynamite or pretend to fall down a fake hole? You've got nothing, Edgar! As usual, *nothing*!!"

Edgar rested his chin helplessly on the side wall of the raft and watched Weedy lord over his friends.

"What else do you have, Edgar, besides a bunch of little tricks? Besides a bunch of little *lies*?" Weedy puffed out his chest in victorious triumph. "Lies are all you got, Edgar! You're like a skunk—all stink, no claw. And man, all that lying won't help you out here in the sea—in a sea like this? A sea like this brings out the truth in people. It *demands* the truth."

"Wait," said Edgar, shaking his head, holding a hand up at Chris Weedy. "This is just a dream." Suddenly he realized this, lifting his chin off the raft, staring out to the sea as a profound peace overtook him and then, magnificently, he was lucid. It was all just a byproduct of his being sun-crazed, food-crazed, and thirst-crazed, and nothing more.

"Now you're using your brain!" said his father, who drifted along behind him. "This *is* a dream, Edgar. And in your dreams, you can do anything you want." His father nodded over at Edgar's hands, who looked down and noticed that they were glowing, like a sort of power was suddenly dancing through his blistered fingertips—like electricity. He smiled at it, because it was really cool, turning them over and watching the electrodes dance. With this newfound power, he rose in the raft and glared across the waters at Chris Weedy.

Weedy, Edgar noticed, immediately saw Edgar's strangely glowing hands and just as quickly, he stopped smiling.

"Let them go," Edgar warned him, "because I have the power now."

"OK! OK!" Chris shouted, surrendering immediately as he lifted his hands in obvious defeat. "You got me, Edgar."

Then, just as soon as he surrendered, he turned and kicked Flounder overboard, tossing the cinder block behind him into the sea, then cackled like a loon.

"NOOOO!" screamed Edgar, as Flounder flopped overboard like dead weight, sinking helplessly down into the depths, the cinder block yanking him under toward the ocean floor like an anvil. Weedy turned and grinned at Edgar, chuckling evilly, a look of furious triumph in his eyes.

"Now *she* goes!" he cried, snatching Shay by the shoulders, who, not going easily, fought and clawed at his face. But he soon fought off her resistance and was able to reach around her body, placing her in a headlock. Then, once he'd restrained her, he flung her overboard into the sea, like a cast net. She crashed into the water but, with one hand, she reached up and snagged the side of the boat, refusing to go down. When he saw this, Weedy cursed violently and stepped toward her, kicking at her hand.

"LEAVE HER ALONE!" screamed Edgar, who, even as he screamed it, knew that words would no longer suffice. Weedy's evil ran marrow deep. He was simply no good, and he was no good to the core.

As some sort of strange, alien knowledge began to stir inside of him, he looked down at his now furiously glowing hands and lifted them up to the sky. From where the power emerged he did not know, but in some strange tongue—maybe Somalian, or maybe the language written on the bricks of the hole back home—he began to speak over his hands that had burst into white-hot mittens of flames.

As the clouds were apparently subservient to his glowing hands, they began to swirl like a whirlpool in the sky: rains and furious winds began churning tempestuously, obeying his direction, ramping higher and higher and higher as Edgar swirled his hands apart and then together, guiding the sea world all around, focusing every bit of pointed energy at the terrible and murderous Chris Weedy.

Then, with a fury, he cast the flames at Weedy's boat and glared with his own evil, delicious grin, shooting his hands, unleashing on Weedy's tiny vessel the horrible storm and all its power. In an instant, Weedy was swept from his feet and flung headlong into the air like a tiny piece of litter in a sandstorm.

"HA!" screamed Edgar, a wild grin emerging, as he began to move Chris Weedy around in the air. As he screamed and pled for mercy, Weedy was bolted across the sky, like a ragdoll kite, as Edgar flopped him around, basking in the sound of his misery. In fact, the more Weedy screamed, the more he tossed him about, because that's what he'd do, wouldn't he, Weedy, the awful, terrible, merciless punk that he was?

Suddenly, from the depths of his trance, Edgar began to hear *other* screams.

This time it was his father. And it was Shay. And it

was even Flounder's voice—all of them were yanked up from the sea by his conjured winds and tossed all about, same as Weedy was. Horrified as they streaked across the sky, right alongside the bully, all upheld by his newfound power, he relented. Flounder's leg was still wrapped in the rope tied to the cinder block and he squealed particularly torturously as it swung him around in the air. Edgar tried to bring Flounder down to the sea with his hands, but suddenly, he couldn't seem to get the controls right. No matter how hard he tried he just couldn't slow down Flounder's erratic sweeping across the sky—nor Shay's, nor his father's. They all spun helplessly in the sky now, like erratic birds, somehow hovering on their own and not coming down. Apparently, there was nothing more Edgar could do. He had lost the power. His hands no longer glowed.

He had lost everything.

"Please!" he asked the sky. "Please let them down! Please let them go!" But the skies refused to listen, as always. Relentlessly, his friends had been flipped and somersaulted in the air, up and down, side to side, and there simply was nothing he could do about it. Apparently he'd created a hurricane now, using only his fury and revenge—a storm even fiercer than any one he'd ever known—one that would doom them all. Soon, he knew, it would even toss him like dead weight into the sea and drown him, and all of them, once and for all.

That's when he realized he was being lifted into the air alongside his friends, the vicious storm carrying them all over the waters now, like leaflets, as they screamed themselves hoarse, jerking in the wind. Finally, without warning, Edgar was cast down by a vast power above and dumped viciously into the swirling sea, and as he plunged deep down, he could feel the pressure suddenly squeezing his temples, and depleting his lungs.

Drowning and choking violently now, he tried fighting for the surface with everything he had in him. It was all such a fight—everything was—from the hospital room to this very moment: everything resisting him, still, with his last breath, he continued to muster every last bit of strength to put up a fight—to press on. To survive the horrible ocean. Clawing to the surface, just as a merciless gale blew down on him from the sky, he finally opened his eyes and woke up, and saw the cause of the gale.

There, hovering just above his raft, was a helicopter, stilled in midair.

A medical stretcher dangled just above him, too, hanging by a rope and lowered from the helicopter. Edgar turned his head to see a masked diver appearing from one side of the raft. The black-eyed man blinked at Edgar, and Edgar blinked wearily back.

"No," whispered Edgar, trying to sit up, but unable to. "Get out of the water, man! There's sharks down there. *Sharks*."

"He's alive!" the man reported on a headset. Then, reaching into a small satchel, he uncapped a small bottle of water and offered it to Edgar, who allowed the man to place it on his blistered lips and pour. Then, as Edgar took a small, painful sip, the water burned his parched throat like acid.

Greedily, Edgar sat up in the raft and strained for another sip, and then grabbed the bottle with his own hands and downed the whole thing.

"Thank you, sir," he mouthed beneath the thundering helicopter blades. The man nodded back and buckled him into the stretcher.

"You're welcome," he shouted over the noise, "but you can thank *them*!" He pointed up at the large aircraft.

As the diver gave the order, he and Edgar were lifted upward to safety, leaving the raft and its half-empty water bottle floating in the sea. He continued to stare at it between his dangling legs as the helicopter lifted him even higher above the waters. As the raft got tinier and tinier by the second, tears filled his sore and bloodshot eyes, and profound waves of thankfulness and relief spread throughout his entire body, like water to desert sands, stretching to each and every last inch of his being.

Somehow, some *way*, he survived.

When the two finally arrived at the helicopter doors, he was corralled and yanked inside and there, shrieking, was his wonderful mother's face.

She'd come to rescue him herself!

"THANK YOU, GOD!" she screamed, grabbing him greedily, snatching him up like he was nothing, smothering his sunburned head with her teary face. Even though it was painful, he didn't care. He laughed and hugged her back with all his strength, which was not much, as his weak arms grasped for her best they could.

"Are you . . . real?" he asked in her ear.

"Of *course* I'm real!" she cried, rocking him back and forth, weeping over him. Squeezing tighter, she suddenly seemed to laugh and cry all at once, and when she finally parted from him, she held him at arms' length so she could study him. He gazed deep into her eyes and his smile faded.

"What about Dad?" he asked. "Did it work? Did I make it rain in Mount Lanier?"

"Oh, Edgar," she said, her eyes filling up with more tears as she burst into a weepy laugh. "Yes!" she exclaimed, nodding crazily. "You did! You made it rain! You put out the fire, you crazy kid!"

He could feel his insides melting with relief. "And Dad?" he asked cautiously. "Is he . . .?"

"He's safe and sound, Edgar, in the hospital recovering, waiting for you! He is alive and in one piece—and has *you* to thank for it!"

With a wild smile, she grabbed him by the back of the head again and pulled him in, cackling joyfully, squeezing him 'til it hurt—but he didn't care. He buried his face in her hair, which smelled like home, and closed his eyes. And when he finally opened them again, he noticed Shay Sinclair was sitting in the back seat, beaming with a smile warm as the sun. She waved at him and smiled, and he lifted five blistered fingers to her in return.

"I was just saving your life," he said to her, "in a dream. I had electric fingers. There was a hurricane." Shay shrugged questioningly, then tapped a big green headset she wore on her ears. Carefully, Milly placed a headset around Edgar's blistered ears so she could hear him.

"What did you say?" came Shay's voice through the headset. It was so good to hear her voice.

"Nothing," he smiled. "I guess you got my letter. Thanks for coming to get me."

"You're welcome," she nodded back. "And you have terrible handwriting."

He grinned and looked beyond at a big man who sat beside her.

"Hello Edgar," he said. "My name is David Sinclair—I'm Shay's dad. I just wanted you to know, the whole town of Mount Lanier will owe you a great debt of gratitude, son."

Edgar's Mom leaned over to him. "Shay's father is one of the most incredible people I've ever met," she explained. "He really helped save your life, Edgar."

Edgar nodded respectfully at the man. "Thank you, sir," he said. "It's very nice to meet you."

Mr. Sinclair nodded back, his eyes lowered in respect.

"One more thing," said his mother, taking him gently by the cheeks. "You are *so* grounded."

Edgar surrendered a big, toothy smile, then burst into

laughter.

Soon he was sipping on water, wearing an I.V., and wolfing down a ham sandwich. It was the best sandwich he'd ever had in his life. As he ate, he and the crew began their long trip back to America, and as the chopper veered and dipped with the oceanic wind currents, his mom pointed at the skilled co-pilot and asked if Edgar recognized him.

"He's a friend of yours," she smiled.

Through the rearview mirror Edgar studied the faces of the pilot and co-pilot, and though he didn't recognize the pilot, there, staring back at him, was the navigator—the same man he'd saved back on the island, the drowning man, the one from the storm, the one from Somalia.

"Oh, wow," said Edgar. "Look at you! I guess you made it out of town, huh?" he chewed. The man, far more robust now than the day they'd met on the island, whose blisters had healed and now seemed much clearer and calmer, nodded.

"I lost your gun," Edgar admitted to him, and the pilot, who looked like a fellow countryman of the navigator, interpreted for Edgar. When he was finished speaking, the navigator nodded at Edgar through the rearview, answering in another tongue.

"My friend say, 'How it shoot?'" interpreted the pilot.

"Ah! Well! It shot fantastically!" said Edgar, the food hitting his stomach and sending ecstatic waves throughout his body.

That's when the man said something else to Edgar, never taking his eyes off him.

"My friend say to you," interpreted the pilot, once more, "'ye smart to catch tha current East, headed for French Islands, was you doin' that?'"

Edgar nodded at him.

"Well," marveled the man, "Cali say to me, ye' near ya'

coordinates you left ya' ma', which means you a natural sail-ah."

Edgar's mother squeezed his shoulder tight, and smiled down at him with pride.

"Cali also say," continued the man, a seriousness taking over his voice, "you two now *even*."

"Yeah," said Edgar in mid-chew. "Yes, *sir*. We're definitely even." He nodded a respectful nod at Captain Cali through the rearview.

After that, as everyone watched him, he finally closed his eyes.

TWENTY-EIGHT

THEY FLEW INTO Mount Lanier in the dead of night. Edgar was wrapped in his yellow raincoat and rushed through the press corps who camped expectantly outside the hospital. He rode on the wide shoulders of Mr. Sinclair, who was flanked by Milly and Shay, and as the journalists stirred and shouted at him, Mr. Sinclair knew exactly how to deal with it. He used to be mayor, after all.

"Commissioner!" they yelled. "Is that the boy? The boy on your shoulders?"

Mr. Sinclair said nothing; he just pushed his way through as they snapped a million pictures of Edgar.

Edgar could hear the cameras from the darkness beneath the coat. It was all very strange.

"Give us something, Commissioner!" they continued to shout. "C'mon, sir!"

"Fellas," he said, when he arrived at the hospital doors, "you'll know what happened soon enough. But not tonight, OK? This kid's had a rough few weeks."

The hospital doors opened for them as Edgar was ushered inside, and soon they were in the hospital room that Edgar's mother had told him about.

The one that held his dad.

As Edgar was placed on his feet and the raincoat lifted off his head, there, lying on a bed just a few feet away, was his father.

In all his weariness, Edgar did not know what to say. He just abandoned trying to speak and simply limped over to his dad.

"Got into my dynamite, huh?" asked his dad, smiling, and reached out a hand to him.

"Every stick," Edgar smiled back.

"Good thinking," said his dad as he broke into a fit of coughing.

Edgar grasped his father's hand and squeezed it tight, hard as he could, as a lump rose in his throat.

"Is he going to be OK?" Edgar said, turning to his mother.

"He's suffering from asphyxiation, exposure, and dehydration," informed the doctor, who also stood nearby—the same doctor who'd tended to Edgar's jellyfish sting, "but we do think he will be OK. Son, I'm not really sure if you know this, but your father's a real hero."

Edgar had heard.

On the plane ride home from Madagascar, there was footage of people telling stories of how his father had navigated them to safety around the burning hillside, using wet tree limbs for walls, gathering foliage from the mountainsides to treat their wounds, predicting wind and weather movements from the skies, and, of course, fishing small streams using crafted spears and even the metal from his jacket zipper.

Like his mother had said: he nearly roasted a wild

boar.

In doing all this, his father had been able to keep the team alive for five days in the fiery wilderness—as well as the young boy they first set out to save—until, in the meantime, as they remained hunkered down, Edgar had brought them rain.

"I lost your tackle box," Edgar confessed. "And also the Abu Garcia."

"Yeah?"

Edgar nodded. He hated that the pole was gone—it was truly the finest rig he'd ever known. It had caught so many fantastic fish. "I think some sharks ate it," he revealed.

"Sharks?" whispered his father. "Oh, wow, you got into a swarm of sharks? What did you do to get out of it?"

"Well, I did what any good sailor would do," he explained. "I killed them with a machine gun."

His dad smiled and grabbed his hand, then shut his eyes and squeezed his hand tight. As he did, the doctor walked over and placed a hand on Edgar's shoulder. "You need to get into bed right now. You need to rest, son. Resting is *healing*." He turned Edgar around and looked down at him sternly, but also, with a smile of respect. "Do you plan to stick around this time?"

He guided Edgar to a bed that was adjacent to his father's and Edgar laid down. Edgar nodded and surrendered to the cool sheets, shuddering at how good it felt. Shay was standing near the door and quietly watched the reunion transpire. Turning to whisper her goodbyes to Edgar's mother, Milly looked down at the girl and warmly opened her arms wide, hugging her with all she had. Then, she turned and hugged her father, with a deep look of affection in her eyes, tenderly kissing both of their cheeks.

"I cannot even *begin to thank you*," she said, her voice suddenly shaky, her eyes filled up with tears.

"Oh, Mrs. Dewitt," said Mr. Sinclair, "the pleasure was all *ours*."

"Can I have a second, Dad?" Shay asked, who, when he nodded, strolled over to Edgar's bedside and looked down at him. He watched as she sweetly brushed the greasy hair from his forehead and gazed down at him. Yanking a corner of the sheet up a bit higher to his chest, she leaned down and whispered in his ear.

"Get better quick," she said. "I've got a huge surprise for you."

He nodded. "I love surprises." Reaching up, he ran a hand through her hair and said, "Tell Flounder to come visit me. I'm bed-ridden, man.'"

She giggled and turned to leave. Then, when the door shut behind her, and as Edgar's family was alone for the first time since his father had gone missing, the three smiled at each other and began to laugh.

Millie walked in between the two beds and took a hand of each of her men, and then, when she did, they formed a chain.

Two SATURDAYS later, Edgar was giving his last interview of the day. This time it was *Rolling Stone Magazine*, and the question was:

"Edgar, now that you know what it's like to be a hero in two different towns: in Mount Lanier, where you put out the wildfire by your . . . clever means, and Bon Secour, where you secretly mailed your fishing profits to the out-of-work fishermen, if you had the choice to live in either, which town would you rather live in?"

Edgar thought about that deeply. "Well, my mom always says we should 'Bloom where we are planted.' So, I guess I can live anywhere. I suppose they're both my hometowns. Is that OK?"

"Sure! And how does it feel to be a hero?"

"Well, it's great," he answered. "Especially when they keep giving you free stuff."

Both towns had given him the keys to the city, and pretty much every restaurant in Mount Lanier declared that Edgar Dewitt got free food forever, since, why not? If not for him, it would have all burned to the ground weeks ago.

Abu Garcia, the rod and reel company, had mailed him a brand new Commander fishing pole—this one with a gold plated reel. He had really loved his father's rig, but this thing was the most beautiful red rig known to man.

He couldn't wait to go try it out.

A note came with the package:

> *Thank you, Edgar, for calling our Commander the 'best fishing pole ever made' when you appeared on* The Tonight Show! *We are so sorry you lost yours to the terrible sharks! But here, have one on us! Happy fishing!*

Shortly after the *Rolling Stone* interview, at a small airport north of town, Edgar rode his bike up to the tarmac and discovered the Sinclairs' passenger plane idling on the runway. *This must be the big surprise.* Shay was standing in the doorway of the plane, waving hugely at him, as beautiful as she ever was.

He rode up and parked his bike in an empty hangar, then jogged up to her and smiled.

"Look who's here!" she said above the roar, jerking a thumb to the back of the plane. There, clinging to the back wall, sat a horrified Flounder, cursing both of their names.

"But we haven't even taken off yet!" Edgar laughed, climbing in and greeting his friend. "What's the matter with you?"

"Listen, Edgar!" said Flounder. "I don't want to be

messed with. You have no idea the horror of this!"

Laughing again, he squeezed Flounder's shoulder and gave it a shake. Flounder was freshly back from California.

"It's good to see you again," said Edgar, elbowing his friend.

"You too," smiled Flounder. "You too."

Flounder added, "My parents want me to tell you something. You get free seafood from now on for the rest of your life, for saving our house. But I told them, 'Just don't let him fillet it because he leaves too much meat on the bone!'"

Once they were airborne, Shay gave the pilot instructions. "Could you please go that way, sir?" She motioned and pointed south.

The pilot swooped down and took them on a route around the grand peak of Mount Lanier, where the plane was nosed down toward the tree line, and circled. From there, Edgar could see the wide, gaping hole in the Earth. *His* hole. Just seeing it again made his heart skip a beat.

Oh man, he thought. *I'd love to go falling right now!* The pilot swooped even lower, giving Edgar a better look.

"Wow," he said. "The cabin's totally gone."

"Yeah," Shay nodded. "It completely disintegrated when the water shot up through it. They said people have been finding planks in their yards as far as four counties away. The cabin, the hole, they're so famous right now, people've been selling the boards for, like, fifty thousand dollars a plank on Ebay."

"Fifty grand *a plank?*" he asked. "Are they crazy?"

He looked down again at all the masses. "Look at all the people," he marveled, pointing down. She nodded in agreement. Around a perimeter, tens of thousands of people had camped in a circle around the hole, who had come from all over the globe to get a glimpse of the wondrous hole. The only thing holding the people back was the healthy line of armed military and government officials and swarming scientists who converged on the hole.

Inside the perimeter, large construction crews had been working tirelessly to seal it off, the hole spewing sea water like a volcanic geyser as each high tide rolled in on the other side of the Earth. Meanwhile, in the Southern Hemisphere, large ships scrambled around the clock to seal the hole there, too.

As they glided by, Edgar noticed the scientists at the hole's edge running samples back and forth to mobile labs that dotted the area. As of yet, nobody could even wager a guess as to why the hole even existed: Who'd dug it? Who'd constructed it in such a way that heat and gravity were impervious to it? When it was dug? And especially, *how* it was dug?

Of course, of greatest interest to them all were the bricks from the hole's walls. The ones with the writing on them. The magical bricks.

Apparently, they were indestructible.

The scientists had not yet discovered a way to so much as *chip* one, rumor had it. They'd used diamonds, lasers, acid—even the largest jackhammers in the world, but nothing was denting them. Every machine that had attempted to break the bricks had been broken themselves.

Of course, the island *around* the bricks was obviously destructible, but not the bricks themselves. Each brick back in the Indian Ocean currently kissing the water's surface remained perfectly intact—had been completely impervious to the dynamite blast.

"Check this out," said Edgar, unfolding a piece of paper for Shay. "It's a letter from Captain Cali. He sent it to me when I was in the hospital."

> *My family is thanking you for saving my life, Edgar Dewitt.*

Please come to Somalia for a visit. I will show
you how to shoot the gun for real!

"You have any idea you were flying around with such a badass pirate hunter?" he asked her, laughing.

"Sure!" she said. "It totally takes a pirate hunter to find an *Edgar Dewitt!*"

"So, hey," he said. "You wanna go to Somalia with me and learn to shoot it?"

Mr. Sinclair, who'd chartered the CH-46 Sea Knight Helicopter, who'd led the search for Edgar and had recruited Captain Cali at the request of Edgar's mother, was the one to finally discover that Ambercod was actually seabass.

And Captain Cali readily agreed to navigate them, since he knew the seas so well and owed Edgar such a huge debt. Cali had brought with him his most skilled pilot, and used his own helicopter, staying in the air for longer than any other search party in their scramble to save Edgar Dewitt. Like Edgar's mother, Captain Cali never even considered that Edgar might be dead.

The boy was magical, he believed: the one who pulled him from the sea and dragged him kicking and screaming down into the center of the Earth.

"It's all dead," shouted Shay, pointing out the window, indicating the wide expanse of scorched ground below. He looked out over the world and saw nothing but an endless swath of deep, dark brown, where sea salt had poisoned everything.

His flood and its destruction stretched across the landscape like a brown plague, as far as the eye could see.

He winced painfully.

"Oh man," he groaned. "I did more damage than the drought."

"Yeah," she said. "But which would you rather have: a brown world, or a living *father?*"

"There's no question," he said, returning his gaze to the wide world of brown.

"Dr. Van Rossum says everything'll grow back anyway," she said, discounting his worry with a wave of her hand. "He says the dead Earth was worth it, too, to see the biggest baking soda and vinegar volcano ever made." She giggled at this and took his arm. "He says you get an automatic A for that."

"An A? Really? Well, his will be the only class I get a passing grade in."

Moments later, when they hit 8,500 feet, Shay tossed him a parachute.

"How are you doing back there?" Edgar called to Flounder, who was currently as pale as an olive-skinned Italian kid can be. A nice, thick sweat was beading across his brow at the moment.

"I hate both of you," Flounder muttered through clenched teeth, "so much."

Edgar giggled and then to the pilot, he said, "Sir? Would you please take this young man to solid ground? I don't think he's airworthy at the moment."

"Roger," said the pilot, grinning.

Shay moved in close and strapped herself to him. "OK," she said. "Just let me know when you want me to pull the cord."

He could feel her warm breath on his neck, which felt exceptionally good.

Stepping to the door, the two gave the pilot a pair of enthusiastic thumbs' up and then, they leapt into the sky.

It was his first jump. But not really.

"Hey!" she screamed into his ear, just after they'd fallen a couple thousand feet. "Isn't this like falling through the hole? It is, *isn't it*?"

The world below him spun delightfully around.

"Yeah!" he shouted. "*Almost!*" He leaned up and gave

her a soft, passionate kiss.

Smiling, they fell back to Earth.

ABOUT THE AUTHOR

Ferrill Gibbs is a writer and singer/songwriter from the Alabama Gulf Coast, whose songs have been featured in *American Songwriter Magazine* and CMJ, material that iTunes has called, ". . . fully arranged pop songs that literate and mature music fans could enjoy."

He graduated a touch beneath summa cum laude in English at Auburn University, widely regarded as the off-off-Ivy League of the South. Clinging to the oft repeated axiom that C students rule the world, Ferrill wakes each day in gleeful expectation of the profits to start rolling in, and has a blog that is highly trafficked by his mother, Linnie.

Having worked in several industries including food service and construction, Ferrill now manages a chain of family-owned convenience stores with his wife, "Fish," in his hometown of Mobile, Alabama, where they live with two wonderful dogs and one feisty kitten.

The Secret Island of Edgar Dewitt is his first novel.

ACKNOWLEDGEMENTS

First of all, I'd like to extend a huge, heartfelt thank you to my wife who steadfastly stood by me in all my pursuits, who believed in this story enough to drag me to seminars and conferences these past few years and who rallied me when I was low and demanded I defy my corrosive self-doubt at each and every turn. How could I thank you enough, sweet Fish?

To Eric Elfman, who taught me how to write for an audience, who urged me to keep up the faith in my darkest hour, thank you.

To Kerry Kijewski, the smartest mathematician I've ever known: thank you for all your help with the Physics. Like Edgar says about the wacky Dr. Van Rossum, Google just can't explain it like you do.

Thank you to my English teachers at St. Paul's Episcopal School: Mrs. Gonzales, Mrs. Davis, Mrs. Strachan, and Mr. Courie. Without your inspiration and creativity, I know I'd be living under a bridge somewhere.

To Mrs. Marsh, how lucky was I to have crossed your path? Maybe, hopefully, I'll get to see you again one day.

To Dennis Braswell, thank you for all you've done, for guiding me in this process and for being an all-around mentor. Now let's go publish that book of your poetry!

To my sisters, thank you for all your inspiration in my life. To Barb, who shared stories with me at a young age, and Carol Anne who taught me piano and how to sing vibrato – you've both made a tremendous difference in my life and made me appreciate all things "artistic." Nothing would be the same without you.

To my Dad, who told me big stories like this one back when I was a kid, like the time he bought a globe and plotted a course for us to set sail from Alabama to Australia, telling me how we could build a raft from pine trees from the front yard and go drift amongst the whales and glowing creatures of the deep like Ahab did - I believed in it for years and it was daydreaming like that that got me living in my own imagination. How could I ever thank you enough, Dad?

To the hard working ladies out at the stores who held things down so I could go play "hooky" and write this book: thank you so much for all you do. To Mrs. Pam, Mrs. Liz, Missy S., Mrs. Erika, and especially you, Mrs. Missy Elsworth – none of this could have been done without you.

To the publishers and editors at Amberjack Publishing – to Kayla, Dayna, and Jenny, and all the crew - thank you for finding me and for finding this story. It has all been a dream come true.

And to my biggest fan, my Mom, who was always the first to visit my blog and who read it faithfully, who shared Edgar's story with all of her friends and never found in it a single flaw, as unabashedly biased in her affection as she was, Mom, you always said I had a book in me and to never give up on it. Well, I'm so glad I didn't. I have very special women in my life.

What would I do without them?